Provenance in Architecture

Uwe Fleckner & Mari Lending (eds.)

Provenance in Architecture
A Dictionary

HATJE CANTZ

Content

Architectural provenance
A preamble
Uwe Fleckner & Mari Lending 7

Acquisition *Eirik Bøhn* 15
Actor *Albena Yaneva* 17
Afterlife *Uwe Fleckner* 19
Agent → Actor
Architectural drawing *Niall Hobhouse* 22
Archive *Albena Yaneva* 24
Artefact *Caroline van Eck* 26
Attribution *Mari Hvattum* 28
Auction → Crisis
Authentication *Christoph Grafe* 29
Authenticity *Erik Langdalen* 32
Authorship *Tim Anstey* 35
Bond *Richard Anderson* 37
Bricolage *Christoph Grafe* 38
Capitalism *Bernd Nicolai* 40
Cargo *Aileen Ramm* 42
Catalogue *Nicholas Olsberg* 44
Celebrity *Uwe Fleckner* 46
Circulation *Craig Buckley* 48
Collage → Bricolage → Pasticcio → Spolia
Collecting *Maristella Casciato* 50
Collective memory *Elif Akyüz* 52
Component *Hugh Strange* 54
Concrete *Adrian Forty* 56
Confiscation → Expropriation
Conservation → Preservation
Construction site *Timothy Hyde* 57
Contract *Chelsea Spencer* 59
Conversion → Transformation
Copy → Facsimile
Copyright *Ines Weizman* 61
Costs *Claire Zimmerman* 63
Counter-monument *Elif Akyüz* 64
Craft *Charles Saumarez Smith* 67
Crisis *Mari Lending* 69
Deaccessioning *Lynn Rother* 71
Decay → Dereliction
Decontextualisation → Displacement
Demolition *Alena Beth Rieger* 73
Demolition auction → Crisis
Depository → Storage
Dereliction *Frank Schmitz* 75
Destruction → Demolition → War
Deterioration → Dereliction
Displacement *Yuning Teng* 77
Dispossession *Markus Lähteenmäki* 79
Dispute *Matthew Mullane* 81
Doppelgänger *Ines Weizman* 83
Drawing → Architectural drawing
Dust *Jorge Otero-Pailos* 85
Element *Nicholas Coates* 88
Exhibition *Wallis Miller* 90
Expropriation *Olivia Horsfall Turner* 92
Extension *Bernd Nicolai* 94
Extraction → Sourcing
Facsimile *Adam Lowe* 96
Finance → Bond
Fire *Espen Vatn* 98
Fragility *Martin Denoun* 100
Fragment *Charlotte Skene Catling* 101
Framing *Flavia Crisciotti* 104
Ghosts *Nicholas Olsberg* 106
Graffiti *Uwe Fleckner* 109
Heritage *Margit Kern* 111
Iconoclasm → Monument, toppled → Vandalism
Image vehicle *Uwe Fleckner* 112
Inhabitants → Residents
Inheritance *Philip Ursprung* 115
Inscription *Uwe Fleckner* 116
Labour *Claire Zimmerman* 117
Lacuna *Uwe Fleckner* 119
Maintenance *Jérôme Denis* 121
Material *Thomas McQuillan* 122
Migration → Image vehicle → Mobility

Mobility *Tim Anstey* 123
Model *Matthew Wells* 125
Modernisation → Renovation
Modification → Transformation
Monument → Counter-monument → Monument, toppled
Monument, toppled *Elif Akyüz* 127
Moveables *Alena Rieger* 129
Network *Albena Yaneva* 131
Obsolescence *Jørgen Tandberg* 133
Occupation *Ingrid Dobloug Roede* 135
Original → Precedent
Palimpsest *Uwe Fleckner* 136
Pasticcio *Nina Lucia Groß* 137
Patina *Erik Langdalen* 140
Photography *Mari Lending* 142
Plagiarism → Precedent
Plaster cast *Mari Lending* 143
Political iconography *Uwe Fleckner* 145
Postproduction *Dag Erik Elgin* 146
Precedent *Eeva-Liisa Pelkonen* 148
Preservation *Jorge Otero-Pailos* 149
Pristine *Erlend Skjeseth* 152
Privilegio *Victor Plahte Tschudi* 154
Production → Postproduction
Prototype → Precedent
Provenience *Nick Walkley* 155
Quarry *Thomas McQuillan* 158
Quote *Mari Lending* 159
Readymade *Hugh Strange* 161
Reclaim → Dispossession
Reconstruction *Erik Langdalen* 162
Recycling *Carson Chan* 165
Reiteration → Type project
Relic → Spolia
Relocation → Displacement → Translocation
Remodelling → Transformation
Renovation *Amandine Kastler* 167
Reparation *Frank Schmitz* 169
Replica → Facsimile
Reproduction *Nick Walkley* 171
Residents *Uwe Fleckner* 174
Restitution *Ella Eßlinger* 176
Restoration *Thordis Arrhenius* 178
Reuse *Richard Wittman* 179
Revival → Afterlife
Ruin *Uwe Fleckner* 181
Sale → Acquisition
Scale → Model
Shipping → Cargo
Sourcing *Charlotte Malterre-Barthes* 184
Spolia *Nina Lucia Groß* 185
Storage *Simon Mitchell* 188
Subtraction *Erik Langdalen* 190
Theft *Chelsea Spencer* 192
Thing-right *Ines Weizman* 194
Transfer *Matthew Mullane* 197
Transformation *Uwe Fleckner* 199
Translocation *Frank Schmitz* 202
Transportation → Cargo
Type project *Richard Anderson* 204
Vandalism *Rosa Lowinger* 205
Void → Lacuna
War *Bernd Nicolai* 207
Warehouse → Storage
Wear → Dereliction
Weathering *Timothy Hyde* 210
Will *Ines Weizman* 211

Bibliography 215
Image credits 226
Contributors 228

Architectural provenance
A preamble
Uwe Fleckner & Mari Lending

Since the word "provenance" was coined in the 1780s (from the Latin *provenire*, to come from), the concept has been used to describe the origins, authorship, ownership and legitimacy of precious and relatively easily movable objects such as artworks, manuscripts, ethnographical and archaeological remnants. Transposed into architecture – scaled up and zoomed in to consider something that apparently sits still – provenance reveals new complexities in the social and material lives of buildings, while reframing questions of movement, migration and circulation. With provenance as a lens, both ownership and authorship in architecture transform: ownership may expand beyond the possession of the object itself towards the sources and resources of its components; while the idea of the singular author splinters in the face of truly multi-authored objects, defined by architects, inhabitants, patrons, custodians, construction workers, maintenance personnel, lawyers, bureaucrats, politicians, historians and others.

Architecture is envisioned, commissioned, contracted, designed, invested in, built, owned, traded, abandoned, expropriated, inherited, debated, overwritten, neglected, monumentalised, repurposed, amended, repaired, destroyed, disseminated, forgotten, repeated, collected, archived, catalogued. Any cut into time will show architecture performing in all sorts of states between complex origins and uncertain destinations. Buildings live interesting lives – lives that may be happy or traumatic, or both, in the course of time.

Buildings are unruly and multi-temporal entities. They consist of materials from many sources and with different life expectancy. On a closer look even the smallest, locally situated structure is the product of networked supply chains within architectural cultures that depend, and have always depended, upon global exchanges of resources, techniques, principles and ideas. Buildings move, and so do architectural artefacts. They move across genre and formats. Consideration of the value, purposes and potentials of architecture, too, are constantly shifting. The insights in this book emphasise the extent to which architecture is produced through and in time. Permanence dwindles as a marker of architectural significance; not even monument designation or listing protocols can arrest a building's history. By nature, and by culture, architecture changes physically, in interpretation and through reception histories.

Architectural provenance unfolds through objects in flux; it exposes where something comes from and where it is heading. Between beginnings and the present there is a whole world, and there is more – provenance may also be a way of imagining the futures of architectural objects.

While traditionally understood as the process that secures an object's authenticity as well as its authentication, and sets its value both aesthetically and economically, provenance is yet to be applied in architectural discourse and practice. Relocating the concept into architecture provides a way to encircle the intricate trajectories of fundamentally composite objects. Together, the entries expose what we may call a politics of provenance: provenance considers value – economic, social, cultural, historical, emotional, artistic and political. Climate change and ecological concerns prompt a radical rethinking of the built world and the future possibilities of the existing building stock within a circular economy. Yet, provenance calls also for a reconsideration of architecture. Its framework reveals new ways of writing architectural history, suggesting that virtual re-inscription and material recycling might be conceptualised as artistic, social and political strategies. As the entry "Afterlife" shows, provenance opens new ways to engage with the past.

Combining the *longue durée* with microhistorical traces and marginalia, provenance reveals how architecture is bought and sold, extracted, distributed, adapted, appropriated, altered, moved or undone according to changing ideals, ethics and politics. The provenance of architectural artefacts opens up an understanding of buildings as multi-trajectorial phenomena rather than as stable entities to be recorded chronologically and retrospectively: "Provenance is a form of memory", as defined in the entry "Fragment"; "Provenance is not just history; it is the consciousness of history", the author contemplates in "Costs". Architectural provenance grasps situated details that tie into global networks of production and transaction. As the entry "Readymade" shows, apparently banal and spectacularly mundane elements create their own "micro-provenance history". By documenting artefactual knowledge, architectural provenance reconsiders core aesthetic concepts such as origins, authorship, attribution, authenticity and authentication, as well as labour and ownership of resources, property and land.

The provenance of architectural provenance

Provenance research, as it has been understood and practised, does not deal with architecture. This is based on the erroneous assumption that buildings are stationary objects that rest in themselves. Our transference of the term towards works of architecture builds on approaches that study how artefacts travel through time and space.

The provenance of things characterises the status and value of cultic or cultural objects. Christian relics, for example, depended on the fact that they could be traced back to the body of a holy person or, at least, to direct contact with such a person; the sentimental as well as the material value of an artefact increases when it has passed through the hands of a prominent personality. Proof of the authenticity of an artwork could also be substantiated by establishing an unbroken pedigree of its owners. In recent decades, provenance research has developed from this kind of historical investigation of evidence towards a globally successful method. It deals with the origin and history of artworks, particularly regarding their acquisition, legal status and the ethical implications associated with their collection and exhibition. Fuelled by the growing awareness of artworks illegally acquired during the National Socialist era, museums around the world began to examine their holdings on the basis of the *Washington principles on Nazi-confiscated art* (1988) in order to clarify the itineraries of objects and, if necessary, initiate restitution to the rightful owners or their descendants. Importantly, provenance research today also serves other contexts of injustice, such as objects translocated in the frameworks of colonisation. This has led to restitution proceedings, which were – and still are – often accompanied by legal, political and ethical challenges.

Although provenance research has increasingly integrated approaches that combine art history, law, political science, ethnology, sociology and other disciplines, it has tended to focus on registering proof-of-ownership chains and often serves only as an auxiliary science in the service of legal interests. Leading academics have lately recognised its methodological narrowness. Thus, our transplantation of provenance into architecture draws on critical perspectives on traditional provenance research itself: anthologies such as Gail Feigenbaum and Inge Reist's *Provenance. An alternate history of art* (2013) and Jane Milosch and Nick Pearce's *Collecting and provenance. A multidisciplinary approach* (2019), are among the significant contributions to make provenance operative beyond merely legal documentation.

In recent decades, art, but also architectural history has focused increasingly on the importance of peripatetic objects. Artefacts might be mobile under their own force, because the motives behind their relocation are inscribed in their genre characteristics (as is the case with coins, medals, stamps, prints, etc.), but also because the iconic power of artworks and their significance in terms of content and material value may trigger a more global sense of desire. One result is the abduction of artefacts – their theft and the global trade that follows such acts of dubious or illegal acquisition. Another is the travelling of variations, editions, copies, adaptations, reproductions and repetitions. Some of this attention to translation, which marks the turn towards provenance also in architecture, was foreshadowed long ago in the work of the German art and cultural historian Aby Warburg. The logics of what Warburg termed *Bilderfahrzeuge* (image vehicles) adumbrate contemporary interest in the circulation of architectural fragments, indeed of entire buildings detached from their original functional contexts.

The phenomenon of provenance is ripe to be rethought on a larger scale. Differently from art, architectural provenance can be discussed as a creative instrument, applicable to understanding unfulfilled and future potentials of buildings by engaging the complex social trajectory of architectural works. We believe this will also have intellectual and methodological consequences for the hitherto static-linear provenance research on works of art. This conceptual expansion encourages a reframing of critical issues in very concrete ways, and a recycling of the meaning and function of buildings spurred on by the complex relationship between thinking and doing that characterises architecture.

While artworks may perhaps more easily be described by fixed points such as origin and destination, architectural culture is a theatre of exchange and circulation. Provenance describes the itineraries that are part of the lives of buildings, whether *en route* or *in situ*: "once architectural experience begins to be understood as something concerned with a built world that is not always stationary, a quality of architectural hypermobility ensues. Because this characteristic emphasises both previous and future destinations, such movement always speaks of provenance", as stated in the entry "Mobility". Architectural provenance provides insight into how material culture in a most concrete sense is distributed, appropriated, altered, reinvented and evaluated.

Defining the world

Encyclopaedias and dictionaries carry some oddly objective connotations. A proud democratic and critical tradition, publications that define what words mean or present specific fields of knowledge, always propose explanations according to contemporary worldviews and position their own historicity. This can take place as a critique of clichéd knowledge – famously in Gustave Flaubert's satirical *Dictionnaire des idées reçues*, the appendix to the novel *Bouvard et Pécuchet* (1881). The colossal French Enlightenment project *Encyclopédie, ou Dictionnaire raisonné des sciences, des arts et des métiers* (1751–1780) represented a veritable rethinking of the definitions of the words that the world is made of, with one offshoot in Voltaire's polemical *Dictionnaire philosophique* (1764). A similar format appealed to the historical avantgarde: Georges Bataille's entries "Abattoire", "Architecture" and "Musée" in the highly idiosyncratic *Dictionnaire* that appeared as instalments in the journal *Documents* (1929–1931) are staples in architectural circles. Some dictionaries, or works that borrow their logic, are all about the impossibility of objectivity and neutrality. Roland Barthes loved to play with the genre, also to expose the random order of the alphabet when trying to make sense of the world in writing. His treatise on love, *Fragments d'un discours amoureux* (1977) undermines the temptation to recount a love story as if it was a coherent, ordered narrative.

Eugène Emmanuel Viollet-le-Duc's nine volume *Dictionnaire raisonné de l'architecture française du XIe au XVIe siècle* (1854–1868) that defined the field from "Abacus" to "Zodiac", and Antoine Chrysostome Quatremère de Quincy's two volume *Dictionnaire historique d'architecture* (1832) are fundamental contributions to the definition of architecture by means of the alphabet. More recently, Adrian Forty's *Words and buildings. A vocabulary of modern architecture* (2000) became an instant classic. The last few years have seen a constant engagement with this tradition. Mari Hvattum and Anne Hultzsch concluded the edited volume *The printed and the built. Architecture, print culture and public debate in the nineteenth century* with a glossary spanning from "Bibliotopography" to "Xylography" (2018); Graeme Brooker's *50/50 Words for reuse*, is a thoughtful consideration of sustainability in architecture (2021); Olivia Horsfall Turner, Simona Valeriani and colleagues furnished *An alphabet of architectural models* from "Ancient" to "Zoom" (2021); Andrea Crudeli introduced the essay collection *Adaptive reuse. Theoretical glossary and design labs* with a lexicon spanning from "Abacus" to "Transition" (2024). In the face of the climate crises, Eva Franch i Gilabert, Mireia Luzárraga and Alejandro Muiño presented the anthology *100 Words for water. A projective ecosocial vocabulary* (2025), while "Ass" and "Zebra" mark beginning and end in *The architect and the animal*, edited by Kostas Tsiambaos (2025), a modern ark of the long twentieth century.

By playing with the alphabet's presumed order within a longstanding, venerable genre, these books propose different ways of describing what constitutes architecture and architectural thinking and, importantly, make strong claims as to what is imperative to discuss and critique in the very present. Dictionaries historicise, define and pose perspectives on objects and phenomena to rethink received knowledge, as well as to reexamine canonical reception history.

A provenance abécédaire

Provenance in architecture. A dictionary historicises, theorises and demonstrates architectural provenance from "Acquisition" to "Will". Architecture is acquired and bequeathed, and between these two economic and legal procedures one hundred entries deal with provenance from oblique and sometimes unexpected angles. They cover notions from across semantic fields, many with clear or latent intersections to other topics, spanning from the logics of the building industry to question of materials, parts and objects, finance and economy, legal matters and ownership, decay, repair and preservation, transport and relocation, media and media dissemination, musealisation and presentation, conflict and iconoclasm, cultures of remembrance, agency and alterity.

This dictionary springs from the international research project *Provenance projected. Architecture past and future in the era of circularity*, based at the Oslo School of Architecture and Design, with more entries contributed by kindred spirits and dear colleagues from all over Europe and the United States. Many of the entries read like microhistories that take specific events or evidence as a starting point to evoke bigger questions. There are no claims of neutrality, the relationship of words and the world are seen from the perspective of the work of the authors, both scholars and practitioners. The result is a polyphonic collection and an architectural history written through episodes from across time and place. Both speculative and concrete, the entries may also reveal the provenance and intellectual history of the words themselves, of concepts, ideas and principles. "Weathering" implicates the historicity of the climate crisis through the unheimlich contemporaneity of John Evelyn's 1661 treatise *FUMIFUGIUM: or The Inconveniencie of the AER and SMOAK of LONDON*; while "Theft" uncovers a fundamental detail: in Michel

Foucault's *Nietzsche, la généalogie, l'histoire* (1971), provenance is defined not as "the erecting of foundations: on the contrary, it disturbs what was previously considered immobile; it fragments what was thought unified". That insight may well serve as one motto for theorising provenance in architecture.

Key provenance terms such as "Authorship", "Attribution" and "Authentication", emerge as messier in architecture than in art. Here, the prominence of the architect as the sole author of a work crumbles, as does the myth of the architect as a controller of processes. Our entry on "Authorship" dates the architect as virtuous author back to fifteenth-century humanist discourse when "the creation of buildings was claimed as an intellectual practice: a building could exist 'complete' in the mind of an architect before ever it was realised in brick or stone". The entry "Network" redefines this established idea of authorship: buildings are "not made by powerful minds (star architects, demiurges, those powerful 'Gods'), but architecture [...] emerges, and gains provenance, as it traces many intricate and hesitant relationships with materials and technologies, skills, bodies and institutions". In our context, architecture materialises as everything but a linear path from an architect's conception to the completed building, which complicates typical provenance phenomena such as attribution and authenticity in the lives of buildings: "Authenticity redefines itself not as a fixed attribute, but as a continuum of care", as the entry "Authentication" observes. The entries "Bricolage" and "Pasticcio" inherently deconstruct simplifying definitions of origins and authenticity, the former as the origins of the elements are "neither here nor there", the latter by "placing equal value on authentic fragments and their reproductions, suggesting a more fluid approach to questions of cultural property and historical authenticity".

Architecture's fundamental practical purpose and constantly changing presents depicts established elements of provenance as continuously negotiated across time. The patron, the client, the person who commissioned the work, may be accounted for in the names of certain buildings: Villa Borghese, Villa Savoy, the Farnsworth House. Yet, the ownership chains that are crucial to traditional provenance research, have been of less interest to architectural historians. In architecture, ownership disputes and changes often imply significant ruptures, and conjure uses and abuses, collective memory and trajectories of emotions as shown in the entries on the ways in which architecture may be owned and possessed – among them "Bond", "Contract", "Demolition", "Deaccessioning", "Dispossession", "Expropriation", "Inheritance" and "Occupation".

Architecture involves a stronger public dimension than most artworks do. Buildings are not only the product of a vast cast of actors over time; different groups may also claim ownership to buildings: "In a world where cultural heritage is threatened by war, economic exploitation and environmental degradation, respecting provenance becomes a matter of justice", as suggested in "Preservation". Provenance in architecture unsettles worn dichotomies and, for instance, shows that the natural resources architecture is made of are cultural products with histories. Provenance may act with actual political force: as "Dispute" demonstrates, "activist provenance" can be conducted by groups that question the official stories of sourcing, to reveal the true origins of materials. Provenance research is itself a specialised field of reception that in our context unfolds far from any anxiety of influence. Also, as stated in the entry "Ghosts", architectural work "inventively unbuilt, and thus timeless and uncertain" gains provenance "through which a possible future world is envisaged and from whose examples its forms might be borrowed". If provenance circumvents the temptation of pinning down architecture to official moments and individual signatures, history becomes more of a "treasure trove to be shared", to be kept alive by "the active quoting and borrowing of the works and ideas of the past", as pondered in "Quote".

Towards a provenance turn

Very differently from art and archaeology, architectural provenance may carry a forward-bound, dynamic and productive significance. Provenance encompasses history and theory on the one side and design work on the other. The reversing of conventional terms of history writing may represent a provenance turn in architecture and architectural thinking, one that presents fragments of other pasts with repercussions for the future. Provenance reconceptualises the architectural object beyond established distinctions of history and practice, culture and nature: "Conceiving architectural design as artefactual design opens the possibility of thinking about architecture not in terms of conformity to the rules of classical theory, but in terms of its provenance, in the manmade history of artefacts and the deep history of nature", as proposed in "Artefact".

Architectural objects leave marks of all sorts on their way from one state to another. Architectural provenance provides a prism through which we are enabled to understand how architecture moves, is destroyed, survives and is transformed, from the macroscopic to the microscopic. In both practice and scholarship architectural provenance may be conceived as a method as well as an ethos.

Acquisition The decennial of 18 Brumaire in 1809 was going to be a many-splendoured thing. Among the projected celebrations, the boundless *Description de l'Égypte* was to mark one of the most prized possessions of the newfound empire – the domain over the classical tradition and imperial authority, and their wellspring in pharaonic antiquity. The ill-fated campaign to conquer Egypt (1798–1801) was a military disaster, but in the exhaustive notes and surveys of the combined French sciences lay the potential for an all-encompassing book that could substitute lost ground. Like so many things Napoleonic, the *Description* blew its budget and overshot its deadline, and when it did come out the next year, its exuberant frontispiece was full of contradictions (fig. 1).

Designed by committee, forged from disparate sources, unrestrained by decorum and vocal in its assertion of historical finality, the enormous engraving epitomised the imperial monument. But strangely, a group of spoils, stacked together beside a token seashore for implicit delivery to France, contradicted universally accepted facts and seemed to rehearse a decade-old humiliation (→ SPOLIA). Dead centre in the image, behind the Rosetta Stone and resting against a carved pharaoh, was a massive slab of stone, the circular astrological ceiling from Dendera.

1 François-Charles Cécile, *Frontispiece*, engraved by Abraham Girardet and Charles Sellier, etched by Jean-Baptiste Réville, from *Description de l'Égypte, Antiquités*, vol. 1 (Paris: Imprimerie impériale 1809)

In reality, most of the things that were rounded up neatly in the frontispiece were either lost or never possessed. The heroic exodus of pharaonic treasures envisaged in advance of the campaign had failed to take place. It was Bonaparte's distinguished army of the recent Italian campaign that was now booted out from France's most promising prospective colony by an Ottoman-British coalition and a ragtag band of saboteurs and assassins. In an ironic reversal of the Treaty of Tolentino, through which the Republic had enriched the Louvre with the masterpieces of the Italian canon, the Treaty of Alexandria of August 1801 dictated that the French now cede their collected treasures to an Ottoman-British coalition. By 1809 and the printing of the frontispiece, the Rosetta Stone was still indexical of French defeat, displayed in the British Museum with an epigraph celebrating its capture from Bonaparte's expedition (→ CARGO). It was a nose-thumbing not soon forgotten. But where the Rosetta Stone had been lost, the Dendera zodiac had never moved an inch, and was still very much *in situ* in the ceiling of the Temple of Hathor (fig. 2).

If the frontispiece was mysterious in its portrayal of ancient treasures in a transitory state, its *explication*, an exegesis printed in the *Description* itself, was outright jiving when it declared that the image showed "the most precious fragments *collected* in Upper Egypt, such as the planisphere of Dendera". An apparent typo, the wording only revealed that possession was a descriptive exercise, a graphic fact.

The polytechnicians that travelled Egypt alongside the expeditionary force were acutely aware of the transcendent nature of their historical mission. For these savants the mission had been a reflexive one: by bringing the rejuvenated and enlightened French sciences to bear on the place of their ancient origins, both would be

2 Édouard de Villiers du Terrage and Jean-Baptise Prosper Jollois, *The circular zodiac of Dendera*, engraved by Louis-Jean Allais, from *Description de l'Égypte, Antiquités*, vol. IV (Paris: Imprimerie royale 1817)

enriched and revealed, bypassing centuries of decadence. What ensued as the military ambition faltered was a race for transcription, analysis and replication that outdid questions of possession in the immediate, material sense. Egyptian antiquity, obscured, inaccessible and buried in lifeless sand as though a metaphor of historical entropy, could be revealed by empiricism spliced with inference and held by description and printing. Accurate → REPRODUCTION, as thing, as image – the enormous engravings of the *Description* were both – could outweigh the whims of warfare and vicissitudes of geopolitical fortune. Knowledge, a permanent record, offered a stronger sense of domain than → FRAGMENTS in a museum.

Vivant Denon was the first to draw the zodiac and he published it in his wildly successful *Voyage dans la Basse et la Haute Égypte* in 1802. But Denon was chiefly an artist and prone to interpretation and enthusiasm, and it was for the impossibly productive ponts-et-chaussées-engineers Édouard de Villiers du Terrage and Jean-Baptise Prosper Jollois to fashion a graphic transcription that could outdo the thing itself (→ ARCHITECTURAL DRAWING). In the fullest awareness of the profundity of their task, the two worked on in the darkness of the temple interior under diminishing supplies of lamp oil till they had exhausted their stock of pencils, fashioning ad hoc replacements by pouring melted bullets into straws. Eminently legible, accessible and indisputably French, the resulting engraving was everything the zodiac was not.

Discovery, transcription and publication was ample claim to ownership of a thing no one could access. And the controversies that immediately followed the first reports of the discovery made the zodiac a ubiquitous presence in France in the wake of Denon's *Voyage*. Dated between fourteen thousand years old or from Roman imperial times, the Dendera planisphere was either a straightforward reiteration of Greek astrology or refutation of biblical chronology and proof of Egypt's deep antiquity, and the pages of the daily *Moniteur Universel* brimmed with opinion pieces. In August 1802, the zodiac was hot, and eyeing ownership of a supreme conversation piece, the editorial commission of the *Description de l'Égypte* requested permission from Interior Minister Jean-Antoine Chaptal to have sculptor and Egypt veteran Jean-Jacques Castex execute a copy in marble in the domestically compliant scale of 1:3. A report estimated its costs to 1,800 francs, and Castex requested lodgings and a studio, into which he disappeared to work on a preparatory wax → MODEL. It was nearly eight years later that the commission, facing imminent publication of the *Description*, followed up with some impatience. Meanwhile, Castex had spirited his model off to Naples, jealously guarding his monument. With thinly veiled concern, the commission gently beckoned Castex and his zodiac to Paris with the reassurance that they were not attempting to deprive him of the ownership of the monument. By now, the best Dendera planisphere was in Southern Italy.

It was long after the fall of Napoleon that Castex' genteel and gleaming white marble zodiac appeared under royal auspices as an artwork at the Salon of 1819. Still, serialisation and beautification had not entirely killed the allure of the thing itself. In an Egypt now ravaged by greedy collectors who specialised in moving the gigantic, the antiquities dealer Sébastien-Louis Saulnier saw an opportunity to achieve the impossible (→ COLLECTING). On his orders, the mason Jean-Baptiste Lelorrain acquired a *firman* for the removal of the zodiac from Ahmet Pasha, the entrepreneurial governor of Upper Egypt, in January 1821. Ownership, and its modern provenance, was in any case long since established. To Saulnier, Denon had claimed the astrological ceiling for France (see Buchwald and Josefowick 2010, p. 11). For Lelorrain, it was the war booty of the French army.

To Bonaparte's savants Egypt had been a landscape resilient to revolution. In a culture in which societal disruption was measured in the destruction of monuments and → VANDALISM was on everyone's lips, Egyptian antiquity, monolithic, cold and rigid, was a bulwark against the destructive forces of time. Ironically, this extended to whatever coveted ornaments were affixed to the giant structures of pharaonic architecture, and the expeditionary engineers had quickly abandoned efforts to detach the zodiac from the temple. Now, it successfully resisted Lelorrain's attempts. Lodged three feet deep in the structure, it weighed 60 tonnes and had to be wrestled from the ancient architectural matrix by force (→ DISPLACEMENT). Employing a workforce of twenty locals, Lelorrain toiled over twenty-two days in the gruelling heat using hacksaws and explosives drilled into the structure to sever the stone slab from the temple. So as not to disrupt the integrity of the monument, a → PLASTER CAST was installed in the ceiling.

When it arrived in Paris in 1822, Jacques-Joseph Corbière, the Minister of Public Instruction and soon-to-be Interior Minister, established a commission comprised by luminaries of the Académie des Sciences and the Académie des Inscriptions et Belles-Lettres to evaluate the importance of the zodiac. They concluded that it was an important piece. In 1822, Louis XVIII purchased the planisphere for 150,000 francs and had it installed in the Royal Library. A commemorative medal was struck, neatly expressing Bourbon domain over the Egyptian and Graeco-Roman past by juxtaposing the zodiac with the king's other recent acquisition, the Venus de Milo. Access to the original zodiac hampered neither reproduction nor discourse, and over the next two years the planisphere was the subject of nine monographs. But what had previously been possessed in reproduction alone was now an auratic, material fact under Louis, and the image that heralded the Napoleonic *Description de l'Égypte* shifted from the portrayal of things distant and contested to things immediate.

Eirik Bøhn

Actor An actor is a participant in the process of architectural production and consumption. The term "actor" typically designates the autonomous entities that play an important role in the making of architecture (see Latour 1987). They can include individuals (an architect, an engineer, a contractor), collectives (the public, the nation), visual representations (plans, → ARCHITECTURAL DRAWINGS, scale → MODELS, budget figures), or non-figurative representations (national spirit, cultural → HERITAGE, procurement system, regulations), → MATERIALS or technologies. To identify the actors, we ask ourselves if the presence or absence of an entity makes any difference.

If we trace the → NETWORKS of architectural practice, we can witness how an actor comes into being rather than taking its properties for granted and as fully defined and assuming the world is composed by a number of known entities. We can define an actor on the basis of behaviour – its performances – manifested in the process of design-making, dwelling, → RENOVATION, → MAINTENANCE and other processes. Performance refers to the specific situation in which an actor emerges and is defined through actions, trails, difficulties and experiences. What describes the actor's profile is not a set of qualities or characteristics defined in terms of essence, but rather the results of these events, trails and experiences – that is, performances.

For instance, a building undergoing renovation is not a mere ostensive object, it is rather unpredictable. To take a specific example, the process of renovation of the seventeenth-century Alte Aula in Vienna (2004–2006) by the Viennese architect Rudolf Prohazka presented the architect and builders with numerous surprises (fig. 1). The building is a part of the university quarter built in 1623 when Emperor Ferdinand IV entrusted the theological and philosophical faculty of the University of Vienna to the Jesuit Order. Its renovation required the massive and coordinated efforts of architects, preservationists, clients and engineers. To fully grasp the renovation of the Alte Aula, we need to follow all these actors at numerous places of planning, discussion and negotiations throughout the whole process until the final completion of the building in 2006 and witness how they engaged in the long-lasting venture of reshaping and redefining it time and again. We need to trace how they expressed their concerns, modify the criteria, communicate their expectations and engage in negotiations. Following these actors, we can recount renovation not as a series of personal "heroic" battles of an architect with the unchangeable "historical substance" of an old building, but rather as a collective venture – tentative, difficult and controversial – to reshape and redefine, rearticulate and re-establish the building of the Alte Aula. Over the course of this process numerous non-human agents (such as the building facade, the natural stone used for the floor, the columns' grid, the fresco and the layers of paints) manifest themselves as important players in renovation.

For instance, the fresco will reveal different yellowish minuscule strata, a new wooden beam will be discovered, and these elements will surprise architects and construction workers in the morning (fig. 2). A surprise can derive from the discrepancy between the received knowledge of the building (preceding the renovation process) and the knowledge that is gradually acquired in the process of renovating it. The architect will stop and wonder, questioning retrospectively the building's fabric: Why was it built so? Why were these wooden parts used? Why were the foundations of the building not laid in the way architects would lay them now? These questions will then trigger a process of corrections and adjustments of the building using the available contemporary techniques and archives.

However, in the course of renovation interventions, the Alte Aula, expected to be a coherent entity, suddenly multiples. Not one fresco but many fresco → FRAGMENTS emerge. Not a single renovation practice, but many diverse practices of intervening and transforming are at stake. The participants in renovation face new uncertainties and engage in new networks. That is the regime of intense and enduring surprise.

1 *Alte Aula, fresco room (old Jesuit theatre)*, 1654, renovated 2004–2006, Vienna. Photo: Albena Yaneva, 2005

2 *Alte Aula*, 1654, renovated 2004–2006, Vienna. Photo: Albena Yaneva, 2005

These multiple surprises show that once reopened, the building starts to act as an agent that enrols more materials, renovation techniques, clients and preservationists. We witness how renovation attends to the multiplicity of the building that cannot be removed from the practices that sustain it. It comes to light as a performative agent that can hardly be mastered by architects, preservationists and planners. Instead, it stubbornly resists interventions, hinders or facilitates specific ways of accommodating the programmatic requirements. In many cases the Alte Aula has no scruples in objecting to the architects' and builders' actions by behaving in undisciplined ways, blocking the renovating operations, obstructing the plans, suspending the builders' deadlines, disappearing from view, disclosing unknown layers of its history and showing a selective "attitude" to different materials. Yet, to argue that a seventeenth-century building is an actor does not mean to claim that it operates as a strange quasi-theatrical machinery from the Jesuit time or that it literally talks to architects and builders. For a building to act, it is to be a part of a network, in which each element relays, prolongs and overtakes the action of the building and the whole collective without either of them ever constituting a source of action in itself.

The fresco or the wooden beams' "objections" that lead to surprises are prolonged by the actions of many agents in renovation. As a result, the capacity of the building to act is the effect of the associations of a heterogeneous network composed of architects, fresco layers, wooden beams, conservators, visitors, visuals, instruments, instead of being assigned to a powerful master architect (→ AUTHORSHIP) or to a single architectural object that could determine the course of action (→ THING-RIGHT). The way architects, builders and clients respond to the objections of a building shows their constant uncertainty over the nature of this entity. No matter how thorough the research on the building history is, the building often happens to reveal a hidden layer; no matter how systematic the knowledge of its materials and construction is, these materials and construction techniques often manifest new properties. The Alte Aula acts (and transforms action) in unexpected ways not merely repeating and relaying it. It distorts and modifies the meaning attributed to it instead of faithfully transporting it through the centuries. Both its history and modalities of action are probed and redefined through the moments of surprise and lead us to question traditional definitions of buildings as static backdrops of activities, as subservient to the laws of technical causality. *Albena Yaneva*

Afterlife In Jacob and Wilhelm Grimm's *Deutsches Wörterbuch* (Leipzig 1852ff.), the noun *Nachleben* (afterlife) has two alternative meanings, on the one hand as "*nachahmendes Leben*" (imitative life), which emulates a role model, and on the other hand as "*nachfolgendes, nachdauerndes Leben*" (subsequent, lasting life), in which the sustainable echo, the after-effect of a lived life or an (emotional) experience is considered. Combining both meanings, afterlife became a category in art history as early as the nineteenth century, when Anton Springer, who counted the young Friedrich Nietzsche among his students at the University of Bonn, investigated the reception of ancient art in the Middle Ages (see Springer 1867, vol. 1, pp. 1ff.). Aby Warburg adopted the term from him and initially used it in his investigations into the afterlife of antiquity, particularly in the Italian and German Renaissance, the lifelong leitmotif of his research. The Hamburg scholar extended the term to other areas and used it as a metaphor to describe how works of art, their iconographies (→ POLITICAL ICONOGRAPHY) or the motifs contained in them (including the so-called "pathos formulae") could continue to operate in various geographical, cultural and social contexts, sometimes changing their artistic form and sometimes their content. Beyond the comparatively simple reception modes of direct copying or → REPRODUCTION, Warburg was especially interested in those adoptions that were the result of more complex processes; he was dealing with the → TRANSFORMATIONS of the objects concerned and their constancy or shift in meaning. The art historian observed with fascination how works of art that were revitalised in this way beyond their original contexts could experience a psychological or political increase in expression (see Didi-Huberman 2002).

In architectural history, the adoption of existing models, as documented for the field of antiquity in the Census of Antique Works of Art and Architecture Known in the Renaissance (see www.census.de), has so far tended to be told as a history of influence. Of course, it has always been recognised that Early Modern buildings, for example, were inspired by stylistic forms and architectural → ELEMENTS from antiquity, that neo-Gothic architecture drew on medieval models and much more. With the concept of afterlife, as Warburg introduced it, such modes of reception can, however, be regarded as essential prerequisites of an art history that is currently increasingly understood as a global network of exchange. In this way, stylistic devices of the architecture of historicism, modernism and postmodernism, such as the use of (simulated) → SPOLIA or other forms of → PASTICCIO, which were previously viewed with scepticism, can also be re-evaluated (see Meier and Jäggi 2021).

In the academic investigation of architectural afterlife, it is essential to distinguish between virtual and actual material afterlife, just as we do with the closely related phenomena of architectural → IMAGE VEHICLES and → DISPLACEMENTS. In many instances, we encounter a virtual afterlife where, for artistic, cultural, political or other reasons, exemplary buildings or styles are referenced or imitated in new contexts. This can occur either as a homage to traditional models, as a take-over of specific meanings or as a gesture of dominance, as frequently seen in colonial architecture. For instance, English colonial rulers transferred the forms and building methods of their native architecture to India, while German colonial rulers transferred them to China. A significant example of this is the residence of the German governor, which the West Prussian-born civil engineer and architect Werner Lazarowicz built in Qingdao between 1903 and 1907 in the "German" style of eclectic monumentalising neo-Romanesque architecture (fig. 1).

1 Werner Lazarowicz, *Residence of the governor of the German colony of Tsingtau*, 1903–1907, Qingdao. Photo: Uwe Fleckner, 2018

The combination of heavy, deliberately rustic, hewn granite blocks with plastered surfaces and half-timbering, the hybrid combination of Romanesque columns and arches with some Art Nouveau decorative forms and individual Chinese → COMPONENTS not only results in an idiosyncratic mixture of styles, but above all it programmatically stages a massive foreign body high on a hill above the city, which dominates the urban landscape of Qingdao with a powerful architectural gesture (see Lind 1998).

On the other hand, the adoption of typical local styles can also result in an afterlife of architectural forms whose use may be perceived as a sign of appreciation or, from a critical perspective, as cultural appropriation, for example in buildings of the so-called Pueblo Revival, as we come across in the New Mexico Museum of Art in Santa Fe, designed in 1917 by the brothers Isaac Hamilton and William Morris Rapp. Here, the style of the local adobe construction method of indigenous buildings was realised in modern → MATERIALS and combined with the requirements of a contemporary museum building. The fact that such imitations have to be considered a form of afterlife is already demonstrated by the term used for this style, which is aimed at revitalisation and which we also encounter in a comparable way in the Mission or Colonial Revival and in non-colonial contexts in the Greek, Gothic or Tudor Revival.

The material afterlife of architecture is given when demolished or otherwise destroyed buildings or parts of buildings are revitalised in new contexts in a manner that transcends mere cost-cutting construction or sustainability considerations alone (→ DEMOLITION, → RECYCLING, → REUSE). This is how the Chinese Pritzker Prize winner Wang Shu designed the Ningbo Museum in 2008, dedicated to the art and cultural history of the Zhejiang province. Its facade consists largely of elements that were left over as rubble from the demolition of the regional village architecture that had to make way for the new building and other structures (fig. 2).

Glazed and unglazed bricks and roof tiles of various colours and formats can be seen on the modern concrete cubes of the museum building, as well as single stone blocks and pottery

2 Wang Shu, *Ningbo Museum, detail of the facade with a brick decorated with the character 壽 (longevity)*, 2008, Ningbo. Photo: Uwe Fleckner, 2019

→ FRAGMENTS; eventually decorative elements, some of which are inscribed, are integrated in the structure of the facade materials. All those pieces, most of which date from the Ming and Qing dynasties, and some even from the Tang dynasty, were inserted using a local craft technique known as 瓦爿 (roughly translated as "split brick"), a recycling method that was traditionally used for the rapid → REPARATION or → RECONSTRUCTION of buildings in the province, which is frequently hit by typhoons. By incorporating demolition materials into the new building, the construction culture that was destroyed by ruthless modernisation is at least given a remnant of dignity and permanence, echoing the highly valued Chinese concept of longevity. On the other hand, using this upgraded rubble in a distinctly contemporary structure means that neither → AUTHENTICITY nor the continued existence of obsolete architecture is deliberately feigned (→ OBSOLESCENCE); instead, its afterlife is realised through the medium of the material. In this way, history, lived experiences and enduring memories are preserved within the building, while the integrated bricks, stones and other fragments undergo an intellectual transformation. Previously, these were local building materials readily available to masons and architects; in the Ningbo Museum, they have become carriers of a distinct memorial significance (→ COLLECTIVE MEMORY).

If we apply Aby Warburg's concept of afterlife to architecture and, under his guidance, examine the phenomena of revitalising adoptions of exemplary buildings or architectural styles, as well as the actual reuse of building materials, then this scientific method contributes to a new perspective on architectural history. It is not primarily the ecological demands of a contemporary circular economy that make this approach fruitful for the provenance history within architecture. Rather, it allows us to conceptualise virtual and material recycling as an artistic, social and memorial means of engaging with tradition within a cultural-historical framework of architectural history.

Uwe Fleckner

Architectural drawing Every drawing of a building by an architect has a double identity: as a sheet of paper carrying marks that are sometimes beautiful, but equally as the singular record of the author's thinking and intention (→ AUTHORSHIP). At the extremes of ownership, this duality becomes irreconcilable – the drawing either fading and illegible on the walls of a museum, or unseen, even unrecorded, deep in an archival vault (→ ARCHIVE, → COLLECTING). On quite rare occasions these double lives can coalesce fully in the physical passage of an individual drawing, across seas and mountains or over time itself, and their eventual safe arrival engenders some seminal event for architectural history (→ IMAGE VEHICLE). "Drawing-as-object" has acted then as the true steward of "drawing-as-idea"; the two holding fast to each other, for the duration of their journey at least, through the specificity of their original purpose or of the audiences to whom they are shown.

On 23 April 1788, Jacques-Germain Soufflot presented a survey of Minerva Medica to his colleagues at the Académie Royale d'Architecture in Paris, with the object of demonstrating that his ambitious dome for Sainte-Geneviève could be built on sound engineering principles. A few months earlier, challenged publicly and in the press by his rival Pierre Patte (→ DISPUTE), he had commissioned his nephew, François Soufflot, called Le Romain, to make record drawings of surviving domed structures in Rome (fig. 1).

Anxious for the attention of a sophisticated Parisian audience, the younger architect took the opportunity to play on the conventions of survey drawing; his study in section, of what was then understood to be a Roman temple, is dressed around in a fictional landscape, that includes himself and a colleague at their drawing boards.

In their minutes, the *académiciens* encouraged Soufflot to continue his research and recorded that the structure "seems suitable to be imitated fruitfully and successfully in many circumstances" (Lemonnier 1911, pp. 341f.). The dome was completed in 1790 to Soufflot's designs, but after his death. The following year the church was rechristened the Panthéon, transformed into a revolutionary temple modelled on the (imagined) Roman original; the dome of Minerva Medica collapsed in 1828.

1 François Soufflot, called Le Romain, *Section of the Roman Temple of Minerva*, 1778, pencil, ink and watercolour, 45.1 × 55 cm. Drawing Matter Collection, London

Charles Robert Cockerell arrived in Athens in the Autumn of 1810 and seems to have wasted no time developing a survey of the paved floor of the *cella* of the Parthenon – an extraordinarily complicated drawing that records both the footprint of the former mosque and, crucially, uses the grid of marble slabs to infer the original location of columns destroyed by the great explosion of Turkish gunpowder in 1687 (fig. 2).

For Mediterranean travellers, good drawing paper was always in short supply, and Cockerell at some point extended the sheet to include the floor of the eastern end of the temple, using the reverse of an earlier drawing that had attempted an arrangement of the recently excavated marbles from the pediment of the temple at Aegina. The architect returned with the drawing to London only in June 1817 and, after being engraved for Peter Oluf Brøndsted's *Reisen und Untersuchungen in Griechenland* (Paris 1826), it became the accepted basis for understanding the original form of the Parthenon amongst succeeding generations of historians. A scruffy and nearly unintelligible drawing had actively stewarded the transfer of critical architectural knowledge – the seeds, indeed, of the Greek Revival (→ AFTERLIFE) – from Athens to northern Europe. Early in the 1840s, Cockerell added a further section of paper on the right, heavy with general notes and observations, and so further repurposed the original diagram to be held up by a gloved assistant as an illustration to his early lectures as professor or architecture at the Royal Academy.

Thirty years later, in 1871, in the same room, George Edmund Street will tell his audience: “In giving my first lectures under the auspices of this Academy, I can hardly forget the first lectures that I ever heard within its walls. They were those of the late Professor Cockerell, an architect so distinguished by his close and careful study of classic art, by his thoroughly artistic and cultivated taste, and by his real earnestness in carrying out what he felt to be good in his work, that none could set before him a nobler example of the course an architect should take. The refinement of his executed works was in full harmony with the length and care of his study of ancient examples; and he proved, if ever anyone did, how necessary such study is to the real success of an architect in Classic or Renaissance buildings, just as much as it is in the case of Gothic buildings” (Street 1871, p. 325). A drawing and a conceptual approach from Cockerell’s youth, over several iterations, still worked as one, but from within the conjured memories of a younger rival pursuing a somewhat different thesis.

2 Charles Robert Cockerell, *Plan of the Parthenon*, 1813, pen and black ink with pencil and grey and orange wash, 82 × 48 cm. Drawing Matter Collection, London

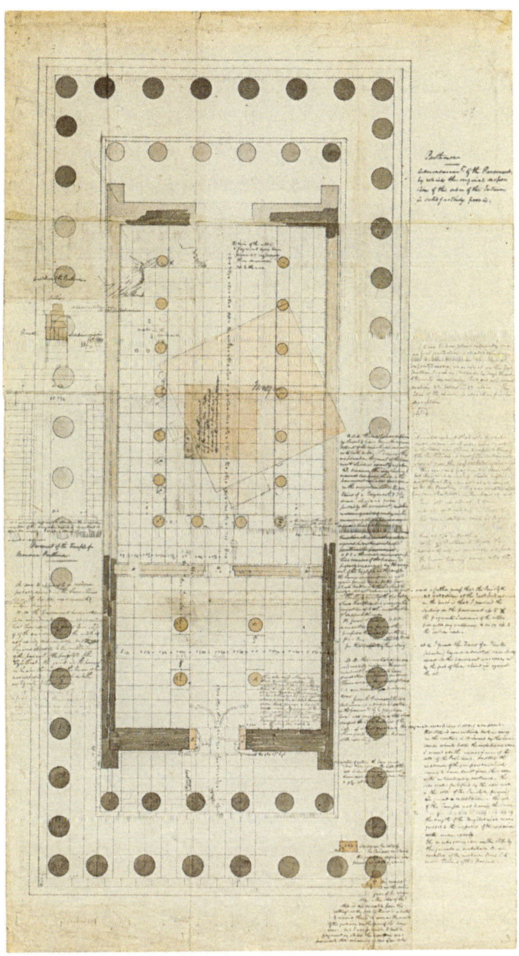

In contrast, after its day out in Paris, Soufflot’s idea and his nephew’s drawing soon went separate ways. If only as a pretty thing, the drawing had a busy afterlife in the collecting market, and belonged for a time to the decorator Armand Ratcau, and later to Olivier Lefuel. Its true history, and importance as a messenger, emerged obliquely only a few years ago to the excitement of scholars. The assemblage of the Parthenon sheets was identified at much the same time, still unattributed and hardly appealing visually, but recognized as perhaps worthy of research (→ ATTRIBUTION).

The lesson is just that the images themselves and the obscure histories related above have always to be retained together, and that value, for their stewards of the longer *durée,* lies in catching them in just those interludes. Ideas are even more fugitive and fragile than the papers, inks and graphite that support them, but they should be understood as the truer content of any collection of architectural drawings. *Niall Hobhouse*

Archive The archive often evokes a musty place full of drawers, dim lights, filing cabinets and shelves overloaded with old documents. It is understood as a place enclosing records, a container of objects and other materials of historical interest, an institution; or as the collection of such materials from which history emerges, like that scent from old books, the "archive-as-source", the origins of history. In both these forms, the archive is not an inert repository of → ARTEFACTS of historical importance or sentimental value. Is it much more than just mute objects and documents – an active and regulatory discursive system, a semantic machine that produces historical meaning, the sure visions of our past. The dual nature of archives as storehouses of dusty objects and as active machines that transform structures and meaning has been the object of many studies by historians and architects.

As Michel Foucault provocatively observed, the archive is neither the sum of all the texts that a culture preserves nor of those institutions that allow for that record's preservation. The archive is rather the "system of statements" that shapes the specific regulations of what can and cannot be said. Thus, it is also "the system that governs the appearance of statements as unique events, that is, as a discursive system" (Foucault 1972, p. 129). More than a repository of documents, a series of images, a batch of correspondence, the archive, for Foucault, is what delimits normality, the average and the field of the possible. As such, the formation of archives and the practice of archiving prevent the amorphous amassing of things, thus controlling, even mastering, one might say, the fear of a frenzied accumulation by establishing an "order of things" (Foucault 1994a, p. 143).

Pointing to another fear, the fear of death, Jacques Derrida argued that facing destruction, and consequently forgetfulness, is what prompts, permits and conditions archivisation. The archive holds the possibility of memorisation, repetition and → REPRODUCTION. The archive always works against itself, as the need to archive is connected to the fear of loss. Yet to archive something, it must be fixed in time, and thus, paradoxically, to archive is also to kill what you fear to lose. Drawing on the analysis of Sigmund Freud's own archive, Derrida coined the term *mal d'archive* (archive fever) to outline that the archive is founded on an instant of death, a moment of passing into the past. In other words, the death drive threatens every archival desire and leads to the destruction of traces and of the archives themselves. The archive, for Derrida, is aporetic: it represents a desire to remember that is founded on the drive to destruction.

If Foucault sees the archive as unequivocally related to discourse production and allowing for a multiplicity of statements to emerge, Derrida in contrast, plays with the double meaning of "archive". The Greek origin of the term, *arkheion*, refers to a house, a domicile, an address, the residence of the superior magistrates, the "archons", those who commanded, but it is also associated with *arkhe*, which is the commencement of history and the command of a people, an authority. Reflecting on the semantics of the term, Derrida regards the archive as having an important "archontic power", as it is what "gathers the functions of unification, of identification, of classification". But he emphasises that this archontic power can be thought only in conjunction with another aspect of the archive, the "power of consignation" (Derrida 1995, p. 10). Consignation, as an act of entrusting, assigning residence, handing over for care, is also an act of consigning, consenting and agreeing through the gathering together of all signs. For Derrida: "There is no archive without a place of consignation, without a technique of repetition, and without a certain exteriority" (Derrida 1995, p. 14). Thus, consignation brings us back to the double meaning of the archive as something on what the dust settles – storage, deposit, house – on the one hand, and, on the other hand, as that active circuit that scatters the dust, a mechanism of discursive formation or sign generation. The archive is, therefore, what gathers things in a place, in a depository, in a building, and what simultaneously generates signs, discourse and an authorised sequence of event.

Architectural archives do not rest frozen in a historical past, to be thawed only for media appearances, for → EXHIBITIONS in museums of art and architecture, in old libraries, in memorabilia concessions, as monuments and memorials, in private albums or on computer hard drives. Instead, they are actively mobilised in the production of architecture and in contemporary thinking about design, and crux to the provenance of architectural matter. While different collections inspire design, the archive is a product of it and is embedded in the design present. Archiving requires an extra effort to organise, catalogue, take inventory, code, preserve and maintain a collection of materials (→ ARCHITECTURAL DRAWINGS, → MODELS, documents). When archive fever (the drive to remember and store related to the fear of death, destruction and forgetfulness) spread into the field of architecture in the 1990s, it triggered reflexivity among practitioners on the formation of archives and the techniques of archivisation, both traditional and novel. Computerisation accelerated these processes, and architectural firms began systematically organising their archives and engaged in thinking about their legacy.

The archive of Álvaro Siza was acquired by the Canadian Centre for Architecture (CCA) in 2015 where it can be consulted and read in transversal dialogue with the *fonds* of other post-war architects such as James Stirling and Aldo Rossi. It was distributed between three institutions: the Portuguese projects stayed in Portugal at the Serralves Museum of Contemporary Art in Porto and at the Fundaçao Calouste Gulbenkian in Lisbon, while the international projects were acquired by the CCA. Yet, Siza's practice began organising the archive long time before this distribution. Siza explained: "I started my practice in '54, and by the nineties, there was a mountain of documents accumulated, and I felt the need to organize them" (Yaneva 2020, p. 137). The archival fever is linked to the messiness of design and the desire to clean the office for new projects. The 1993 Pritzker Prize recognition for his work led to more commissions, more "mountains of paper" piled up, the need for archiving became even more pressing.

Chiara Porcu, a young architect, was appointed as archivist in the 1990s and she spent thirty years organising the archive of the firm. At the time, there were a number of influential projects in the office such as the Faculty of Architecture at the University of Porto, the Chiado and the Toren van Siza, and it became difficult to search for materials in the piles. This prompted the need to organise the archive, introducing an original order that closely reflects the knowledge of the firm's projects, of Siza's unique drawing style, the different collaborators and the overall working methods and organisational habits of the firm (fig. 1).

In 2015, the archive travelled to Montreal and many archivists engaged in rehousing the material, placing them in acid-free folders and establishing new connections through physical displacement (fig. 2). To understand the material,

1 *Álvaro Siza's archive*, Porto. Photo: Albena Yaneva, 2018

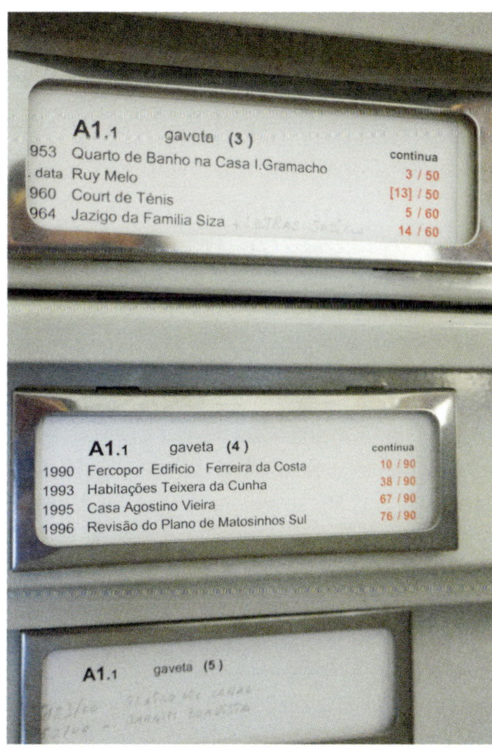

2 *Fond of Álvaro Siza*, Canadian Centre for Architecture, Montreal. Photo: Albena Yaneva, 2019

archivists at the CCA questioned the arrangement introduced by Chiara Porcu and tried to grasp her reading of Siza's work as well as his own interpretation of how his work is to be archived, structured and understood. This dialogue and the knowledge acquired through the rehousing of the material gradually led towards the production of the CCA map of the Siza fonds.

The archive is not just the reflection of the mind of an architect. It is rather a complex additive entity that takes inspiration from design as a collective, heterogeneous and social process. The archive in practice allows architects to re-examine old projects and intervene and has competing reversible temporalities: the times of the aging buildings, aging architects and the vibrant living library of ideas that extends the technical memory of the design firm.

While organising archives for → COLLECTING institutions, archiving is an important tool for extracting, correcting and interpreting knowledge that will form the epistemological basis of architectural scholarship. Archiving is never about a specific object, but about architectural material of larger social and epistemic importance for the discipline. The situated and local practices of arranging, → CATALOGUING, care taking and preserving happen to produce larger structuring effects in an archive. Effects that resonate with greater epistemological anxieties in the discipline and the profession. *Albena Yaneva*

Artefact "The object is the simplest prejudice with which we can work in our experiential world", according to Hans Blumenberg (Blumenberg 1986, pp. 262–263). But once we start thinking about artefacts, things turn out not to be so simple. Take for example a nautilus cup that was made in 1602 in Utrecht and is now in the Metropolitan Museum (fig. 1).

The shell, polished to a silky sheen, is placed on a layered pedestal in which an egg-and-dart border supports a depiction of the waves of the ocean; the pedestal also has small excrecences that might be handles (if they were not so small) of grotesque ornament growing into alert animal heads. The shell itself is clasped, so to speak, on the front and back by female herms sporting volutes, and on the right side by a sea animal that expands from its flat tail into a full-sized monster that spits out a tiny male figure who dives into the cup; and all this is crowned by the reclining figure of Neptune. On the left side a grotesque satyr's head has grown from a stem flanked by spikes that recall both the bare branches of a tree and the bones of a large fish. Architects, it is well known, create buildings, not artefacts. But as this object shows, even decorative artefacts have an architecture and use typical architectural features such as the pilaster as a way of figuring the metal support for the shell. So what happens when we start to think about the artefactual nature of architecture?

In conventional ontologies the artefact is close to things and objects, but distinct from them because it is man-made and by that very fact artificial. The word literally means something made by art and thus carries with it a long pedigree, going back to Aristotle's distinction between things made, or actions performed, without empirical knowledge of cause and effect, and those based on knowledge and experience. In the Renaissance *arteficia* would become collectors' objects, to populate their *Wunderkammer* (→ COLLECTING). With the emergence of empiricism and of the modern public museum a distinction between works of art and artefacts was put in place. In Vienna for instance the artworks from the *Wunderkammer* in Ambras were transported to the Kunsthistorisches Museum, whereas the objects now dismissed as curiosities disappeared into the reserves or were banished to ethnographical collections (→ STORAGE). The industrial revolution added another layer of distinction: artefacts increasingly became mass-produced, part of the realm of technology, and if at all of art, then of industrial design (see Schlosser 2021).

But the Nautilus cup embodies in the most pregnant form a number of tensions that are always present in the notion of artefacts. There is the opposition if not conflict between art and nature. One can read this Nautilus cup as a staging of the transformative powers of nature as well as human art: both the shell and its metal framing are the result of transforming primary materials, but also display the constant transformation of tendrils into rams' heads, tree trunks into satyrs, or vegetal motifs into a seamonster. The cup not only thematises transformation, the essence of the workings of Nature and the artificer, but also its own deep history – in the depths of the ocean and in the silversmith's forge, but also in widely-held beliefs in the Renaissance, going back to Ovid's *Metamorphoses*, that the essence of reality is constant transformation. Other specimens also present their own provenance more literally when

1 *Nautilus cup*, 1602, nautilus shell with gilded silver mounts, 27.9 × 16.8 × 10.8 cm. Metropolitan Museum, New York

they include → INSCRIPTIONS in Chinese for instance. In all cases, these Nautilus cups are travelling objects that cross borders – between parts of the world, realms of nature, human ontologies and artistic genres. They carry the evidence or the scars, of their migrations, and by these marks they invite the viewer to write their biography (→ IMAGE VEHICLE).

Another conspicuous feature of these cups is what Claude Lévi-Strauss would call their *entassement*, the limitless and endlesly varied piling-up of heterogeneous elements. This is an aspect that returns in the work of the artist who in my view most consistently thought about the artefactual nature of architecture: Giovanni Battista Piranesi. In his late colossal candelabra of the 1770s (fig. 2) similar features as in the Nautilus cup return: a pedestal employing elements of the classical orders, transforming vegetation and a strong insistence on animal presence (see van Eck 2023).

They do not feature shells, but as is well known, in the slightly earlier preface to the *Diverse maniere* (1769), Piranesi argued that the origins of Ionic ornament go back to the shapes of shells. In the facade of Santa Maria del Priorato, his only executed architecture design, he also performs an aetiological conjuring trick that recalls the play on origins and provenances we have seen in the Nautilus cup. In Rome he shows in the ornament → FRAMING of the oculus how the egg-and-dart motif grows from the tail of a snake. Now Piranesi had a term for a class of artefacts that included chimney pieces, lamps, dress, vases, furniture and candelabra: *piccola architettura*. They are architecture because they are made of stone and the product of design; at the same time they had never been the object of architectural or art theory. But they are of great interest for a provenance perspective of architecture, because they are all – in the artist's last publication, *Vasi, candelabri, cippi, sarcofagi, tripodi, lucerne, ed ornamenti antichi disegnati ed incisi dal Cav. Gio. Batt. Piranesi* (1778) – part of his investigation into the material origins of Roman architecture. The captions often list their provenance: from the ethnographical Museo

2 Giovanni Battista Piranesi, *Marble candelabrum*, 1770s, Roman elements of the fifteenth and eighteenth centuries, height 3.53 m. Musée du Louvre, Paris

Borgiano in Velletri to the princely collections of the Lungara or the Barberini. Conceiving architectural design as artefactual design opens the possibility of thinking about architecture not in terms of conformity to the rules of classical theory, but in terms of its provenance, in the man-made history of artefacts and the deep history of nature. *Caroline van Eck*

Attribution After nearly thirty years of debate, a failed architectural competition and dozens of rejected proposals – in the spring of 1860, Norway's new parliament building seemed further away than ever. A few years earlier, the young Swedish architect Victor Emil Langlet had been commissioned to design the building, yet the ministry, not trusting the inexperienced Swede, had also commissioned a project by the Danish architect Hansen, whose drawings were shown to the Norwegian public that very spring (fig. 1).

Confusion soon arose. Not only was Hansen's project one of so many parliament proposals that the public could hardly keep track; it was also not entirely clear which Hansen had made it. Conservative newspapers raved about the famous architect Hansen, praising his work in Athens and Vienna. The radical press, on the other hand, pointed out that this was not the celebrated Theophil Hansen, who was just making his mark as the starchitect of the Vienna Ringstrasse (→ CELEBRITY), but rather his lesser-known brother Christian, who after some much-praised works in Athens had withdrawn to a more parochial existence as a Danish building inspector and later professor at the Academy. Had the ministry commissioned the wrong Hansen? "Why the Ministry landed on just this man is not easy to grasp", opined the newspaper *Christiania-Posten* on 5 May 1860: "Prof. Chr. Hansen is not such a big figure in the art world, although his *brother*, Theophilus Hansen, does have a name. That the incompetent Ministry may have confused the two, is not beyond the realm of possibility." The confusion had in fact been anticipated already the year before by the critic Emil Tidemand, who in in an exasperated outburst in *Morgenbladet*, 9 May 1859 – set in quotation marks as if to underline the absurdity of the situation – asked "Who is Mr. Hansen?"

The Hansen confusion was used for what it was worth by his defenders as well as his critics. If conservative Hansen-supporters ascribed Theophil's projects to Christian in order to boost the latter's fame, the radical press did the

Nr. 20.] Illustreret Nyhedsblad. 87

Om Storthingsbygningen.

Musik og Literatur.

1 Christian Hansen, *The parliament project*, engraving, from "Om Storthingsbygningen", *Illustreret Nyhedsblad*, 13 May 1860

opposite – stripping Christian of all fame and attributing the elder brother's major work to Theophil. Critic Emil Tidemand tried to end the confusion by publishing translated entries from *Nordisk Konversationslexicon* on Christian and Theophil Hansen respectively, making it clear that *both* brothers were exceptionally famous and accomplished, and that it would be an honor for the Norwegian nation to have a parliament by either one. To no avail, as it happens. Langlet's project was approved in Parliament on 18 May 1860, leaving Christian Hansen with only sour grapes and a protracted quarrel with the Norwegian Ministry whom he accused – not without reason – of contractual negligence.

The brothers Hansen may not have gotten to build anything in Norway, but they remained remarkably famous and were frequently reported on in the Norwegian nineteenth-century press. Not seldom with erroneous attribution. In a reportage from the 1873 world exhibition in Vienna, for example, the newspaper *Correspondenten* praised Theophil Hansen's Ringstrasse monuments and footnoted with some pride that this was the man who had made a proposal for the Norwegian Parliament some twelve years before. After the devastating 1884 → FIRE at Christiansborg Palace in Copenhagen, the Norwegian press ran long articles about Theophil Hansen's → RECONSTRUCTION project, wrongly attributing the burnt-down palace to his brother: "It is a curious play of fate, that Theophilus Hansen is likely to resurrect the work of his brother – the deceased minister Heinrick Hansen – reviving it like a Phoenix from the ashes in a rejuvenated and beautified form – for it was the latter who made the plans for the re-erection of the now destroyed Christiansborg Palace" (Anonymous 1884).

Sadly, Emil Tidemand (who had died in 1865) was not around to clarify this triple misattribution. It involved not only two Hansen brothers, but three, as well as another (and totally unrelated) architect Hansen. For the architect of the Christiansborg Palace that had burnt in 1884 was not Hendrick Hansen as the Norwegian journalist asserted, but Christian Frederik Hansen, Denmark's great neo-classicist and by far the most famous Hansen of them all. Neither did Theophil seem to have had a brother by the name Hendrick. The brother he did have, Christian, was, however, for a period minister, and he was also, as the anonymous writer stated, dead, perishing in the spring of 1883. How three real architects Hansen plus one fictitious brother came to merge into two larger-than-life master builders of the Danish royal palace on the pages of a provincial Norwegian newspaper, is not to be known. Attribution is power, and the subtle effects of misattribution are incalculable. *Mari Hvattum*

Authentication The history of art history harbours a particular necessity – to attribute works of art to specific authors, to identify them and finally to authenticate them. All these processes are based on the concept of the author and operate within the prevailing tradition of attributing certain works to certain people, usually men (→ AUTHORSHIP). The genre of artist and architect biography, popularised by Giorgio Vasari, is closely linked to the desire to guarantee → AUTHENTICITY and eliminate doubts about → ATTRIBUTION. The biographer's pen, like the forger's brush, is a tool of mythmaking. And both the celebration of the author and a seemingly watertight authentication provide a necessary element for establishing the value of a work of art on an emerging art market. Stories of dodgy dealers and dubious experts have accompanied the trade ever since buyers who were not commissioners appeared on the scene. And the allegation of faulty authentication does not stop with the dealers. The scholarly origins of art history in eighteenth-century Italy are curiously suffused with stories as flamboyant as a true crime thriller.

Take for instance Pierre-François Hugues, who under the pseudonym Baron d'Hancarville produced one of the most ground-breaking works on William Hamilton's collection of vases, a tour de force that established the fame and reputation of the collector among European connoisseurs, while blurring the lines between academic accuracy and roguish intrigue (fig. 1).

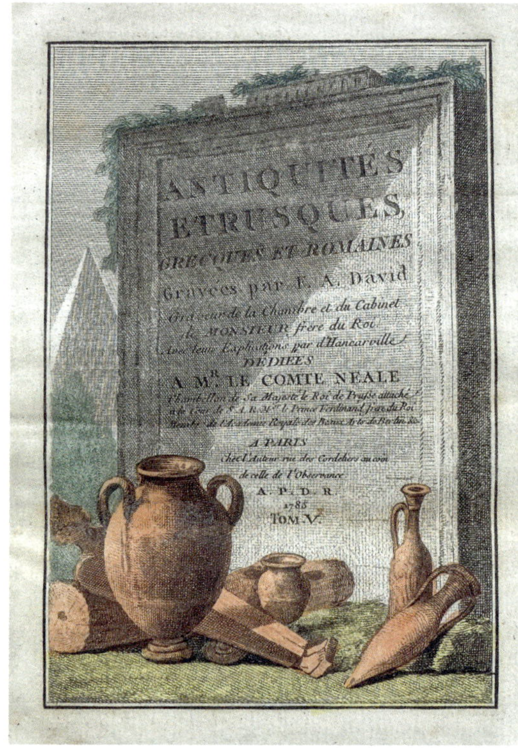

1 François-Anne David, *Frontispiece*, 1785, from Pierre-François Hugues d'Hancarville, *Antiquités étrusques, grecques et romaines*, vol. v (Paris: David 1787)

Always on the run from his creditors, this ingenious charlatan and friend of Johann Joachim Winckelmann also earned an extra income with popularised pornographic illustrations on gems, which he claimed had been collected by Roman emperors (see d'Hancarville 1782). The fifty feculent illustrations in this moderately priced book were modern fakes, invented by the author (see Haskell 1982, pp. 185f.). In this case, the liberal provenance research went well beyond the attribution of authenticity: by also depicting the secret rites of Roman women, d'Hancarville in passing fabricated an early history of sexuality.

Joseph Duveen (1869–1939), later equipped with the official recognition as the 1st Baron Duveen, successfully bought works of art from short-strapped European aristocrats and sold them to American nouveaux-riches. Duveen's dealings relied on one of the leading art historians of the day, Bernard Berenson (1865–1959). Their collaboration was successful; their alliance, a masterclass in the manipulation of traces and clues, exposes the moral fissures beneath the edifice of art history.

Berenson's judgement about the originator and authenticity of a work of art caused its value to de- or increase (see Secrest 1979). As his judgements favoured intuition over facts and data, Berenson, recent scholars have argued, certified questionable attributions, especially for paintings from the Quattro- and Cinquecento, for which Duveen paid him handsomely. Indeed, Berenson's willingness to associate paintings with a clear identification allowed Joseph Duveen to market them to clients whose concept of art history relied on the concept of works of art produced by single masters, and not of workshops involving a good deal of collaborative activity. Both were trafficking in the theatre of legitimacy, selling pedigrees rather than paintings to American magnates hungry for the patina of aristocracy.

Together, they instrumentalised the trace, bending it to the logic of capital. Everyone won: the art dealer realising value, his clients (including Henry Clay Frick, Andrew W. Mellon, John D. Rockefeller and Henry E. Huntington) and the art historian, whose status as one of the most influential representatives of the emerging discipline was founded on his status as a major authenticator. Recent scholarship, with its infrared eyes and dendrochronological scalpels, has unveiled these suppressed histories. Yet the market resists. For what value resides in a bottega when the buyer craves a master? Berenson was perfectly aligned with the market's hunger for myth.

There is, indeed, an element of the thriller in histories of authentication. Carlo Ginzburg relates the story of Giovanni Morelli (Ivan Lermolieff), who suggested studying the minor, "most negligable" parts of faces and bodies in order to find the clues as to who had produced a painting: ear lobes, fingernails, the shapes of toes. The art connoisseur turns into a detective following in the footsteps of Sherlock Holmes examining cigarette ashes or footsteps in the mud. The reading of traces – of fingerprints – becomes part of crime fighting, and the control of the potentially criminal (which is everyone). The trace, as Ginzburg reminds us, is never neutral; it is a battleground where power, monetary interest and knowledge collide (see Ginzburg 1979).

Does authentication hold any value at all in the field of architecture? After all, the procedures in this discipline are even more diffuse and collective than in the visual arts. Art historians trace brushstrokes for proofs of provenance. Architectural authenticators examine plans, marginalia and tender documents in search of the maestro's mysterious imprint. Establishing authorship and authenticating it obscures a chaotic reality. It eliminates traces rather than revealing them. In keeping with Leon Battista Alberti (who, as Marvin Trachtenberg suggests, modelled the architect on Petrarch's elevation of the individual writer and the associated concept of immortality through the work), the architect became an intellectual who set himself apart from the lowly bricklayers and carpenters (see Trachtenberg 2010, pp. 87ff.).

Is that infamous sketch by Le Corbusier, or is it a trace of Charlotte Perriand's unrecognised participation? And the spidery drawings showing the Villa d'all Ava as a bare stage set: Are they really by Rem Koolhaas while the more precise ones, struggling to organise structure and material, are by one of his unnamed collaborators? The irony here is palpable: Koolhaas, who always describes architecture as a collective endeavour, also has his work dissected for autographical peculiarities because the researchers want it that way. Or does he want it as well?

Just as its counterpart in the art world, authentication in architecture is a performance of exclusion. The authenticator's judgement is therefore not just a recognition, but the assignment of value that transforms bricks and mortar into a cultural currency. After all, the market has little appetite for complexity: When the investor René Benko (who was investigated and taken to custody for fraud in 2024) starts to build the Lamarr department store in Vienna, it is announced as the work of a Pritzker Prize winning star architect (→ CELEBRITY), not as the collective work of an Office for Metropolitan Architecture with its draughtmen and -women and the craftspeople who were involved in the process (fig. 2).

The attribution of the project was part of the advertising campaign for the store, before the collapse of the client reduced economic ambitions to match the design's banality. Perhaps this is where Ginzburg's paradigm of evidence shows its fangs: the trace is not neutral, but a weapon used by those who control the narrative.

2 *Lamarr luxury department store advertised on the fence of the construction site*, Vienna. Photo: Christoph Grafe, 2022

A price may have to be paid for emphasising authentication in architecture. It comes at the expense of authenticity which, after all, is also the tangible remnant of collective production, of the messy reality of bricks and mortar, of shovels and trowels. Such cancelling out is not new. It is the consequence of a longstanding project of disentangling intellect and muscle power, patron and craftsman. Is there another version? An emerging culture of repair, driven by the urgency of climate crisis and the rejection of throwing things away, creates a counter-narrative (→ REPARATION). After all, repair is an inherently intimate affair. It always involves confronting the traces of time: the cracks, the → WEATHERING, the wear and tear. When repairing a building, the layers are inevitably exposed; the quick fixes of the subcontractor, the manoeuvres of the craftsman, the tweaks of those who inhabit it (→ MAINTENANCE). Authenticity emerges not as a static testimony, but as something that is alive: an object onto the surfaces (and deep structures) on which people, time and weather leave inscriptions. Repair involves a dialogue with past presences. It is a forensic investigation of the → LABOUR that has gone into the walls and the ground.

The culture of repair challenges not only authentication but the myth of the flawless original (→ PRISTINE). It accepts that buildings, like life, are characterised by accidents, compromises and interventions. The anonymous weld seam gains value not as a defect to be concealed, but as evidence of the worker who has left it. Authenticity redefines itself not as a fixed attribute, but as a continuum of care. In a finite world where → REUSE is no longer optional, the survival of architecture could depend on this change. A repaired building with its visible scars and hybrid histories becomes a manifesto of sorts: a discovery of the traces of people and the more-than-human creators of cities and buildings. *Christoph Grafe*

Authenticity Centred above the main podium of the semi-circular assembly room in the Storting, the Norwegian parliament designed by Emil Victor Langlet and inaugurated in 1866, hangs a large painting depicting a group of seated men in a modest, brightly lit room decorated with spruce garlands, observing an elegantly dressed man making a declaration (fig. 1).

The painting by the artist Oscar Wergeland, commissioned and presented to the parliament by the medical officer and businessman Lorentz Reinhold Boll Ring, is among Norway's most reproduced artworks. It constantly appears in news reports and history books, on stamps, bills and souvenirs as well as → REPRODUCTION in private homes (→ IMAGE VEHICLE). The scene is set on Wednesday 11 May 1814, and takes place in the upper floor's central hall of the Eidsvoll Manor House, an hour's drive north of Oslo. It portrays eighty-four of the 112 representatives who worked out the Norwegian constitution after the personal union of Denmark-Norway was dismantled as a consequence of the Napoleonic Wars.

Recent scholarship has evidenced that the painting, universally believed to be an accurate restaging of the moment when Christian Magnus Falsen (considered the main author of the document) proclaimed the constitution to the assembly in 1814, is rather a comment on a political controversy of the early 1880s when the political left and right parties debated whether or not the ministers should be allowed to meet in the parliament, a dispute that paved the way for parliamentarism (see Torkjelsson 2015, p. 40). Proof is found on the sheet of paper in Falsen's left hand where "Paragraf 115" is worded, dating the painting to 11 May when the representatives debated the paragraph that specifies the conditions for making changes to the constitution, an aspect core to the debate of 1882.

Equally interesting is the painting at large, representing Wergeland's attempt to reproduce the historic location of 1814 more than six decades later. Before functioning as a temporary assembly room in 1814, the so-called Rikssalen (Hall of State) at Eidsvoll was a rough and unfinished space, originally planned by the owner Carsten Anker as a picture gallery and a banquet hall. It was painted, furnished and decorated for the deliberations in 1814. When Wergeland visited it in the early 1880s in preparation for his painting, the building had altered status, ownership, use and look (→ TRANSFORMATION). Immediately after the assembly, the benches, podium and the garlands were removed, and the space was turned into a picture gallery as originally planned. When Anker was bankrupted and the building auctioned off in 1829, it fell into decay (→ DERELICTION). In 1837, it was designated a national monument, in 1851 the Norwegian state purchased the building, and in 1864, for the fiftieth anniversary of the Norwegian constitution, the Rikssalen was wallpapered in green to house the national picture gallery. Based on what he observed on site, as well as in oral and written sources, Wergeland constructed what would become the official emblem of the pivotal event of 1814 (see Risåsen 2005).

In 1897, astonishingly, while preparing for the centennial in 1914, the painting became the model for the → RECONSTRUCTION of the building itself. The wallpaper was removed, the walls were painted white, three rows of benches installed, and garlands and curtains put in place. The 1964 restoration followed up with the installation of rococo furniture, a new layer of paint and the garlands were adjusted in accordance with the painting to heighten the "authenticity" of the room.

The → RESTORATION prior to the bicentennial of 2014 was based on thorough investigations of material evidence and archives not conferred earlier; inventories, → FIRE tariffs, auction → CATALOGUES and correspondence. In the case of the Rikssalen, the blueprint of Wergeland's painting was abandoned in favour of an archival-based version of the space: the rococo stairs and one row of benches were removed, while the 1964 layer of oil paint was scraped off the walls and replaced with composition paint. The curtains were removed, the white-painted floor returned to its original untreated pine, the forty-eight squared window replaced with the original grid of twelve, the argent lamps moved to the longitudinal walls, and the garlands supplemented with white drapes. Although the roughness of the original wall planks had evened out during the former restorations, the room appeared to be more authentic than ever, giving the visitor the feeling of how it had been to attend the deliberations in the "primitive" setting of the 1814 Rikssalen.

"Authenticity" is a slippery term. Derived from the Greek αὐθεντικός, signifying something original, genuine and principle, it has commonly been used to qualify something as

1 Oscar Wergeland, *Eidsvoll 1814*, 1882–1885, oil on canvas, 2.85 × 4 m. Parliament Building, Oslo

real and true, as opposed to fictitious and false. In → PRESERVATION it has traditionally been used in the validation of → MATERIAL substance, yet has gained a broader meaning when engaged in more complex settings: "The past as we know it is partly product of the present; we continually reshape memory, rewrite history, refashion relics. [...] To revise what actually happened, as distinct from our ideas and its traces, is impossible, yet ardently desired. Three main motives impel would-be time travellers to tamper with history: to improve the past itself or the lot of those who lived in it; to better present circumstances by changing what has let up to them; and to ensure the stability of the present by altering (or protecting) the past against interferences by others" (Lowenthal 1985, p. 26). David Lowenthal famously emphasised how the past is reconstructed, interpreted and shaped by present-day concerns, values and ideals. Authenticity is as such not an absolute entity but a matter of perception and context. The historian states that the desire for "authentic" experiences often conflicts with the very nature of historical preservation, leading to practices that alter the original form and meaning of → HERITAGE sites. Lowenthal suggests that the desire for authenticity is not seeking exact replicas of the past (→ FACSIMILE), or the original physical state of an object, but rather a connection to it – one that evokes a sense of continuity, truth or identity. He argues that authenticity should be understood as something fluid and often shaped by the intentions behind preservation processes and the meanings that individuals and societies attach to them.

2 *Eidsvoll Manor House, Rikssalen*, after the 2014 restoration. Photo: Guri Dahl

The question of authenticity relating to the Rikssalen at Eidsvoll is a complex one. Today, the material authenticity of the hall is high, with original floors, walls and ceiling (if partly obscured by new layers of treatment). The room displays reproductions of original furnishing, materials and techniques, and gives access to the feeling of "roughness" of the short-lived space of 1814, while arguably adding depth and value to the constitution itself (fig. 2). The 2014 version is perhaps the most correct version of the space of 1814 but lacks traces of the many (celebrated) restorations it has undergone and has lost its ambiguous relationship with the iconic painting. The last restoration claims a high degree of authenticity but can hardly be evaluated in isolation. In 1968, Jean Baudrillard stated that "no matter how fine it is, an antique is always eccentric; no matter how authentic it is, there is always something false about it. And indeed, it *is* false, in so far as *it puts itself forward as authentic within a system whose basic principle is by no means authenticity but, rather, calculation of relationships and the abstractness of signs*" (Baudrillard 1996, p. 74). The restored Rikssalen can be described as both authentic and false, pointing to the ambiguous nature of the term.

The Wergeland painting is a national icon, but unavoidably bound to the physical space. Acting as a blueprint for the visitors, the painting will remain the "original" due to its position in the → COLLECTIVE MEMORY. The contemporary, actual space remains secondary. The 2014 restoration deviates significantly from Wergeland's edition, and one risks what could be called an authenticity rapture, in which the discrepancy between expectation (set by the painting) and the space become too large.

The relationship between the painting and the Rikssalen hints at the complex and fluid structure of authenticity and the sometimes-conflicting versions of historical circumstances. Neither the painting nor the space is authentic or are authenticating proofs (→ AUTHENTICATION) of the events that took place in 1814. Yet together they constitute a truly eccentric and authentic whole, as a conglomerate of misunderstandings, uninformed decisions, political controversy, material experiments, archival evidence and shifting preservation ideologies. *Erik Langdalen*

Authorship Along the entablature of the Pantheon in Rome an inscription almost a metre high reads: "M AGRIPPA•L•F•COS•TERTIUM•FECIT" (Marcus Agrippa, son of Lucius, Consul three times, made it). The implications of this statement are complex (fig. 1). Like the equally famous "R. Mutt" inscribed on a piece of early-twentieth-century sanitaryware, "M AGRIPPA ... FECIT" describes a territory of authorial possibility rather than any precise authorial ownership (fig. 2).

The bronze letters on the Pantheon date from 1895. The incisions they are placed in are as old as the building. Up until the 1880s, that structure was thought to have been erected by Agrippa himself during the 20s BCE, endowing it with a wonderful imperial pedigree. Victorious general at the Battle of Actium, Governor of Transalpine Gaul, Agrippa's reported intent was to dedicate the temple to Augustus, Rome's inaugural emperor and his life-time benefactor. During the nineteenth century, this association gave the Pantheon special significance. From 1870, as Rome became the capital of a reinvented secular Italian state, the national government made moves to strip the rotunda of the accretions produced during 1,200-odd years as a Christian church (→ TRANSFORMATION). It then served as a mausoleum for King Vittorio Emanuele, titular head of the new regime, after his death in 1878. Agrippa's authorship tied tight a radical association in this proposal: laying Vittorio Emanuele to rest in a temple originally intended for Rome's

1 *Pantheon inscription*, 1895, Goodyear Archival Collection, Brooklyn Museum Archives, New York. Photographer unknown

most august emperor shone a divine, ancient and imperial light onto a fragile, new, political construction.

Between 1889, when the permanent royal tomb was completed within the rotunda, and 1895, when the bronze lettering was set up, other implications of inscription began to undermine the clarity of authorial connection at the Pantheon (→ INSCRIPTION). The size and grammatical precision of "M AGRIPPA ... FECIT" bore no resemblance to anything else produced during Augustus's reign. Surveys during 1892 and 1893 recorded stamps on the building's brickwork, contemporary barcodes that revealed both the bricks' makers and their date of manufacture. These obstinately dated the fabric to the second century CE. Scholarly opinion began to identify the Emperor Hadrian as the builder. That "M AGRIPPA ... FECIT" was inscribed by the grammatically picky Hadrian onto a structure Agrippa could not possibly have "made", suggests sophistication, double meaning and ambivalence. Hadrian never signed the Pantheon. But his claim to have built it might be as significant as Agrippa's, just as, for Jorge Luis Borges, Pierre Menard's twentieth-century authorship of *Don Quixote* was as monumental an achievement as that which produced the *Don Quixote* of Cervantes. Secure → ATTRIBUTION melts into something less certain.

Agrippa and Hadrian, Marcel Duchamp and Borges. Where were notions of authorship, architecture and provenance first explicitly brought together? The link goes back to Leon Battista Alberti, who created a body of theory to describe architecture using tropes from humanist discourse in fifteenth-century Italy. His formulations, made in *De re aedificatoria* (c.1452) and the Italian translation of *De pictura* (1436), linked authorship and architecture in contrasting ways. In a development that reflected contemporary reassessments of the art of painting, the creation of buildings was claimed as an intellectual practice: a building could exist "complete" in the mind of an architect before ever it was realised in brick or stone (see Anstey et al. 2007).

Following Alberti, the provenance of any building, as the provenance of any painting, could be thought to involve an origin point in the mind that contained this vision. Whether buildings moved literally or in media (→ DISPLACEMENT, → IMAGE VEHICLE, → MOBILITY), whether they changed hands or were abandoned (→ ACQUISITION), whether the discussion concerned "Brunelleschi's dome for S. Maria dell Fiore" or "Le Corbusier's Chapel at Ronchamp" or "Jean Prouvé's Maison Tropicale", this fundamental link between authorship and provenance remained: the value of the work, its status as an object whose provenance was of interest, lay to an extent in the assignment of an author function that described the virtuosity of one individual in its construction.

2 Marcel Duchamp, *Fountain*, 1917, 291 Art Gallery, New York. Photo: Alfred Stieglitz

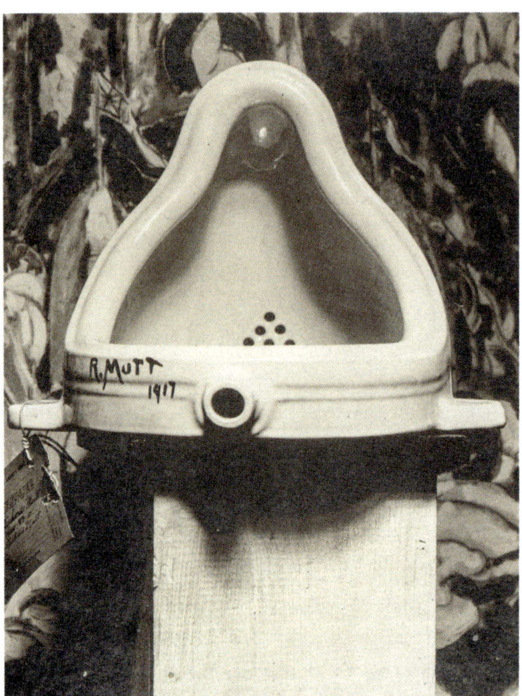

This author-function has often been claimed to distinguish architecture from "mere building". But it always embeds some uncertainty. One can ask, "Who authors?": Alberti was militant in his claim that authorship, in terms he was deriving from legal and humanist theory, remained with the architect, who owned a building in a way that neither a patron (an Agrippa or a Hadrian) nor an artisan (a brickmaker or carpenter) could. But before and after Alberti the diversity of authorial claims to building blur this clarity. Names such as *Thermae Agrippae* project a sense of authorial ownership by a patron that is equally valid to that claimed by their architect. Almost anyone connected with processes of construction would dispute the possibility that buildings can exist complete in any single mind outside the context of procurement and delivery. Brick stamps also have an authorial claim to make. One can ask, "What is authored?": this "what" might be an → ARCHITECTURAL DRAWING or → MODEL, an → ARTEFACT with an indexical relation to a permanent building. But Alberti's introductory celebration of the architect's skill suggests that it might as well be processes, that architects design sequences of action as well as static structures. Indeed, "what is authored" might be the effect of altogether more fluid factors based in history, interpretation and mediation. Agrippa's proclaimed patronage of a Pantheon he didn't build, or Hadrian's decision not to implant his name into an authorial inscription he probably commissioned, are both examples of that complication.

Tim Anstey

Bond Investment instruments articulate time and space in the production of architecture. Their role in the emergence of tall buildings in the United States demonstrates the agency of finance as an element of architectural provenance. The birth of the skyscraper has been attributed to many factors: urban density, the development of new construction techniques and to the discovery, noted by Cass Gilbert in 1900, that it was a "machine that makes the land pay" (Willis 1995, p. 19). Form follows finance, in Carol Willis's memorable phrase, but it is also true that finance appeared in many forms.

European observers marvelled at the prices land could fetch in places like New York City. The German architect Otto Rappold reported in 1913 that the land beneath the Singer Building cost about $1000 per square metre and that a narrow sliver of land at Broadway and Wall Street sold for the highest price he had ever seen at $6000 per square metre (see Rappold 1913, p. 28). It was not uncommon for the land beneath a building to cost more than the structure itself, as was the case with Daniel Burnham and Co.'s Fuller – or "Flatiron" – Building. Such expensive land dictated the seemingly endless stacking of floor atop floor – the reproduction of the world, as Rem Koolhaas would say – to ensure a return on investment (see Koolhaas 1994, p. 82).

In many cases, the process of financing of land → ACQUISITION and construction was similar in the USA and Europe. Private investors, banks, architectural firms and contractors typically had to raise between thirty and forty per cent of the total sum required before a bank would finance the remainder.

But the US market also created forms of financing that were hitherto unknown in European cities. The German building engineer Karl Fritz Stöhr described the process of fundraising through the issuance of mortgage bonds that he had witnessed during his work at Daniel Burnham & Co.'s Chicago office between 1912 and 1914. In this process, business plan and architectural design are sublimated into a new form – the bond, a promissory note secured against the idea of a building and a scheduled yield of interest.

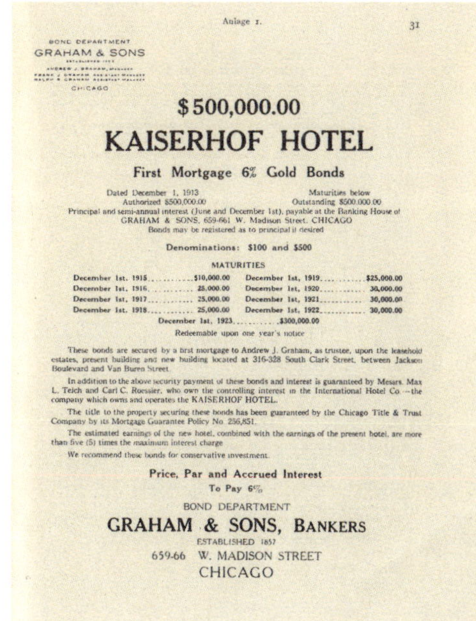

Anlage 1. 31

BOND DEPARTMENT
GRAHAM & SONS
CHICAGO

$500,000.00

KAISERHOF HOTEL

First Mortgage 6% Gold Bonds

Dated December 1, 1913 — Maturities below
Authorized $500,000.00 — Outstanding $500,000.00
Principal and semi-annual interest (June and December 1st), payable at the Banking House of GRAHAM & SONS, 659-661 W. Madison Street, CHICAGO
Bonds may be registered as to principal if desired

Denominations: $100 and $500

MATURITIES

December 1st, 1915	$10,000.00	December 1st, 1919	$25,000.00
December 1st, 1916	25,000.00	December 1st, 1920	30,000.00
December 1st, 1917	25,000.00	December 1st, 1921	30,000.00
December 1st, 1918	25,000.00	December 1st, 1922	30,000.00
December 1st, 1923	$300,000.00		

Redeemable upon one year's notice

These bonds are secured by a first mortgage to Andrew J. Graham, as trustee, upon the leasehold estates, present building and new building located at 316-328 South Clark Street, between Jackson Boulevard and Van Buren Street.

In addition to the above security payment of these bonds and interest is guaranteed by Messrs. Max L. Teich and Carl C. Roessler, who own the controlling interest in the International Hotel Co.—the company which owns and operates the KAISERHOF HOTEL.

The title to the property securing these bonds has been guaranteed by the Chicago Title & Trust Company by its Mortgage Guarantee Policy No. 256,851.

The estimated earnings of the new hotel, combined with the earnings of the present hotel, are more than five (5) times the maximum interest charge.

We recommend these bonds for conservative investment.

Price, Par and Accrued Interest
To Pay 6%

BOND DEPARTMENT
GRAHAM & SONS, BANKERS
ESTABLISHED 1857
659-66 W. MADISON STREET
CHICAGO

1 *Prospectus for bond issue for Kaiserhof Hotel*, 1913, from Karl Fritz Stöhr, *Amerikanische Turmbauten* (Munich: R. Oldenbourg 1921)

Stöhr had seen this play out in the extension to Chicago's Kaiserhof Hotel. Seeking to add an eighteen-story annexe to the original premises of the 1889 building on Van Buren Street, the owners of the Kaiserhof turned to the banking house of Graham and Sons to issue $500,000 of first-mortgage bonds at six per cent interest. Issued in denominations of $100 and $500 in 1913, the bonds had scheduled maturity dates on the first of December every year until 1922. The innovation of this financial structure lay not only in the issuance of bonds to private persons but also in the method of fundraising. Stöhr reported that once the business plan had been created for bond issue, it was then reproduced in the form of posters, newspaper announcements, prospectuses and other forms of advertising. A prospectus for the Kaiserhof Hotel reproduced in Stöhr's study of skyscrapers demonstrates how this worked (fig. 1).

The document appealed to potential investors through arithmetic, building description and architectural imagery. Tables documenting the value of assets (the existing building, the new

2 *Rendering of proposed extension from the prospectus for bond issue for Kaiserhof Hotel*, 1913, from Karl Fritz Stöhr, *Amerikanische Turmbauten* (Munich: R. Oldenbourg 1921)

building, etc.) and income from operations attested to the solidity of the enterprise. The prospectus pointed to the experience of the architects, Marshall & Fox, in building other hotels and tall buildings across the country as merits of the project. The document also included a perspectival rendering of the new Kaiserhof as intended to be built, the annexe towering above the broad existing structure and demonstrating elegant "German Renaissance" details at the grand entry and on the pinnacle of the tower (fig. 2). The image's caption included the physical address of the soon-to-be-built structure and a message from the bank: "We own and offer $500,000.00 First Mortgage 6% Gold Bonds" (Stöhr 1921, p. 33). The idea of the building and the idea of profit coincide in this juxtaposition of image and text.

Born of the distribution of risk and the promise of reward, the addition to the Kaiserhof Hotel illustrates the intermediary work that the mortgage bond has played in the production of architecture. The bond is one of the sites where architectural design and business acumen intersect in the translation of ideas into the physical space of the city and the fiscal calendar of accountants. It shows us that buildings arise not only through the → LABOUR of talented architects and skilled builders. Through the medium of the bond, buildings become manifest as investment vehicles before they ever make the land pay. *Richard Anderson*

Bricolage What happens if a practice emerging out of pure necessity – in, say, building a chicken shed in the back garden – turns into an artistic or intellectual principle? In their original context the → COMPONENTS may have reached the end of their half-life. Now they reappear in a new context. Sometimes, even the most innocent practice of building or making things – improvised tinkering – can develop into an interplay of purpose and aesthetics. What was to ensure survival may have become an unintended work of art. Only then intention may creep in. Bricolage might, following Claude Lévi-Strauss, become wild thinking: like mythological thought, it relies on "résidus et des débris d'événements", the fossilised reminders to the history of an individual or a society (Lévi-Strauss 1962, pp. 35f.). The origin – or should we say: the provenance – of the → ELEMENTS is neither here nor there. It is the potential of elements to be used, in their contextual effectiveness, that counts.

Architecture, meanwhile, traditionally meets such tinkering with scepticism. Admittedly, there is a venerable history of the → REUSE of building components, of → SPOLIA, ranging from ancient columns in mediaeval churches to → RUINS left over from → WAR action during the post-Second World War → RECONSTRUCTION. Yet at least since Leon Battista Alberti, who defined the conceptual unity of the building as the core of architectural → AUTHORSHIP, the coherence of the design retains its inviolability. The hierarchy and harmony of the parts are to reflect the will of a creative spirit – an ideal that contradicts the fragmentary logic of the makeshift. Cesare Brandi, who otherwise does not appear particularly dogmatic, was adamant that in a work of art, each part ought to be attributed the status of a work of art separately. Only then, it is suggested, the totality and the unity of the work is safe (see Brandi 1963, p. 65).

There is a countermodel to this: Mannerism with its preference for the ruptured, the exaggerated and the hybridised. Or, alternatively, building out of simple necessity, which harbours no ambition to be included in the canon. It follows its own economy of means, in which functionality and improvisation triumph over dogmatic clarity. While in architecture this generally remains marginalised, the visual arts have established collage and its related bricolage as radical forms of expression since the early twentieth century. The beauty of an unexpected encounter of things: "As beautiful as the chance meeting of a sewing machine and an umbrella on a dissection table" (Comte de Lautréamont, *Les chants de Maldoror* 1874, VI,1). The surrealists, whose attitude towards collage and the fragmentary was borrowed from Lautréamont, were to celebrate this "interplay" of heterogeneous elements, hoping to be freed from convention. Operations are invariably about the destabilisation of meanings and the ironic resistance to the tyranny of the perfect work in itself – not about necessity, as we see in Luigi Rossinis etching *Casa di Cola di Rienzi*: an ur-bricolage in the idiosyncrasy of its logic, defying both structural and compositional rules, establishing what could be described as a difficult yet simple whole (fig. 1).

1 Luigi Rossini, *Avanzo della Casa di Cola di Rienzo*, 1820, etching, 36.7 × 46.2, cm. Private collection

Possibly the aversion to bricolage in architecture has another, more banal reason. Whereas the process of combining disparate elements in the visual arts is ennobled with the creation of a new constellation of meanings – in other words, authorship is not undermined, but rather reinforced through ironic distance –, bricolage is never absent in architecture regardless. Architecture is always compromise and, as Hermann Czech wrote, it is always *"Umbau"*, a conversion (see Czech 1998). Alberti too was condemned to tinkering. The readymade building from a single hand became a reality only under the production conditions of the second industrial revolution. And even then only partially – remember Le Cobusier's complicated concealment of all kinds of patchwork in the production of the white villas of the period before the Second World War. The logic of bricolage in a disorderly practice – an art that has to reconcile itself to circumstances – remains that of pragmatic assembly: rather *utilitas* and perhaps *firmitas*, rarely *venustas*; not even a reinterpreted one.

A few years before he introduced the term "postmodernism" into architectural discourse and reinterpreted it as a primarily stylistic battle cry, Charles Jencks presented a much more complex concept for the architecture of the consumer society: "adhocism" (see Jencks 1973, pp. 28ff.). The lack of formal coherence, the random combination of elements that do not seem to fit together appear in Jencks's judgement of buildings as essential, unavoidable characteristics of architecture that offers functional and semantic openness. An architecture, Jencks suggests with explicit reference to Karl Popper, adjusted to an "Open Society". It was only later that bricolage found its way into architecture more broadly, arguably through the preparatory work of OMA (Office for Metropolitan Architecture) in the 1980s. Here, this was an expression of an aversion to the intellectual deficits of both modern heroes and postmodernism.

The principle really came into its own in Belgian architecture at the turn of the millennium. Here, in the homeland of Northern

European Mannerism and one of the main centres of Surrealism, it really could become a strategy for architecture in a finite world. In times of limited resources, the traditional duality of perfection and novelty, which ultimately stems from material abundance and the product quality of serial production processes, must be called into question. The acceptance of chance, of using scavenged or recuperated components in an intentional assemblage, reveals the inevitability of a new conceptualisation of the unity of a work. A work that sees itself as a web of influences and decisions. Instead of the concept of completion, a state of continuous unfinishedness and constant becoming opens up. The operation of bricolage, which only was temporarily a game, becomes a necessity again, but also something created with relish from different production logics. *Christoph Grafe*

Capitalism Capitalism as a current paradigm in the economic culture dominated by the Global North, including China, is a contested term. As Nancy Fraser in her part of the introductory dialogue of *Capitalism* states, "the use of the word 'capitalism' is mainly rhetorical, functioning less as an actual concept than as a gesture toward the need for a concept" (Fraser and Jaeggi 2018, p. 2). Harald Wolf defined capitalism as "a concept of motion that expresses the dynamic of the modern economy: its tendency of unlimited growth, rapid increase, and incessant mobility [...]. The concept expresses at the same time the tensions and conflicts within this motion" (Wolf 2004, p. 76).

Aside from these discursive debates, historically, capitalism emerged in seventeenth-century England, although the term was not commonly used until 1900 by authors like Max Weber and Werner Sombart. In Great Britain, the old aristocracy and the gentry, followed by the bourgeoisie, began to trade on a global scale, based on private property, investment and commodification. Starting with the Atlantic Triangle with the slave trade from West Africa to the Americas, cotton was produced on an unprecedented scale and manufactured on an early industrial level in the mills of the British Isles. This patriarchal system of capitalism was based on global trade, colonialism, slavery, inequality and capital accumulation, alongside real-estate speculations and huge architecture and infrastructure investments such as the railroads (see Piketty 2014). Capitalism is also associated with the Enlightenment and democracy, culminating in the French Revolution. Its concept varies between laissez-faire or free-market capitalism, state capitalism and welfare capitalism. It was Adam Smith who called for free trade as the basis of *The wealth of nations* (1776). Capitalism was associated with economic and social progress, hygiene, new infrastructure and urbanism. From the nineteenth century onwards, new building-types appeared, such as stock exchanges (shares and → BONDS), department stores and → EXHIBITION halls (commodities), industrial buildings using steel-iron constructions and working-class housing estates.

1 William Simpson, *Interior of Joseph Paxton's Crystal Palace*, 1851, watercolour, 71 × 99 cm. Victoria & Albert Museum, London

Industrialisation also brought challenges, as the European working classes (→ LABOUR) didn't benefit from economic growth and organised themselves politically in socialist parties, theoretically based on the writings of Karl Marx and Friedrich Engels (*Das Kapital* 1867–1894). To combat socialism, the welfare state was imposed in Germany, for example, in the 1880s, preventing an imminent revolution, which only took place in "backward" Russia in 1917. In this context, architecture served as a tool of precedent. Le Corbusier, in his manifesto-like book *Vers une architecture* (1923), used the slogan "architecture or revolution" to emphasise the social dimension of the new architecture. The New Deal building programme in the US, the fascist infrastructure programmes and the welfare state housing projects of postwar Europe must be seen against this background.

One outstanding example of early capitalist architecture was the Crystal Palace at the first World's Fair in London in 1851, the *Great exhibition of the works of industry of all nations* (fig. 1).

The exhibition was not only a global effort to highlight the supremacy of the British Empire, but more importantly, it introduced a new mode of displaying goods and established the sequence of World Fairs to the present day. As *spiritus rector* Prince Albert asserted in a speech given at a banquet at the Mansion House on 21 March 1849: "The products of all quarters of the globe are placed at our disposal, and we have only to choose which is the best and the cheapest for our purposes, and the powers of production are intrusted to the stimulus of *competition and capital*" (Martin 1876, p. 248). The competition for the building was launched by the Building Committee, headed by William Cubitt, and accompanied by the Royal Commission, chaired by Prince Albert himself. Both committees were prototypes of a public-private partnership, led by the railway companies and the construction industry with engineers, architects and managers (see Anthony 1992, p. 23). Because of his eminent

2 *Downtown Dubai, Business Bay*. Photo: Sergei Gussev, 2017

network, Joseph Paxton launched his functional project out of competition and succeeded. The innovative character of the Crystal Palace lay in its sheer size of 567 by 137 metres, its modularity (→ COMPONENT) and its prefabrication. The size of the largest panels available (25 by 120 centimetres, produced by Charles Brothers) was constitutive for the module of the entire building, which was built by Fox, Henderson & Co. with 5,000 workers and 4,000 tonnes of iron. It was not a steel skeleton, as is often claimed, nor did it have a curtain wall. With its transparent, "crystal" facade, it was an unprecedented building that created a perceptual shock and opened the way to glass buildings. Lothar Bucher described the new phenomena as an eyewitness: "The sidewalls are too distant to be caught in one glance, and instead of finding an opposite wall, the eye moves upward along an infinite perspective, the end of which blurs into a blue haze. We do not know whether the building is suspended 100 or 1,000 feet above us [...]. It is a piece of a summer night dream in the midday sun" (Bucher 1851, p. 10f.).

Another project leads us to the current state of capitalism and architecture under a neoliberal economy that has come to an end due to the current policies of the United States: Dubai, with its ambitious iconic architectural projects based on oil and real estate, was catapulted from a tribal society to high capitalism in a very short time (fig. 2). The emirate takes its leading position through a series of megaprojects (the world's tallest building (Burj Khalifa), the world's largest theme park, the artificial palm islands, which helped create Dubai as a prototype of the globalised city, a "'perfected' synthesis of shopping, entertainment, and architectural spectacle on a pharaonic scale" (Davis 2007, p. 54). With the establishment of an international hub in the 1990s and the opening of property ownership to foreigners in 2002, large-scale real-estate projects and signature architecture have become a leitmotif. This is part of a broader economic strategy for the post-oil condition in the Gulf to ensure Dubai's leading position: "You shouldn't look at these projects as crazy individual projects. It's part of building a brand" (Davis 2007,

p. 53). Dubai grew out of an alliance to create a tax haven and special economic zones, and it attracts investment to a place where the sheikh could guarantee a golden future based on global business, leisure and a high-class lifestyle.

Dubai's entirely new coastline stretches over 40 kilometres, with three artificial palm trees islands, two likewise artificial archipelagos (the "World" and the "Universe") and finally the Waterfront City, designed by Rem Koolhaas (OMA). The emblematic dimension of this project is also reflected in its representation on Google Earth, where it is difficult to decide whether to look at a satellite image or an animated rendering. Despite all these computer-designed projects and renderings, the shape of the real city of Dubai has never been the task of architects, but of developers like Nakheel and Emaar, due to the social and political conditions of the sheikdom. Waterfront City evokes the character of Dubai as a built stage set, an *ex nihilo* image, a city of wonders, first introduced in George Lucas' film *Stars Wars* with its capital Coruscant City. Gerhard Burs emphasises the fact that all major projects in Dubai are based on a themed "scripted space" in which architecture is used as branding, merchandising and a media backdrop: it "creates virtuality and perceptions through this constructed virtuality. The subject itself is dispersed" (Burs 2017, pp. 125 and 205). This goes far beyond architectural → AUTHORSHIP in the Global North and demonstrates the highly symbolic significance of the entire Dubai project seen in the light of the actual state of capitalism. *Bernd Nicolai*

Cargo In the context of armed conflicts, colonisation and the travels of wealthy tourists, there has always been a geographical → DISPLACEMENT of cultural assets. This → TRANSLOCATION to new countries often has an impact on the reception and effect of cultural assets and occurs for a variety of reasons. Architecture was – and is – also affected by these changes of location. Shipping buildings and → COMPONENTS as cargo is a complex and costly process. In most cases, it leads to new ownership and often raises questions about the rightful proprietor of the architecture. Cargo, from the Latin word *carricare* (to load), refers to objects that are transported by land, air or sea.

While the loading and transport of smaller architectural → ELEMENTS such as columns or caryatids is similar to that of other cultural → ARTEFACTS, paintings or sculptures, entire pieces of architecture such as temples, houses or obelisks pose more complex problems (see Anstey 2024). Regardless of whether it is cargo that has to be transported by ship or airplane, rail or road, such an undertaking incurs significantly higher → COSTS and requires more → LABOUR. Technical problems can also arise, both during removal from the site and during transport and re-erection at the destination. In the past, for example, hydraulic devices and new types of carriers had to be designed to transport architectural works. The so-called Cleopatra's Needle began its journey to London in 1877 inside a specially built "cylinder ship" (fig. 1), the hull of which was constructed around the obelisk (see Müller 2018).

The journey of such monuments was often extensively documented in contemporary travelogues (see Bankes 1830, vol. 2, pp. 295ff.; Wilson 1877). Reasons for such a deliberate effort include the research interests of individuals or countries as well as saving cultural assets from → DEMOLITION and → DERELICTION. Cleopatra's Needle was also in danger of being turned into building

1 *The cylinder ship Cleopatra with the obelisk at Westminster Bridge*, wood engraving, from *The Illustrated London News*, 16 February 1878

material (see Iversen 1968–1972, vol. 2, p. 99). The collector's passion of the buyer or travelling explorer could also be a decisive factor (→ COLLECTING). More negatively connoted motives include the appropriation of cultural property as a symbol of the colonisation of the country of origin, a self-representation fabricated by ancient artefacts or a political demonstration of power in the event of a victory over a nation (→ SPOLIA).

An interesting example of architecture as cargo is the Philae Obelisk, which was brought to England in 1821 (fig. 2). Built between 131 and 116 BCE under Ptolemy VIII, Cleopatra II and Cleopatra III at the Temple of Isis and decorated with hieroglyphics and Greek inscriptions, the monument became the focus of research and public attention due to its discovery and subsequent displacement to England. Located in 1815 by William John Bankes on the Upper Egyptian island of Philae, the traveller immediately attempted to have the obelisk transported to his estate in the county of Dorset (see Iversen 1968–1972, vol. 2, p. 70). Bankes had quickly recognised the scientific value of the artefact and wanted to ensure that the object went to Britain and not France (→ ACQUISITION). Competition in the decipherment of Egyptian hieroglyphs led to disputes between the two countries at this time, as was the case with the Rosetta Stone (London, British Museum).

Despite Bankes's wealth, exporting the cultural giant was therefore anything but easy. The French consul general Bernardino Drovetti protested vehemently against the seizure. Although the English consul general Henry Salt and the governor of Egypt Muhammad Ali Pasha supported the English politician, the journey was not without incident (see Bankes 1830, vol. 2, pp. 308ff.). The obelisk was transported as cargo on board the *Cangia*, first to Luxor and from there to London. Once there, it was reloaded and hauled overland to Dorset on a carriage (normally used for cannons and other heavy artillery pieces). The journey turned the obelisk into an → IMAGE VEHICLE and placed it in a new cultural and political context in England. Bankes did not use the monument in its original religious-political function, but primarily for self-promotion: through the obelisk, he was able to distinguish himself as a widely-travelled, fearless explorer and scientist of a still-new discipline, hieroglyphic research (see Jasanoff 2004). Salt also used it to document Britain's victory over France and his own victory over Drovetti (see Iversen 1968-1972, p. 72). As cargo, the Philae Obelisk brought both the hieroglyphs and the design of this kind of architecture to Britain, where both were copied on a large scale in the course of Egyptomania (see Lending et al. 2018; Versluys 2020).

2 *Philae Obelisk at William John Bankes' Manor*, Kingston Lacy, Dorset. Photo: Clemens Franz, 2016

The example of the Philae Obelisk is just one of many in which architecture initially becomes cargo in a very practical sense and then becomes an image vehicle that itself transports its own cultural freight. With regard to provenance, this often has complex consequences: when architecture becomes mobile, ownership claims often become contradictory and various parties are vying for the cultural artefact. These include the collector and his descendants, the owner of the land on which the architecture stands, the nation of its origin, the nation of its actual location or even current occupying powers. Removal can save a building from decay and destruction, but it can also, as in the case of the Philae Obelisk, tear apart a structural complex such as the Temple of Isis. Architectural elements shipped abroad, for example the Elgin Marbles (London, British Museum) or the Ishtar Gate (Berlin, Pergamon Museum), are therefore highly controversial in today's restitution debate and many of the countries of origin are demanding the return of the cultural artefacts. Ultimately, this would mean that their architecture would once again become cargo. *Aileen Ramm*

Catalogue The term κατάλογος has been used to categorise descriptive registers of things since the time of Homer, whose list in verse of ships bound for Troy was so named. It came into modern use in the sixteenth century, most commonly employed (as it still is) to lend dignity to lists of goods at sale and to describe a printer or publisher's forthcoming titles. It was gradually adopted in the eighteenth century to describe scientific compendia, notably in botany and astronomy, eventually coming into use for library and museum registers, a notable early instance being the two-volume *Librorum impressorum [...] catalogus* (London 1787) of printed books in the British Museum. Catalogues played a central role in nineteenth-century international → EXHIBITIONS, the massive catalogue of London's *Great exhibition of the works of industry of all nations* of 1851 establishing a standard for illustrated registers of works of art and industry. This was then applied to exhibitions and collections of art (→ COLLECTING), with the large *Art treasures of Great Britain* exhibition in Manchester of 1857 printing a catalogue both in book form and in a series of illustrated handbooks and magazines. The tradition of the French yearly Salons, which had been content since their inception in the late seventeenth century simply to issue pamphlet lists in the form of *livrets*, was thus superseded, and by the end of the nineteenth century, fine art cataloguing with expertise attached was well established.

Cabinet collections of → ARCHITECTURAL DRAWINGS and prints, largely incorporated into library and museum settings, have generally followed the cataloguing practices of the fine arts; and in these cases, provenance data recording the passage from creator to final repository is one among a number of fundamental elements of description, providing much of what an archeologist offers by locating a piece within the sector of a given dig (→ PROVENIENCE). But the description of larger and more recent architectural collections presents problems to which any approach based on cataloguing at the level of the item or short series is inadequate. Architectural works, even for a single project, derive from different phases and functions, and documents follow an instrumental path which requires recording. The archivist in the course of description and inventory therefore eschews the catalogue approach in order to list works as elements in a structured hierarchy, showing their relationships, and charting their movements from the point of creation – not so much from source to collection as from hand to hand, from sketch to → CONTRACT drawing, and from schematic document to builder's instructions. This is captured in the archival use of the word provenance, a fundamental tenet of archival methodology which emphasises analysis of the character and purpose of a document and of the graduated place it held within the layers of a larger cohort (→ ARCHIVE).

To the archivist, for many generations the catalogue entry suggested only the brief description of a large group of materials that might be reported to a general guide or union register. But collections have become increasingly obliged through market and institutional conditions to adopt library and gallery catalogue systems – based on the briefest description of a single object – in order to capture digital images for reference, and have come to rely upon that image to catalogue itself, as if it were self-descriptive. Respect for archival provenance in description therefore diminishes, and visual documents begin to float in a private vacuum of their own making.

In the other sense of the catalogue as the printed record of a body of artistic work, a unique and marvelous tradition applies in architecture, where the *opera completa* – comprehensive illustrated catalogues of works – have established through their long provenance a scientific biography of the discipline, the essential archive of its landmarks and, for many years, the core body of reference for architects in training. It is a continuing practice, in which the basic format persists: a catalogue by project, in which a summary representation of the work (either perspective, elevation or photographs) is presented in relation to didactic plans reproduced from the architect's drawings, so that the ideation and the result can be seen in relation to each other (→ PHOTOGRAPHY, → REPRODUCTION).

The provenance of the form originates with Sebastiano Serlio, who, having established through four books, the first published in 1537, the classical origins and character of fundamentals, turns in the three books prepared from 1545 to a retrospective catalogue of modern examples that illustrate the classical principle at work. A second great catalogue of architectural work is then famously folded into his treatise on form by Andrea Palladio as the second volume of *Il quattro libri dell'architettura* (Venice 1570). Appearing in many editions in many languages well into the eighteenth century, Serlio and Palladio establish the models both for the retrospective survey (or *catalogue raisonnée*) and for the architect establishing a printed *oeuvre catalogue* as a permanent record of their own work.

With growing refinement in the book arts, the sharp lines produced by etching on metal plates replaced the woodcuts of the renaissance printer, and thus works of ever greater refinement, dimensions and resilience, allowing for

1 Charles McKim, Wiliam Mead and Stanford White, *Casino at Newport*, 1881, Rhode Island, from *A Monograph of the Work of McKim, Mead & White, 1879–1915* (New York: Architectural Book Publishing Company 1915)

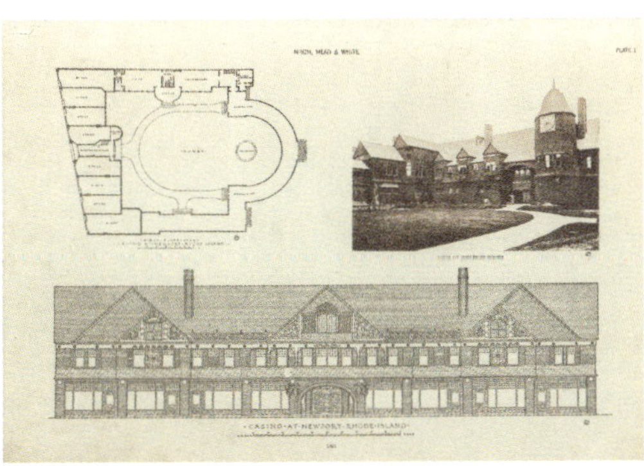

substantial print runs, followed. We can see the trend culminating in the France of the Directoire, first with such flamboyant works as Charles Percier's *Maisons et autres édifices modernes à Rome* (Paris 1798), and then in the massive, scientific reconstitution of Giacomo Barozzi da Vignola's works by Louis-Hyppolite Le Bas and François Debret, produced in Paris in fascicules from 1815 to 1823. This explored the Renaissance master's built works in depth through engravings derived from their own meticulous observational drawings, and justifiably carried the title – perhaps the first catalogue to do so – of *Oeuvres complètes de Jacques Barozzi de Vignole*. The *Vignole* moved the tradition towards establishing a library of historic reference for students entering the new Beaux-Arts system of architectural emulation (which Le Bas himself would lead for many years). It was to be famously followed by Paul Letarouilly's three volumes of *Édifices de Rome moderne* (Paris 1840–1857) which remained until well into the twentieth century a near-biblical source for those training or trained in the Beaux-Arts tradition to draw upon.

Examples from the American century represent different aspects of the continuing tradition. Among those formed by the Beaux-Arts school was the prolific American partnership of McKim, Mead and White. They were among the first modern studios to present to the profession a comprehensive lasting catalogue or monograph of their works, establishing their own remarkable Architectural Publishing Company of New York to do so. There were four volumes, each with a hundred plates of photographs and newly prepared drawings (each one with the → COPYRIGHT mark introduced by US law in 1909), laid out in relation to each other in a large portfolio format, and covering the period from the establishment of the firm in 1879 until 1915 (fig. 1).

A selective student edition entitled *Works* was produced in 1925, by which time the Architectural Publishing Company had taken an essential place in the production of scholarly illustrated catalogues by expanding the Beaux-Arts corpus with surveys of Mexican, Colonial

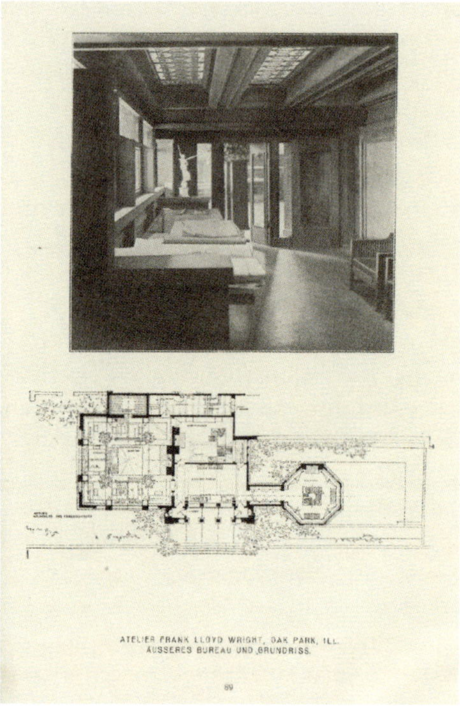

2 Frank Lloyd Wright, *Studio of the architect*, 1889, Oak Park, Illinois, from "Frank Lloyd Wright. Chicago", *8. Sonderheft der Architektur des XX. Jahrhunderts* (Berlin: Ernst Wasmuth 1911)

and other work that grounded in meticulously reconstructed provenance the rich revivals – in New England and California especially – of the 1920s (→ AFTERLIFE).

Entirely divorced from the Beaux-Arts system, and speaking for a new and indigenous school of architecture was Frank Lloyd Wright, whose first collected works appeared in two forms in 1910–1911. Wright's aesthetic sympathies, initially derived from Louis Sullivan, who had trained in Germany, lay with the Dutch, with the Vienna of Wagner and Olbrich, and with the Jugendstil of north Germany. It was not surprising therefore that the invitation to publish his early work in catalogue form came from Europe, first in the form of a lavish portfolio of drawings, the *Ausgeführte Bauten und Entwürfe von Frank Lloyd Wright* (Berlin 1910), and then in a much more modern and informative bound catalogue of twenty-six principal built works, presented through highly innovative photographs – inside and out – and a small number of newly made expository drawings. The portfolio, exhibited in Berlin, created a sensation and its plates are much prized – though the bulk of copies sent to America for sale were lost to → FIRE. But it is the catalogue, in a dedicated issue (or *Sonderheft*) of an anthological series devoted to the new architecture, that best records his early work (fig. 2).

Indeed, one can think of the great "collected works" – even more than the indispensable and often more seductive manuscript and drawing collections – as the central archive in the culture of architecture: a clear, objective, self-conscious documentation of what has been done and imagined either by one studio as in Le Corbusier's singularly titled *Oeuvre complète*, or by one movement at one time and place as Letarouilly reconstructed it. It is here that the truest archive of the discipline, drawing on the longest provenance, resides. *Nicholas Olsberg*

Celebrity The entertainment industries of the twentieth century gave rise to a new type of personality in the form of the star, who garnered special public attention through their achievements in film, music and sports. Marilyn Monroe, Elvis Presley and Muhammad Ali, for example, were the subject of a celebrity cult that certainly had traits of religious veneration. Their images were disseminated in the media, and their autographs and memorabilia were collected as veritable "contact relics". In the meantime, painters and writers, fashion designers, chefs and hairdressers, even the Real Housewives of Beverly Hills have become the celebrities of a multiple media society. And the gain in distinction that seemed to have been attained through their omnipresence in the public sphere has long since been so worn out by the sheer frequency of the phenomenon that categories such as world star, superstar and megastar have had to be introduced to hierarchise the legions of stars and starlets.

Some architects are also among those people who enjoy the greatest reverence today. Although there have always been famous representatives of their profession, the media dissemination (→ IMAGE VEHICLE, → REPRODUCTION) of their buildings in the twentieth century has meant that not only the extraordinary achievements of architecture, but also the people themselves, their lives and fates, have become the focus of attention. For these – mostly male – architects, such as Frank Lloyd Wright (about whom T. C. Boyle wrote his novel *The Women* in 2009), Ludwig Mies van der Rohe, Frank Gehry and Daniel Libeskind, the portmanteau term "starchitect" was created to linguistically propagate their new social status. This cult of stardom is also associated with provenance aspects such as → AUTHENTICITY or originality, and today many cities still strive to ennoble their urban landscapes with buildings by celebrity architects.

Interesting social and cultural-historical constellations arise when celebrity architects are confronted with other celebrities as clients or buyers of their buildings. In autumn 2021, rap musician Kanye West purchased a beach house in Malibu for $57.3 million, which star architect Tadao Ando had built for a financial expert and art collector in 2013. However, the building, which with its rigorous geometry, delicate → CONCRETE surfaces and wide-open window frontage facing the ocean bore the typical signature of the Japanese Pritzker Prize winner, did not quite fulfil the wishes of the new owner. West, an avowed anti-Semite, misogynist, conspiracy theorist and admirer of Hitler and Trump, quickly embarked on a remodelling of the house – and so fate took its course (see Parker 2024).

What might have been planned as a → RENOVATION or → TRANSFORMATION turned out to be an at least partial → DEMOLITION, indeed an act of → VANDALISM: the grey limestone floor, some walls, marble wall cladding and concrete, wooden and glass fixtures, the kitchen, chimneys and all bathrooms fell victim to the sledgehammer, electrical wiring, heating and sanitary facilities were ripped out and finally even the windows were removed (fig. 1).

Although the musician had claimed that Tadao Ando was the "greatest living architect", he obviously thought he was an even better designer when he destroyed the masterpiece of the man he supposedly admired. Kanye West has since lost interest in the sad remains of his → ACQUISITION and is now putting the → RUINS back on the property market, with photographs taken before the demolition and of course with reference to the famous provenance of the house. Ironically, his real-estate agent praises the destroyed building as "an everlasting beacon of permanence", as an "exceedingly rare architectural achievement that should be seen as a masterful work of art, rather than just a residence" (https://ogroup.com/listing/24844-malibu-rd/).

Buildings by famous architects, such as Marcel Breuer's Geller House on Long Island (1945, demolished 2022), Richard Neutra's Maslon House in Palm Springs (1963, demolished 2002) or Kisho Kurokawa's Nakagin Capsule Tower in Tokyo (1970–1972, demolished 2022), have been destroyed time and again by the philistinism of authorities or private proprietors. The star cult that these and other architects enjoy has not prevented their buildings from being wrecked for commercial or other reasons. On the other hand, the fact that so-called celebrities among homeowners are always keen to call the residences of famous architects their own, only to then ruthlessly destroy them, as in the case of wannabe designer Kanye West, is a particular tragicomedy of provenance history. *Uwe Fleckner*

1 Tadao Ando, *Former Sachs Residence*, 2013, partially destroyed 2021–2024, Malibu. Still from a video by Spencer Lowell for *The New Yorker*, 2024

Circulation In 1871, Charles Garnier imagined a world of elegant spectators ascending and descending a grand staircase in a first-class theatre, one that closely resembled the *escalier d'honneur* (fig. 1) he had designed for the new Paris Opera: "If the grand central staircase is a sumptuous and lively place, if the decorative arrangement is elegant, if the animation that reigns on the steps makes for an interesting and varied spectacle, there will be profit and advantage for everyone. If one disposes the lateral walls of the staircase in such a way that they are opened broadly, the people circulating on each level may distract themselves as they please with the sight of this great vessel and by the ceaseless circulation of the ascending or descending crowd" (Garnier 1871, p. 85).

His ideal of distracted and leisurely circulation was erected on a scaffold of hypotheticals, each clause and sentence beginning with a conditional. Drawn from a chapter of his treatise *Le théâtre* concerning the principles to be used in designing theatre stairs, Garnier's description hinges on what was at the time a relatively new term in architectural theory, "circulation". The term was more than a synonym for movement or flow, it marked a moment of heightened aesthetic reflexivity in which architecture afforded mobile subjects the opportunity to contemplate the very movement of which they were a part.

1 Charles Garnier, *Grand Escalier d'Honneur. Vue en perspective*, steel engraving by Alphonse Riquois (after Jean-Joseph Sulpis), from *Le nouvel Opéra*, vol. 2 (Paris: Ducher 1880)

The theorisation of circulation within *Le théâtre* belonged to an initial effort on Garnier's part to ensure that the new opera was itself circulated in print form, a project that would continue over the next decade through an extensive campaign that enlisted painters, photographers, engravers and publishers to meticulously document and reproduce nearly every detail of the building and its construction (→ PHOTOGRAPHY, → REPRODUCTION). The flood of books, folios, pamphlets, prints and newspaper and magazine articles that ensued made the new Paris Opera into arguably the most widely disseminated building of its era. As Martin Bressani and Peter Sealy have argued, this process of mediation did not consolidate the building's perception into a monumental unity; mass reproduction rendered it more fragmentary and heterogenous (see Bressani and Sealy 2011). Such a tension speaks to a paradox inherent to notions of circulation, a term that denotes both a movement that returns regularly to its point of origin and forms of dispersion that travel outwards in multiple directions simultaneously.

As the leading Garnier scholar notes, circulation was a preeminent category for the architect's theory of composition, yet it was also a term he never defined (Mead 1991, p. 120). For Garnier it was essential that composition realise *"une bonne circulation"*; form was to be a bulwark against encumbrance, obstruction and confusion. Yet Garnier's extensive deployment of the term is relevant less for being paradigmatic than for the oppositions and discrepancies it highlighted. Garnier published his vision of circulation at a moment when the new opera remained under construction, its future uncertain. Paris had just endured a months-long assault by Prussian troops (→ WAR) followed by the rise of the revolutionary Commune and the horrors of its violent suppression. His effort to theorise circulation in terms of reflexive aesthetic unity worked to disavow the more paradoxical and divisive aspects of → MOBILITY; a theory which can be read as a compensatory bourgeois antithesis to a city so recently defined by siege and barricades, tactics for controlling urban space by impeding the movement of goods, people and troops.

Drawn from the Latin *circulatio,* the term's roots lay in the circle as a figure of ideal cosmic order. The earliest uses of "circulation" in French and English describe such things as the orbits of celestial bodies and the motions of the holy spirit. By 1628, William Harvey in *Exercitatio anatomica de motu cordis et sanguinis in animalibus* (translated into English as *Anatomical exercise on the motion of the heart and blood in animals*, 1653) coined this term to denote the way blood moved from the heart out through arteries and veins and back again. By naming this closed loop "circulation", Harvey transferred the term's cosmological associations to the visceral realm of the body. In the eighteenth century, the term made its way into emerging fields such as economics and natural history. No longer confined to celestial motion and internal pulsations, "circulation" was now used to describe the movement of opinions, knowledge and currency by means of the relatively new printed media of books, newspapers and paper money. In the eighteenth century, a treatise like Pierre Patte's *Mémoires sur les objets plus importans de l'architecture* (1769) highlighted the *"libre circulation des voitures"*, arguing that unencumbered vehicular traffic was indeed essential to the beauty and convenience of any modern city (Patte 1769, p. 11; see Adams 2019). Architects only began to use circulation to describe spaces internal to buildings, as Adrian Forty has shown, in the mid-nineteenth century, where it functioned as a scientific metaphor allowing spaces for movement to be conceptualised as quasi-autonomous organs independent of the rooms and spaces that they supplied (see Forty 2000, pp. 87ff.). The adoption of the term within architectural theory contributed to a double reification; if circulation was rendered an autonomous element of composition it also tended to transform the movements of a whole range of bodies, fluids and objects into things that could be subject to design.

To question such reifying tendencies, we might consider not only circulation's metaphorical status, but the operations supporting the articulation of circulatory ideals. Garnier's *bonne circulation* was nominally opposed to stoppage and obstacles, yet his own theory demonstrated that the mobility he envisioned arose from a capacity to arrest and differentiate moving bodies. Circulation concerned more than the fluid, elegant or efficient movement it sought to name. While the term is often used as a synonym for flow or dissemination, more attention should be paid to what we could call "discrepant circulation", those operations that differentiate mobilities by means of pathways and diversions, openings and closures, differences constituted within historically unequal relations of power and knowledge. From this perspective, we might ask how concepts of circulation have served to regulate (while also being structured by) formations of class, race, caste, ability or gender.

The design of Garnier's grand staircase was premised on a pair of axioms that he tellingly described as a "circle from which one can never hope to escape" (Garnier 1871, p. 60). The first was that every spectatorial space contained better and worse seats, and that this difference tended inevitably toward hierarchical organisation. The second was that a hierarchical division of the audience required the strict division of pathways leading to these different places. Garnier's ideal circulation managed this hierarchical division of spectators, who were to arrive by means of different entrances to be conducted to their places via carefully distinguished routes. The *escalier d'honneur* in which the circulating spectators were to enjoy the spectacle of the crowd was reserved for spectators with luxury seats. Spectators with "ordinary" seats were to take secondary stairs (see Garnier 1871, p. 59ff.).

What Garnier calls circulation enacted and operationalised the distinction between different classes, choreographing the audience's hierarchical division. It is not only a question of what kind of circulation we encounter here, but of the matrix that makes it possible. The matrix of circulation included stairs and passages, but also ushers and printed tickets, each of which was checked at the threshold to such spaces, filtering the audience into different channels: a form of movement conditioned by stoppage and controlled access. From this perspective, the moment of reflexivity that Garnier described can be read in a different light. Perhaps what the imagined spectator contemplates is not their immersion in the circulating crowd, but the effect of a matrix of stratification that lay just beyond the frame of Garnier's scene. *Craig Buckley*

Collecting The art of collecting has been closely linked with twentieth-century architecture. By the late 1970s, significant collections had emerged, comprising → ARCHIVES and individual → ARTEFACTS such as → ARCHITECTURAL DRAWINGS, → MODELS, office documents, photographs, correspondence and ephemera. This trend led to the establishment of architecture museums, research institutes and university programmes dedicated to the field. These developments significantly influenced the discipline, transforming the creative works of architects, designers, planners and architecture scholars alike.

The impact of collecting extends beyond mere → PRESERVATION. It has dynamically transformed our perception of the built environment, prompting reconsideration of power relations in terms of gender rebalancing, social justice concerns and global political engagement. While for centuries collecting primarily focused on protecting documents and traces of the past, contemporary approaches have shifted dramatically. Today, archives are no longer viewed as static repositories of frozen artefacts. Instead, they are seen as inspirational and creative tools – works in progress that continually evolve through new interpretative projects and → ACQUISITIONS, which can redirect the original assets. This shift in perspective allows archives to play a more active role in shaping our understanding of architecture and its societal impact.

The archives of photographer Julius Shulman (1910–2009) illustrate how collected materials can be reinterpreted and repurposed to generate fresh insights into architectural history and practice. When the Getty Research Institute (GRI) acquired Shulman's archive of architectural photographs two decades ago, it created an astonishing resonance with the institute's existing holdings from visionary Southern California architects such as Neutra, Lloyd Wright, Lautner, Koenig and Kappe. Throughout his long career spanning from 1935 to 2009, Shulman documented Los Angeles' evolution into a vast metropolis. His photographs captured not only the essence of architecture but also its context and the story each frame narrated. The impressive collection included 537 linear feet (more than 260,000 vintage and modern photographs, approximately 70,000 prints, negatives, transparencies and related printed material). The most significant outcome of this acquisition was the establishment of a new Department of Architecture at the GRI. This department has since contributed to greater scholarly attention to mid-century modernism's legacy and transformed Los Angeles into a centre for the study of twentieth-century architecture and design.

Recently, the donation of an extensive documentation on Richard Neutra's inaugural project in Palm Springs, the Miller House (1936–1937), was offered to the GRI. While Neutra designed two more houses in that region during different phases of his career, it's often his masterpiece, the Kaufmann Desert House (1946), that receives the most attention. A decade before the Kaufmann building, Neutra's Palm Springs work began with a unique commission from Grace Lewis Miller. Her journey from Saint

Louis to Palm Springs was motivated by a desire to start a new life in Southern California after becoming a widow and single mother of two children. She aimed to build a home that would serve as both a residence and a studio for teaching the Mensendieck system of exercise, leading her to select Neutra to create a space meeting these unconventional requirements.

How does this connect to Shulman? Having developed a keen interest in architectural → PHOTOGRAPHY, Shulman had just met Neutra who, impressed by his early work, decided to hire him as the office photographer. The assignment to photograph the Miller House was one of the most fortuitous encounters for both men. This project helped solidify their professional relationship and marked the beginning of a close friendship that would prove beneficial to both of their careers. Shulman's photographs of his friend's works, including the Miller House – commonly known as Mensendieck House (fig. 1) –, played a crucial role in cementing Neutra's place in architectural history.

When the donor approached the GRI, the initial reaction was a straightforward refusal due to the overwhelming number of documents already received from the photographer himself. What could this new donation possibly contribute? Considering that what was offered was the documentation held by the client herself, it quickly became evident that the intersection of these two professionals with Grace Lewis Miller represented a significant moment in both architectural history and photography.

The archive addition arrived with unexpected treasures, among other documents were approximately eighty letters exchanged between Neutra and Mrs Miller, underscoring crucial phases in the design process, which was largely managed through correspondence with construction documentation exchanged remotely. More than a dozen of photographs mailed by Shulman to the client, not only signed by the photographer but also fully annotated on the reverse, commenting on architectural details, spatial fluidity and efforts to make the cactus garden a unique feature of the indoor and outdoor landscape, allowing a → PRISTINE gaze of the land the Agua Caliente Indians built (fig. 2).

Fifteen gelatin silver prints of Neutra's visits to the → CONSTRUCTION SITE, twelve of which include annotations on the verso by Grace Lewis Miller herself are part of the donation . These historical materials undoubtedly enrich our understanding of the design process and the early stages of Shulman's career as an architectural photographer. They highlight the importance of archival documentation and its role in shaping the visual narrative of modern architecture.

1 Richard Neutra, *Mensendieck House*, south-facing elevation seen from the desert, with native plants in the foreground, 1936–1937, Palm Springs. Photo: Julius Shulman, 1937

2 Richard Neutra, *Mensendieck House*, Grace Lewis Miller sitting inside the porch with east view onto Agua Caliente Reservation land, 1936–1937, Palm Springs. Photo: Julius Shulman, 1937

This dynamic view of collecting aligns with the contemporary quest for decolonising the archives. By treating archives as living resources, we can better leverage historical knowledge to inform current and future architectural practices, ensuring that the discipline remains responsive to evolving societal needs and environmental concerns. *Maristella Casciato*

Collective memory When Maurice Halbwachs introduced the term *mémoire collective* into sociology in the 1920s, he did not set out to craft a theory for interpreting architecture, yet the built environment remains one of the most striking materialisations of memory and a medium of collective memorising in public space. Indeed, ever since the publication of his 1925 study *Les cadres sociaux de la mémoire* and the posthumous fragment of his seminal work *La mémoire collective* in 1950, the study of memory and its relationship to cultural communities has grown into an expansive and highly heterogeneous field, spanning disciplines from history to cultural studies to art history and architecture.

While Halbwachs does not provide a generally fixed definition of the term "collective memory", he implicitly unites two distinct yet interrelated perspectives that are crucial to his observations: the first considers collective memory as the framework within which individual memory develops and is shaped by a shared social and spatial context. The second moves away from the single individual and emphasises the role of discourse, myths, oral narration and social structures in how a group of individuals collectively recalls and interprets the past in an ever-dynamic process of constructing a shared cultural identity (see Erll 2017, p. 12). In this way, Halbwachs liberated the concept of memory from the partly ideologically engaged, bio-psychologically oriented definitions of his time, as well as from the then-dominant psychoanalytic approach that located experience within the sphere of the individual's unconscious. His shift from individual recollection to a spatially and actively constructed memory allowed for application of the theory to both material and immaterial culture. This reconceptualisation, later extended through a distinctive understanding of the two spheres of communicative and cultural memory, also demonstrates that in terms of architecture, built structures can function as a medium to both of these spheres (see Assmann 1995). More recent critical perspectives have highlighted the tensions that arose within contemporary memory culture, addressing what has been described as a "new unease" surrounding practices of rememberance (see Assmann 2013).

The close relationship between the concepts of material culture and collective memory has been a central topic in cultural studies since the early twentieth century. In particular, the interplay between memory, space and social structures inspired scholars to explore how the built environment serves as a framework for collective remembrance. The Place de la Concorde in Paris, a site deeply intertwined with the French Revolution and historically inscribed by the execution of Louis XVI on 21 January 1793, or Berlin's Reichstag building, whose glass dome was reconstructed by British architect Norman Foster in 1993 (→ RECONSTRUCTION), turning it into both a historical reminder and symbol of democratic transparency, are just two among countless other examples. Similarly, the Palazzo della Civiltà Italiana in Rome, originally built under Mussolini's fascist regime, now housing the headquarters of the fashion label Fendi, or the removal of the faces symbol on several facades around Italy, that once symbolised this dictatorial episode in the country's history (→ POLITICAL ICONOGRAPHY), stand as reminders of bygone totalitarian aesthetics, while the reinterpretation of these memorial markers in contemporary use underscores the complex interplay between architecture and historical memory.

All these examples can be understood as mnemonic topographies, or so-called "mnemotopes": landscapes or urban spaces that inscribe and sustain a group's identity through visible traces of the past. Such spaces demonstrate that memory is not merely temporal but fundamentally spatial, embedded in the environment as both a framework and a performative site of collective identity (see Pethes 2015). The symbolic meaning of the Berlin Reichstag building, for instance, has shifted from an imperial structure to a democratic icon, while at the same time it frequently functions as a site for political demonstrations. The United States Capitol in Washington DC likewise epitomises this performative dimension: long serving as a symbol of democratic stability, it was violently contested during its storming in January 2021, exposing the vulnerability of democracy and demonstrating how built environments can become the focal point of competing narratives about a nation's past and future (fig. 1).

Architecture thus not only passively reflects memory but also actively shapes and mediates processes of remembering, and importantly also those of forgetting, as built structures are continuously part of reinterpretations and appropriations (→ COUNTER-MONUMENT).

In contrast to other important notions on collective memory and space, like Pierre Nora's theorisation of the *lieux de mémoire*, which emphasises specific topographical sites as vessels of memory (see Nora 1989), Italian architect Aldo Rossi employed the concept of collective memory to support his theoretical argument for an intrinsic continuity in the environment. In *The architecture of the city*, first published in 1966, Rossi draws on Halbwachs' concept of collective memory to reject the idea that memory is confined to monumental or commemorative sites. Instead, he argues that the entire urban fabric accumulates and preserves collective experience over time. In his explications Rossi uses the term "urban artefact" (Rossi 1982, pp. 130ff.), referring to architectural forms that endure beyond their original function and acquire new meanings as they persist through social and historical transformations. These → ARTEFACTS, such as theatres, cemeteries or residential blocks, anchor the memory of a city's inhabitants and represent the resilience of the built environment as a repository of collective identity (→ RESIDENTS). For Rossi, this spatial persistence constitutes a city's collective memory, demonstrating that ordinary urban structures, no less than iconic monuments, serve as carriers of the past and contribute to the lived continuity of urban life.

1 *A scene from the storming of the United States Capitol,* 6 January 2021, Washington DC. Photo: Tyler Merbler

Coinciding with Halbwachs' approach in the 1920s, another pioneering figure in memory studies, though emerging from a different disciplinary tradition, is the German art historian Aby Warburg. While the French theorist's concept foregrounds the social frameworks of memory embedded in communicative as well as cultural structures in society, Warburg's focus lay on a more image-centric concept of remembrance, to which he referred to with terms like *"soziales Bildgedächtnis"* (social image memory) or metaphorically used expressions like *Engramme leidenschaftlicher Erfahrung* (engrams of affective experience) (see Warburg 2010, pp. 629ff.). His investigations were driven by the conviction that images are carriers of memory across time, encoding collective emotional and cultural experiences. His notion of the *Pathosformel* (pathos formula) is central to this idea: it refers to specific visual motifs and gestures that recur across different historical periods, transmitting affective states such as suffering, ecstasy or mourning. These visual expressions embody an → AFTERLIFE or recurrence of cultural memory, revealing the persistence of archetypal emotional experiences within the visual languages of European art and beyond. Furthermore, the neologism *Pathosformel* illustrates that cultural memory is not merely a linear transmission of knowledge but a dynamic field, where affective and symbolic forms continuously resurface and are reinterpreted across time. In his unfinished project *Bilderatlas Mnemosyne*, named after the Greek goddess of memory and mother of the nine muses, he assembled photographic → REPRODUCTIONS of artworks, books and architectural ornaments to trace the migration and transformation of visual memory across cultures epochs (→ IMAGE VEHICLE). This idea found architectural expression in Warburg's Kulturwissenschaftliche Bibliothek in Hamburg, where the elliptical reading room symbolised his belief that artistic production oscillated between the bipolar qualities of rational order and unordered human creativity, which in the newly built library became a spatial representation of what he saw at the core of human culture (fig. 2).

The Warburg Institute today, after its emigration from Nazi Germany to London in the 1930s, retains the elliptical form, maintaining it as a spatial reference to Warburg's epistemological vision: since 2024 the refurbished building introduced the elliptical reading room as a contemporary rearticulation of a collective memory attached to the institute's original site in Hamburg (→ DOPPELGÄNGER), underscoring the continuing interplay between spatial form and the dynamics of cultural remembrance. *Elif Akyüz*

2 *The elliptical reading room of the Kulturwissenschaftliche Bibliothek Warburg*, 1926, Hamburg. Photographer unknown

Component The distinctive pointed arches, ribbed vaults and flying buttresses of Gothic architecture constitute → ELEMENTS of a system demonstrating the remarkable paradox achieved in the great cathedrals of the age whereby an overall organic unity combines with a compositional looseness through geometric consistency. While there appears to have been little proportional or geometric consistency across the medieval cathedrals, within each building a rigorous series of numerical relationships existed between the various parts and the whole. A sense of geometric harmony results, each component understood in relation to the overall through a combination of repetition and subdivision, a quality described by Erwin Panofsky as "progressive divisibility" (Panofsky 1957, p. 48).

Similarly, during the early Renaissance, the radical innovation of Filippo Brunelleschi's architecture was the interpretation of the classical language as a modular system of building parts. The architectural elements inherited from the Romans of arch and column become grammatical components of a syntax. Always considered in relation to the whole, they are also extendable in the manner of a framework (see Aureli 2014, p. 19f.). The subsequent theorisation by Alberti of this development focused on the harmonious balance between part and whole. Both Gothic and classical examples suggest that while architectural components might variously be considered as parts, elements or pieces, they always relate to an idea of a whole. They are, in effect, constituent components.

While the sense of a component as a part or element of a whole remained, the advent of machine production nuanced the idea of the component towards that of the module or the unit, towards the mechanical. The division of → LABOUR, serialised production and the assembly line all emphasise the processes of separation and disaggregation. In the reading of a component as a part of the whole, a subtle shift occurs in emphasis from the whole, to the part: the pointed arch and the doric column are subsumed within the overall effect of the resultant entity, but the fabricated modern building component, when assembled, retains its own distinct character apart from the whole.

Joseph Paxton's development of a glasshouse construction system culminating in the Crystal Palace in 1851, exemplified the evolution of the component as mechanical → ARTEFACT. Over a series of greenhouses at the Chatsworth estate in Derbyshire, England, most notably involving the construction of the Great Stove and the much smaller Victoria Regia House, Paxton perfected a roofing system which pioneered a series of innovations, namely the profiled sash bar, the ridge-and-furrow roofing profile and the so-called Paxton gutter. The innovations to the performance of each construction component led to a system of roofing that integrated the requirements of the structural, weather protection, drainage and the transmission of light into a unified solution. The Paxton gutter in particular was a unit of construction that combined the function of beam and gutter into a single building component. After the initial design work to the Crystal Palace had been completed, but before it had been published, Paxton submitted his timber roofing system to be patented in 1850, using the title, "Certain improvements in roofs" (fig. 1).

While relating to the Chatsworth buildings and the Crystal Palace, the patent recognised

1 Joseph Paxton, *Patent specification for roofing improvements*, 1850, enrolled by the Patent office 22 January 1851. Drawing Matter Collection, London

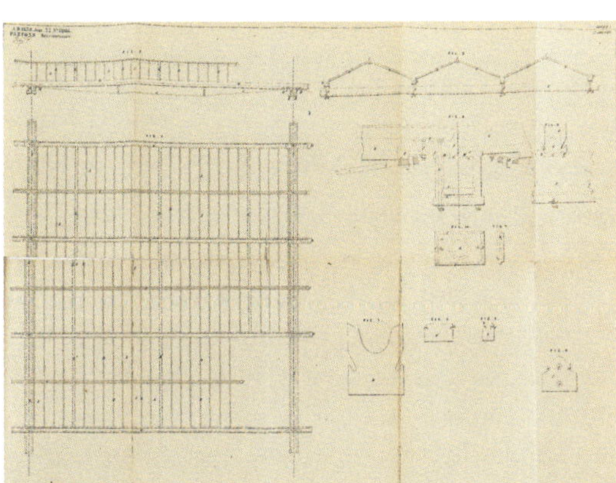

2 *Meccano construction set*, display board for the use of toy dealers, c.1955

the universal applicability of the cladding. No longer conceived as an element that was inherently part of a spatial whole, the component became the focus of the architecture – here was a system of standardised components, produced through a system of serialised industrial production. The origins and provenance of such prefabricated components (→ READYMADE) can therefore also be included in the construction history of these buildings, seemingly defined by their assembled parts.

While Paxton's patent demonstrated the primacy of the machine-made component over the idea of a spatial whole, it was with the High-Tech British architects in the twentieth century that the idea of the component truly flourished. This architecture of technology heralded an architectonic language derived from the component: the kit of parts, modules and nodes, the promise of flexibility through re-configuration, the articulated and over-articulated joining of fabricated units, all heralded an architectonic language derived from the component. For a generation of architects who grew up constructing with Meccano (fig. 2), the component had triumphed. *Hugh Strange*

Concrete The *Denkmal für die Märzgefallenen* (Memorial to the dead of March) that we see today in the cemetery at Weimar is a → RECONSTRUCTION. The first memorial, designed by Walter Gropius – and built of concrete – was put up in 1922 to commemorate the seven trade unionists who had died in the successful resistance to the 1920 right wing Kapp *putsch*. In 1936, the memorial was destroyed with explosives by the Nazis, to whom its symbolism was repugnant, although the official reason given was simply that it was "ugly" (→ DEMOLITION, → MONUMENT, TOPPLED). Ten years later, in 1946, it was rebuilt in a careful and almost precise reproduction of the original by the Soviets, in one of the very first acts of reconstruction in the Soviet sector of postwar Germany (fig. 1). It is thus a double memorial, commemorating both the victims of the 1920 *putsch*, the destruction of the memorial in 1936 and all that had ensued thereafter (see Fuhrmeister 2001; Forty 2012).

In the ten years between 1936 and 1946, the entire meaning of the memorial was recharged. Not only had the successful resistance to the Kapp *putsch* become a victory that contrasted with the failure of the trades union movement to prevent Hitler's rise to power in 1933, giving the original victims a now heroic status, but the fact of its being made of concrete, which had originally been a default decision for reasons of economy, had acquired, in the intervening years

1 Walter Gropius, *Denkmal für die Märzgefallenen (Memorial to the dead of March)*, 1946 (reconstruction), Weimar. Photo: Adrian Forty, 2004

since 1936, a superadded meaning. It is no surprise therefore that such meticulous care was taken to reproduce exactly and minutely the concrete mix and finish of the original memorial – although at the time of its making in the early 1920s, these properties had been of no great account.

The construction of the first memorial had been very much a Bauhaus project, supervised by Josef Hartwig, one of the Bauhaus masters, and some of the → LABOUR was provided by Bauhaus staff and students. The choice of concrete, instead of Gropius's original intention to use limestone, ran up against the local building code, which prohibited the use of concrete in cemeteries unless it was mixed with natural stone aggregates. Accordingly, when construction began in September 1921, the concrete was mixed with crushed limestone from nearby → QUARRIES, but also some terrazzo was added, thus combining a natural with a synthetic aggregate. The most skilled part of the work lay in the finishing of the concrete. The cement surface left from the casting process was removed with hammer and chisel to expose the stone and terrazzo aggregates beneath, and the edges finished, as in traditional stone masonry, with a five-centimetre wide tooled margin, leaving narrow ridges perpendicular to the edge (fig. 2). The result was remarkably delicate, showing that despite the coarseness of the → MATERIAL, manual skill could transform it into something refined.

The concrete mix (though without the addition of the crushed terrazzo), the bush-hammering and the tooled margin were all carefully reproduced in the 1946 → FACSIMILE. The fact of its having been made of concrete had by now become a celebration of socialism, a meaning that it had not had in 1922. Whereas the concrete of the pre-war memorial was unremarked upon, in 1946 this was seen as of great significance, and there was extensive discussion of this aspect of it. Commentators remarked on the seamless, unbroken form as not personalised, without trace of individual, only collective effort. Furthermore, the

2 Walter Gropius, *Denkmal für die Märzgefallenen (Memorial to the dead of March)*, 1946 (reconstruction), detail of concrete surface finish, Weimar. Photo: Adrian Forty, 2004

material itself was seen as the result of a chemical bond between the different components, producing a product stronger and harder than any of the individual elements – an analogy that Fyodor Gladkov had used in his classic 1925 Russian socialist realist novel *Cement* to describe how, in a socialist society, individuals come together to form, with invisible bonds, a collective unity. Unlike stone, which is the result of a long process of sedimentation, concrete is formed rapidly at the moment it sets, and this, it was said, was analogous to the historical formation of the socialist republics, born instantaneously from the shock events of the moment, rather than was the case with other regimes that had developed over long periods of time. With the recalibration of concrete as a "socialist" material, the reconstruction of the *Märzgefallenen* memorial in 1946 was an explicit celebration of the victory of communism over fascism (→ POLITICAL ICONOGRAPHY). It is easy to see why, even before the construction of the many subsequent memorials commemorating the victory of the Red Army, the Soviets chose to replicate this memorial in its historically loaded location of the Weimar cemetery where stand nearby the tombs of, amongst others, Herder, Goethe, Schiller and Liszt, a virtual pantheon of German art and literature.

Replicas are generally seen as less than originals, or occasionally equal to them; while replicas in concrete, with its reputation as a "poor" material, are invariably inferior. The *Märzgefallenen* memorial is rare in being supercharged beyond its original – and furthermore, manages this not despite its concrete, but because it was made of concrete.

Adrian Forty

Construction site Rare, or perhaps nonexistent, is the construction site whose provenance does not involve some considerable measure of distance. Physical distance, as in the route travelled by planks of mahogany sailing from the West Indies to be reconstituted as doors or panelling in the stately homes in Europe, but even in an instance of a construction site that gathers materials close to hand, there likely remains a distance in the provenance of techniques that are being put to use. It is a temporal distance, in that the provenance of techniques of masonry, carpentry or simply measuring, hoisting or mixing, lie in a past quite removed from the present of that construction site. While the provenance of any construction site can always be assessed in terms of the specifics of origin and destination – sand from here to make concrete there, capital accumulated in this domain to pay wages to labourers in that local script – the more profound quality of the provenance of the construction site is simply distance as such.

A singular demonstration of this quality of distance stands today on the shoreline of the continent of Antarctica. Modest in architectural terms – a simple hut less than 3 metres high and only 58 square metres in plan – the provenance of its construction site reveals an extremity of distance. This building is the Shackleton Hut, which housed the fourteen members of the British Antarctic Expedition from February 1908 to March 1909 (fig. 1).

Located on a sloping site, the structure was fixed into place with wood foundation posts, clad with wood planking and felt insulation and reinforced structurally with wrought-iron straps and tie rods. Each one of these → ELEMENTS arrived at the building site from a distance, for the inhospitality of the Antarctic continent is not only a matter of ruthless climate, but also the lack of useful building resources. Ice and a permanently frozen ground are the materials that stretch across the continent. The only local → MATERIALS used in any Antarctic architecture were rocks to serve as windbreaks, ice caves for storage, and in one or two buildings, seaweed to provide a slight improvement in insulation.

The materials for the Shackleton Hut all arrived aboard the expedition ship *Nimrod*, which had set sail from London six months before it anchored at the Antarctic coast on 3 February 1908 and the expedition began unloading. Each building material had thus travelled at least from London – 24,000 kilometres – though some had travelled further (→ CARGO). The deal wood came from forests elsewhere in Britain, the felt and the tie rods

1 *Shackleton's hut at Cape Royds, Ross Island, Antarctica*, 1907–1909, Joseph Kinsey Collection, National Library of New Zealand, Wellington. Photographer unknown

from factories, although the provenance of the iron could also be seen to include the mines deep underground from which the coal had been extracted to produce the wrought iron used to manufacture them. And as for temporal distance, then, it is not only the six months of ocean travel, but the deep geological time of the seams of coal that were then brought into juxtaposition with the ice layers of Antarctica, not as old as coal but still with a duration exceeding a human lifespan.

Humans were of course part of this construction site as well. None of the fourteen expedition members were practiced in construction, though one was the carpenter and others had mechanical skills. Anticipating the challenges of building, the expedition had commissioned a prefabricated building, so that the work of the construction site would be limited for the most part to assembly and simple carpentry.

The foundations, however, proved more difficult. In the vivid recollection of the expedition leader, the holes for the posts had to be drilled into ice and bedrock with a hammer and chisel, and the posts themselves set into place with a cement of volcanic earth and water set to freeze. Seen as a temporal distance the provenance of the building site collapsed the most immediate time of pairs of frozen hands attempting to chip away ice and rock with the far more extended time of the technique of hammering used across millennia by human societies.

To ask "What is the provenance of the construction site?" is to pose an inquiry into distance, and into the commensuration of distance. For what is remarkable about construction sites and their varied provenances is not only the routes and itineraries traced by individual materials and bodies to arrive and appear in construction, but the manner in which a construction site gathers together provenances. Each construction site gathers distances – geographic, temporal, economic, social – setting them into relations which in turn can reveal dissonances, resolutions or potentials. Distance is the provenance of the construction site.

Timothy Hyde

Contract Cass Gilbert's copy of the building contract for the Broadway-Chambers Building, dated 1 March 1899, is a dirty document (fig. 1). The strikingly polychromatic office building, still standing on a corner in Lower Manhattan, was constructed by the George A. Fuller Company for the wealthy Boston widower Edward R. Andrews. A critical instrument of the landmarked building's architectural provenance, the agreement between Andrews and the Fuller Company is framed by a boilerplate form, a legal-sized folio of four pages, and includes two lengthy typescript addenda. The margins of the form are smudged, the paper brittle and torn. Three deep accordion-style folds, made over a century ago to bundle the pages for pigeonhole filing, have not yet yielded to its years spent in an archival box (→ ARCHIVE). It simply won't lie flat. These grimy traces hint at the life of a working copy of more sacred originals, which, now lost, were likely kept in fire safes.

Most of the contract's terms were fairly standard, indeed standardised. In 1888, the American Institute of Architects (AIA) and the National Association of Builders had hashed out the terms of the first nationally standardised building contract in the United States. Copyrighted and licensed to a single printer to control its contents, the 1893 edition of the Uniform Contract consisted of twelve preprinted articles interrupted by ruled blanks, all elegantly laid out to frame and elicit the filling-in of details and the signing of names. Gilbert, a good AIA man, would not have contemplated using anything but the official Uniform Contract, which was the industry standard in any case by the turn of the twentieth century. Yet Gilbert himself was not bound by any building contract, a two-party agreement between owner and contractor. Rather than signed at the bottom of the page, his name was typed at the top in the space reserved for naming that quasi-judicial authority, "architect", under whose "satisfaction and direction" the contractor's work was to be performed.

As for the contractor, the man who signed on behalf of the Fuller Company was Harry S. Black, vice president (and the boss's son-in-law). Black was an adventurer, not a builder. Before joining the firm, he had worked in a general store, joined a surveying party, sold woolen goods and started a bank. As colleagues remembered him, Black was "a business genius, a gambler, a financial juggler", who knew nothing about construction and thought the "idea of slamming in a figure on a big hotel overnight was great stuff" (Starrett 1938, p. 69 and p. 80). Years later, Gilbert would harangue his AIA colleagues about the threat of large, highly capitalised construction companies like Fuller (see Gilbert 1907, pp. 89ff.). But for almost three years before the Broadway-Chambers contract was signed, he worked closely with Black to arrange a financial scheme for the project and coax Andrews into the investment.

The single most important expectation stipulated, and reiterated, in the contract was the completion date: 1 May 1900, just twelve months after the contractor was to take possession of the site, on the customary "moving day" when leases across New York City expired simultaneously. Article 6 was the designated place for such information in the Uniform Contract. So important was this temporal horizon, however, that it was written into the very identity of the Broadway-Chambers project itself, defined emphatically in Article 1 as "the construction and erection of a *completely finished* first-class fire proof office building [...] on or before the first day of May, in the year 1900".

In a trade-press article titled *Building skyscrapers*, published several weeks after this all-important date, Gilbert laid out the vulgar economic conditions of modern realty finance that shaped the temporality of skyscraper construction: "The building", he famously quipped, is "merely the machine that makes the land pay" (Gilbert 1900, p. 1091). For owners, Gilbert explained, the building process was a costly interval during which rental income was suspended and interest on capital invested in the land continued to accrue – to say nothing of the manifestly expensive operations at the job site (→ CAPITALISM, → COSTS, → LABOUR). It was thus incumbent on architect and contractor both "to make the enterprise begin to earn as soon as

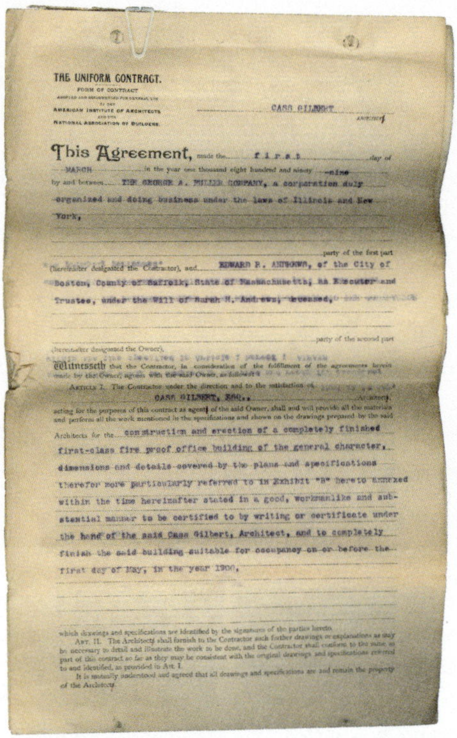
THE UNIFORM CONTRACT.
FORM OF CONTRACT
AMERICAN INSTITUTE OF ARCHITECTS
NATIONAL ASSOCIATION OF BUILDERS.

CASS GILBERT
Architect

This Agreement, made the first day of MARCH in the year one thousand eight hundred and ninety -nine by and between THE GEORGE A. FULLER COMPANY, a corporation duly organized and doing business under the laws of Illinois and New York,

party of the first part (hereinafter designated the Contractor), and EDWARD R. ANDREWS, of the City of Boston, County of Suffolk, State of Massachusetts, as Executor and Trustee, under the Will of Sarah H. Andrews, deceased,

party of the second part (hereinafter designated the Owner),

Witnesseth that the Contractor, in consideration of the fulfillment of the agreements herein made by the Owner, agrees with the said Owner, as follows:

Article I. The Contractor under the direction and to the satisfaction of CASS GILBERT, ESQ., Architect, acting for the purposes of this contract as agent of the said Owner, shall and will provide all the materials and perform all the work mentioned in the specifications and shown on the drawings prepared by the said Architects for the construction and erection of a completely finished first-class fire proof office building of the general character, dimensions and details covered by the plans and specifications therefor more particularly referred to in Exhibit "B" hereto annexed within the time hereinafter stated in a good, workmanlike and substantial manner to be certified to by writing or certificate under the hand of the said Cass Gilbert, Architect, and to completely finish the said building suitable for occupancy on or before the first day of May, in the year 1900,

which drawings and specifications are identified by the signatures of the parties hereto.

Art. II. The Architects shall furnish to the Contractor such further drawings or explanations as may be necessary to detail and illustrate the work to be done, and the Contractor shall conform to the same as part of this contract so far as they may be consistent with the original drawings and specifications referred to and identified, as provided in Art. I.

It is mutually understood and agreed that all drawings and specifications are and remain the property of the Architects.

1 *Copy of the Uniform Contract between Edward R. Andrews and the George Fuller Company for the construction of the Broadway-Chambers Building*, 1 March 1899. Cass Gilbert Papers and Architectural Drawings, New York Historical

possible". It was for these reasons, "and not for the purpose of making a record in rapid construction", that construction was ideally to be completed within a year (Gilbert 1900, p. 1091).

The occasion for this article was, ostensibly, the timely completion of the Broadway-Chambers Building weeks earlier, the triumphant story of which Gilbert narrated in the past tense. At the very same moment, however, Gilbert was acutely aware of the acrimonious tension that had been building between Andrews and Black about the meaning of the words "completely finished" and their financial implications. By the first of May, as scheduled, office tenants had begun moving into the Broadway-Chambers, only to find the premises "entirely unfit for occupancy", much less for transacting dignified business (New York Historical, Cass Gilbert Papers and Architectural Drawings, C. P. Fraleigh to Frederick Southack and Alwyn Ball Jr., 8 May 1900, box 51, folder 7). They wasted no time in complaining to the building's leasing agent. Owing to a → FIRE in the workshop that was to supply dynamo engines, the building was still without electric lights, and it was not entirely clear when they would be installed. The elevator service was, tenants complained, "simply outrageous". Of the four elevators, one was unfinished, another had been entirely commandeered by wall painters, and the remaining two were so busy with the up-and-down transit of workmen and furniture movers that clients of the tenants found themselves whooshed past their floor only then to be conveyed back down to the lobby, sometimes more than once, before finally arriving at their vertical destination. Moreover, in lieu of marble doors yet to placed, the hoistway entrances were covered with muslin cloth, a makeshift arrangement that, according to an exasperated representative of the US Life Insurance Company, allowed a chill to pour in from the elevator shaft, "bringing dirt and dust" and causing "several of the clerks [to be] laid up with colds, to say nothing of the damage resulting to our records". Lime and marble → DUST coated everything, paint fumes wafted into executive offices, and the water closets reeked. Perhaps worst of all, workmen were in the lobby and the halls and the elevators and the stairs, rubbing shoulders with clerks and clients.

Given these conditions, office tenants were "quite surprised" to receive a bill for the full month's rent. When it became clear that the rents would be uncollectible in many cases, Andrews wrote to Black on 16 May 1900, insisting that he had "no choice" but to "look to you to make good the rents which the tenants refuse to pay, so far as you are responsible for the unfinished state of the building, as per the terms of your contract" (box 51, folder 7). From the contractor's perspective, this was a creative construction of those terms, to put it mildly. In a letter to Gilbert, Black rejected any implication that his company was accountable for the tenants' troubles, which he believed were "principally imaginary" (box 51, folder 12).

Modern skylines were, and still are, built on the promise of contract: a legal instrument for synchronising the vicissitudes of building with the anticipatory temporality of finance, overlaying its risks and uncertainties with the appearance of smooth, predictable lines. But of course, buildings do not lie flat. Between projection and concrete, contingencies waft in, ruffling and warping the terms of agreement. *Chelsea Spencer*

Copyright The emergence of modern architecture strangely coincides with the development of copyright law. The development of modern architecture, its production, seriality and export across seas and that of copyright laws are entangled. The question of copyright is challenged by new modes of architectural production. Artificial intelligence, computer-generated work and ever-larger → NETWORKS of production put pressure on the notion of → AUTHORSHIP and ownership. Paradoxically, the more networked and diffused architectural production becomes, the more the concept of the "starchitect" emphasises the absolute nature of authorship (→ CELEBRITY). These paradoxes must be challenged by a proposition for a new mode of architecture and modes of critical appropriation should be debated by architects, lawyers and intellectual property activists. Partly as response to such debates and partly as its catalysts, a fascinating variety of appropriations, copying practices and architectural → DOPPELGÄNGERS challenge the legal confines of the profession (see Weizman 2012a, 2012b and 2018). Architectural copies can be easily ignored or dismissed as low art, or they appear irrelevant for truly disturbing the nature and esteem of an "original". The difference between production, copying and faking lies in the position the object has in relation to the law. Architecture features in many types of legal processes – as a scene of a crime, as a cause for damages, in property law or as evidence for crimes, even war crimes (→ WAR). At the centre of this investigation is the way copyright law is applied to architecture.

Copyright is generally understood as the consequence of a certain conferring of an identity of a maker on an object, a thing, a structured assemblage or a building. It is the right to copy, replicate, duplicate and receive the financial benefits of this act (→ FACSIMILE). Perhaps one could argue that it was in fact copyright law that allowed architecture to be copied, replicated, mass produced and exported across the world (→ IMAGE VEHICLE). Just like prints, photographs, films or digital files (→ PHOTOGRAPHY), the architectural copy is both a product of the media and a media form in itself, reflecting the existing means of production and → REPRODUCTION.

The state defines the right of authors in their lifetime and beyond death. In international law copyright is applied in accordance with the country in which the author is a citizen, but not outside of its borders unless the country is a signatory of an international convention. The Berne Convention for the Protection of Literary and Artistic Works (adopted in 1886) defines a minimum duration for the legal copyright protection that is calculated as fifty years after the death of an author. Many countries have raised this figure to seventy-five years, which somehow aligns the life of a copyright protection to the average lifetime of a person. We could think of this protected term of a creative work of art as its second life. As this field of copyright often becomes complicated and obscure, one could say that within these fifty or seventy-five years (here death is the only stable baseline), artistic work exists in an ambiguous terrain of ownership. When its copyright protection expires, the work falls into the public domain, and the work has effectively become public property and may be used freely. At that point, the work enters its third life, which should, in principle, be infinite (→ AFTERLIFE).

In the early 2000s, we entered an era of "modernism's third life", the period past the seventy-five-years-long second life of the works of those authors that died pre-Second World War, including modernist authors such as Hermann Muthesius (d. 1927), Charles Rennie Mackintosh (d. 1928), Lars Backer (d. 1930), Adolf Loos (d. 1933), Hans Poelzig (d. 1936) and Bruno Taut (d. 1938). In no other field is this question more pressing than in modern architecture, which sought to distance the author from authorship, the building from uniqueness, and potentially tried to undo the individual from mass production. Finally, seventy-five years after the first generation of modern architects died their second death, modernism has fulfilled the dissociation of the work from their person. We could even say that only in its third life the work can become truly modern. In modernism's third life, we have for the first time a freely reproducible architecture. As we enter the first life of architecture to give it its third life, modernism can finally be fulfilled. In this third life we might see architecture turn into things. In thing-world, copying is the means of reproduction, and copyrights are thus the most fundamental and inalienable of → THING-RIGHTS; potentially beyond and inspite of those of their makers.

In 2008, to mark the expiry of the copyrights of the works of the Viennese architect Adolf Loos (d. 1933), one of the famous modernists of the first generation, I attempted to set foot on this new terrain of the third life of modernism. I was invited to design a villa as part of the Ordos 100 project, a master plan for one hundred residential villas in Ordos, Inner Mongolia, curated by the artist Ai Weiwei. Seventy-five years after the death of the author, I proposed to build a facsimile of Loos's 1928 unbuilt house for the legendary Black-American performer Joséphine Baker in Paris (fig. 1).

1 Ines Weizman, *Proposal to realise the 1928 House Baker project by Adolf Loos in Ordos*, 2008, collage

The project stimulated new questions and retrospectives and evoked a chain of unexpected claims over the Loos estate. The larger the file of documents grew, the more it needed the insights and consultancy of experts, lawyers, historians, architects, collectors and self-acclaimed heirs of the Loos estate to realise a copy of a project that in fact had no original. Two results were *Repeat yourself. Loos and the culture of the copy*, examining the implications of the passing of Adolf Loos's work into public domain, and *Of all the gin joints in all the towns in all the world...*, containing a film essay on Joséphine Baker's perilous travels through North Africa and the Middle East.

In 1964, at the initiative and financial support of Oskar Kokoschka, two art historians, Gustav Künstler and Ludwig Münz, published *Der Architekt Adolf Loos. Darstellung seines Schaffens nach Werkgruppen*, translated into English in 1966 as *Adolf Loos. Pioneer of modern architecture* (see Münz and Künstler 1964). Surprised and disappointed by being left out of the credit lines of the Loos estate, Elsie Altmann-Loos, the second wife of Loos (→ WILL), started a series of legal → DISPUTES with the Albertina in Vienna that had just created the Adolf Loos Archive. In the years before her death in 1984, she by chance met Adolf Opel – a Viennese filmmaker, novelist and dandy – in a hotel in Buenos Aires where Altmann-Loos earned her living as a receptionist. Charmed by his courtesy, the old lady decided to confer Opel her rights over the Loos assets. This was controversial with her daughter Esther Gonzales-Varona, who until the 1990s contested this fact, but all her claims failed in front of the court in Austria.

Meanwhile, Adolf Opel began to collect, edit and publish the writings of Loos, claiming to be the rightful owner of the Adolf Loos Archive. He reconstructed his own collection of Loos's writings, reproducing what had been published in earlier collections (*Ins Leere gesprochen*, 1921; *Trotzdem*, 1931). Today, most writings by Adolf Loos have been published by Adolf Opel. However, Opel also claimed the rights over the documents and drawings. When I interviewed him in

2012, Opel stated that he owned the Loos copyrights and that all reproductions of Loos' works need his permission. He seemed oblivious of the fact that, quietly and without fanfare, in 2008, seventy-five years after the death of Loos, the work has slipped into its third life and the public domain. *Ines Weizman*

Costs Costs are variables; they change with the vagaries of any given moment and are often lost to memory in the roll of time. Land costs go up and down. The costs of building → MATERIALS and → LABOUR fluctuate around forces well outside any given building project, subject to global capital markets and local or nonlocal supply and demand. The costs of money itself rise and fall around larger economic flows that index global anxiety and opportunism (→ CAPITALISM). And the monetary value of buildings also changes dynamically around market fluctuations. Yet each of these trajectories could be traced, at least theoretically, were available data tabulated and made accessible. What might the fluctuating costs of architecture say about provenance? A graphic diagram of relative costs for any given building over time indexes its value: social value, economic value, historical value, political value. A proposition, then: provenance – the source of things, or where they come from – records cost and value over time. Just as provenance has been poorly understood in the history of architecture, so has cost, as one metric of a building's value.

Take, for example, four acclaimed houses: the Villa Savoye (1928–1930), the Tugendhat House (1928–1930), Fallingwater (1935–1938) and Case Study House # 8, also known as the Eames House (1949) – all by well-recognised *architecte-auteurs*. According to *The sunny days of Villa Savoye*, Le Corbusier's building cost about 800,000 French francs in 1929 (see Delhomme and Savoye 2020, p. 24). The Tugendhat House in Brno cost infinitely more a year or so later: several scholars give the costs as 5 million Czech crowns or 3,800,000 francs (see Moore 2012, converted for 1930). Sticking with francs as a metric, Frank Lloyd Wright's domestic magnum opus, Fallingwater, cost 5,355,250 in 1938 francs, or $155,000 (to an original budget of $30,000) according to *Guardian* columnist Jonathan Glancey (see Glancey 2001). In *Fallingwater aid. Architecture in detail*, Robert McCarter gives $147,000 (see McCarter 2002, p. 59). Charles Eames noted that in 1949 the 2,500-square-foot Case Study House # 8 in Pacific Palisades "would normally have been $11.50 per sq. ft., or the equivalent of good residential construction with traditional framing in California. But since his usable square feet in about half the house are 17 ft. tall, Eames' estimate brings the cubic foot cost down to a very economical $1!" with an additional 5,000 for the site's retaining wall (Blake 1950, p. 94).

The median house price of $9,564 in California, recorded in the 1950 census, might be generously adjusted upwards for this case, and still not exceed one tenth of Fallingwater's cost – even without correcting for inflation between 1938 and 1949. Each of these houses is a "canonical" example of modern domestic architecture – equalised in certain respects by their status as manifesto buildings about which young architects should learn. But only the last of them was proposed as a type – a possible solution to the high costs of housing. And only the last of them was remotely *preiswert*, "economical".

While Le Corbusier's manifesto was expensive (and cost must be lodged contextually, in this case around other bespoke houses in the countryside around Paris in the late 1920s), the Brno house was infinitely more so. The onyx wall inside the Tugendhat House reputedly cost fully as much as the entire Villa Savoye, built at roughly the same time. Fallingwater was also expensive. All of them have been painstakingly restored after periods of relative neglect, adding further expense to their histories (→ DERELICTION). The Eames House, however, breaks the mould, locating "architecture" in a low-cost building (fig. 1).

A low-cost building on the front end, its history makes it a high-value building today, particularly so after its survival from the

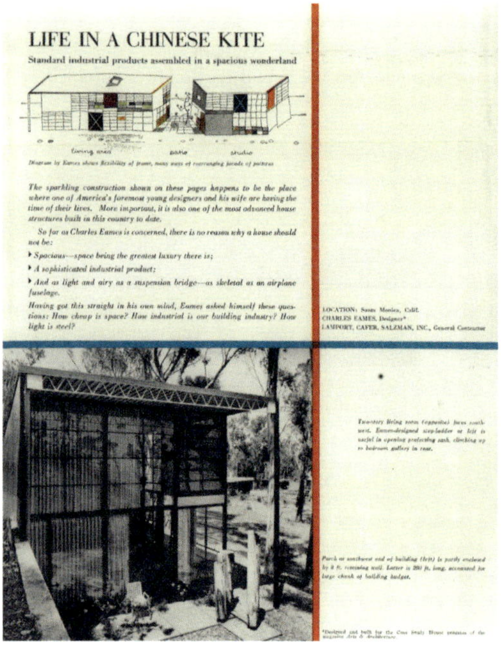

LIFE IN A CHINESE KITE

Standard industrial products assembled in a spacious wonderland

living area patio studio

Diagram by Eames shows flexibility of frame, many ways of rearranging facade of pattern

The sparkling construction shown on these pages happens to be the place where one of America's foremost young designers and his wife are having the time of their lives. More important, it is also one of the most advanced house structures built in this country to date.

So far as Charles Eames is concerned, there is no reason why a house should not be:

- *Spacious—space being the greatest luxury there is;*
- *A sophisticated industrial product;*
- *And as light and airy as a suspension bridge—as skeletal as an airplane fuselage.*

Having got this straight in his own mind, Eames asked himself these questions: How cheap is space? How industrial is our building industry? How light is steel?

LOCATION: Santa Monica, Calif.
CHARLES EAMES, Designer*
LAMPORT, CAFER, SALZMAN, INC., General Contractor

Two-story living room (opposite) faces southwest. Eames-designed step-ladder at left is useful in opening projecting sash, climbing up to bedroom gallery in rear.

Porch at southwest end of building (left) is partly enclosed by 8 ft. retaining wall. Latter is 200 ft. long, accounted for large chunk of building budget.

*Designed and built for the Case Study House program of the magazine *Arts & Architecture*

1 Peter Blake, *Presentation of Case Study House # 8 (Eames House)*, 1949, from *Architectural Forum*, vol. 93, no. 3 (1950)

cataclysmic Palisades → FIRES of 2024–2025. In this case, weighing costs in the assessment of architectural value reminds us that money cost and value are irregularly coordinated in architecture.

What does the general topic of building costs add to the study of provenance in the built environment? Initial construction cost relates a building directly to its original context by indexing the materials, labour, land and finance costs that went into it. Later, as buildings age, costs associated with their → MAINTENANCE, conservation, retrofitting or → RESTORATION provide other concrete metrics of their perceived value at a given moment in time. Provenance is not just history; it is the consciousness of history. Researching provenance encourages curiosity about the → SOURCING of building materials; about the history of land ownership; about the character of the labour force; about the occupation of a building over generations (→ RESIDENTS). For all of these, cost provides an index of change over time and a useful tool of provenance studies. *Claire Zimmerman*

Counter-monument The twentieth century was marked by a profound skepticism toward the concept of monumentality, as artists, critics and philosophers questioned both its supposed permanence and the authority it had accrued as an artistic and political form in earlier times. From Friedrich Nietzsche's 1874 watchword "Away with the monuments!", to Lewis Mumford's 1937 proclamation of their "death" and continuing into contemporary debates on "toxic" monumentality, this aesthetic as well as epistemic skepticism reflects a global and ongoing reevaluation of how societies construct and preserve memory. In the final decades of the twentieth century, the critical discourse coincided with what scholars have described as the "memory boom", which is a paradigmatic trend that refers to a surge of academic and public interest in all forms of remembrance as a framework for engaging with history, shaped by concerns over collective amnesia and the loss of historical consciousness. This intellectual climate fostered the emergence of the counter-monument (or anti-monument), which, as a term, encapsulates artistic responses to traditional memorialisation.

When examining the evolution of this concept, two pivotal developments must be considered: first, the rise of the notion of "counter-memory / counter-history" within postmodern discourse, particularly through Michel Foucault's theorisation of historiography, which interrogated the ways dominant ideologies construct and sustain normative historical narratives while marginalising alternative perspectives (see Foucault 1977). Second, the theoretical shift intersected with a growing public reckoning with national memory, particularly in relation to the atrocities of the Second World War. The late twentieth century saw an intensified global focus on the collective processing of the Shoah, catalysed by popular events such as the American television series *Holocaust* (1978), which brought the urgency of remembrance to mainstream audiences. Within this context, the counter-monument emerged not only as an aesthetic reaction to traditional commemorative forms but also as a response to the broader epistemic

→ CRISIS concerning how history is constructed, who controls its narratives and how societies engage with collective trauma.

As a reactive tendency in public art, the term "counter-monument" was formally introduced in the early 1990s by James Edward Young in his analysis of what he called "Germany's Holocaust Memorial problem" (Young 2002, p. 65). Remarkably, the scholar would later serve as a member of the commission jury for the much-debated *Memorial of the murdered Jews of Europe* in Berlin, a project that was entrusted to American architect Peter Eisenman and completed in 2004. Young, a major contributor to the discourse on postwar memorial culture, described counter-monuments as works that are ethically committed to remembrance yet "aesthetically skeptical" of traditional forms of commemoration (Young 1992, p. 271). Counter-monuments therefore reject the monumental as a stable and authoritative form, instead employing strategies used in contemporary art of the 1970s like those of ephemerality, participation and performative elements to destabilise conventional modes of memory.

Indeed, Young's advocacy for counter-monuments resonates strongly with Foucault's notion of counter-memory, which seeks to challenge dominant historical narratives with an anti-genealogical perspective on discourse. Counter-memory or counter-history, unlike revisionist historiography, does not simply propose new theories or uncover hidden facts; it explains and deconstructs the way in which dominant ideologies impose a normative order, subjugating and silencing marginalised groups. This approach aligns with the function of counter-monuments, which do not merely reject traditional memorial forms but actively work to reveal their limitations, problematising their claim to permanence, universality and authority. Furthermore, these works, by embedding memory into everyday spaces (→ RESIDENTS) or adopting ephemeral forms, critique traditional architectural permanence and encourage viewers to question the provenance, authority and ownership of → COLLECTIVE MEMORY. Those conceptual aesthetic/artistic approaches also have to be defined in contrast to broader political debates on the removal and physical deconstruction of existing monuments in the urban space that are perceived as being tied to histories of oppression. In recent debates this opposing approach can be exemplified by cases such as the dismantling of Confederate statues in the United States, the toppling of colonial-era monuments in Europe or even the claim for removal of contested works of art from museums (→ MONUMENT, TOPPLED).

Emerging primarily in Germany in response to Holocaust commemoration (Young, in his 1992 essay, names a few significant positions of the initial movement), counter-monuments have since become an international artistic and architectural strategy for challenging dominant narratives of history and power. Their influence extends beyond postwar memory culture, shaping broader debates about the role of monuments in contemporary societies reckoning with histories of violence, imperialism and oppression. Early examples of strategies which challenge the permanence and authority of conventional memorials include Austrian artist Alfred Hrdlicka's *Gegendenkmal* (Counter-monument) of 1985–1986, a sculptural contextualisation of a heroic First World War memorial erected during the Nazi regime in Hamburg (see Fleckner 2007, pp. 86ff.), or the *Mahnmal gegen Faschismus, Krieg und Gewalt* (Monument against fascism, war and violence) by Esther Shalev-Gerz and Jochen Gerz installed in Hamburg's Harburg district in 1986 as a participatory conceptualisation of the topic (fig. 1).

The lead-coated column of the latter work was the visible → COMPONENT of a complex mechanism that gradually lowered the twelve-metre pillar into the ground in an eight-stage process, during which visitors were invited to scratch their names and place → GRAFFITI on the column's surface. The signed portion, covered all over in scribbling, finally disappeared beneath a bronze plate as the pillar finally vanished completely in 1993 (see Fleckner 2007, pp. 166ff.). A text panel at the site, which was a

1 Esther Shalev-Gerz and Jochen Gerz, *Memorial against fascism, war and violence*, 1986–1993, lead-coated column with aluminium structure, text panels, 12 × 1 × 1 m, Harburger Ring, Hamburg. Photographer unknown

central element to the artist's concept, transformed the monument's performative act into a democratic gesture. Written in an appellative tone in seven languages, it read: "We invite the citizens of Harburg, and visitors to the town, to add their names here to ours. In doing so we commit ourselves to remain vigilant. [...] One day the column will have disappeared completely and the site of the Harburg monument against fascism will be empty. In the long run, it is only we ourselves who can stand up against injustice." By inviting collective participation, the inscription turned individual voices into the symbolic manifestation of a group standing against fascism. In general, these types of memorials transformed remembrance into an ongoing communal act rather than a passive encounter.

The focus on participation and impermanence reflects a broader aesthetic tendency in contemporary counter-monuments, but the definition of the term has become increasingly fluid in the twenty-first century (see Widrich 2020; Kölmel 2023). In recent years, such public works of art have expanded beyond physical interventions to include digital and augmented reality technologies that challenge traditional notions of presence and materiality in memorial culture. One notable example is Marc Quinn's *A surge of power (Jen Reid)*, a temporary intervention installed in 2020 on the empty pedestal of slave trader Edward Colston's toppled statue in Bristol (fig. 2).

The sculpture, a 3-D scan of protestor Jen Reid with her fist raised in a Black Power salute, was printed in black resin and placed overnight without official permission, making it both a counter-monument and an act of protest. Quinn, who has also contributed to the Fourth Plinth programme at London's Trafalgar Square with a comparable work, explores tension between absence and presence, questioning how architectural spaces can accommodate

2 Marc Quinn, *A surge of power (Jen Reid)*, 2020, 3-D print, resin, steel, 230 × 70 × 70 cm, The Centre, Bristol. Photographer unknown

social-debate-driven counter-histories. However, his intervention has also been criticised as opportunistic, aligning with prevailing cultural trends rather than fundamentally challenging debate. Such works demonstrate the conflicts within more recent interpretations of the counter-monument concept today, as they sometimes oscillate between radical critique and aestheticised engagement with contested histories, especially in the digital age, where commemoration risks becoming a spectacle rather than a sustained critique. *Elif Akyüz*

Craft In December 2016, Alan Hughes and his wife, Kathryn, the third-generation owners of the Whitechapel Bell Foundry in east London, announced its impending closure. It was one of the most important sites of historic craft practice in London, preserving the manufacture of church bells in a way which was not substantially different from how they had been made since the Middle Ages (fig. 1). They had sold the building to a property developer, Vince Goldstein, for £5.2 million (→ ACQUISITION). Goldstein sold it on to a New York venture capitalist, Bippy Seigal, for £7.9 million, through an investment vehicle, Raycliff Capital, which financed the purchase through bank loans.

Divergent views emerged in the architectural and → HERITAGE community as to what should happen. The → PRESERVATION agency, SAVE, thought that since there are hundreds of small factories in warehouses and sheds in London and elsewhere, it was pointless to try and protect the original use of one of them as a representative example of its type (see Saumarez Smith 2020; O'Brien 2021).

Historic England, the government's preservation agency, was under pressure from the government to adopt a more creative policy towards historic buildings, to work with developers on plans for redevelopment. There are some good examples where historic factories have been kept in operation through alternative use, including the adaption in 1987 of Salt's Mill in Saltaire by a Bradford-based property developer, Jonathan Silver, who successfully converted it into a mixed use development of shops, offices and an art gallery, preserving the structure of the building, not keeping it in operation as a textile mill (→ TRANSFORMATION). When Vince Goldstein, the developer, first requested permission for the conversion of the Whitechapel Bell Foundry into a restaurant, Mike Dunn, the officer responsible for making a judgment on whether or not this was a legitimate change of use, recommended approval to the London Advisory Committee.

By February 2017, there was a third possible approach to the building involving a coalition between two parties who had not previously worked together: the United Kingdom Historic Buildings Preservation Trust, otherwise known as the Prince of Wales's Phoenix Trust, has been responsible for the preservation of a big working pottery in Stoke-on-Trent called Middleport Pottery, a good model of how to keep alive the original use of a building for tourism and local

1 *The street facade of the Whitechapel Bell Foundry in its state of disrepair*, London. Photo: The Gentle Author, 2025

employment; and Factum Foundation, the charitable arm of Factum Arte, a company based in Madrid responsible for maintaining and developing a range of historic craft skills but often by using the latest digital technology (→ FACSIMILE). They proposed a scheme for keeping the Whitechapel Bell Foundry as a working foundry but adapting it in such a way that it would work with artists and use new technology to keep alive the craft skills previously employed by the foundry.

Instead of investigating whether or not the original use of the Whitechapel Bell Foundry could be kept alive, before allowing – indeed, encouraging – its change of use, Historic England took the view that it was not viable to retain it as a working bell foundry and that once the original business had closed, it opened an opportunity for alternative use. They therefore supported investment into keeping as much as possible of the original fabric of the building, while allowing it to be converted into a private members' club, restaurant and boutique hotel (fig. 2).

The arguments surrounding how to preserve the Whitechapel Bell Foundry provide a way to examine different approaches to the protection of historic buildings. The first is the anti-preservationist view unexpectedly adopted by some of the historic preservation agencies: the world changes; processes of manufacture change; London has not for a very long time been a manufacturing city, so one should allow the world to change. The second approach was that the fabric of the building is sufficiently important to try to preserve it as far as possible intact, but the use of the building is irrelevant to the fabric of the building. So long as the historic fabric of the building is preserved, then it does not matter if there is a change of use; it is part of the changing ecology of the building. The architectural interest of a building lies in its construction, not what happens inside.

2 *The interior of the Whitechapel Bell Foundry taken shortly before its closure*, London. Photo: Shahed Saleem, 2016

The third approach was adopted by Re:form and Factum Arte. This is that the historic interest of a building lies at least as much in the way it was originally used as in its built form. The way we understand and perceive the past is about looking at, studying and preserving the ways that people have worked in the past and that craft skills are worth trying to preserve and protect at least as much as the fabric of buildings, even if one allows, and actually encourages, the evolution of these skills by the use of new technology (see Swenarton 1989; Casey and Hayes 2023).

There could have been a fourth approach which would have been to have kept the Whitechapel Bell Foundry going more precisely as it was, using an agency like the National Trust, where you would have kept the building in operation making church bells not as a commercial operation, but, following the model of places like Ironbridge Museum in Shropshire and Styal Mill in Lancashire, for the benefit of historical archaeology and tourism. It became difficult to recommend once all the working equipment had been sold in April 2017 and the people who had worked in the foundry had been made redundant.

These discussions and debates concern the idea that the interest of a historic building lies not just in its architectural form, but in the changing patterns of its use – thinking about how buildings change and how they evolve through time; how far it is worth trying to protect and preserve the patterns and patina of their historic use; or how far one should be non-interventionist and simply allow buildings to evolve even if, as in the case of the Whitechapel Bell Foundry, the craft involved and the ways of working are now extremely rare and themselves worth preserving. *Charles Saumarez Smith*

Crisis Auctions signify crises, pauses, reversals and ruptures in the lives of both buildings and their owners, who besides being deceased, bankrupted or scandalised, were sometimes also beheaded (during the French Revolution property, architecture and luxury goods travelled intensively through European auction houses). Both the personal misfortunes publicised through auctions and the destiny of the ill-starred owners' estates evoke a conception of crisis that originates in Hippocrates' definition of cκρίσις (*krisis*) as the turning point in an illness, where the patient either recovers or dies. Architecture sold at auction experiences critical moments that result in life or death, survival or demise.

In fact, crises are everywhere to be found in the world of objects that change hands under the hammer. → CELEBRITY memorabilia thrives from crises with lethal outcomes, far from the happy ending that Charles Dickens rehearsed: "Oliver opened his eyes; he felt cheerful and happy. The crisis of the disease was safely past. He belonged to the world again" (*Oliver Twist*, 1838, ch. 12). In March 1767, for example, James Christie sold a signum "composed of diamonds, rubies, sapphires, emeralds, onyx, pearl, etc. worn by Mary Queen of Scots the morning she was beheaded", or so read the provenance stated in the catalogue.

Yet, architecture behaves differently from more easily portable treasures, and not least in the longstanding tradition of → DEMOLITION auctions. Some of the biggest demolition sales took place under the reign of Henry VIII during the dissolution of the monasteries when architectural features and building → MATERIALS were often repurposed elsewhere. There was no salvage in sight when Richard Neutra's Maslon House in Palm Springs (1963) sold at Sotheby's in 2002; a month later the house was bulldozed.

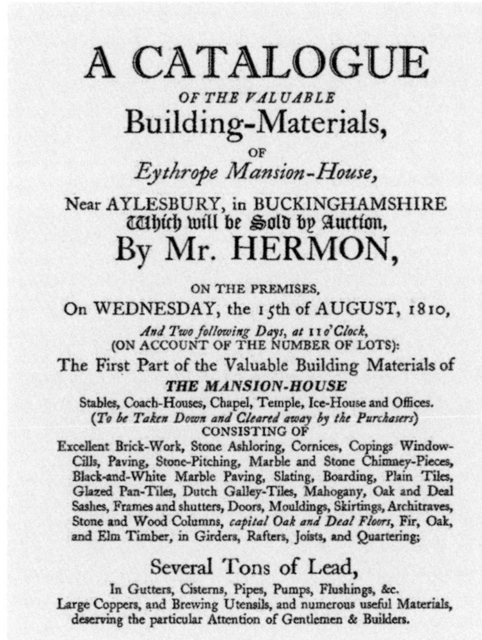

A CATALOGUE
OF THE VALUABLE
Building-Materials,
OF
Eythrope Mansion-House,
Near AYLESBURY, in BUCKINGHAMSHIRE
Which will be Sold by Auction,
By Mr. HERMON,
ON THE PREMISES,
On WEDNESDAY, the 15th of AUGUST, 1810,
And Two following Days, at 11 o'Clock,
(ON ACCOUNT OF THE NUMBER OF LOTS):
The First Part of the Valuable Building Materials of
THE MANSION-HOUSE
Stables, Coach-Houses, Chapel, Temple, Ice-House and Offices.
(*To be Taken Down and Cleared away by the Purchasers*)
CONSISTING OF
Excellent Brick-Work, Stone Ashloring, Cornices, Copings Window-Cills, Paving, Stone-Pitching, Marble and Stone Chimney-Pieces, Black-and-White Marble Paving, Slating, Boarding, Plain Tiles, Glazed Pan-Tiles, Dutch Galley-Tiles, Mahogany, Oak and Deal Sashes, Frames and shutters, Doors, Mouldings, Skirtings, Architraves, Stone and Wood Columns, *capital Oak and Deal Floors*, Fir, Oak, and Elm Timber, in Girders, Rafters, Joists, and Quartering;
Several Tons of Lead,
In Gutters, Cisterns, Pipes, Pumps, Flushings, &c.
Large Coppers, and Brewing Utensils, and numerous useful Materials, deserving the particular Attention of Gentlemen & Builders.

1 Auctioneer Hermon, *Catalogue for the building materials of Eythrope House*, 15–17 August 1810

Crisis signifies an essence in architectural provenance; moments when change is imminent. Crises mark transitional states in which architecture is revaluated, negotiated, recomposed, gains new status, meaning and connections, and when new owners and authors (→ AUTHORSHIP) are inscribed in a building's often unpredictable → AFTERLIFE.

"All transitions are crises", as Goethe put it (see Koselleck 2006, p. 367). Some such critical transitions unfolded in the series of demolition auctions of British country houses, accompanied by → CATALOGUES, erratic → TRANSFER, → REUSE, as well as the public exposure of privacy and personal crisis. In August 1810, at a time when building materials were much in demand due to the Napoleonic Wars, the 5th Earl of Chesterfield had Mr Hermon auction off Eythrope House in Buckinghamshire on the premises (fig. 1).

A fraction of the title page of the *Catalogue of the valuable Building-Materials* (graphically characteristic for the genre with its many typefaces and letter sizes) read: "Stables, Coach-Houses,

Chapel, Temple, Ice-House and Offices. (*To be taken Down and Cleared away by the Purchasers*) CONSISTING OF Excellent Brick-Work, Stone Ashloring, Cornices, Copings Window-Cills, Paving, Stone-Pitching, Marble and Stone Chimney Pieces, Black-and-White Marble Paving, Slating, Boarding, Plain Tiles, Glazed Pan-Tiles, Dutch Galley-Tiles, Mahogany, Oak and Deal Sashes, Frames and shutters, Doors, Mouldings, Skirtings, Architraves, Stone and Wood Columns, *capital Oak and Deal Floors*, Fir, Oak, and Elm Timber, in Girders, Rafters, Joists, and Quartering; Several Tons of Lead, In Gutters, Cisterns, Pipes, Pumps, Flushings, &c. Large Coppers, and Brewing Utensils, and numerous useful Materials, deserving the particular Attention of Gentlemen & Builders."

When a crash in the Jamaican sugar market forced William Beckford to sell his secluded Gothic Revival haven, the ensuing auctions at Fonthill Abbey became highpoints of spectacle, scandal and publicity. The preview for the auction in September 1822 attracted crowds of domestic tourists that would not under any other circumstance have set foot in the house. Although this auction was cancelled at the last minute when a gunpower millionaire bought the house, he auctioned it off again the next autumn. The collection was dispersed and the buildings razed. The Fonthill Abbey auctions produced a battery of publications, including Christie's one guinea *Catalogue of the magnificent effects at Fonthill Abbey* in 1822 and massive news coverage. Less known, perhaps, is the fact that Beckford auctioned off his father's Neo-Palladian country house, completed around 1770, for demolition in 1807 while working on his own building project on the same estate.

Another critical highlight is the Hamilton Palace auctions. Most of the art collection was sold over seventeen days in 1882, in a sale where art dealers made a solid presence. In November 1919, Christie, Mason & Wood's catalogue offered "The Remaining Contents of the Palace", after which the house disappeared from the face of the coal-rich earth it had been sitting on (fig. 2).

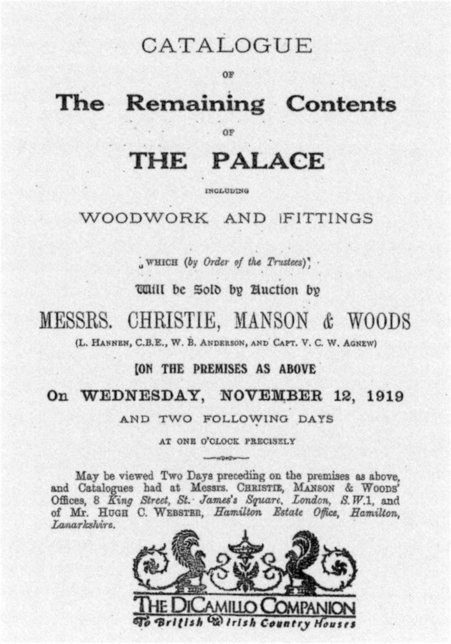
CATALOGUE

OF

The Remaining Contents

OF

THE PALACE

INCLUDING

WOODWORK AND FITTINGS

WHICH (*by Order of the Trustees*)

Will be Sold by Auction by

MESSRS. CHRISTIE, MANSON & WOODS

(L. HANNEN, C.B.E., W. B. ANDERSON, AND CAPT. V. C. W. AGNEW)

ON THE PREMISES AS ABOVE

On WEDNESDAY, NOVEMBER 12, 1919

AND TWO FOLLOWING DAYS

AT ONE O'CLOCK PRECISELY

May be viewed Two Days preceding on the premises as above, and Catalogues had at Messrs. CHRISTIE, MANSON & WOODS' Offices, 8 *King Street, St. James's Square, London, S.W.*1, and of Mr. HUGH C. WEBSTER, *Hamilton Estate Office, Hamilton, Lanarkshire.*

2 Christie, Manson & Woods, *Catalogue of the final sale of Hamilton Palace*, 12–14 November 1919

That did not end the trajectory of auctions of this stately home, however, nor the → CIRCULATION of its grand rooms. Agents and art dealers were among the bidders in 1919, and numerous interiors crossed the Atlantic where many of them entered the collection of the American media tycoon William Randolph Hearst (see Harris 2007). Suffering a financial crisis during the Depression, Hearst auctioned off huge parts of his collection in the spring of 1941. The auction took place on the fifth floor of the Gimbel Brothers department store in New York: "People are a little terrified at going into an art gallery. They feel that they are surrounded by professionals who make them timid. But no one has ever had an inferiority complex about going into a department store", the organizing gallerist Arnold Hammer explained to *TIME* magazine (Anonymous 1941). "The Hamilton Palace Dining Room, XVIII century, paneled and carved in wood, with fireplace" figured as lot 96 in the auction catalogue; the ducal room was installed between the fourth and sixth floor of the department store on 33rd Street and Broadway.

More rooms from the grandest country house in Scotland were offered under the category "Buildings and Parts" in the Hearst *catalogue raisonné*: "A Collection of Six Panelled Rooms from Hamilton Palace, Seat of the Duke of Hamilton, Reigning Peer of Scotland, at Lanarkshire, Scotland, Ranking among the Finest Oak and Georgian Rooms in Existence and they are truly magnificent" (Hammer Galleries 1941, p. 323).

"Life is short, and art long, the crisis fleeting; experience perilous, and decision difficult. The physician must not only be prepared to do what is right himself, but also to make the patient, the attendants, and externals cooperate", reads the first of Hippocrates' *Aphorismi* (c.400 BCE). Rather than preconfiguring the idea that individual lives are only brief occurrences whereas artworks may aspire to permanence, Hippocrates' maxim ὁ βίος βραχὺς, ἡ δὲ τέχνη μακρή (*ars longa, vita brevis*) points to the importance of τέχνη (*techne*), of textbooks from which skills could be taught and learned (handed down as "art": Horace's *Ars Poetica* or Ovid's *Ars Amatoria* advises on how to compose a poem or seduce somebody). The surgical biopsies and prostheses created by the dismantling and transplantation of entire interiors, facade elements and building materials hovers between life and death. Yet, as post-demolition transformations they, like Oliver Twist, belong to the world again; involving odd skills, perilous experience, difficult decisions, bizarre manipulation and publicity. *Mari Lending*

Deaccessioning The term "deaccessioning" generally refers to the formal process by which a collecting institution, usually a museum or university, voluntarily removes an item from its permanent holdings (see Gammon 2018). Despite being a common practice in North American museums and historically in pre-war Europe, the voluntary disposal of objects has remained largely unexplored – even within the recently emerging field of provenance studies, which readily focuses on concepts of → DISPOSSESSION and → RESTITUTION in contexts of injustice while overlooking institutional divestment. Art history, too, leaves us with conspicuous absences. While its counterpart, → COLLECTING, has long been historicised and theorised – even if often in surprisingly euphemistic terms – deaccessioning continues to lurk in the shadows of institutional memory. In the rare cases where museums incorporate deaccessioning into their official histories, the narratives are typically sidetracked: they focus on the → ACQUISITIONS made possible through such disposals, as evident in the cases of Vincent van Gogh's *Starry Night* (1889) and Pablo Picasso's *Les Demoiselles d'Avignon* (1907), both acquired by the Museum of Modern Art in New York, instead of focusing on the exchange procedure or the discarded objects and their new contexts. Museums' uncanny proximity to the art market and their proactive economic role – revealed through their practices of exchanging, dealing and trading artworks – may explain why mainstream art-historical discourse has largely avoided examining deaccession processes.

If we turn to philosophy, following Krzysztof Pomian's theory on the origin of museums, which defines collecting as the withdrawal of objects from the sphere of practical utility in order to grant them symbolic or cultural value (see Pomian 1988), we might understand deaccessioning as the inverse gesture: the removal of symbolic or cultural value by reintroducing the discarded objects into functional, transactional or otherwise utilitarian realms. This line of thinking might hold when we consider museums as gatekeepers for the art historical canon, from which discarded objects are deliberately expunged by the experts who authorise their removal and relegate them to a different context and uncertain future in private or less prominent museum collections. But can this perspective hold when we acknowledge deaccessioning as a provenance phenomenon across the arts, including architecture, which is typically more constrained by functional necessities and cannot as easily be discarded?

Architecture can be transformed and reused (→ TRANSFORMATION, → REUSE), destroyed and replaced (→ DISPLACEMENT), or abandoned and left to decay (→ DERELICTION, → RUIN), but we should also consider the moment when architectural structures serve similar purposes in seemingly inferior ways or are repurposed by other user groups or for other uses, in which case the context usually changes, but the location rarely does – unlike in the case of mobile artworks (→ IMAGE VEHICLE, → MOBILITY, → TRANSLOCATION). A paradigmatic example of such architectural deaccessioning is the 945 Madison Avenue building in New York, designed by the Bauhaus architect Marcel Breuer and completed in 1966 (fig. 1).

Currently known as the "Breuer building", paying tribute to the Hungarian-American architect and the building's first provenance, it acquired this name only after undergoing a sequence of institutional reassignments that reflect shifting curatorial, economic and urban dynamics. Its trajectory from museum to auction house reveals how deaccessioning can function as a form of institutional metamorphosis, wherein architecture itself becomes a medium of historical and ideological transformation.

For the longest time in its existence, the icon of brutalist architecture was well known as the Whitney Museum of American Art, the very institution that commissioned the modern architect to house its twentieth-century collection. Its

1 Marcel Breuer, *Former Whitney Museum of American Art*, 1966, 945 Madison Avenue, New York. Photo: Lynn Rother, 2025

inverted ziggurat form and austere, modernist → MATERIAL palette helped define the Whitney's institutional identity and positioned the museum as a champion of postwar American art. The Upper East Side building lost its original context when the Whitney relocated to a newly designed space by the Italian architect Renzo Piano in the Meatpacking District in 2015, marking a decisive shift toward broader audiences and a more expansive curatorial mission. Although framed as a logistical necessity, this departure constituted a symbolic deaccessioning, in which the building was no longer deemed adequate to represent the institution's evolving vision.

In 2016, the Metropolitan Museum of Art reopened the building to the public, rechristening it the "Met Breuer". This occupation was intended to showcase parts of the Met's modern and contemporary collection – long considered the weakest link among the institution's holdings – but also served as an experiment in institutional expansion. However, the Met soon found the programme financially unsustainable and terminated the originally conceived eight-year lease of the building in 2020. The brief tenure was marked by critical ambivalence, revealing tensions between the building's formal language and the Met's traditional identity.

From 2021 to 2024, another Upper East Side neighbour, the Frick Collection, temporarily relocated to the building while its Fifth Avenue home underwent renovation. The Frick's Old Master paintings and decorative arts were thus placed in deliberate juxtaposition with Breuer's brutalist architecture. The result of the so-called "Frick Madison" was a curatorial experiment that drew attention to the dissonance between content and container and again underscored the building's status as a decontextualised architectural object. The Frick's explicitly temporary occupation further alienated the building from its original purpose and reinforced its identity as a flexible institutional shell.

In 2024, the building was acquired by the auction house Sotheby's, marking its first transfer from a nonprofit cultural institution to a for-profit commercial entity. This final shift dramatises the stakes of architectural deaccessioning: a building designed to house and elevate cultural heritage for the public good is now enlisted to facilitate the monetisation of such heritage. In this context, deaccessioning becomes a lens through which to view the transformation of public cultural infrastructure into privatised commercial assets.

Yet, inverting Pomian's theory of collecting is too shortsighted to understand such deaccession processes. Neither are cultural and symbolic values simply removed or exchanged for economic values; they are rather used and even instrumentalised. Moreover, deaccessioning cannot simply be understood as a diminishing value transformation, as the removal of discarded objects might make us believe. Instead, deaccessioning must be viewed through Igor Kopytoff's concept of the "cultural biography of things" (see Kopytoff 1986) and the anthropological lens of Arjun Appadurai's theory of the "social life of things" (see Appadurai 1986). Thus, it is to be understood as a moment within a larger continuum of object histories, where value, meaning and function are not fixed but continuously negotiated.

For both theorists, commoditisation is not a static category but a process that objects may enter and exit throughout their lifespans. Buildings, like portable cultural goods, may shift between regimes of use, display, reverence and exchange, accumulating different layers of significance along the way. The architectural deaccessioning of the Breuer building exemplifies this fluidity as it moves through a succession of cultural, curatorial and commercial contexts that reshape its institutional meaning. Each deaccessioning decision marked a phase transition in the building's "biography", in which its status changed from core institutional asset to a dispensable surplus.

When the Sotheby's deal hit the news, it wasn't the former Whitney that the auction house bought for approximately $100 million – it was "the Breuer building": real estate which, thanks to a sequence of deaccessions in the form of institutional reassignments, now carries its iconic status as a modern architectural site in its name (→ CELEBRITY). It is ready to be further capitalised upon when Sotheby's opens its newest flagship. As the building's provenance continues to evolve, it reveals the mutable nature of institutional identity and the market's enduring appetite for architectural aura. *Lynn Rother*

Demolition People walk in sped-up time while buildings melt, thrash and explode more slowly than you might expect in the music video for Queen and David Bowie's 1981 hit *Under Pressure*, directed by David Mallet. Like the vocal tracks of Bowie and Freddie Mercury, the four-minute video is assembled from parts (fig. 1).

Under Pressure is a critical portrait of 1981 told through found footage of crowds, failures and phantoms from the past decades, a collage of demolitions, soup kitchens, trench-coated workers and riots. Mercury's first exasperated "pressure!" comes as a car motor shatters in slow motion, filling the screen with dust and debris. Minute one ends with towers in free fall, one after another, until a final collapse suddenly, smoothly, whiplashes back into architectural form.

The speed here is worth paying attention to: people gain momentum, demolitions are prolonged, tension is built in through tempo. The early 1980s was a celebratory moment for demolition. What had once been

1 Queen and David Bowie: *Under Pressure*, 1981. Still from the video by David Mallet

merely a shadow of the construction industry was now an advancing profession receiving serious interest. Much of the attention directed towards the industry focused on its efficiencies: demolition was a cost-saving solution ("Blasting scheme saves $6 million", *Engineering News-Record*, 1977) with increasing precision (a three-part series on "Control and demolition" was published in the journal *Planner*, 1974–1975) and research potential ("Demolition offers rare collapse data", *Engineering News-Record*, 1979). But most important for the growing profession ("Cut throat industry, but good prospects", *Civil Engineering*, 1984), was its newfound speed of destruction ("Downtown Dallas block razed in 11 1/2 seconds", *Engineering News-Record*, 1980; "Right equipment speeds demolition", *Highway and Heavy Construction*, 1981).

A history of cinematic collapses would substantiate this fascination with tempo and trajectory. Demolition appeared on screen early with *Démolition d'un mur* by Louis Lumière (1896), a short silent film in which the destruction of a building wall is played forward and then rewound – a technique later echoed in "Under Pressure".

Side by side, these two show the changing methods of destruction, from hand wrecking with jackscrews and picks to firing up explosives and stepping back. Most of the explosive demolition scenes in *Under Pressure* would appear again on screen just one year later with the release of the much-loved documentary *Koyaanisqatsi* by director Godfrey Reggio and cinematographer Ron Fricke (1982). Like *Under Pressure* the acceleration and efficiency of modern life are underlined by the speeding and slowing of footage. At a duration twenty times that of the music video and substituting the musical genius of Phillip Glass for that of Queen and Bowie, the film is known for inducing a sort of trance-like state among its viewers. An especially iconic scene pans around the condemned thirty-three, eleven-storey-high Pruitt-Igoe towers as small explosions set off a chain reaction of collapses. Questions of speed and destruction were not only present in these films, they were prescient. The events were part of a generation of demolitions mostly performed by the connoisseurs of building "implosion": Controlled Demolition, Inc. The company would go on to correspond with artist Gordon Matta-Clark about their shared interest in the demolition "choreography" (→ INHERITANCE), shed the modernist skin of Las Vegas through a series of demolitions which drew spectators out of performance venues and into the streets, and work with Hollywood productions to bring captivating destructions to the big screen. Demolition contractors often mediated between the desires of building owners and movie producers – offsetting → COSTS of demolition with sales to film rights and essentially displacing the costs of demolition onto cinema-goers. Indeed, much of the value of the demolition industry lay in its production value.

Consider how many cinematic demolitions are presented in slow motion. These scenes are slowed to enhance the clarity of fast-moving explosions, by making visible what would otherwise be obscured by speed. We take it for granted that demolition happens quickly. Development favors speed, destruction, change, but demolition can be slow and innocuous, too.

Demolition seems to be slowing – not *en masse*, but in duration. Controlled demolitions increasingly take place not in minutes but over years. Take the recently condemned Grenfell Tower in Central London. After a tragic → FIRE which killed seventy-two people and an ensuing eight years of uncertainty, a decision from the government to "take down" the tower stipulates that this process will be a "careful and sensitive progressive deconstruction" lasting "over a two-year period" and hided "behind the wrapping" of the facade, as reported in *The Guardian* (Grierson and Walker 2025).

If 1980s filmmakers sought to direct attention to the acceleration of society, then there is a certain pride in slowness today. Demolition – once fast, explosive and performative – seems to have quieted. A now-popular genre of time-lapse YouTube videos depicts the gradual reduction of towers through actions that reverse the patient process of construction. This real-life speed adjustment presents an apparently reformed aesthetics of demolition. Reluctant demolitions disappear through slowness rather than speed.

If slowing the images of demolition could make them more readable, then slowing the process might also provide insight into an industry intimately connected to architecture. Demolition plays a decisive role in the history of architecture, as it often reflects a shift in styles, functions and social values. These moments of buildings in → CRISIS might be interpreted as a symbol of progress or the loss of cultural → HERITAGE. Demolition not only enables the creation of new spaces and structures, but also a critical examination of past inflection points and their influence on the present.

The video compilation for *Under Pressure* is an iconic characterisation of accelerated life, but viewers will notice an optimistic undertone. By minute three, demolitions reverse. Anonymous, accelerated crowds give in to deep kisses. Bowie and Mercury sing of love. *Alena Beth Rieger*

Dereliction In the architectural context, dereliction refers to the gradual physical and aesthetic decline of a building due to ageing, → WEATHERING, lack of → MAINTENANCE or improper use. This process can manifest itself in structural damage, material fatigue and an impairment of the original functionality and appearance (fig. 1).

Dereliction can lead to a significant loss of substance and usability, turning a building into a → RUIN. In contrast to → DEMOLITION, there is usually no direct intention of destruction in the case of dereliction. In *Buildings must die*, Stephen Cairns and Jane M. Jacobs distinguished between different modes: dereliction can initially manifest itself in the superficial deposition of → DUST from the air or substances from rainwater (see Cairns and Jacobs 2014). At the same time, corrosive forms of dereliction can occur in which surfaces oxidise, for example by the formation of verdigris on copper.

Buildings can also be infested and eroded by living organisms, including lichen, mould or plant growth. In the long term, dereliction is accompanied by loss of substance, be it the superficial peeling of paint on a wall, the slow erosion of stones by rainwater or the flaking of a plaster facade. Massive and often irreparable damage is caused by internal decay processes, especially in organic → MATERIALS. However, inorganic building materials can also experience material fatigue; for example, steel can develop minimal cracks over time and lose its stability. In the case of reinforced concrete, the penetration of moisture can cause the reinforcements to rust and expand, which in turn causes the concrete to crack (→ FRAGILITY).

The reasons for the dereliction of architecture can be manifold. The owners of a building may be physically or financially unable to maintain it. Purposeful neglect is also conceivable, when the owner of a listed building deliberately fails to maintain it until its → RESTORATION is physically impossible or economically unreasonable, so that the owner can get away with demolishing it. In addition, there are social, political, economic and ecological reasons that lead to the abandonment of entire settlements, cities or regions and thus to the dereliction of the buildings there. Historians refer to this

1 *Former Hotel President in the state of decay*, Berlin. Photo: Frank Schmitz, 2025

phenomenon as "desertification". In Germany, for example, the withdrawal of Soviet troops in the 1990s meant that the former barracks were left to decay until only a small proportion could be converted into civilian housing estates. In addition to political shifts, climate change is also increasingly causing vacancy and dereliction. Rising temperatures are making many regions around the world uninhabitable due to heat and drought. Even in the high mountains, thawing permafrost is leading to landslides and posing threats to local buildings, which have to be abandoned in extreme cases. With regard to the Alps, for example, the question has already been raised in the media: "Does Switzerland have to abandon Alpine villages?" (*Weltspiegel*, ARD television, 24 November 2024).

Buildings are susceptible to phenomena of dereliction to varying degrees, with modernist buildings since the nineteenth century often being particularly vulnerable. In their study *On Weathering*, Mohsen Mostafavi and David Leatherbarrow point out that new building materials and production techniques lead to "a great degree of unpredictability in the life of buildings after construction" (Mostafavi and Leatherbarrow 1993, p. 17). The buildings of the "white" modernism of the 1920s and 1930s are also particularly susceptible to weathering. Their gleaming white cleanliness (→ PRISTINE) is not very resilient to the streaks of running rainwater and other phenomena of dereliction (fig. 2).

2 Le Corbusier and Pierre Jeanneret, *Villa Savoye*, 1928–1931, Poissy. Photo: René Burri, 1959

Le Corbusier categorically rejected the traces of time in architecture, as well as the → PATINA and dirt associated with it. Cairns and Jacobs refer to Le Corbusier's trip to America in 1935, during which he glorified the modernity and cleanliness of a city like New York as an expression of national virtue (see Cairns and Jacobs 2014). On the other hand, he was critical of practices in Europe, where dust and dirt were cultivated and patina and cracks in historic walls preserved. As Corbusier famously pointed out, medieval cathedrals were also originally white.

Accordingly, the phenomena of decay have long been negated in architectural theory. The Vitruvian *firmitas* implies that architecture is stable and therefore unchanging. Design theory also long assumed that works of art and architecture were realised according to a consistent design, such that, in the words of Heinrich Wölfflin, "nothing could be changed or shifted, but everything must be as it is" (Wölfflin 1920, p. 133). According to this understanding, every change caused by weathering or plant growth – that is decay – is to be understood as deficient. → CAPITALISM also influenced modernism's negative connotation of signs of aging in architecture. The capitalist logic of circulation and continuous production of new goods was transferred to architecture, rendering it a consumer good: the new and unused is always seen as the best functioning, and so in the real-estate sector, too, the new often promises more prestige than the already used.

According to other ways of thinking, the ageing of architecture is viewed more favourably or even understood as an integral part of the life cycle of buildings: for example, weathering should not be understood only as a → SUBTRACTION, such as a stone surface is eroded by rain. Rather, the accumulation of material in the form of patina, lichen or moss contributes the "finish" to both a building and its environment and could "productively modify a building over time" (Mostafavi and Leatherbarrow 1993, p. 42). This understanding is implicitly based on a biologistic interpretation of the building, implying that it is born, develops, becomes deficient and can ultimately reach the end of its life cycle. These organic analogies go back to the architectural theory of the Renaissance period, as Cairns and Jacobs pointed out with regard to the Italian theorist Filarete (see Cairns and Jacobs 2014, p. 26). Dereliction and loss, as well as the repair of buildings (→ REPARATION), are therefore not just an accident and a necessary evil, but fundamental to the nature of the built environment. The acceptance of decay was a central element in the concept of *Alterswert* (age value), which the art historian Alois Riegl made an essential component of his fundamental theory of monuments (see Riegl 1903, p. 20ff.). According to this theory, imperfection and a lack of coherence are key characteristics that indicate the age of a building. If a building is also to be considered a monument, this legibility is even expressly desired and constitutive of its monumental value.

Today, dereliction is often explicitly accepted by the users of architecture and is given a positive connotation. Moreover, there are isolated approaches in architectural design to incorporate dereliction as an element searching for the "aesthetics of an unaesthetic ruined space" (Nieszczerzewska 2015, p. 387). Devices such as roof overhangs, cornices or water drains, which have been used for centuries and are intended to minimise weathering caused by rain, are sometimes actively negated. A studio building erected in 1995–1996 for the artist Remy Zaugg in Mulhouse, France, for example, was deliberately designed by architects Herzog & de Meuron in such a way that rainwater leaves clear streaks on the concrete walls and thus "completes" the building. *Frank Schmitz*

Displacement The term "displacement" refers to the movement of buildings from their original location and context. Due to their → MOBILITY, various kinds of displaced architecture, such as temples, tombs, memorial halls, houses and monuments, can act as → IMAGE VEHICLES (Aby Warburg), resulting in turning decontextualisation into recontextualisation and thus altering → COLLECTIVE MEMORY. Physical displacement can involve moving entire structures from their original sites to new grounds, as happened, for example, with the preservation-driven → TRANSLOCATION of the Abu Simbel Temples in the 1960s due to the creation of the Aswan Dam, as well as with the transfer of the Ishtar Gate to the Pergamon Museum in Berlin, which sparks ongoing debates about cultural → HERITAGE, ownership and repatriation. In those cases in which it is understood as part of the phenomenon of image vehicles, displacement can also encompass representing structures in the form of copies or → FACSIMILES in various contexts to recontextualise architectural → ELEMENTS, as seen in the exchange of garden design between Asia and Europe since the eighteenth century. Notable examples include the Chinese pagoda at Kew Gardens and the influence of European styles like those from the Palace of Versailles in the Old Summer Palace (圆明园) in Beijing. Thus, displacement is a complex phenomenon that intertwines multiple aspects – spatial, stylistic and symbolic – across different cultural contexts. It represents the dynamic processes through which architectural elements and structures are moved, transformed and reinterpreted beyond their original settings.

The case of the so-called Ketteler Monument in Beijing exemplifies this complexity, as it encompasses various dimensions of displacement in form, meaning and political utilisation. The monument initially commemorated German minister Clemens von Ketteler (1853–1900), who was killed during the Boxer Rebellion (1899–1901). As part of the humiliating terms of the *Final protocol for the settlement of the disturbances of 1900* (the Boxer Protocol) between the Qing Empire of China and eleven foreign powers, its establishment marked a dark moment in early twentieth-century China. The court was compelled to convey apologies to the German Emperor for Ketteler's murder and to build a monument at the site of his death, inscribed in Latin, German and Chinese to express the Qing Emperor's regrets (fig. 1).

The Germans insisted on a design resembling a traditional Chinese memorial gate, *paifang* (牌坊), modelled after the largest stone archway in the Ming emperors' tombs, instead of a Western-style statue. By appropriating traditional Chinese architectural forms, the monument, featuring a "four-columns-three-gates" structure topped with blue glazed tiles, leveraged the grandeur of a royal grave archway to symbolise Western dominance.

The Ketteler Monument stood at the scene of the assassination on a street in Beijing's city centre for fifteen years until Germany's defeat in World War I. In 1919, it was removed and relocated to Beijing's first public park, the Zhongshan Park, three kilometers from its original site. Original → INSCRIPTIONS were erased, and the structure was renamed the Victory of Justice Gate (公理战胜坊) to celebrate the Allied victory of the war. In 1953, it was renamed again to Protection of Peace Gate (保卫和平坊) to commemorate the Peace Conference of the Asian and Pacific Regions held in Beijing (fig. 2).

The displacement of the monument into a park largely eliminated its colonial symbolism from collective memory and provided significant opportunities to imbue the structure with new meanings that emphasise the achievements of new regimes and national pride, visually reflecting the country's political change. For example, the archway's form gained specific iconographic meaning after the park became the temporary resting place of Sun Yat-sen, the founder of Republican China, in 1925. Since then, it has been incorporated into memorial spaces for Sun Yat-sen, such as his large mausoleum in Nanjing, and frequently replicated in many commemorative parks named after him throughout the Sinophone world.

Later, statues and posters of national heroes and political leaders were strategically placed around the monument to reshape its political meaning. For instance, during China's Cultural Revolution, Mao Zedong's portrait and quotes occupied the entire structure, making it appear like a bulletin board for Maoist propaganda. Since the 1980s, large flowerbeds have been annually set in front of the monument to celebrate China's National Day on the first of October, turning the site into a beloved spot for citizens to take selfies and family photos, which appear in countless family photo albums. Thus, the monument's original association with any specific historical figure has become blurred, as it connects more closely to people's everyday lives, transforming into a "people's monument", used by the people and endowed with personal meaning (→ TRANSFORMATION). From its origins as a colonial symbol erected on a city street, intended to warn and assert dominance over the public, to its role commemorating victory, peace and the

1 *Dedication of the Memorial Gateway Arch (Ketteler Monument)*, 1903, Mishi Street (renamed Kettelerstraße), Beijing. Photographer unknown

2 *The Protection of Peace Gate (former Ketteler Monument)*, moved in 1919, renamed 1953, with sanitation workers taking selfies in front of the flowerbeds they have cultivated, Zhongshan Park, Beijing. Photo: Yuning Teng, 2023

nation's prosperity within a park, and finally to its current status as a "people's monument", the Ketteler Monument's displacement illustrates the complex social and historical changes that have unfolded in modern China. However, it is important to note that, whether one hundred years ago when German soldiers celebrated their invasion of China under this archway, or today when sanitation workers take photos in front of it with the flowerbeds they have built, the interpretation of this monument's significance has always been controlled and guided by political authority, never fully opened to public discussion.

As demonstrated by the Ketteler Monument, displacement reveals the ways architectural structures can be repurposed and redefined through geographical relocation, reflecting shifts in power, society and identity. Thus, as numerous other case studies could demonstrate, displacement is not merely a physical movement but a transformative process that reshapes political narratives and collective memory across time. *Yuning Teng*

Dispossession Dispossession may easily seem a terrifying prospect. But what if the possessions were unrightful or if property makes little sense to begin with? What can and should be owned and by whom? To whom does the forest, the steppe or the mountains belong? Or the sea, the sky, the wind and the clouds? Such considerations may be a slippery slope, but often they are also a necessity. In (post)colonial and imperial situations, dispossession may appear not simply as a tool of depriving someone of their possessions, but of reclaiming and → RESTITUTION. This is the stuff of → WAR and conquest, of revolution and de-colonisation.

What, then, is the architecture of dispossession? This is perhaps best understood through extreme examples. Architecture is one essential instrument in the toolbox of colonisation and a key substance of the imperial repertoires that have marked conquest-driven dispossession of land and territory throughout history. Military construction, fortifications, camps and settlements, triumphal arches and monuments, buildings in uniform style displaying the power of centralised rule; such architectures appear as signs of conquest and power in newly acquired territories as well as in colonial centres. Or they may appear as monuments to the very act of dispossession and the loss that came with it.

A more important consideration is how architecture can counter the dispossession by oppression, how can it act as a de- and re-constructive force? In times of revolution and de-colonisation, confronting the monuments of past regimes is often part of the regime change (→ COUNTER-MONUMENT, → MONUMENT, TOPPLED). Sometimes the most powerful and persisting acts of architectural dispossession are those that do not replicate the oppressive tactics of conquest and takeover, erasure and removal, but seek more regenerative paths through reclaiming and disarming them. After the French Revolution of 1789, the claim for imperial and religious monuments took aggressive forms of removal, but also scientific forms of action, where the → COLLECTING, cataloguing and study of monuments historicised them (→ CATALOGUE). The new category of "historic monument" helped to disarm them, providing new frameworks for critical observation (see Delbeke 2017).

Other architectural tactics were also devised amidst the revolutionary furore of destruction, such as festivals, music and poetry, as well as the garnishing of old monuments and the erection of new ones (see Ozouf 1976; Smyth 2016). As religious buildings were targeted across France during the anti-Catholic fervour of 1793, the iconic single completed spire of Strasbourg cathedral came under attack as a structure of religious excess. Between the anti-religious ambition to bring down and what must have been the inevitable attachment to a local, intergenerational icon, an unexpected solution materialised. Instead of tearing down the imposing tower, the local craftsmen and women knitted a giant Phrygian cap – a symbolic garb of the Revolution – to be put on top of the spire (see Glaser 2004). Gargantuan in scale and powerful as an act, but fleeting as a material gesture, the knitted cap attempted to redefine, reclaim and reframe rather than replace. This symbolic act of disarming is the architecture of gentle dispossession.

Similar tactics proliferate across revolutions, although often they are overshadowed by the more daring acts in the history books. The architects of the revolutions in the Russian Empire, too, often sought to reclaim and redefine the inherited imperial monuments rather than to erase them. In Saint Petersburg, this became particularly tricky, as the entire city, up to its name, was a prime symbol of empire. Artists devised temporary edifices and huge canvases that during celebrations of the new rule would cover the facades of imperial palaces and monuments (see Geldern 1993; Tolstoy et al. 1990). They were similarly fleeting in their presence, and the destruction of the entire city was hardly an option.

In the midst of the heroic attempts to imagine something entirely new, there were others, who sought to employ tactics of disarming and reclaiming, powered by dispossession. One example is the very first Russian revolutionary monument, designed by the young Lev Rudnev in 1917, and erected in the middle of the former imperial capital on its main military parading grounds, the Field of Mars (fig. 1).

Instead of proposing new formal ideas, it took the classical idiom of the surrounding city and repurposed it in order to undo its meaning.

1 Lev Rudnev, *Monument to the Heroes of the Revolution*, 1917, postcard, Pochtovaia otkrytka, Leningrad. Mogily revoliutsionerov na pole im. Zhertv revoliutsii (b. Marsovo pole) (Moscow: Izogiz 1929)

Instead of a figure on a pedestal, the form of the monument makes a foundation, leaving empty the space on top as well as inside its perimeter. The monument repurposed its granite from the embankments of a recently destroyed harbour storage facility, designed by Thomas de Thomon and revered as an icon of the city's neo-classical architecture. Rudnev emphasised how this → MATERIAL transferred by a collective effort performed an inversion of the meaning of the city: from the periphery to the centre, inside-out, replicating the inversive (and dispossessing) promise of revolution (see Lähteenmäki 2020 and 2022, pp. 87ff.).

The monument's foundational and open form, the collective act of its construction embedded in its materiality and its constant use as a space of congregation during revolutionary festivities, exemplifies architectural dispossession, disarming and reclaiming with regenerative means. Rudnev's monument undid the entire form and format of an imperial monument, and by repurposing the classical idiom and materiality of the imperial city, it sought to readjust the meaning of the entire city, diverting its essence from the old edifices of power to the potential of the empty space of the square as a foundational space of revolution. This monument turned dispossession into an instrument of de-imperialisation of the city, its space and architectural → HERITAGE.

The twenty-first century calls for acts of dispossession in the former imperial centres to face their own violent pasts, as well as in the colonised territories that are seeking new ways to relate to their past. Few architects have managed to propose strategies that succeed.

Asif Khan is one of them. His (rejected) redesign of Hamburg's former Museum für Völkerkunde (renamed Museum am Rothenbaum – Kulturen und Künste der Welt in 2018) proposed to put the museum itself on critical display by → FRAMING it with a glass structure (fig. 2).

The museum collection and institution are entangled with European colonialism – as is any such museum – and, infamously, also with the development of racial theories during the Nazi

2 Asif Khan, *Proposal for the redesign of Hamburg's Museum am Rothenbaum – Kulturen und Künste der Welt*, 2024

regime. Simultaneously, it is the home for wonders of Indigenous knowledges from across the world. Performing a material, spatial and intellectual reframing of the museum, the design also proposed to open the old facade of the building and surround it with a new landscape inside the glass case, creating an alternative, open and natural context to the treasures it houses.

Another building by Khan, completed in 2025 in Almaty, Kazakhstan, reimagines an old Soviet cinema as a space for a future Kazakh culture (see www.asif-khan.com/project/tselinnyi-centre-of-contemporary-culture-almaty/). The 1960s' cinema was originally built according to Soviet standard designs (→ TYPE PROJECT) and named Tselinny, or "Virgin Lands", after a slogan of a Soviet campaign to turn the Kazakh steppe into a site of extraction for the benefit of Moscow. Instead of simply rejecting or erasing, the new Tselinny reclaims the name and the space. It reframes the difficult layers of the past and redeems those lost underneath them by evoking the clouds that bring rain to the steppe and act as their real and mythical regenerative force.

For the thinking of how architecture could reclaim the colonial concept of Tselinny, the cloud acts a veil of possibility that encircles the existing structure making the past into a ground to build a better future. These are cases that show how – through architectural dispossession, disarming and reclaiming – buildings with difficult provenance can be harnessed to make a difference. *Markus Lätheenmäki*

Dispute A protest banner reads: "No Rainforest Destruction for Tokyo 2020 Olympics" (fig. 1). The message seems reasonable, but what rainforests are in Tokyo to be destroyed? The threatened trees are not the sacred groves in Meiji Shrine or the forests in Okinawa, but in fact a string of sensitive rainforests 4,500 km to the country's south-west.

Beginning in 2016, the Bruno Manser Fonds, Rainforest Action Network and a constellation of aligned groups in Asia and Europe coordinated petition-signing campaigns and demonstrations to protest the use of illegally sourced timber in Olympic building projects. Activists sounded the alarm after discovering that Japanese contractors were using → MATERIALS produced by Shin Yang and Korindo, two companies that have long been accused of illegal logging in Malaysia and Indonesia. While protestors delivered petitions in Germany and Switzerland, a small group of monkey-mask wearing protestors gathered at the suspected crime scene in Tokyo: Kengo Kuma's National Stadium (fig. 2). Were the stadium's supposedly green timber roof and eaves ripped from protected rainforests?

The controversial construction of the National Stadium was preceded by controversy over its selection. Kengo Kuma and Associates took over the project after Zaha Hadid's winning competition entry was cancelled due to concerns about budget overrun, the design's parametric refusal

1 *Protestors outside of the Palace Hotel during an IOC Executive Board Meeting*, 2016, Lausanne. Photographer unknown

2 Kengo Kuma and Associates, *Japan National Stadium*, 2019, Tokyo. Photographer unknown

to blend into its urban context and the size of its estimated environmental impact. Kuma won a smaller second competition with a project that countered each of the criticisms leveled at Hadid. It would be more cheaply built, blend into the city and utilise sustainable materials. The Tokyo Organizing Committee celebrated the new stadium as the jewel of their rigorous sustainability campaign and a national symbol of Japan's broader adoption of the UN's Sustainable Development Goals. To emphasise the new design's national rootedness, Kuma proudly announced that the stadium's signature timber canopy and exterior eaves would come from trees located in all of forty-seven of Japan's prefectures. Despite this curious display of arboreal nationalism, the stadium, like most stadiums, is mostly reinforced → CONCRETE. And this concrete requires a different type of wood whose origins were not so proudly publicised by the architect: plywood formwork made from protected forests in Southeast Asia. Though the visible beams were sourced from Japanese cedar and larch, sharp-eyed sleuths investigating building sites around Tokyo spotted plywood with Shin Yang and Korindo logos at Olympic → CONSTRUCTION SITES, including the National Stadium. Like a connoisseur's stamp, the logo and production numbers helped activists trace the materials' journey from specific plywood mills in Southeast Asia to Japanese importers who sanctioned the trade.

"Japanese architecture" is synonymous with the visible tactility of wood found in Shinto shrines, Buddhist temples and rustic tea houses. But it is the hidden and disposable plywood used in concrete formwork that has supported the country's explosive growth since the end of the Second World War. After domestic production dipped, Japanese companies began importing huge quantities of Southeast Asian timber in the 1970s that made both anonymous infrastructure and bespoke designs possible. The Japanese plywood trade changed significantly following the banning of Indonesian and Malaysian log exports in the 1980s and the establishment of industry-wide verification systems to guarantee the origins of stock. Nonetheless, Japan remains the top importer of Southeast Asian timber in the world, and plywood continues to flow to the country's construction sites through a network of intermediary trading companies. The effects of this trade are staggering. In Sarawak, the epicenter of Malaysian logging in northern Borneo, decades of deforestation have displaced Indigenous communities, threatened endangered orangutans (hence the masks worn by the Tokyo protestors), perpetuated abusive → LABOUR relations and accelerated the collapse of ecosystems.

In early 2018, the Tokyo Organizing Committee publicly admitted that 87 per cent of plywood formwork used in the National Stadium's construction originated from Indonesian and Malaysian rainforests. The oversight was in part due to differing definitions of provenance. The Olympics' self-enforced Timber Sourcing Code traced timber products to supposedly reputable suppliers, but not to the actual forests of origin. The code was updated, but activists identified obvious loopholes that could be exploited to maintain the status quo. The controversy highlights the difficulty of identifying the true source of materials in a multilayered supply chain overseen by governmental and regulatory bodies with different, and often competing, interests. Architecture's imbrication with these extractive industries is so plain that it is sometimes ignored, or worse, seen as inevitable. When confronted with the human and environmental → COSTS of their work, architects often throw their hands up and say, "I was unaware". Frustratingly, this is not always incorrect. Kuma could have asked about the provenance of plywood from construction companies, supervising contractors and Olympics officials, and he would have been given assurance from all involved that the plywood met sustainability regulations and was legally sourced.

The true origin of the National Stadium's plywood formwork was only revealed through activist provenance. The purpose of activist provenance is to dispute the credibility of otherwise-interested claims to an object's origin. To effectively dispute the provenance of a material requires not only boldness and bravery, but also a convincing body of evidence. Groups such as Global Witness produce in-depth reports that combine on-the-ground journalism with historical and legal analysis to track the often murky and corrupt movement of construction materials. Research is then distributed in a variety of ways, including news articles, formal legal complaints, protests, policy recommendations and so on. This myriad output is a rich para-architectural history that productively differs from disciplinary formats such as university press books and peer-reviewed articles. Where the analytical historian attempts to understand the contextual factors that allowed a building to come into being in the first place, activist provenance hunters dispute statements by architects, industry regulators and governments in the public realm. Importantly, such activist dispute is not merely a relativising gesture meant to cede responsibility to architecture's "infinitely complex" being. It is, instead, a way to point fingers, name names and present counterevidence that substantiates the purposefully hidden violence of architecture. *Matthew Mullane*

Doppelgänger During the German Romantic movement at the end of the eighteenth century, writers and readers alike became infatuated with the doppelgänger, a term reputedly first used by Jean Paul in his 1797 novel *Siebenkäs* (see Pizer 1992). The appearance of a man's double (we never come across a single instance of a woman being haunted by a doppelgänger) added a layer of deep anxiety and psychological disturbance to the portrait of the individual, reflecting the sense of a world in turmoil. What's more, the copy, both mysterious and mechanical, seemed to be a kind of super-human that inspired dread. With its extraordinary, "uncanny" talents, it was certainly superior to the "original", who was forever limited by his human frailties. Sigmund Freud studied the states of dream and unconsciousness described by the Romantics (alongside Shakespeare) while developing his theories of human psychology, and it is true that writers such as Novalis, E.T.A. Hoffmann, Adelbert von Chamisso, Annette von Droste-Hülshoff, Gottfried Keller and Theodor Storm created ambiguous characters riddled with anxiety about their fate and plagued by memory-loss and guilt. Most doppelgänger novels culminate in murder, others trace flights from reality, later diagnosed as forms of insanity.

Around the same time as Freud, August Strindberg began to explore the unconscious and the nature of dreams. The hero of his 1890 novel *I havsbandet* (By the open sea), for example, labours for a month, cutting down trees and shifting great piles of earth to recreate a Tuscan landscape on a Swedish island in order to please his lover. The effect is so perfect, captured at the precise moment when the garden is reflected, mirrored on the surrounding sea that everyone present (including his lover) falls on their knees in amazement.

The appearance of truth and the truth of appearance are curiously linked. Architectural doppelgängers, similarly, are also realised fantasies of impossible manoeuvres, the products of Fitzcarraldian determination, of extreme passion, of a readiness to accept enormous risks, and more often than not, yes, of love (see Weizman 2012b). And by exploring the double both in the discursive field of media and the law – "original" or "copied", "legal" or "illegal" – we can gain a sense of the potential power of the doppelgänger.

Art historian Hillel Schwartz ponders our uneasy preoccupation with doubles, likenesses, → FACSIMILES, replicas and re-enactments in his book *The culture of the copy*. A large section is devoted to twins, conjoined twins and doppelgängers, described as "the archetypes of unreasonable facsimile: images of ourselves that arouse consternation; omens of the peril of relentless copying" (Schwartz 1998, p. 49). For Schwarz, the "evil twin" promises companionship and familiarity but also threatens the other's individuality. The solution, he says, is for the two to live within the creative tension between the "original" and the "copy"; those of us who are not twins also have to accept the inherent ambiguity of our doubleness.

A sequence in the 2010 film *Doubletake* by Johan Grimonprez, takes a different stand, combining archival footage of a large meeting of twins with an eerie voiceover scripted by the novelist Tom McCarthy and performed by Alfred Hitchcock's doppelgänger: "They say that if you meet your double, you should kill him, or that he will kill you. I can't remember which. But the gist of it is that two of you is one too many. By the end of the script, one of you must die."

In architecture, an analogous murder of precisely this sort took place with the forced demolition of an unauthorised replica built in Zhengzhou in 2004 (fig. 1). In response to a lawsuit brought by the Le Corbusier Foundation, a court had ruled that a fast-food restaurant built in the image of the Ronchamp Chapel was in breach of → COPYRIGHT and it was demolished in 2008. Before the architectural community could testify to the simulacrum's concrete existence and study the versatility of Le Corbusier's plans, the "bad" copy was destroyed in order to ensure the "proper" → PRESERVATION of a piece of European → HERITAGE.

Another doppelgänger to the Ronchamp Chapel, the Bank of America building in downtown Palm Springs, by the Beverly Hills-based architect Rudy Baumfeld, was spared the attentions of lawyers. Completed in 1959, only four years after the inauguration of the original church, the bank is today a Class 1 Historic Site, a designation embraced by local realtors, who in these lean times market properties in the manner of architectural historians (fig. 2).

The bank seems to have been built as a genuine gesture of homage, but does this argument trump copyright law? Architectural doppelgängers are usually found far apart from each other, or more precisely, they emerge out of a condition of distance, from a kind of shadow economy with no exact records, no statistics, no "central" planning agency, no → ARCHIVE, no lawyers, no powerful institution to protect the original.

Interestingly, when plans were made to reconstruct Ludwig Mies van der Rohe's Barcelona Pavilion in the 1980s, when the archives were opened and the original documents reexamined, no coherent evidence of the building could be found. An archaeological dig unearthed only one cruciform column fragment. The architect commissioned to reconstruct the pavilion, Ignasi de Solà-Morales, was forced to rely on preliminary drawings, photographs and various texts (→ ARCHITECTURAL DRAWING, → PHOTOGRAPHY) extracted from the famous surveys of modern architecture by Philip Johnson, Henry-Russell Hitchcock and the Museum of Modern Art's first director, Alfred Barr. However, when the architectural historian George Dodds reviewed these "eye-witness accounts", he discovered that none of these scholars had actually visited the building during the exhibition in Barcelona (see Dodds 2005).

A further crucial piece of evidence, reproduced in virtually every monograph and article on Mies, were the *Berliner Bild-Bericht*

1 *Doppelgänger of Le Corbusier's Ronchamp Chapel*, 2004, demolished in 2008, Zhengzhou. Photographer unknown

2 Rudy Baumfeld, *Bank of America Building*, 1959, Palm Springs. Photo: Carol M. Highsmith, 2009

masterprints from Mies's personal collection. Looking at these drawings, Dodds found that some details had been cut off, while in others the prints had been airbrushed with light grey paint, masking elements or surface imperfections that Mies apparently considered distracting. In the past, permission to make copies of the prints was directly controlled by Mies himself. Today, as the rights to reproduce images from Mies's collection are expensive and controlled exclusively by MoMA, publishers tend to use new colour photographs and drawings of the reconstructed pavilion. In one such instance, in *Morning cleaning*, exhibited in the Mies van der Rohe Foundation in Barcelona in 1999, it took the Canadian artist Jeff Wall more than twelve days to capture the brief-yet-optimal early morning sunlight when George Kolbe's bronze sculpture could be perfectly glanced through the pavilion windows (see Fried 2007, pp. 507ff.; Conley 2009). Was this laboriousness and attention to detail a way for Wall to comment on the difference of the tinted glass of the original with the plain, transparent glass of the replica? Or was he inspired by Rem Koolhaas holding the mop in his 1986 Milan Triennale reconstruction of Mies's pavilion which he had turned into a body building studio? Did the replica destroy the original? And if so, what was the original, the drawing, the archaeology buried in the ground, the retouched photograph? Here again the copy emerges at the intersection of media technologies and techniques of representation.

We could perhaps then imagine buildings like the skyscrapers in Madelon Vriesendorp's illustrations – buildings who after making love get up out of their Manhattan beds and head towards a courthouse, where they present a case, where they are called to testify, doing cross-examinations, delivering verdicts. Here, architectural representations – drawings, animations, → MODELS – are not presented, but presenting, not disputed as evidence in a courtroom, but disputing. The objects of architectural representation turn the courtroom into a critical arena of architectural debate (once this arena was urbanism). Architecture's rights could then potentially exist beyond and regardless of the right, reputation and financial interests of the architect. Sometimes architecture might even need protection from its architect. A re-evaluation of the architectural doppelgänger might help us to understand the architect no longer as the sole creator or uptight regulator of the work. It might open up a way to understand architecture as an interpretative act, a medium in matter. For only in this way will it be relevant. *Ines Weizman*

Dust All things turn to dust. If that's true then they must be made of dust, or so thought Lucretius when he observed in his *De rerum natura* in the middle of the first century BCE that the surface of monuments wore off at the places where people touched them. He could not see any particles of dust coming off on people's hands, but the evidence was clear that some of the → MATERIAL was being removed through the action of touch. He thought he had finally observed those particles when, sitting in a dark room, he saw specs of dust suspended in the air, against the sun's raking light. He found it unusual that, instead of falling slowly to the ground, the dust was floating in random directions. Lucretius theorised there must be smaller invisible particles colliding with the larger visible motes of dust and keeping them afloat. His scientific observations, written as poems, were inspirational for scientists researching what we now call the atom, especially after 1417, when the humanist scholar Poggio Bracciolini rediscovered Lucretius in a long-lost medieval manuscript – under a thick layer of dust. Centuries of research inspired by Lucretius followed by the likes of Michel de Montaigne, René Descartes and Isaac Newton until John Dalton formulated a modern theory of atoms as the indivisible parts of matter (see Dalton 1808). We have dust to thank for rousing the scientific imagination to observe the smallest visible things, to speculate on how they fit together to form larger things, and conversely to contemplate how matter breaks down into dust.

It was not until the late 1840s that, amidst the Romantic appreciation for architectural → DERELICTION and picturesque → RUINS seen from afar, John Ruskin got up close to decaying building surfaces to document, among other things, their dust. His patient field recording of these surfaces involved measured pencil and watercolour drawings that carefully registered the colours of various dusts. He also took daguerreotypes, which he used to continue his observations indoors (→ PHOTOGRAPHY). Ruskin was particularly fond of Venetian architectural stone surfaces, which moved him to write *The stones of Venice* (1851–1853) and the companion visual aid of his → ARCHITECTURAL DRAWINGS presented in the luxurious folio *Examples of the architecture of Venice, selected and drawn to measurement from the edifices* (1851). The folio opens with a photogravure of his mezzotint *The Ducal Palace, twentieth capital*, an astonishing study of how dusts settle on carved architectural surfaces (fig. 1).

His drawings belie a compulsive obsession with the Doge's Palace's dusty Gothic surfaces, a building that housed the rulers of the maritime Venetian Empire from the ninth century until 1797, when it was conquered by Napoleon.

As Ruskin's eyes inquired into the decaying surfaces of this Venetian imperial seat, he documented an unexpected phenomenon: some of the dust on the surfaces was in the same colour as the stone underneath it, clearly indicating its immediate provenance. But other streaks of dust were of entirely different colours than their substrate, indicating that they came from elsewhere. Ruskin was mostly interested in the painterly effects arising from the superimposition of fields of these variously coloured dusts, which rainwater had washed down the surfaces, and the sun had baked on, in a natural process that watercolouring seemed perfectly designed to imitate, since it involves using the brush to move watery suspensions of coloured dusts over the page in successive washes. In these early studies of dust, he associated it with decay. Not knowing where the dust came from, he claimed its provenance to be time itself, describing them as "time-stains" which darkened building surfaces "into fields of rich golden brown, like the colour of seaweed when the sun strikes on it through deep sea" (Ruskin 1853, p. 69).

1 John Ruskin, *The Ducal Palace, twentieth capital*, photogravure of mezzotint, from *Examples of the architecture of Venice, selected and drawn to measurement from the edifices* (London: Smith, Elder & Co. 1851)

As the industrial revolution advanced, it became obvious to Ruskin that those dark washes on buildings were not time-stains but man-made stains: particles of soot from burning coal, much of which is so small as to be nearly invisible and to remain suspended in the air for long periods of time, in a similar way to the dust observed by Lucretius. After rains, these particles floating in the air adhered to the moist facade of the Doge's Palace. The moisture was acid rain which dissolved a microscopic layer of the limestone, turning it into liquid gypsum at the very moment when specs of soot were adhering to the surface (→ WEATHERING). When the surface dried, the result was thin veil of black gypsum over the stone's surface.

Still, Ruskin always opposed cleaning buildings, especially because in his days it was often done by scraping the surface with steel brushes or even chisels to reveal the colour of fresh cut stone, causing more harm than good. Once the darker dust became identified as pollution, some preservationists began to break ranks with Ruskin and to call for cleaning it (→ PRESERVATION): "We must scrupulously and religiously respect the color of time", wrote Camillo Boito, perhaps Italy's most well-respected preservation architect of the late nineteenth century, but we must clean "extrinsic, superficial and casual soot" (Boito 1893, p. 102). Boito drew a distinction between the → PATINA, or the colour cut stone acquires after it comes into contact with air, oxidises and starts to decay, and the colour of stone under a veil of soot. At the heart of the distinction was a question of provenance. It was only acceptable to conserve dust that could be traced directly to the building's materials. Any dust with a non-architectural provenance was to be cleaned and forgotten.

Boito's assertion that soot is extrinsic to architecture is debatable. If we define an architectural material as that which is required to create and sustain architecture in working order, then coal, whether in rock form or dusty soot, can certainly be considered an architectural material, as burning coal was, and continues to be, required to manufacture every other construction material, erect buildings and keep them warm, electrified and inhabitable. Coal dust could even be considered a condition of possibility for the very existence of architecture. Therefore, Boito's theoretical justification for cleaning soot is not entirely convincing. Neither is the common practical justification, which argues that soot must be removed in order to conserve the underlying surface. Cleaning facades do not address the root cause of the decay, which is acid rain, not dust (→ MAINTENANCE). This is why the column capitals that Ruskin drew have now been removed from the facade of the Doge's Palace, brought indoors to the *Museo dell'Opera* where they are protected from acid rain, and replaced by copies outdoors (→ FACSIMILE).

After two decades of writing on dust as evidence of architectural decay, Ruskin turned his own view of dust on its head and began thinking of it not as the end, but as the beginning of architecture. The turning point came as he drew the monumental masses of stone that are the Alps and wondered how they formed. Dust he argued, under enough heat and pressure, became stone. Different kinds of dusts became different kinds of stones. A pure dust produced a pure stone in the shape of a crystal. For example, pure Quartz (SiO_2) forms into hexagonal crystals. He imagined heterogeneous mixes of dust and marvelled at how they must have sorted themselves into multiple kinds of pure crystals imbricated in each other, but individually recognisable, as they are in granites and marbles. Dust generated stone, and by extension architecture. An intrinsically generative material, dust offered lessons to artists and architects on how to create the interlacing geometric forms he so admired in Gothic architecture.

He gathered his observations in the form of a play titled *The ethics of the dust* (1865), an attempt, similar in intention to Lucretius' but different in every other way, to theorise dust as the indivisible particles that make up stone. Ruskin was interested in how and why dusts arranged themselves into ordered crystals. He

2 Jorge Otero-Pailos, *The ethics of dust: Doge's Palace*, 2009, cast of dust from the Doge's Palace in Venice, Arsenale, 53rd Venice Art Biennale

believed crystallisation was the expression of a divine moral order, where dust embodied the seeds of beauty and virtue. By contrast, Lucretius viewed dust as visible evidence of the random, ceaseless chance collisions of atoms forming structures without purpose or divine guidance. While Lucretius might be closer to our modern secular sensibility, we must recall that when Ruskin wrote *The ethics of the dust*, crystallography was still largely a descriptive science focused on the external geometric forms of minerals, without a clear atomic understanding of crystal structure. The modern scientific understanding of crystallisation – based on internal atomic lattices and bonding forces – only fully developed after the discoveries of X-ray diffraction in crystals by Max von Laue in 1912 proving the periodic arrangement of atoms, and the simultaneous development by William Henry Bragg and his son William Lawrence Bragg of X-ray crystallography as a method to determine the atomic structure of crystals. For Ruskin, a man that lived in a constructive culture in which stone was the primary and most prized building material, the task of revealing dust to be the source of stone was tantamount to uncovering dust to be the origins and provenance of architecture itself.

While in addition to coal we now have oil, airborne pollution, the kind of soot that sullies buildings, remains the condition of possibility for erecting and maintaining buildings. In this sense, our constructive culture is much closer to Ruskin's than we like to think (fig. 2). Ruskin viewed dust as the material origin and ending of architecture, connecting it to a larger geology, ecology and the key to its regeneration.

His lessons, the result of his prescient scholarly and artistic attention to dust, remain particularly poignant today as we reimagine architecture in terms of its material provenance, supply chains, material consumption and enduring dust. Jorge Otero-Pailos

Element In a conversation in February 2025, the manager of the Norwegian Siporex factory in Abidjan, Côte d'Ivoire, during the 1970s shared a story about a little-known part of the global repercussions coming from the Norwegian building industry. He talked about how Siporex – a building element stemming from a Swedish patent in 1924, created in Gullaug, a small town 45 minutes south of Oslo, made of raw materials from the United Kingdom, France, Denmark and Trøndelag in Norway – was loaded on a boat from Copenhagen, assembled by Ivorians and plastered by a man from Hønefoss, Norway, in order to create Norwegian-produced and financed homes in Abidjan for more than 100,000 people. Through these homes, the element Siporex set a lasting imprint on the inhabitants and urban fabric and claimed a both elusive and distinct → AUTHORSHIP in a capital city on a different continent.

In the 1930s, this new building element was introduced to the market in Sweden, making its way to Norway shortly thereafter. Autoclaved aerated → CONCRETE, under its tradename Siporex, was an incredibly lightweight element that transformed the building industry. Siporex elements had unparalleled strength, were → FIRE safe, and could be used to insulate due to their porosity. More importantly, however, was the fact that the material's lightweight nature made transportation a cinch (→ CARGO). Systematised into a variety of sizes, these elements created the opportunity for buildings to be constructed in record time and with the most basic set of tools (sold separately), as

1 *Advertisement for Siporex-Ytong Element-System*, from *Byggekunst*, vol. 50, no. 5 (1968)

exemplified through advertisements such as "A Siporex villa constructed, under roof, and plastered in seven days", printed, among other places, in the Norwegian architecture journal *Byggekunst* over decades (fig. 1). The properties that set Siporex apart from the competition catapulted this element into popularity, first in Scandinavia, followed by the rest of Europe, before expanding around the globe from harbour to harbour and project to project.

Postwar demand and housing shortage, an increased production capacity and an emergence of new materials coalesced to form a new way of producing architecture; one that was an assembly of elements and components rather than crafted *in situ*. This way of creating architecture shifted its production from the → CONSTRUCTION SITE to the assembly line. Elements could come from all over the globe, each with their own history and provenance.

Siporex elements of 60 by 15 by 240 centimetres formed the module for the homes built in Abidjan in the 1970s (fig. 2). Piece by piece, these elements were assembled to rapidly complete construction projects – projects made possible by financing and loan guarantees from NORAD, the Norwegian Agency for Development Cooperation, while simultaneously leading to record profitability for Ingeniør F. Selmer, the company tasked with leading the building projects in Côte d'Ivoire (see Steen 1975, p. 18). As exemplified by headlines such as "F. Selmer has a daily turnover of one million kroner" (Anonymous 1973, p. 6) and "Norwegian Housing Fairytale in Africa" (Christensen 1973, p. 16), constructing housing in Abidjan from Siporex elements was a lucrative business. In 1975, F. Selmer established a factory in Abidjan, providing a new base for the production and distribution of these building elements.

The Norwegians left Abidjan in the early 1980s. Today the factory is closed and the Siporex elements are hidden beneath plaster, but its significance lives on, imprinting the provenance of this close-to-invisible architectural element across urban landscapes far from its patented origins (→ AFTERLIFE). Through names that stick behind across Abidjan, such as that of an ice cream shop, *Glacier Siporex*, that of a place of worship, *Siporex Mosque*, or that of a shopping mall, *Sicomex Siporex*, the movement of this material can be traced, from factory floor in Gullaug to an unsuspecting neighborhood in Côte d'Ivoire, aptly named, Youpougon Siporex. *Nicholas Coates*

2 *Siporex housing project in Abidjan*, from Øyvind Steen, *I første rekke. Ingeniør F. Selmer A/S 1906–1981* (Oslo: F. Selmer 1981)

Exhibition Being stuck in customs is no good for anyone or anything. But in one instance, a confrontation with border regulations became a taxonomic lesson about architectural exhibitions and their objects, even before the duties were paid. At the end of 1967, a → MODEL of Berlin's future Neue Nationalgalerie tried to make its way from the German Pavilion at Montreal's Expo '67 to the Art Institute of Chicago and a retrospective of Mies van der Rohe's work (fig. 1).

The model's role at both exhibitions placed it at the centre of a network of important institutional → ACTORS: the Neue Nationalgalerie, the Art Institute of Chicago, the commissioner general for Germany at Expo '67, the German government and Mies's office, all of whom were anxious to hear that it had arrived safely in Chicago (→ CARGO). But looming import duties transformed the model into an orphan. Although the model had successfully crossed borders to get to Canada, its provenance needed to be documented to enter the US, which involved determining who owned it, who fabricated it and even its identity. Not equipped to deal with architecture "on the move", US customs did not know how to assess duty rates for an object that was fabricated in one country (at Mies's office in Chicago), exhibited in three countries (Germany, Canada and the US) and might be owned by any one of three parties (the Stiftung Preussischer Kulturbesitz, the Art Institute or Mies). Further complicating the issue was that the commissioner for the German Pavilion at Expo '67 knew that the German government owned the model but wrongly assumed that it was made in Germany. The Art Institute, responsible for the shipping, was unsure about this, asking Mies to verify that the model was made in his office in Chicago (Art Institute of Chicago, Archive). Practically speaking, it was unclear who would have to pay the customs duties or if there would be a bill at all. And no one was willing volunteer the money to ensure that the model reached Mies's exhibition.

Not only ownership and → AUTHORSHIP but also the model's status and purpose drew scrutiny. The problem lay in its association with exhibitions. The customs officials needed to know if the model would only live as long as the exhibition, where it would represent something that was absent (a building or a design) or if it could be considered a work of art in the Art Institute's collection (→ COLLECTING). The regulations revealed that objects made for exhibitions had little integrity outside of the events. Objects generally regarded as substitutes rather than "works of art", especially common in the case of architecture, had even less. According to Mr Bass, the shipping agent responsible for getting the model from Montreal to Chicago, the expedient solution (a likely way to avoid the duties) would be for the Art Institute to acquire the model so it would be considered a "permanent exposition as a work of art representing architectural design". Crossing a border to land in the collection of an art museum would bestow the architectural model with integrity by casting it as art and giving it a home, thereby annulling other claims to ownership, whether through commission (the German government) or authorship (Mies). For the customs agents, the condition would make the model invaluable and impossible to assess in monetary terms. Otherwise, Bass explained, it

1 *Model of the Neue Nationalgalerie*, 1963, exhibited at Expo '67, Montreal, and the Mies van der Rohe retrospective, Art Institute of Chicago, 1968. Chicago History Museum

would fall into the category of "materials from an exposition" (Art Institute of Chicago, Archive). Possession, in the terms set by the laws of international trade, was beyond the grasp of exhibitions, especially architectural ones, due to their temporary nature and the preponderance of representations, which evoked the spectre of buildings but left nothing "real" to possess. In these terms, a model's value was limited to its short-term utility and easily quantified by the fabrication costs. Denied the validation determined by possession for reasons beyond utility or authorship, exhibition objects were ready targets for US customs inspectors, eager to collect the tax.

Well before the Neue Nationalgalerie model faced obstacles in crossing a border to reach an exhibition, architectural objects had already tangled with borders and had their identity called into question within exhibitions. At art exhibitions in particular, architectural objects repeatedly crossed disciplinary borders, confounding conventional ideas about what "belonged" to a specific kind of art. A prominent example is the recurring exhibition at the Prussian Academy of the Arts in Berlin in the late eighteenth and nineteenth centuries, where exhibitions of architecture upset notions of disciplinary ownership and authorship and ultimately raised the same question about the identity of the architectural object that was raised at the US/Canadian border a century later. Was a model a work of architecture or applied art? Was a plan a work of architecture or a drawing? If they were works of architecture, did they have artistic integrity or were they exhibition → ARTEFACTS, assembled to substitute for a building, which was the work of art that could not be put on display?

The answers changed frequently. In the 1789 exhibition → CATALOGUE a footnote appeared in tiny print at the end of the list of works of architecture. It explained that, although → ARCHITECTURAL DRAWINGS were listed with paintings, drawings and engravings, they were exhibited with models. By the early nineteenth century, the disciplinary ambivalence had yielded to decisiveness. The architectural drawing had become the work of art identified with architecture, preserving the one-to-one correspondence between an object and a discipline, definitive for the Art Academy, while models whose obligation was to represent buildings disappeared from the architecture exhibits. Nonetheless, buildings still appeared in object form but had migrated to other disciplines. A series of cork models by the model maker Antonio Chichi were considered architecture (and Chichi acknowledged as an architect) in the 1798 catalogue, but by the nineteenth century cork models had crossed the border to applied art, where they were displayed with buildings rendered in all sorts of materials, including soap (in 1828), as works of art in their own right. Karl Friedrich Schinkel's works were not immune to these transformations. In 1839, a folded paper model, exhibiting a bookbinder's talent in the category of applied art, represented Schinkel's Berlin Schauspielhaus. Schinkel only exhibited architectural projects early in his career; later, they were represented in other sections as the work of painters, engravers and sculptors as well as craftsmen, with occasional mention of his name. Meanwhile, the architecture section had been all but abandoned, a consequence of the politics that led to the migration of state architects and their prominent commissions from the Art Academy to their own Bauakademie. At this point, architecture hardly "belonged" to art.

Just in time for the Art Academy's centennial in 1886, the Prussian state architects realised the value of public audiences and returned to the art exhibitions, but they still resisted artistic convention. They showed contemporary architecture in a range of media (architectural and projective drawings, models and photographs) to emphasise that the objects collectively represented buildings (→ PHOTOGRAPHY). At the same time a section devoted to "Historic Architecture" acted as a counterpoint, respecting the conventions of art by using original architectural drawings to showcase the *"künstlerische Handschrift"* (artistic handwriting) of some of Germany's greatest architects, as Karl Emil Otto Fritsch, the editor of the *Deutsche Bauzeitung,* explained (Fritsch 1886a, p. 306). But the section could not escape the influence of the contemporary exhibits, which asserted the uniqueness of architecture's material culture. Although the historic drawings were important for their authorial → AUTHENTICITY, the pull of the building and the public led the organisers to include photographs of completed projects to give the drawings more relevance. As a result, Germany's architectural → HERITAGE was celebrated as an equivocation between works of art and representations and between respecting and flaunting the boundaries of convention. The exhibit of two buildings by Gottfried Semper, one of Germany's most modern thinkers, displayed the ambivalence most clearly. According to Fritsch, Semper's son Manfred insisted on the inclusion of photographs of the buildings alongside the drawings to call attention to "the consistency between the execution and the designs" and therefore to Semper's "decisive contribution to the individuality of those buildings" (Fritsch 1886b, p. 341.). Drawings and buildings – or photographs of them – validated each other. The display of Semper's work reflected the significance ascribed to his architecture: while both documented an important past, they also looked forward, demonstrating the complexities that accompanied the emergence of a modern point of view. *Wallis Miller*

Expropriation The English Reformation cast a long shadow. Even over a century after the confiscation and repurposing of ecclesiastical lands and properties by the Crown under Henry VIII, the lay ownership of former Church estates and the exploitation of erstwhile monastic buildings as → QUARRIES of ready-hewn stone pricked at the conscience of the pious Protestant nobility and gentry.

Sir Henry Spelman (c.1563–1641) was chief amongst them. Although best known as a legal historian and antiquary, he was also the author of two polemics: *De non temerandis ecclesiis* (London 1613) and the posthumously published

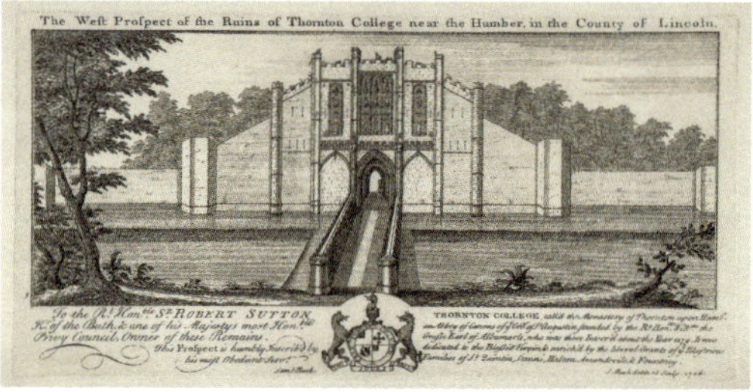

1 Samuel Buck, *The west prospect of the ruins of Thornton College near the Humber in the county of Lincoln,* 1726, engraving, 18.2 × 36.7 cm. Private collection

The history and fate of sacrilege (London 1698). They recount how the expropriation, or impropriation, of Church lands – that is, the taking away of the Church's proprietary rights by laymen – resulted in divine judgement against those who made, or benefitted from, the confiscation.

Spelman's own experiences prompted these treatises: in 1594 he purchased the leases to former priories at Blackborough and Wormegay in Norfolk, but became embroiled in expensive lawsuits that eventually dispossessed him of the former monastic holdings (→ DISPOSSESSION). With much self-reproach, he interpreted this outcome as proof of the "infelicity of meddling with consecrated places" (Spelman 1698, p. 259). His conclusion also stemmed from the experience of his uncle, who found himself "much crost" in his attempt to build on appropriated glebe land. Spelman warned his uncle that the undertaking was impeded because "God was not pleased with it, insomuch as it tended to the defrauding of the Church" (Spelman 1613, dedicatory letter).

Defining sacrilege as "invading, stealing, or purloining from God, any Sacred thing", Spelman charted this offence chronologically, from Eve plucking an apple in the Garden of Eden to Henry VIII suppressing the monasteries in the 1530s (Spelman 1698, p. 1). Spelman enumerated the consequences of expropriation, including loss of wealth, failure in business, mental decline, lack of progeny or even death (often by slow or violent means). Alongside these misfortunes, he also cited thwarted building projects as an indication of divine opprobrium. The very stones revolted against their misappropriated use. At Binham Priory, Norfolk, the poet and amateur musician Edward Paston "was desirous to build a Mansion-house upon or near the Priory", but when he tried to clear the ground, falling masonry killed one of the workmen. Paston was so "perplexed with this Accident in the beginning of this Business" that he abandoned his intention "and would by no means all his Life after be perswaded to reattempt it", instead building a house at Appleton (Spelman 1698, p. 253).

In Kent, St Radegund's Abbey came into the possession of Sir Thomas Edolph, "who did lately build a fair House upon the Site of the Monastery, and it hath fallen down three times" (Spelman 1698, p. 279). At Rainham, Norfolk, Sir Roger Townshend intended to build "a goodly House" using the stone of Coxford Abbey as his quarry (Spelman 1698, p. 268). When demolishing the steeple, the first stone to be removed broke a man's leg, and the steeple later collapsed entirely resulting in one fatality. Townshend persisted, but having raised the walls using abbey stone, they began to split from the cornerstones, a phenomenon that Spelman saw with his own eyes. At this point Townshend conceded and began construction on a new site with fresh stone. Apparently under Spelman's guidance, he built a parsonage for the parish church and new walls for the churchyard with the spoliated abbey material – the stones complied (→ SPOLIA).

Another building collapse ascribed to sacrilegious transgression (not mentioned in Spelman's treatises but well known because the house was designed by a named architect), is that of Thornton College, built out of the → RUINS of Thornton Abbey, Lincolnshire. Founded in 1140, the Augustinian priory was one of the wealthiest in England, and is still renowned for its gatehouse, built between 1377 and 1382 (fig. 1).

In 1602, the site was purchased by Sir Vincent Skinner (1542–1616), a staunch Puritan who was knighted for his services to Oliver Cromwell. Skinner demolished most of the abbey buildings, leaving only the gatehouse (→ DEMOLITION). Around 1607, he used the abbey stone to construct an ambitious house, known as Thornton College (fig. 2), to designs by surveyor and architect John Thorpe (1565–1655), which survive in Sir John Soane's Museum (see Summerson 1966; Roberts 1984).

The house was still standing in 1611 but did not endure. In an account of 1697, the Lincolnshire diarist and antiquary Abraham de la Pryme recalls the "hall, when it was finished, fell quite down to the bare ground, without any visible cause and broke in pieces all the rich furniture that was therein" (de la Pryme 1870, p. 145; see Oswald et al. 2010). It is also possible that – before or after a collapse – it was dismantled by one of Skinner's creditors to whom he had pledged the house as security against a loan. In either case, the house came to a bad end, as did Skinner who died, disgraced and intestate, in a debtor's prison.

2 John Thorpe, *Ground plan for Thornton College*, from *The Book of architecture of John Thorpe*, T67, c.1607, ink on paper. Sir John Soane's Museum, London

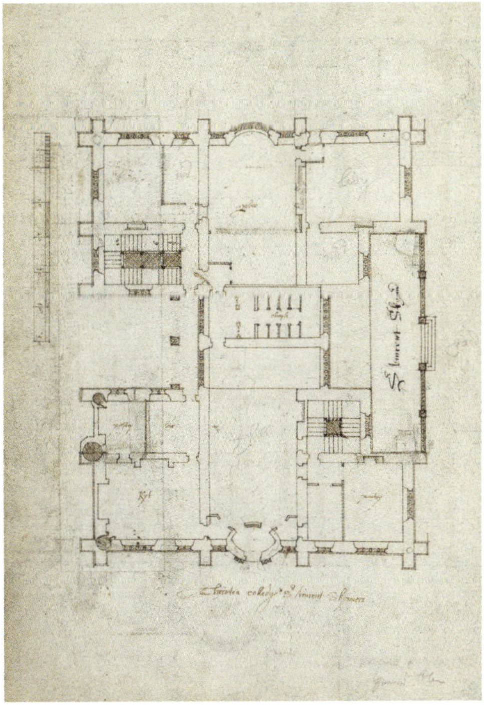

First projected in the 1610s, *The history and fate of sacrilege* lay unpublished for decades "lest it give offence to the nobility and gentry" whose right to possess former monastic lands it called into question. In 1698, however, it was finally published "for the terror of evil-doers" (Spelman 1698, titlepage).

Meanwhile, *De non temerandis ecclesiis* (published privately by Spelman in 1613 in order to test the market for his expanded study), appears to have had a significant impact on the elite of Norfolk and beyond. According to Jeremiah Stevens, Spelman's good friend, Sir Baptist Hicks, Sir Roger Townshend and John Scudamore, 1st Viscount Scudamore, all took advice from Spelman on how to mitigate their ownership of former ecclesiastical lands. As Spelman observed, the evidence of "God's Judgments and Severities against Sacrilege" were enough to "affrighten all Men" (Spelman 1698, pp. 54f.) from possessing anything with a monastic provenance. *Olivia Horsfall Turner*

Extension Extension in architecture is a common practice to enlarge and modify a building in order to implant new functions or meanings. Since the Neolithic period, farmhouses have been extended and grouped into typical granges, often due to new ownership or a new generation of → INHABITANTS. Greek and Roman sites, such as the Acropolis, the Fora in Rome or the spa district at Bergama in Turkey, underwent extensions over centuries. Military and public buildings, castles or town halls, were enlarged to represent wealth and power or ever more ambitious political claims; ecclesiastical buildings, for example cathedrals, were extended due to the growing wealth or influence of the respective parish or diocese. With the advent of the industrial age, factories were a → PRECEDENT building type for extension: the General Motors car factories in Detroit, the AEG electrical factory in Berlin or chemical and pharmaceutical plants such as Hoffmann La Roche in Basel are well known examples of capitalist expansion also of the spatial means of production (→ CAPITALISM).

Two typologies have recently been subjected to spectacular extensions: the library and the museum, which took over a status sacred buildings enjoyed for centuries. The earliest example is the transformation of the Royal Palace in Paris into a *musée universel* during Dominique-Vivant Denon's directorship in the early nineteenth century. Large parts of the Seine wing of the Louvre, the *Grande Galerie*, became part of the Musée Napoléon displaying art treasures looted in Italy, the Southern Netherlands and Germany during the Napoleonic conquest (→ COLLECTING). After the First French Empire and the era of revolutions, in 1852, the Louvre as museum of art and archeology was more than doubled in size by Louis Visconti and Hector Lefuel with the Cour Napoléon as part of the north wing towards the Rue de Rivoli.

The Musée du Louvre served as a model for huge museum complexes in Europe, notably the Victoria and Albert Museum in London and the collections on the Museum Island in Berlin. Aesthetic education, art historical and archaeological presentation and scholarship went hand in hand with imperial representation and competitive architectural programmes. The Berlin collections followed the idea of a universal art museum, extending the Museum Island complex, originally established by Schinkel's Altes Museum (1823–1831), with August Stüler's encompassing Neues Museum (1842–1854) and Ernst Ihne's Kaiser-Friedrich-Museum (1894–1904), topped by Alfred Messel and Ludwig Hoffmann's neo-classical Pergamon Museum (1907–1930), which was an early architectural museum displaying parts of ancient buildings such as the Pergamon Altar, the Market Gate of Miletus and the Babylonian Ishtar Gate translocated from colonised countries (→ DISPLACEMENT, → TRANSLOCATION). The British Museum responded to this imperialist approach with the Duveen Galleries, designed by John Russell Pope (1931–1938), to house the so-called Elgin Marbles from the Parthenon.

Pope also designed the National Gallery of Art in Washington (1937–1941), which was extended by Ieoh Ming Pei's East Wing (1968–1978), who transformed the neo-classical style of the old building into a sculptural, almost brutalist structure, softened by a highly functional, light-filled plaza-like interior (fig. 1).

It was the Chinese-American Pritzker Prize winner's architecture that closed the circle of important museum extensions, when Pei built his famous glass pyramid as the centre and new landmark of the so-called *Grand Louvre* (1985–1989), one of the *grands projets* of president Mitterand's Paris, and part of the many museum expansions at the turn of the twenty-first century.

The list of worldwide significant museum extensions in the late twentieth and early twenty-first century is long: it ranges, to name but a few, from David Chipperfield's extension of the Neues Museum in Berlin (1997–2009), which had been badly damaged during the → WAR, to Herzog & de Meuron's remodelling and extension of the Tate Modern in London (1997–2002/2005–2012). What these projects all have in common, however, is that they demonstrate the growing cultural power, ambition and hegemony of their mostly state clients through architectural extension and → TRANSFORMATION – comparable to stately and ecclesiastical architecture of earlier eras.

Two libraries may illustrate this transformative nature of extensions. The study centre of the Herzogin Anna Amalia Bibliothek in Weimar, which was severely damaged by a → FIRE in 2004, is not only the result of an extension of the baroque building, but also a reworking of the traditional type of the book tower in the shape of a four-story cube with internal galleries (fig. 2).

The study centre, designed by Karl-Heinz Schmitz and Hilde Barz-Malfatti, was inaugurated in 2005 and transformed the traditional library into a multi-use location for research and events. An even bigger project was launched in 2017 by Rogers Stirk Harbour and Partners with the extension of the British Library (to be built in 2026–2032). As a public-private partnership with an investment of more than £1 billion, it will serve as one of the world's largest knowledge centres, including the National Centre for Data Science and Artificial Intelligence, in combination with public, commercial and office space covering 55,000 square metres.

In both cases, it is exemplary that we are not only dealing here with the expansion of existing usable space, but that both a significant functional expansion and – not least – representative buildings are to be created with which the state clients want to respond to the political, social and intellectual challenges of their time.

1 Ieoh Ming Pei, *East wing of the National Gallery*, Washington DC, 1968–1978. Photo: Gunnar Klack, 2014

2 Karl-Heinz Schmitz and Hilde Barz-Malfatti, *Herzogin Anna Amalia Bibliothek, study centre*, 2000–2005, Weimar. Photo: Bernd Nicolai

Thus, expansions add an additional layer to the extended buildings (→ PALIMPSEST), and in terms of provenance they emphasise the vital existence of architecture over the *longue durée* of time with many authors involved in the lives of buildings (→ AUTHORSHIP). *Bernd Nicolai*

Facsimile The root of the word "facsimile" (*fac-simile*) lies in the act of making, while "copy" is linked to profusion and abundance; a cornucopia, the form from which all things flow. Making a facsimile is a form of realism in the tradition of Zeuxis and Parrhasius, where paint or other materials assume the qualities and materiality of something else. "Facsimile" is a mid-seventeenth-century term in English; coined at the time when the fundamental distinction between primary and secondary qualities, between what the body is made of and how it appears, was established (see Lowe 2020).

An object has material properties that make it specifically what it is. A facsimile is a copy of an object that replicates its look and superficial characteristics so that the two objects appear identical under normal display conditions (→ DOPPELGÄNGER). A facsimile is not just a printed copy, it is a "re-materialisation". It must be true to the source reference in terms of scale, surface, colour and reflectivity (fig. 1).

Its role is to verify the appearance of an object at a specific point in time and assist with the long-term → PRESERVATION and understanding of the original object. It does not aim to falsify or mislead, it reveals and verifies.

A facsimile is a creative performance of an original object striving for objective accuracy. Like a performance of a play or a musical score, it can be made in a way that enhances our understanding of the source, or it can focus on the performer or the means of production. The former tends to be enriching, the latter impoverishing. A facsimile that does not add to the career or provenance of an object, leading to a digital connoisseurship that extends a collective understanding, is a copy or → PASTICCIO. Marcel Duchamp and Andy Warhol's interventions, for example, do not add to an understanding of Leonardo's Mona Lisa, they engage with and enhance its → CELEBRITY status. Richard Hamilton's recreation of Duchamp's *Large Glass* sought to replicate the qualities of the original even though there are significant differences between the two objects.

A facsimile of a physical object requires a physical presence while a facsimile of a digitally generated work should mimic the qualities of the digital source. The digital data can exist in diverse virtual forms and can be handled within a digital space, but lacks physicality. The recording of a physical object to create a facsimile needs to focus on documenting information in as many ways as possible: albedo photography (representing the inherent diffuse reflectance of colour without glare or shadow), normal mapping (pixel-level description of the orientation of each point on the surface of the object), depth mapping (representing the relative distance of each point of the surface as tonal information) and shaded mapping (the simulation of the object under different lighting conditions for digital display). It is also useful to have multispectral data to help understand how the image was made (X-ray, Infra-red, Ultra-violet, etc). Historical photographs (→ PHOTOGRAPHY) and other sources of philological information can help reveal the biography of an object and how

1 Factum Arte, *Facsimile of Paolo Veronese's "Wedding at Cana" of 1563 in Palladio's refectory*, San Giorgio Maggiore, Venice. Photo: Grégoire Dupond, 2007

it has changed over time. This data, when layered together, archived and made accessible online, is essential for the preservation of the original object.

The data required to produce a facsimile differs from the information needed by restorers or forgers (→ RESTORATION). In both cases, the materials used to make an object are critical. Scientific analysis (both destructive and non-destructive) can record invisible layers of information that reveal different aspects of the process of manufacture. All objects reveal that originality is a process in a state of flux. All material objects change with time in different ways depending on location, atmospheric conditions and use. These changes can be rapid (the → FIRE in the Notre Dame Cathedral, Paris) or slow (the tombs in the Valley of the Kings before tourism). They reveal how the object has been made, valued and cared for. Material objects are articulate. Forensic analysis and educated inspection reveal subtle details embedded within their physicality.

A facsimile is situated in time and should look identical to the source at the time it is recorded and made. To achieve this verisimilitude, it will not necessarily be made of the same materials. The virtue of the facsimile is that it unambiguously draws our attention to the material conditions of the encounter with the object. It is a representation that has the same shape and superficial qualities as the object being analysed and re-produced (→ REPRODUCTION, → RECONSTRUCTION). A facsimile of a marble sculpture will not be made from the same type of marble as this natural material will not have the same veins and characteristics.

The same is true for a facsimile of a manuscript on vellum where the scribe will have responded to tears and scars resulting from the preparation of the organic material. A facsimile of a drawing by Raphael needs to contain the incised lines that came before the marks in pencil and ink that leave a visible trace on the surface of the paper. The relationship between the surface and marks on the surface are of central importance in the production of a facsimile. The facsimiles of two of Raphael's cartoons made for the Victoria and Albert Museum in London revealed significant details that suggest the artist instructed them to be copied. It was these copies (fragments exist in the Musée Condé at Château de Chantilly) that were cut and used to make the Vatican Tapestries.

A facsimile will result in objectively accurate knowledge about an object. The great experimental scientist James Nasmyth in his autobiography stated that "the eyes and the fingers – the bare fingers – are the two principal inlets to sound practical instruction [...]. Gloves, especially kid gloves, are perfect non-conductors of technical knowledge" (Nasmyth 1883, p. 97). To know something is to handle it and gain an intimate knowledge of its qualities. Objects seen behind glass and at low light levels do not reveal their true nature and significance. They need to be shared and discussed in order to become complex subjects. And they require time to reveal this complexity. The role of a facsimile is to provide the time and direct access for thoughts, ideas and concepts to be projected onto the facsimile and cross-referenced with the original.

Originality and → AUTHENTICITY are two concepts that are evolving, as the presence of a facsimile can mimic the appearance of the original. Walter Benjamin, writing at a time when off-set lithographic printing was the means of mediation that gave public access to objects in the private domain, was aware that surface qualities were missing in this means of reproduction. The surface of the object is now "printable" adding three dimensionality to the printed copy. Once image and materiality are merged, the attention focusses on the qualities of both surface and colour. If the character of either diverges from the source, it results in an impoverished copy rather than an enriching facsimile.

An exact facsimile in its original location and viewed with the intended light source will never be more original than the source, but it can acquire more authenticity than an original in the wrong location, with incorrect lighting, displayed at the wrong height and as a discrete "museum" object rather than a complex subject.

Throughout history, humans have used the process of copying to deepen understanding and facilitate communication. We now inhabit an increasingly polytechnic world in which the professional distinctions between science and art, nature and culture have dissolved. In this environment the value of an object does not reside primarily in its commercial potential, it reveals itself in its context and its trajectory. Objects are important because they are primary evidence that define modern, socialised human interaction. They are dependent on a system of customs, behaviours and technologies used to negotiate relationships with the environment we inhabit and the people with whom we engage (→ NETWORK). This is mediated through instinctive, verbal and visual language.

Privileged access was once the domain of the rich and powerful. Today the democratisation of knowledge is possible. The Museo del Prado in Madrid sells a visually identical detail of one of Goya's Black paintings. In the Valley of the Kings an exact facsimile of the tomb of Tutankhamun asks visitors a basic question: Do they want to visit the original and contribute to its destruction, or do they want to visit a facsimile and enhance their understanding while helping in the preservation of the original? The aim of a facsimile today is to give privileged access to the largest number of people.

Within a region whose material culture is largely defined by impermanent objects, the Sacred Cave of Kamukuwaká provides a vital insight into ancient Xinguan cosmogonic and ethno-historic cartography. Following a project with People's Palace Project, a replica of the cave (fig. 2), made by Factum Foundation, was created and installed at the Cultural and Territorial Monitoring Center in Ulupuwene village, Upper Xingu, Brazil (see Factum Arte 2019).

2 *Inauguration of the Sacred Cave of Kamukuwaká*, Ulupuwene, Brazil, 2024. Photo: Alaor Filho

The community has now declared that the original cave on contested land outside the reserve will remain as a → RUIN and a reminder of the changes that are happening, while the digitally restored and reconstructed cave will continue to function as the vehicle to transmit the traditions and historical knowledge to the community (→ IMAGE VEHICLE): "These actions of restoration are not artificial", declares indigenous activist Shirley Djukurnã Krenak: "What is artificial is having to fight against deforestation, against weapons of war, against agrotoxics, against bad people" (Waurá et al. 2020, p. 116).

Digital Restoration is an emerging subject that does not alter the original but can assist in facilitating multiple points of view to be projected onto the object. If the facsimile and the original are identical under museum conditions is our modern Western prejudice about the relationship between originality and its aura the only thing that separates them? *Adam Lowe*

Fire California is as much a state of mind as a place, a symbolic landscape of eternal sunshine and a prospect of a better life. Modernism put on its swimsuit there, lifted its ideological anchor and became free when it arrived on the Pacific Coast. The dream of a light, futuristic life materialised in the Case Study Houses (1945–1966), where steel and glass promised a new era of freedom and comfort, accompanied by the hum of air conditioning. Under the palms and blue skies, one could imagine life with a martini glass in hand, Hollywood → CELEBRITIES as neighbours and a world free of worries. Today, infernal flames lick the glass panes, the expansive horizon is blocked by black smoke, while these houses face the threat of being engulfed by wildfires. Designed by architects such as Richard Neutra, Charles and Ray Eames, Pierre Koenig and Craig Ellwood, the Case Study Houses were not just homes, but stage sets for a modern, hedonistic lifestyle (fig. 1).

These homes were meticulously choreographed for a specific idea of middle-class life. Glass walls and open floor plans turned the home into a kind of stage, where daily life – from dinners at the Eames dining table to cooling moments by the pool – became a performance involving both → RESIDENTS, their guests and the readers of magazines. The houses framed a specific idea of modernity, a life free of clutter, filled with elegance and control. While the Case Study Houses are tied to California's specific climate and culture, they also carry universal ambitions of progress, harmony and control. Modernism sought solutions that could be applied across geographies, but the specific – the landscape, the fire hazards, the intensity of the sun – continues to challenge the universal.

These houses were extensively documented by photographer Julius Shulman (1910–2009), who highlighted the theatrical qualities of the buildings with the vast metropolis of Los Angeles and a spectacular nature as a backdrop (→ COLLECTING). Glass walls and sliding doors allowed a seamless fusion of indoors and outdoors, where cocktail party guests flowed effortlessly in and out. Shulman's photographs captured this lifestyle in houses floating above Los Angeles, bathed in light and expectations for the future. The swimming pools, later painted by David Hockney, became visual metaphors for freedom and its underlying darkness.

Martha Rosler's series of photomontages *House beautiful: Bringing the war home* (1967–1972 and 2004–2008) shows another side of this American architectural culture (fig. 2). Through

1 Pierre Koenig, *Case Study House #22*, 1960, Los Angeles. Photo: Julius Shulman

the glass doors, flames are visible – wildfires as well as the threats of → WAR and destruction. Rosler's work displays the vulnerability of modernism's dream of a seamless connection between indoors and outdoors. The mid-century idyll, including Alvar Aalto's Paimio armchair from 1932, which can be seen in *The gray drape* from 2008, for example, is threatened by the cruel reality of the Iraq war, just as nature threatens the buildings in the Hollywood and Santa Monica mountains in our present day. The urban structures of modernism have proliferated here in wild provenance, while nature strikes back ever harder. And so the whipped back "gray drape" reveals that the history of architecture is not just a history of building, but always also a history of struggle, conflict and loss.

Today, the seamless modernist transition, has become a cliché repeated in real-estate ads and television shows. What was once an attempt to unify architecture and nature has become a pathologically repeated commercial slogan. More importantly, events like the increasingly frequent wildfires remind us of the fragility of

2 Martha Rosler, *The gray drape*, 2008, photomontage as C-print, 101.6 × 76.2 cm, from the series *House beautiful: Bringing the war home*, edition of ten

this relationship. Designed to be exposed to nature, the glass houses are defenceless against its forces. Nature has proven to be anything but a docile pet. The images of houses surrounded by flames in January 2025 prompted a reflection on how modernist ideals meet the challenges of our time. Videos of Californian glasshouses brutally surrounded by flames resembled those hyper realistic depictions of a fireplace on flat screens. California is also about living with the complexities that accompanies dreams. Rosler's flames and the war outside the glass walls show how threats assumingly left behind in the old world have reemerged, and now inside the gate. The Case Study Houses are not only monuments to a promising future but mirrors reflecting our inability to act even when the → CRISIS is just outside the glass pane – or broadcast on the screen in front of us. *Espen Vatn*

Fragility Fragility is not a condition but a propensity to tear, crack and break. As such, it is not an intrinsic property, but a situated behaviour. No → MATERIAL or building can escape it completely. Claims to escape it by inventing magical materials are always deceptive (see Rubio et al. 2025). To illustrate the importance of the way we conceive of fragile architecture, let's take a look at a building that is supposedly robust: a nuclear reactor. A paroxysmic technoscientific architecture of the post-Second World War era, nuclear reactors were described by their promoters as modern Egyptian pyramids or as cathedrals that would bring radiance to modern powerful nations around a new faith in progress.

More prosaically, they emphasised the fact that nuclear reactors, as robust techno-scientific buildings, would be around for a long time. They are usually characterised by the number of "solid" materials that they contain. But let's see them in a different light: as fragile buildings. From the outset, these colossi of steel and → CONCRETE (but also of water, electrical cables and many other materials) have been threatened by microscopic phenomena: micro-cracks caused by corrosion (fig. 1). This has recently become a major concern in France.

In August 2021, nuclear pipes in France's newest reactor were checked with ultrasound. After twenty-three years of operation, the Civaux power plant was shut down for its second major check-up (fig. 2). The workers

1 *Example of stress corrosion cracking phenomena, tested in stainless steel in the nuclear industry*, 2020. Photographer unknown

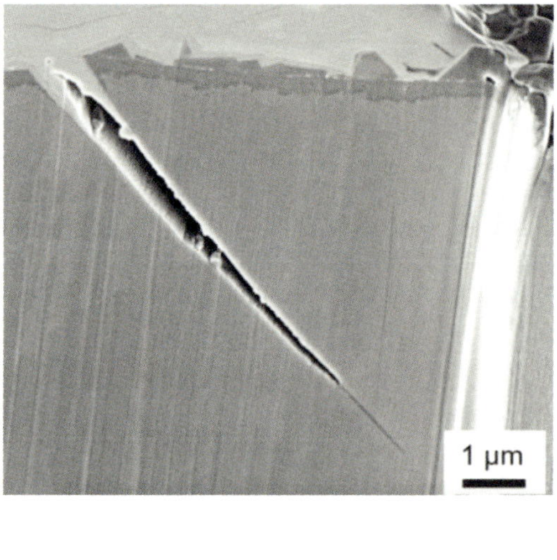

inspected the primary circuit, the most radioactive part of the reactor. In their uncomfortable suits, they had to be quick but precise when fitting sensors. Performing an echography of the pipes in a highly irradiated environment, the operators had to interpret the signals in real time, the dosimeter around their neck pulsing. Strange signals, impossible to make sense of, appeared on the controllers' screens. The signals were so bizarre that they decided to cut up the pipe and send it to the laboratory. Analyses revealed cracks linked to a stress corrosion phenomenon that had been "excluded at the design stage" – a very French safety approach, and a fragile one. In other words, these cracks, theoretically, should never have occurred. However, a few months later, the French public operator noticed that such cracks were appearing in all the pipes of the same type in all fifty-six reactors, each time with a different shape and length. While it was assumingly not possible for them to appear, the cracks appeared everywhere and with no legible pattern.

Suddenly, we see new, different buildings. Soon, the French fleet of nuclear reactors, which has been presented as very safe and well-maintained, was described as very fragile. No change in management had caused the cracks. But unexpected cracks of a few millimetres have changed the way safety officers see the reactors, they no longer know the reactors they thought they knew, the reactors have become something else. It is a matter of recognising that they are fragile. Yet fragility is pervasive. The detection of the many cracks reveals the fragility of the rules and methods, the regulations, the control of the supply chain and the monitoring of materials. The fragility of the materiality of buildings spreads to the fragility of the management of buildings. And then it spreads further to the fragility of perception: How to see what we didn't see or didn't expect to see? How to look where we think nothing will take place?

We are touching on yet another characteristic of fragility. Once something is perceived as a fragile entity, there is no way back. Fragility is a

2 *Civaux nuclear power plant*, 1997, Vienne, aerial view 2005. Photographer unknown

matter of both knowledge and care (→ MAINTENANCE). These cracks in the pipes show that things are materially fragile in part because knowledge is fragile. After decades of research in departments dedicated to corrosion around the world, after almost four years of tremendous effort by the French operators and authorities, the nuclear industry doesn't really understand how these cracks could occur in such different circumstances in every single French reactor – and never anywhere else, except in very few cases. When the materials and knowledge on which we build are fragile, practices of care become essential. The focus then partly shifts from beliefs that suppress fragility to practices of care that are able to recognise and support it, all the more so at a time when nuclear infrastructures are ageing. As a result, fragility is not something that can be eliminated, but something that can be accompanied. And the architectural politics of fragility depends on the choices, rarely discussed, that are made to accompany it. *Martin Denoun*

Fragment A fragment is a small piece or part, from the Latin *fragmentum*, a remnant, literally "a broken piece", or "a piece broken off" from *frangere* (to break). Fragments are mysterious, evocative and tantalising; parts of a greater whole which no longer exists. The inversion of a "phantom limb", here the body is the ghostly presence that signals to the shattered relic.

The erotic architectural treatise *Hypnerotomachia Poliphili* (1499) describes in great, sensual detail the buildings, landscapes and pagan pleasures Poliphilo encounters on the quest for Polia, his elusive beloved. The transition from the real into the dream-world takes place in a landscape strewn with architectural fragments (fig. 1): "epistyles and capitals, excellently designed and roughly carved; cornices, zophori or friezes and arched beams; huge, broken statues missing many of their brass details; niches, shells and vases of Numidian stone and porphyry, ornamented with various marbles; great baths and aqueducts, and a host of other fragments that lay shattered here and there, nobly carved, but reduced, as it were, to their first elements, so that one could not tell what they had been when they were whole" (Colonna 1999, p. 22).

From these remains, Poliphilo progresses into a dream-world of spectacular architecture. The fragments transport him to a place of infinite beauty and wisdom; they take him on a philosophical journey. The *Hypnerotomachia*'s elaborate, ekphrasic descriptions, the woodcut illustrations and curious text made up of fragments of different languages and quotations, became a primary source for Renaissance conceptions of architecture and gardens. It also focused attention on provenance as a generative resource, simultaneously retrospective (recalling an unknowable past) and prospective (in suggesting a possible future).

1 *Poliphilo surrounded by antique architectural fragments*, woodcut, Francesco Colonna, *Hypnerotomachia Poliphili* (Venice: Aldus Manutius 1499)

Provenance is a form of memory. The relationship between architecture and memory is profound, and buildings, real or imaginary, served as mnemonic devices, particularly before widespread printing. In the case of ancient memory theatres, and Renaissance revivals (→ AFTERLIFE), the architecture was conceptually complete, but speeches were fragmented, to be deposited as discrete "chunks" in various architectural spaces, then recalled in the order of the mental route taken through the building (see Yates 1966).

Early modern philosophers used elaborate plural compositions of architecture and landscape, combining allegorical images, text and organised symbolic systems to explain complex theoretical concepts. In 1614, French friar Martin Meurisse and engraver Léonard Gauthier created the *Artificiosa totius logices descriptio* (Artificial description of logic in its entirety). These broadsides are extraordinary acts of compression; the earlier *Hypnerotomachia* could be an expanded account of a journey through the philosophical landscapes they encapsulate. Like a memory theatre brought to throbbing life in the space of a single page, key relationships within the field of logic are laid out, enabling the student to follow a specific route from a state of ignorance outside the walled space of the symbolic architecture or garden, towards wisdom at the centre, acquiring knowledge along the way (see Berger 2017).

Meurisse's publication contains an image of a man with a wooden leg and large stick carrying a basket of human limbs on his back as he approaches the entrance to the central enclosure and path towards wisdom. Included among these fragmented body parts is, perhaps, his own leg. This memorably grisly figure illustrates Boethius's sixth-century *De Divisione*, a foundational text in medieval scholasticism which transmitted the Aristotelian doctrine of division: "For you divide the body of a human this way into its parts: into a head, hands, chest, feet

[…] or in any other way that makes a correct division in respect of the proper parts" (Berger 2017, p. 162). On other philosophical broadsheets of this period, scattered feet, hands and other body fragments also illustrate concepts of incomplete versus complete entities, *entia incompleta* and *completa*, with the "complete" represented by a whole person. "Mereology" is the philosophical study of "part-whole" relationships such as the division of a genus into species, or a house into walls, floor and roof. The aim of division is to define.

"Spoliation", from the Latin *spolium* (war booty), is a practice with ancient origins where fragments of quarried or cut stone are taken from an old construction and reused in a new one (→ SPOLIA). In late antiquity entire structures could be demolished for → REUSE, driven either by ideological or pragmatic motives, or both. Spoils or booty could be reconstituted in architectural form in symbolic triumph over the conquered, or simply used expediently to save the → LABOUR and energy of recutting stone for construction. Spolia had spiritual potential for protective magic. Often marks were cut into repurposed surfaces; crosses or other symbols were carved into consecrated pagan structures to ward off the demons that might linger in the stones. Reorientation could also signify a shift in power; a vertical statue is made prone and subservient through being laid on its side.

Examples can be found all over the world, in every culture, from every epoch. The San Marco Basilica in Venice, Italy, is encrusted with book-matched marble panels looted by the Venetians from the interior of Hagia Sophia, Constantinople, during the Fourth Crusade. San Marco turned Hagia Sophia inside out. These precious stones are now external cladding, pinned to the surface like butterflies or flayed skin, facing the Lagoon, exposed for centuries to the heat, cold, wind and rain. The four embracing Tetrarchs, petrified Saracens of darkly gleaming porphyry, protectively enfold the corner of the Treasury, strategically placed between the Basilica and the Doge's Palace, bridging Church and State. Porphyry is the most valuable of stones for its beauty, strength, rarity and association with imperial births and coronations. In Venice, trophies were both mineral and human: the looted Pietra del Bando was used as a platform for announcing public executions and the Pillars of Acri for displaying severed heads.

From 1927 to his death in 1940, Walter Benjamin used fragments and quotations to construct an alternative non-linear history in a work that is itself often regarded as a "torso" or a "monumental fragment". *The arcades project* was to be a "magic encyclopaedia", constructed from the refuse and detritus of history to create a constellation that reveals hidden traces of the daily life of the collective through patchwork (see Benjamin 1999a). The immense range of montaged fragments span from Crystal Palace and georamas to mirrors, iron constructions and dream houses. From these many thousands of pieces, Benjamin constructed a labyrinthine dream city, an infinitely shifting, phantasmagorical architecture. Their combined effect is kaleidoscopic and dazzling (→ PASTICCIO).

Kurt Schwitters described *Merz*, his method of working, as having developed out of the shattering effects of the First World War: "In the war, things were in turmoil. What I had learned at the academy was of no use to me […]. Everything had broken down and new things had to be made out of the fragments; and this is Merz. It was like a revolution within me, not as it was, but as it should have been" (Dietrich 1993, pp. 6f.). The catharsis after trauma in finding a means that enabled expression began in the early 1920s with the installations he made in his family house in Hanover, combining sculpture, montage and collage. After his first son died within a week of his birth, Schwitters incorporated his death mask in the *Merzbau*, referred to as the K.d.e.E. (*Kathedrale des erotischen Elends*), the *Cathedral of Erotic Misery* (fig. 2). It was destroyed in 1943 by Allied bombing raids. A poor copy exists in the Sprengel Museum, Hanover.

2 Kurt Schwitters, *Merzbau (Kathedrale des erotischen Elends)*, 1923–1937, mixed media, Hanover. Photographer unknown

The Merz works are psychological collages where layers of fragments of found objects relate to personal experiences, and those with painful or traumatic associations Schwitters often physically buried beneath those with more benign or happier ones. Ultimately, he declared, "Merz means to create relationships, preferably between all the things in the world" (Schwitters 2006, p. 18).

T. S. Eliot's 1922 *The Wasteland* is a literary montage where fragments of text bring resonant meaning with extreme economy of means. In the disillusioned aftermath of the First World War, Eliot forges a poem where fragmentation provides the theme and structure, but also the language and emotion. Like Benjamin and Schwitters, Eliot abandoned linear narrative, shifting instead between characters, times and places, creating "A heap of broken images" (Eliot 1922, p. 11). Each quotation carries with it the profound associations of the original, that releases with the depth-charge of a high intensity explosive in its new context. Voices drift in and out like echoes in the aftershock. From Sanskrit, to the archaic, through Ovid, Chaucer, Dante, Webster, Shakespeare, Wagner, Baudelaire, biblical allusions, popular song and tarot, emerges a dream portrait of modern consciousness and new meaning.

We are defined by our necessarily partial, fragmentary experience and memories of the world. There can be great beauty in these fragments, and in the ways in which they can be reassembled to create new forms. Fragmentation can also be the result of a violent blow; physical, personal or societal. *The Wasteland* ends with, "These fragments I have shored against my ruins" (Eliot 1922, p. 49). *Charlotte Skene Catling*

Framing At the 1934 International Museum Conference, the director of the Rijksmuseum in Amsterdam, Frederik Schmidt-Degener, explicitly refered to framing when discussing how to valorise works of art. This direct link between enhancing museum heritage and framing evoked the etymological meaning of the verb "to frame" (from the Old Frisian *framia*), which could be traced back to "benefitting" or "advancing" something (see Schmidt-Degener 1934, p. 201). The frame allowed for a harmonious presentation of the collection by guiding and modulating the spectator's attention toward specific works, according to Schmidt-Degener. But it was the prominent twentieth-century conservation theorist Cesare Brandi who fully articulated the original sense of "framing". He described it not only as a means to benefit the visibility of an artwork, but crucial in extending its life – an essential step in collection care and what is now recognised as preventive conservation (→ COLLECTING, → PRESERVATION). Framing mediated between the past and the present, shaping what the viewer could see, experience, and know about the original work.

This reflection must be considered in relation to Brandi's lifelong endeavour to promote virtuous conservation practices through exhibitions. From his appointment as director of the

1 *The original Istrian stone frame encasing Bellini's San Giobbe altarpiece*, San Giobbe, Venice. Montage by the author

Istituto Centrale per il Restauro in 1939, Brandi organised temporary shows to inform the public about the methodologies that were employed in the institute's laboratories. For the first exhibition at the Istituto Centrale in May 1942, he experimented with a framing technique that left the edges of Sienese Renaissance masterpieces visible. This framing "defined a gravitational field around the paintings without attempting to reconstruct their original proportions" (Brandi 1942, p. 367). A similar presentation method had already been employed by architect Franco Albini for contemporary artworks. Brandi's innovation lay in applying to Renaissance art a framing clearly distinct from the original, with the aim of preserving the paintings' legibility: the edges of the artworks held valuable information about the construction of the support and the preparatory layers. By exposing details that were usually visible only to the conservator, Brandi offered a broader public the opportunity to engage with the materiality of art.

By 1953, following the publication of two seminal studies reassessing seventeenth- and eighteenth-century frames, Brandi had reconsidered his stance. Speaking at the International Congress of the History of Art in Pisa, he admitted: "I am the author of an example I now regret – the abolition of frames" (Brandi 1954, p. 97). If the original frame was lost, laying bare the edges of Renaissance masterpieces was a mistake because it compromised their intended appearance. Instead, he advocated for a visible, honest reframing that reflected its own time while avoiding falsification. More importantly, and at that same congress, Brandi extended the concept of framing to architecture: "A frame is essential in mediating between the spatiality of the image and that of the surrounding, lived-in space" (Brandi 1954, p. 97). Coming from a significant voice in the Italian establishment, this comment highly resonated among those architects who had been engaged in reframing Old Master paintings as part of their remodelling of museum interiors. Their approach had often been criticised for clashing with the ancient artworks.

Over the following decade, Brandi's idea took shape, providing a consistent theoretical reference point for Italian architects. His influence is evident when Albini lectured at the Politecnico di Torino in 1954 and described framing as a spatial "intermediary between image and environment [...], a volume of air assigned to the painting, almost a zone of influence within its pictorial space" (Albini 2006, p. 73). Brandi's concept ultimately found its fullest expression in the closing chapter of his *Teoria del restauro* (1963), where the removal of frames was examined as a restoration issue.

This is the context for architect Carlo Scarpa's framing that took into account the provenance of the artwork as well as its history of reception. Consider, for instance, his reframing between 1950 and 1957 of Giovanni Bellini's San Giobbe altarpiece in Venice (fig 1), which had been transferred to the Gallerie dell'Accademia in 1815. Its move was part of a broader Venetian trend of relocating artworks from churches to museums to protect them from environmental damage (→ DISPLACEMENT, → TRANSLOCATION). On a first glance, the large altarpiece appeared completely decontextualised: framed by a thin gilded profile, it floated against the dull, ivory-white walls of the Gallerie dell'Accademia in Venice. Upon more careful consideration, one realises that there is something in the gallery space that recalls the altarpiece's original setting – a staircase Scarpa designed in Istrian stone (fig. 2).

In the church of San Giobbe, the altarpiece was conceived in harmony with its Istrian stone frame, exemplifying the Renaissance symbiosis between painting and architecture. In the Accademia, the altarpiece was reframed in a standardised gilded profile in order to ensure coherence among diverse → ACQUISITIONS – a practical choice that nonetheless diminished its site-specificity. Scarpa's intervention preserved the nineteenth-century gilded profile while subtly referencing the altarpiece's original frame through the stone he selected for the staircase. This sophisticated reference in the form of an architectural → ELEMENT introduced a shift in the concept of framing that went beyond the familiar dualism of inside and outside, contained and unbound, and that instead drew architecture into its logic. In seeking to integrate the surroundings, the framing ceased to be mere ornament, and began, in a kind of reversal, to encompass the room within its own limits. *Flavia Crisciotti*

2 Carlo Scarpa, *Staircase of the Gallerie dell'Accademia*, referencing the original frame of Bellini's San Giobbe altarpiece, 1951, Istrian stone, Venice. Photo: Gianantonio Battistella, 2004

Ghosts We live among them always, the remnants of other times and former people, in layers of memory, forgetfulness and varying degrees of knowledge (→ AFTERLIFE). I am writing in the window of a *pousada* in Gharb al-andalus. It was once a convent, set down upon the crest of an *alcáçova* that had itself been built above the foundations of Phoenician houses. We are looking out on a church that carries the domes of a mosque, across to the old city of new Tavira, whose white dwellings, built after the catastrophic temblor of 1755, propped themselves against all that was then left standing to lean upon – the red stone towers of the Moorish fortress, whose turrets punctuate the urban panorama and break almost at random the path of modern steps or roadway. This or something like it is the sequence – the provenance – of many towns, though at their largest and most prosperous it lies buried, invisible and unremembered for aeons, like the temples and conduits of ancient Londinium. Yet through the names we give to places and by the shapes we give to things of use and the figuration deployed in decoration (like the beakers, *azulejos* and embossed silver trays of Portugal), patterns from the lives lived in those remains persist, like the primordial echoes that sound in the well-known words and habits of modern life.

Even when invented, these reappearances and recollections offer archetypes that lend a sense of apparent familiarity, age and reassurance to a newly built world around us. Architects in our time have not been shy to dream up and display such a long provenance where none is evident: Gino Valle reconstituting the ancient-sounding walls and paths and lapping waters of Venice in

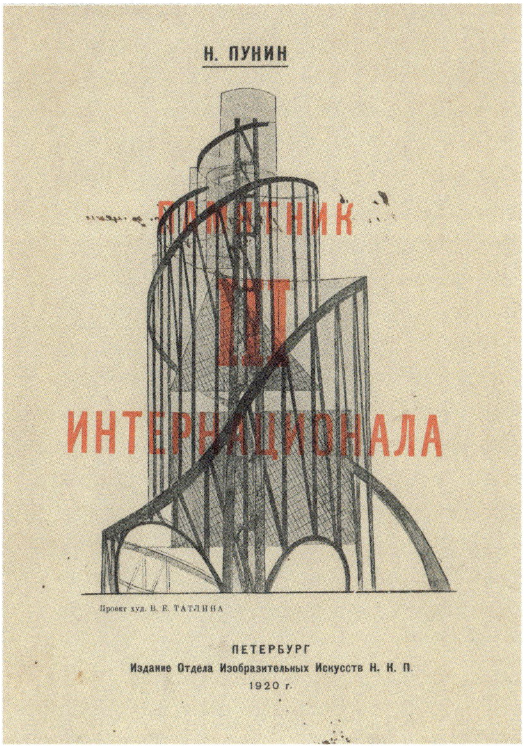

1 Vladimir Tatlin, *Pamiatnik III Internatsionala (Monument to the Third International)*, cover from Nikolai Punin, untitled pamphlet (St Petersburg: Izo NKP, 1920)

his acoustic design for housing on the Giudecca (1984–1986); Carlo Scarpa installing an imaginary archaeology into the gardens of Querini Stampalia (1959–1963), and weaving a set of infinitely archaic symbolic forms – perhaps Etruscan or Pharaonic – into the landscape of his cemetery for the Brion family (1968–1978); Peter Eisenman evoking universal prehistoric stone assemblies to evoke grief, regret, remorse and remembrance in his Berlin Holocaust Memorial (1997–2005); and Álvaro Siza threading through the sparkling white new town at Malagueira (1973–1977) the grizzled stone form of an ancient aqueduct that neither is nor ever was – inventing an origin-myth of place for the displaced lives of a hygienic modern world constructed in no place and *de novo*.

Many perceive in the later works of Louis Kahn a conscious echo of lost worlds and remote monuments, a sort of ghostliness in which a studied incompleteness of design evokes the Attic ruins and Sienese towers his travel studies rejoiced in. But perhaps the most haunting instance of the reconstitution of immemorial archetypes is the unbuilt Danteum (1938) of Giuseppe Terragni and Pietro Lingeri, in which each mysteriously drawn chamber was to evoke the atmosphere, light, shadows and tones of Dante's progress through Purgatory, Paradise and Inferno. Like their earliest work together – the first study for a Monument to the Fallen of Como in 1926 – the architects would shape the container in a near-primordial language that reduced to its essence the Roman architecture known to Dante's guide, the poet Virgil, and called upon by Mussolini to assert the national character of his modern state by evoking the ghosts of its ancient precursor (→ POLITICAL ICONOGRAPHY).

The Danteum, imagined again and again through film and digital animation from our own time, is a ghost in another sense: one of those unbuilt works of the twentieth century – not fantasies but realisable and often very nearly built – that have joined with imaginary architecture like Giovanni Battista Piranesi's *Carceri* and the megastructures of Étienne-Louis Boullée to become the ghostly archetypes through which a possible future world is envisaged and from whose examples its forms might be borrowed and developed. Their number is legion, and their persistence as points of reference suggests that in a discipline so bound to provenance and → PRECEDENT it is sometimes the work inventively unbuilt, and thus timeless and uncertain, turning and returning fresh in the mind rather than the modern monument sitting fixed on a changing landscape that lays the imaginative groundwork for the new.

One thinks of Vladimir Tatlin's *Monument to the Third International* of 1920, a tower calling on medieval imaginaries of Babel and intended to rise from a bank of the Neva to exemplify the skyward train of aspiration through which the working people of the world might find a new life to float above the masonry prison of street, chimney, factory and slum, a contrast between light and dark, framework and block, beautifully illustrated on the cover of Nikolai Punin's pamphlet advancing it (fig. 1).

It was never commenced and the → MODEL, though exhibited in Petersburg and carted through the streets in a Moscow parade, soon lost. First recreated by Pontus Hulten in Stockholm in 1968, the model has since appeared again in many forms, including such equally and subtly polemical evocations as those of Dan Flavin and Ai Weiwei. The early 1920s have left us numerous other invocations of a newly vertical and transparent modernity – like the submissions of Adolf Loos, Walter Gropius and Adolf Meyer and Bruno Taut for the Chicago Tribune Tower competition (1922) and the long enquiry, starting in 1921, of Ludwig Mies van der Rohe into the shape and structure of towers of glass – forcefully and sometimes even literally revenant in skyscraper dreams of the late-modern and postmodern era, from Bertrand Goldberg to Michael Graves.

Another famous ghost appeared forty years later in 1961 as the idea for Cedric Price's proposed Fun Palace for Joan Littlewood in London began to form. This was another permeable structure, intended to last for ten years and made of nothing more than a lightly covered framework through and within which indeterminate activities and temporary structures might be channelled or housed (fig. 2).

From May 1964, when the press took it up, it was projected for many sites from Bishopsgate Station to West Ham, Euston Square, Camden, south London and the Lea Valley, before being shelved in 1968 when Littlewood adapted its ideas into a more plastic form to house this adult playground in her Bubble City – elements of which were built by Bruce Lacey for the festival of London and by Ken Turner in his highly interactive Plastic Garden, the first of the Serpentine Pavilions. The concept of a short-lived permeable open-ended mega-block was infectious from the start. the *Guardian* called an exhibition of student designs for rethinking the public house "well on its way to the Fun Palace" (McCarthy 1965, p. 9). Its spirit found its way to Milton Keynes in the abortive plan for a City Club (1970), a permeable leisure centre in which many blocks of the utopian grid were to be covered by canopies under which happenings could include everything from a sort of cybernetic fun fair (with a chamber of "the mad scientist") to a free-flowing sports field. The Fun Palace was never about its physical framework but always about establishing intersections or urban pathways leading to unpredictable possibilities for action, movement, inquiry and performance. As such it is closer not to a Centre Pompidou, or to the wave of High-Tech Architecture that so often cited it as a progenitor, but to such other generous, fluid and indefinite ghosts of the time as Hans Hollein's Communication Interchange, Ron Herron's series of Loose Packages, or Constant's New Babylon.

There are ghosts too of modern → RUINS and losses, like Aldo Rossi's Teatro del Mundo (1984–1985), a fantastical barge of pungent vernacular city forms housing a display of propositions for the new city. Built as if for a Venetian masque of the seventeenth century and celebrating common archetypes as the primal shapes to generate new architecture it was an elegiac rationalisation of echoes we hear all around us. I see it as a ghost itself, floating away from Venice to cross the Adriatic to Dubrovnik, as amazingly it did, and then being lost forever. And I think of Minoru Yamasaki's World Trade Center, whose mysteriously separated twin towers, always evanescent and uncertain, even in conception, have somehow

2 Cedric Price, *Fun Palace for Joan Littlewood (project)*, Stratford East, London, 1961, perspective sketch, mixed media, 16.5 × 40.3 cm. Museum of Modern Art, New York

never left us, retaining an invisible mnemonic presence on the skyline to all who knew New York when they were standing and as they fell (→ COLLECTIVE MEMORY), like phantom cypresses rising in the mind to shade all those who were then there lost. *Nicholas Olsberg*

Graffiti Since time immemorial, man has felt the need to leave evidence of his own existence, his resentment and his desires in mostly public places. The history of such → INSCRIPTIONS, signs or pictorial representations, which can be summarised under the Italian term "graffiti" (modified from the Latin word *graphium* for stylus), can therefore be traced back to ancient times and is documented, for example, by prehistoric petroglyphs, Egyptian temple inscriptions, pornographic scratchings from Pompeii or the Inscription Rock in the El Morro National Monument in New Mexico, which has been marked by travellers since the early seventeenth century. As a subcultural form of expression in today's sense, graffiti has been developed since the 1960s, primarily in major US cities, from where it spread to the punk, hip hop and sprayer scenes around the world.

Initially applied illegally to house walls, vehicles and structures of public transport, graffiti encompasses various techniques (writing, scratching or stencils) and genres (tags, throw ups or pieces). Partly legalised – and thus domesticated –, graffiti has also been used to decorate youth centres, schools and commercial properties, for example. Occasionally, its more aesthetically motivated manifestations are even recognised as Urban or Street Art and thus bring into question the merely subcultural character of graffiti. Artists such as Harald Naegeli (the "Sprayer of Zurich") and Banksy, who is only known under his pseudonym, also utilise the medium of clandestinely applied pictures, or, like Keith Haring and Jean-Michel Basquiat, adopted stylistic features of Street Art in their works, which are highly appreciated by the art market. Irrespective of this, however, the various genres of graffiti were – and are – globally used as an expression of social or political protest; they spread slogans and counter-slogans, mark the spheres of influence of different groups or gangs and call for public action. However, in their wild, often overlapping and conflicting accumulation, graffiti are still mostly perceived as acts of → VANDALISM.

Regarding a provenance history of architecture, graffiti can be interesting for various reasons. On the one hand, they are often an indicator of the neglect or → DERELICTION of buildings; on the other, they draw attention to precarious social or political urban situations. Not infrequently, however, inscriptions also comment on the architecture itself on which they are sprayed. In the early 2000s, for example, the subversive insight "clean walls – higher rents" (seen in Luckauer Straße) was written on a freshly renovated wall in Berlin's Kreuzberg neighbourhood. Also in Berlin, a scathing remark – "Bonjour tristesse" – on an apartment house that the Portuguese architect Álvaro Siza had built shortly before in

1 Álvaro Siza, *Apartment building*, 1982–1983, with inscription of an unknown sprayer, 1984, Schlesische Straße, Berlin. Photo: Uwe Fleckner, 2025

Schlesische Straße to close a → LACUNA torn by the Second World War in the old building stock became famous in 1984 (fig. 1).

The short text, partly in mirror-inverted letters and quoting the title of a 1954 novel by French author Françoise Sagan, was placed on an arch in the attic zone of the otherwise rather unimaginative building. Although the text laconically refers to the monotonous "tristesse" (dreariness) of the facade design, the architect reacted wisely to the unwanted criticism, respected the inscription and even ensured that the now iconic commentary was restored several times, at least for some years (see Akcan 2011).

The mechanisms of the culture industry have led to a situation where phenomena of youth and protest culture can also be appropriated by commercial interests (see Adorno and Horkheimer 1947, pp. 144ff.). Even those forms of illegal graffiti or Street Art that have consciously rebelled against the "clean" aesthetics of modern urban architecture have not been spared this fate. Just as the appearance of punks, hip-hoppers and other members of underground movements has been taken over in fashion, for example by the British designer Vivienne Westwood or so-called "heroin chic", the mock vandalism of graffiti is also occasionally used today to lend a certain "street credibility" to the buildings on which it is applied or to the companies or institutions housed in them.

An interesting example of this can be found on Kantstraße in Berlin's upmarket Charlottenburg neighbourhood. There, on the ground floor of an inconspicuous apartment building from 1959–1960, we find a glass front completely covered by wildly colourful tags, which reveals only to the initiated that it conceals one of the city's finest and best Asian restaurants (fig. 2).

Only a tiny neon sign ("893 料亭") indicates the name of the gourmet temple, which refers to the so-called *ryōtei*, a special type of Japanese private restaurant that traditionally offers particularly exquisite dishes and serves as discreet meeting places for business people and politicians. The interior design of the restaurant,

2 Hans-Dieter Bolle, *Apartment building*, 1959–1960, with shop front of the restaurant 893 Ryōtei, 2017, Kantstraße, Berlin. Photo: Uwe Fleckner, 2025

created by Allen Kaufmann Architects in 2017, which is virtually invisible from the street thanks to the one-way mirror glass front, deliberately takes up the allusion to the underworld and gangster milieu conveyed by the graffiti and, at the owner's request, resulted in an exclusive place reminiscent of the aesthetics of Japanese yakuza films by the → TRANSFORMATION of a former drug store (see www.archdaily.com/946014/893-ryotei-bar-allenkaufmann-studio).

Graffiti therefore cover architecture and monuments of all kinds with a → PATINA of contemporary traces of reception. They use the surfaces of buildings as carriers of different messages and thus occasionally also document the changing appreciation or rejection that these structures have experienced over the course of time. Beyond the aesthetic or functional determinations intended by their architects, owners, users and → RESIDENTS, they are thus overwritten with → PALIMPSESTS of social, political or artistic statements and can be fundamentally altered in their character in this way. Even if these buildings naturally do not leave their respective plots of land, their intellectual locations within the urban fabric of a city shift in the sense of an expanded concept of provenance. *Uwe Fleckner*

Heritage "Heritage is our legacy from the past, what we live with today, and what we pass on to future generations. Our cultural and natural heritage are both irreplaceable sources of life and inspiration", according to the UNESCO World Heritage Convention. Without connecting heritage to a specific location, the definition still links → AUTHENTICITY and continuity of heritage to ideas of irreplaceability. This indeed applies to architectural heritage, as → RECONSTRUCTION, in general, is not considered an adequate substitute for the "original" building. The ideal of irreplaceability is often extended to the surroundings, as architectural heritage and authenticity is associated with site-specificity (see Kaspar 2007).

Moving architecture from its site of origin can be interpreted as decreasing the heritage value or the *Denkmalwert* (monument value) of a building (see Kaspar 2018). This differs only gradually from reconstructions, as part of the irreplaceability of an architectural heritage object – its site – is exchanged (→ DISPLACEMENT, → TRANSLOCATION). The Burra Charter of 1979, adopted by the ICOMOS Committee Australia (revised 2013), explicitly formulated a heritage

1 *Mora cottages*, Skansen, postcard (Stockholm: Axel Eliassons Konstförlag c.1900)

conservation standard: "The physical location of a place is part of its cultural significance. A building, work or other element of a place should remain in its historical location. Relocation is generally unacceptable unless this is the sole practical means of ensuring its survival" (The Burra Charter 2013, Art. 9.1).

Translocations become critical moments in the biography of a monument, as its value conventionally hinges on its relationship to the original site. Essential parts of the authenticity of historical buildings are lost by repositioning. Originality and historical authenticity depend on the state of → PRESERVATION, but also on the location.

However, architecture may achieve high-standard heritage status after translocation, for instance when a relocated building is accompanied by narratives and attributions of being "characteristic" for the building cultures of a certain region or a nation, which can be represented with the help of this particular example. Constructions of regional or national architectural canons, usually based on architectures of rural → PROVENIENCE, often happened by translocations at the turn of the twentieth century. Exhibitions of representative buildings were compiled in often parklike environments and perceived as idealised embodiments of national or regional architectures (see Jöchner et al. 2023). Replicas of vernacular architecture appeared in world → EXHIBITIONS; a model further developed into open-air museums. Such architectural exhibitions were favoured due to the rapid transformation of both cities and countryside in the face of modernisation and industrialisation, the latter being seen as homogenisation and standardisation within international entanglements. Such narratives link modernisation with a loss of local specifics and tradition, factors that were indispensable for the construction of national identities.

At the open-air museum founded by Artur Hazelius in Stockholm in 1891, buildings from various regions of Sweden were transferred and rebuilt at Skansen, part of Nordiska Museet (fig. 1).

2 *Shooting of the movie "La estrella del Rey" by Luis María Delgado and Arduino Maiuri*, 1957, Poble Espanyol, Barcelona. Photo: Jack Metzger

With this process of transference, the buildings lost the surroundings which characterised them as historical and architectural individuals. However, they gained a new status by being authenticated as architectural heritage representing a specific region or a specific type of building in carefully curated ensembles. Like taxidermy specimens in natural history museums, they no longer represented themselves, but a type. Only in this deliberate canonisation could the claim to visualise the heritage of a region or a country be credibly embodied. Discarding the specific, the individual and the contingent, they aspired to be more than one thing in the here and now, and become representative of architectural → ARTEFACTS from elsewhere. This extension of meaning came at the price of detachment from the original space. It was no coincidence that the specific curatorial activity of defining and exhibiting the characteristics of architectural heritage took place in the vicinity of national art museums, which were also given the task of reifying, materialising and defining national heritage.

The Poble Espanyol, the Spanish Village at the 1929 Barcelona World Fair, consisted of reconstructions of buildings from different regions across Spain. Compiled into a village, it was erected near the Palau Nacional (today's Museu Nacional d'Art de Catalunya), displaying Spanish art and national history (see Wunderwald 2023). The change of name from the intended "Iberiona" to "Poble Espanyol" shows that the ensemble was not meant to epitomise the villages of Spain, but the Spanish village par excellence (fig. 2). The buildings were transformed into an emblem of architectural heritage in rural Spain to create a vision of national unity in an era of political conflict. Margit Kern

Image vehicle The term "image vehicle" is a metaphor coined by Aby Warburg to explain his view of → ARTEFACTS as movable phenomena. We first encounter it in a note in which the German art and cultural historian stated in 1906 that printed → REPRODUCTIONS on the walls of bourgeois homes had taken on the role of manorial tapestries (see https://bilderfahrzeuge.hypotheses.org/3329). In the course of his research, he expanded the formulation and spoke explicitly of "automobile image vehicles" (Warburg 2000, p. 5), with which visual facts are disseminated across spatial and temporal distances. His inimitable sense for descriptive linguistic points, which he often drew from the semantics of modern technology, thus created a term that precisely corresponded to his concept of art history as a dynamic process of cultural exchange (→ AFTERLIFE).

Warburg devoted individual case studies to the global migration of artefacts – in this context he spoke of an "international wandering of images" – as well as his famous *Mnemosyne* atlas. Using the adjective "automobile", i.e. self-moving, he made it clear that, in his view, it was the aesthetic, social or even political expressive power of artefacts that was responsible for the → MOBILITY of works of art (or their reproductions, copies or replicas). According to this theory, specific artefacts move actively through space and time and can no longer be regarded as merely passive objects. Warburg initially thought of artefacts of specific genres, such as prints, leaflets, coins, medals or stamps, which are inherently mobile (→ MOVABLES). However, he himself, and above all the current reception of his ideas, ultimately extended the concept to all areas of artistic production (see Beyer et al. 2018; Fleckner and Tolstichin 2020).

Even works of art history that are commonly referred to in German as "*Immobilien*" (real estate, literally: immovable entities), i.e., architecture of all kinds, can under certain circumstances take on the character of image vehicles. Buildings are of course easy to circulate in the medium of their reproduction, be it as images in paintings and drawings, but above all in specially published albums with prints of architectural views, in books, magazines and encyclopaedias, as well as in photographs (→ PHOTOGRAPHY), which were already being distributed in the nineteenth century by agencies such as Alinari (founded in Florence in 1852). Moreover, → PLASTER CASTS of individual buildings or their → FRAGMENTS also made it possible to establish a global canon of architecture (see Lending 2017). Today, the worldwide dissemination of knowledge of architecture is largely ensured by the new media, and three-dimensional replicas are created by companies such as Factum Arte (founded in Madrid in 2001) using digital surveying and state-of-the-art 3-D printing processes (→ FACSIMILE).

In fact, buildings themselves are also repeatedly set in motion. On a profane level, this happens when houses are moved, usually for reasons of monument → PRESERVATION, in order to protect them from → DEMOLITION, although this does not necessarily turn them into image vehicles in Warburg's sense. More interesting are those → TRANSLOCATIONS or → DISPLACEMENTS in which architecture or architectural → ELEMENTS were removed from their original setting due to their artistic, cultural or political significance in order to be integrated into museum collections, for example (→ COLLECTING). This has happened, among others, with a number of medieval sacral buildings that form the core collection of The Cloisters in New York; individual buildings such as the Ishtar Gate (Berlin, Pergamon Museum) or the Temple of Dendur (New York, Metropolitan Museum) have also been migrated in this way. Copies or replicas of famous buildings are also used to fulfil different, mostly touristic or commercial functions as landmarks, for example in the Paris Las Vegas casino hotel, whose building complex includes scaled-down replicas of the Eiffel Tower, the Arc de Triomphe, the Louvre, the Musée d'Orsay and the Paris Opera.

The complex consequences of relocating an edifice can be illustrated by the example of a simple residential building that once stood in an underprivileged neighbourhood of Detroit (fig. 1). The civil rights activist Rosa Parks lived here from 1957 to 1959 after she was forced to leave her hometown of Montgomery, Alabama (→ RESIDENTS). On 1 December 1955, she refused to give up her seat on a bus reserved for white passengers ("whites only"). The incident sparked fierce protests, non-violent resistance actions were organised and finally a lawsuit in the United States District Court led to a ruling that racial segregation on buses was unconstitutional. As the instigator of the protests, Rosa Parks was threatened with death and eventually moved in with relatives in Detroit, to the very house that had stood the test of time and could have become an important monument to the Civil Rights Movement as a place of escape and resistance (see Fleckner 2018).

Decades later, a niece of the activist tried to prevent the demolition of the dilapidated building (→ DERELICTION). She finally turned to the Berlin-based American artist Ryan Mendoza, who dismantled the building in September 2016 and shipped its → COMPONENTS to Germany. He rebuilt it on a plot of land in the Wedding neighbourhood, a district with a high proportion of migrants, developed a sound installation for his project with historical and current sound documents on the Civil Rights movement and finally presented the building to the public (fig. 2).

Since April 2017, the building has thus been located between tall apartment blocks in Berlin exile (see McGrane 2017). The transport of the building from continent to continent brought with it a number of shifts in meaning (→ CARGO). If the house of Rosa Parks in the US could have kept alive the memory of the historical but still necessary struggles for equal rights and at the

1 *Former home of the McCauley-Parks family*, South Deacon Street, Detroit. Photo: Fabia Mendoza, 2016

same time documented the economic and social decline of the industrialised areas in the north of the country, in present day Germany there was also a reflection on the pressing issues of migration and (political) asylum. Overall, the relocated building drew attention to the topicality of the debate on colonial history and racism, political emancipation and forced expulsion.

It was only through the loss of its original location, only after it had become a work of art itself, that the house of Rosa Parks was able to develop its well-deserved radiance in a foreign country that it was denied in Detroit. Having become an image vehicle, the building was temporarily transported back to the US and exhibited at the WaterFire Arts Center in Providence, Rhode Island, in 2018, then in the courtyard of the Palazzo Reale in Naples from 2020 to 2022. On its odyssey around the world, the house keeps alive the memory of the fact that mobility has played and continues to play no small role in human endeavours for freedom and equality. Long before Rosa Parks' courageous efforts helped to abolish racial segregation in public transport, Black activists were already fighting for the right to free travel and trying to build national networks in their struggle against racism and oppression with the help of stagecoaches, steamships and railways (see Pryor 2016). The house from Detroit can now also lay claim to such mobility: in the service of memorial consciousness, the image vehicle began its journey around the world, saved itself from demolition and oblivion by virtue of the subversive energies stored in it and, through its translocations, became a revitalised testimony to political commitment. In exile and in its new locations, it could, can and will remind us of the courage of a remarkable woman, but also of the devotion of many supporters to anchor the memory of the conflict-laden struggles for the rights of African-American citizens deeply in the historical responsibility of the US. The house of Rosa Parks, in whose weathered facade (→ WEATHERING) decades of social reality have been inscribed, can no longer be erased from the visual memory of humanity (→ COLLECTIVE MEMORY), to which Warburg devoted his entire life as art historian.

Aby Warburg researched the wandering of artefacts not only because it allowed him to trace the pedigree of images: he was particularly interested in the shifts and increases in meaning

2 Ryan Mendoza, *Rosa Parks' House*, former home of the McCauley-Parks family and sound installation, Wriezener Straße, Berlin. Photo: Uwe Fleckner, 2017

that a work of art underwent through the process of its migration. This makes the concept of the image vehicles interesting for theoretical considerations dedicated to provenance phenomena within architecture. If buildings are removed from their original contexts, their essential character changes even if they are rebuilt unaltered in their new location. As social artefacts, buildings cannot be viewed in isolation and are always defined by their urban context too. And even the mere dissemination of architecture in the media of reproduction or replication has an effect on the exemplary buildings if the process of reception modifies the understanding of the building, of its position in the architectural canon or of its social structure. The metaphor of the image vehicle thus not only describes the actual or virtual mobility of a building, but also encompasses the intrinsic change that necessarily accompanies its translocation. *Uwe Fleckner*

Inheritance Gordon Matta-Clark died in 1978, at the age of thirty-five. His father Roberto Matta survived him for twenty-four years. Gordon could not inherit anything from the fortune of his father, an immensely successful surrealist painter who, "like every good communist owned about seven castles", as Jane Crawford, his daughter-in-law and Matta-Clark's widow, once told me. On the other hand, he inherited his father's way of making a career. Like Matta the Elder who worked with Le Corbusier in Paris after studying architecture in Santiago de Chile, Matta the Younger initially studied architecture at Cornell. Like his father, he left architecture and started a brilliant career as artist. Only after beginning to practice as artist, he added the name of his mother Anne, née Clark – also an artist who divorced soon after his birth – to his name and became Gordon Matta-Clark.

While Matta-Clark did not inherit a fortune, he had financial support from his father during his studies and grew up in the core of the New York art world. He never mentioned the topic of inheritance. But it is plausible that his focus on working with what is already existing, → RECYCLING trash to build *Garbage wall* (1970), cutting into the facade and floor of an empty warehouse for *Day's end* (fig. 1) or climbing the chimney of an industrial → RUIN in Kassel for *Jacob's ladder* (1977), was motivated by the idea that everything was inheritance. After all, Matta-Clark's art never starts from scratch, but rearranges what is given (see Lee 2000).

Matta-Clark never owned seven castles. But thanks to his father he could afford to take risks and fail. If real estate, or rather, inherited real estate, is the substructure of architecture, the issue of inheritance is, at least latently, omnipresent in his oeuvre. Is his masterpiece *Splitting* (1974), a single-family house cut in two, a comment on the unending saga of inheritance dispute? Is the series *Reality properties: Fake estates* (1974), collages of documents referring to leftover lots of land purchased at auction a critique of the greed of speculators? Is *Bingo* (1974), the dismantling and discarding of sections of another single-family house, a play with the drama of squandering an inheritance? Most of the earlier work by Matta-Clark happened in a loose collective of artists, architects, dancers and musicians. If one looks at the photographs, films and videos of their activities – for instance the performance *Tree dance* (1971) in the branches of a large tree or *Open house* (1972) in an improvised shared flat in an open container on the street – one cannot but think of a group of young people who play carefree with what they inherited.

The starting capital for the collectively run restaurant *Food* (1971–1973) in fact stemmed from the inheritance of his girlfriend. With *Food*, an artists' diner in Lower Manhattan, where artists cooked for fellow artists, Matta-Clark returned back to his inheritance, to architecture. Everything in the restaurant is carefully designed, from the exuberant menu to the business plan, the cooking, the serving, the eating. Robert Frank, the most famous photographer of his generation, was the cameraman for the film *Food* (1973) that captures even the smallest detail of this project. Matta-Clark worked with

1 *Gordon Matta-Clark documenting "Day's End"*, 1975, building cut at Pier 52, New York. Photographer unknown

leftovers, but he made sure that every moment of creativity was documented and made fruitful and that no idea was wasted. After a couple of years, the restaurant went bankrupt, and the inheritance of Matta-Clark's girlfriend was gone. But as a legacy *Food* left the concept of fusion cuisine, the open kitchen – and the gentrification of Lower Manhattan – to the next generation.

One can, of course, renounce an inheritance. *Anarchitecture*, the name of a group show held in 1974 by the collective around Matta-Clark, was a signal in this direction. *Window blow-out* (1976), a performance in the exhibition *Idea as model* in Peter Eisenman's Institute for Architecture and Urban Studies in New York that culminated in shooting at the windows of the exhibition space, was another critical manifesto. The ephemerality of Matta-Clark's performances, the processual nature of his works and the emphasis on trash, debris, fragments and ruins all manifest his desire to challenge the status quo, property, and the gravitational pull of real estate through art. However, this artistic freedom and independence are difficult to envision without the inheritance, guarantee and security provided by earlier generations and, so to speak, by architecture itself. The art of Gordon Matta-Clark reflects back on architects, evoking both optimism and melancholy. It reveals what they could become if they chose to renounce their inheritance. *Philip Ursprung*

Inscription In the autumn of 1779, Nicolas Edme Restif de la Bretonne once again embarked on one of his lonely nocturnal rambles through Paris. He feels old, even though he is only in his mid-forties, his poor health torments him as much as his dubious lifestyle. And he wants to share his fate, his weariness perhaps, with the people of the city to which he moved for good as a young printer about twenty years ago. Secretly, anonymously, he begins a series of urban inscriptions that will accompany him for the decades to come: "It was in 1779, on 5 November, when I started writing on stones on the Île Saint-Louis, suffering from stomach pains. The first inscription is on the tenth stone, on the left of the Pont-Rouge as you enter it from the island. I did it because I wondered whether I would still be able to see this mark next year. It seemed to me that if I saw it again, it would give me a feeling of joy, a joy that comes so rarely in the autumn of life that it seemed permissible to bring about such an occasion. This note contained only the words: *5â 9bris malum* (5 November pain)" (Cottin 1889, p. 3). Countless others were to follow, hundreds more, written on the walls, scratched with sharp tools, scattered across the architecture of that *vieux* Paris between the market halls, the Marais, the Île de la Cité and the Île Saint-Louis, which was the setting for this quite unusual existence, meticulously documented in the diary of the prolific writer, which was only published posthumously.

And so it is hardly surprising when we read that Restif renewed his inscription in the following year: "I wrote it down before I returned to the first one, which I thought had been erased; but I found it again later and saw it with the sweet feeling of joy that overcomes a man who has escaped death. My soul blossomed and I rejoiced: 'I still exist! Death, the terrible death, has not taken me away. I still see the light of the sun, I still see, O Seine, your waves as fleeting as the days that have passed since I engraved this stone. I want to engrave it once more!' And I wrote, *bis anniversarium mali* (second anniversary of pain). Since then, I have refreshed the inscription every year, adding *ter* the third time, *quater* the fourth, *quinquiès* the fifth and *sexiès* last year" (Cottin 1889, p. 13).

Restif used the buildings of his city as carriers of enigmatic messages. He scratched dates, Latin words and sayings, often abbreviated in idiosyncratic ways, into the stone skin of the urban body. His inscriptions represent a very peculiar case of the early history of → GRAFFITI; they set what he hoped would be the immortality of inscriptions against the fugitiveness of his own lifetime. An autobiography – quite literally – carved in stone of his mental and physical states was thus created and was intended to document his life, the scandalous life of a novelist and pornographer, a social utopian and chronicler of the lowest milieus of the French capital. Today, all but one of these inscriptions have disappeared: "1764 Nicolas" can be read in Antiqua majuscules on the pillar of an arcade located on the Place des Vosges (fig. 1).

It was created a good dozen years before the "first" mark on the Ile Saint-Louis, which he himself recalled in his diary. In its laconic brevity, it still defies the times, unnoticed by the numerous tourists who visit the square, which was called Place Royale during Restif's epoch, and only visible to the connoisseur who strolls through the city as the author of the inscription, this *spectateur nocturne* and early flâneur, once did.

1 Nicolas Edme Restif de la Bretonne, *Scratched and dated inscription*, 1764, Place des Vosges, Paris. Photo: Uwe Fleckner, 2025

If they were still there today, these testimonies of nocturnal wanderings, they would be part of that urban → PALIMPSEST, of that architexture in which inscriptions of all kinds are interwoven and superimposed: street names, the names of houses, shops and hostels, official announcements and subversive slogans on political posters (→ POLITICAL ICONOGRAPHY), which were joined much later by the colourful advertising messages of the billboards, Litfaß columns and neon signs, whose inscriptions authors like Louis Aragon in his novel *Le paysan de Paris* (1926) and Alfred Döblin in his *Berlin Alexanderplatz* (1929) or Walter Benjamin in some fragments of his *The arcades project* (1927–1940) used as semantic → QUARRIES for their (literary) monuments of the two metropolises. The provenance history of architecture also includes the fact that the constitution of a city can be read not only from its social structure, but also from the state of its architecture, from the tangible appropriation of the buildings by their → RESIDENTS, who inscribe their own existence into them by means of diverse traces of life. *Uwe Fleckner*

Labour The word "labour" came from Latin *labor* into Middle English *labour* by way of French; as a loan word, "labour" travelled in company with "travail" and "toil", all synonymous with "hard work" from the late fourteenth century and long predating "effort", which arrived a full century later (see Vezzosi 2025, p. 1069). Tracing the appearance of "labour" from late Middle English, a typical → CONTRACT for the construction of the Corpus Christi Chapel in Cambridge in 1579 illustrates the association of the word with building work. According to the contract for the slating of the Chapel, the contractor must "ffynd all manner off stuffe that is needffull to them for the workmanshippe and Layinge off the sayd slate uppon a Chappell newelye to be erected and builded within the sayd Colledge, as Lyme, sande, Lathe, cowe dounge, horse dounge, slatepyne, and nayles, Ladders, Lynes, Cordes, and rouffe tyle: and the said Raffe and Jhon [...] shall fforthwith [...] dresse the sayd slate and ffynd all manner off Labor and workmanshippe, [...] without anye intermission or leaveing off, off the sayd worke, vntyll it be so perfitlye slated and finished" (Willis and Clark 1886, p. 312). Distinct from workmanship or → CRAFT, labour is toil.

"Labour" is a noun and a verb at once. While it originated as hard work or toil, its meaning came to diverge from mere "work". For David Hume in 1752, labour represented individual purchasing power, from which satisfaction could be gained: "Everything in the world is purchased by labour, and our passions are the only causes of labour" (Hume 1906, p. 8). For Adam Smith, labour might be aggregated as "the wealth of nations" (see Smith 1776), whereas for Karl Marx, by contrast, labour was a very motor of → CAPITALISM, along with geography, weather and time. And for Hannah Arendt in her 1958 *The human condition*, labour was distinct from work, and both differed from action in a hierarchical schema that placed labour closer to the activities of animals.

The provenance of labour in Western architecture, then, sits within a constellation of meanings that accrued to the term over centuries. Architecture discourse has tended to adopt Arendt's distinction, ascribing action to the activity of design (see Arendt 1998, pp. 7ff.); work to the production of documents in preparation for a building, and labour to the men and women who erect buildings on → CONSTRUCTION SITES (fig. 1-2).

Such a schema was questioned in the 2010s, as light shone on "Who builds your architecture?" (http://whobuilds.org/). And young architects have asserted their right to be seen as labourers, not workers or activists. The reason is that "labour", in the wake of recent reinvestments in Karl Marx's political economy, has become a glorious term, a righteous assumption of the predicament of the working class by those trained in institutions of higher education. It may represent solidarity by those who merely "work" with those who actually "labour".

Yet in today's terms, the necessity for such solidarity lies in the wholesale degradation of employment in Western society, whereby greater rights accrue to those with disproportionate power, while the constrained power of the working class creeps ever upwards in the socio-economic spectrum. For many academic architects in North America, this creep now

1 *Workers constructing the Packard plant*, 1906, Detroit, Albert Kahn Associates Records, Bentley Historical Library, Ann Arbor, and Albert Kahn Associates, Detroit. Photographer unknown

2 *Workers constructing the Packard plant*, 1916, Long Island Albert Kahn Associates Records, Bentley Historical Library, Ann Arbor, and Albert Kahn Associates, Detroit. Photographer unknown

threatens the system that has protected academic work for decades. Neoliberalism, we learn, threatens to downgrade action into work, and work into labour.

Labour in architecture has a narrative and a history quite separate from the travails of contemporary academic architects, or privileged practitioners of the profession. The status of labour on building sites has changed drastically since "Raff" and "Jhon" contracted to slate the roof of the Corpus Christi Chapel in 1579. Changing building technologies present opportunities to change the economic equation of building construction; in the history of architecture and especially in the period of modern industrial capitalism, construction evolution has consistently tended to disadvantage workers, not employers.

Sergio Ferro identifies a structural affinity between serial manufacture on building sites, as one team of craftsmen followed another, and non-hierarchical socio-political organisation in which differing professional competencies helped balance social relations through David Harvey's "monopolizable trades" (Harvey 1982, p. 59). Ferro notes, however, that "workers' exclusive possession of the know-how necessary for construction became problematic for capital in the 19th century" (Ferro 2024, p. 9). Metallic structure and reinforced → CONCRETE construction, in the first case made in factories and in the second made according to a set recipe, disenfranchised craft workers on building sites, substituting unskilled or semi-skilled labour for craft labour guilds.

Adrian Forty notes that "concrete offered a chance to bypass the traditional trades altogether, to break their monopoly over construction, by making it possible to build without any need for them at all" (Forty 2012, pp. 226f.). This classic case of labour deskilling resembles that identified by Harry Braverman in *Labor and monopoly capital* (1974) and later confirmed by Thomas Piketty's assessment of the movement of capital in *Capital in the twenty-first century* (see Piketty 2014). If tracing the provenance of labour in architecture suggests that the transit of modernity tends towards ever-increasing subjection, the solidarity of workers at the drawing table and on the building site suggests that another future is possible. *Claire Zimmerman*

Lacuna The history of architecture is also a history of decay, destruction and loss. Time and again even important buildings disappear through → DEMOLITION; time and again entire cities, neighbourhoods or streets are razed to the ground by → FIRES, natural disasters or the devastating → WARS of mankind. Academic disciplines such as archaeology and art history have therefore always devoted themselves also to the vanished buildings of past epochs, attempting to explore their appearance, function and significance by studying relics and → RUINS, with the help of written sources, building plans or depictions in paintings, with → ARCHITECTURAL DRAWINGS as well as → PHOTOGRAPHY. The list of such losses is endless: it includes buildings such as the ancient Library of Alexandria, the Babri Masjid in Ayodhya, India, built in the sixteenth century and demolished in 1992 during religious conflicts, the Royal Palace of Benin destroyed by the British colonial army at the end of the nineteenth century and the Crystal Palace in London, which burnt down in 1936. In quite a few cases, however, lost edifices were rebuilt or replaced by replicas (→ FACSIMILE, → RECONSTRUCTION).

In contrast, the voids left behind by destroyed architecture, the voids within urban landscapes, have hardly ever become the subject of academic study themselves. If, on the other hand, the history of architecture is understood as a history of its provenances, then both these empty spaces and the artistic and architectural measures that were used to react to the loss of buildings without replacing them come increasingly into focus. In order to distinguish it from other types of buildings that no longer exist, the phenomenon of lacuna is defined here as a visible (or visualised) empty space in an existing, usually closed and otherwise intact building stock.

1 Robert Venturi and John Rauch, *Benjamin Franklin residence and print shop (Ghost Structures)*, 1976, Franklin Court, Philadelphia. Photo: National Park Service, 2010

As a design task beyond reconstruction or replication, gaps between buildings and other urban voids always come to the fore when they appear suitable for serving a mostly politically motivated culture of remembrance. For example, an attempt was made to transfer the synagogue on Bornplatz in Hamburg, which was destroyed by the National Socialists, to the → COLLECTIVE MEMORY by having its floor plan marked in the ground at its original location by the artist Margrit Kahl in 1988. In doing so, the violently induced empty space, which was used as a car park prior to the artistic intervention, was consciously respected so as not to camouflage the historical crime through a "repair" (see Fleckner 2007, pp. 96ff.). Even following the nearly complete demolition of the Berlin Wall in the years after 1989, its course has been marked in various ways in the pavement. However, such and similar "disembodied" monuments can hardly be described as architectural solutions (→ COUNTER-MONUMENT); moreover, they cover the empty spaces if not with buildings, then with designed elements.

The approach to urban lacunae is different when the paradoxical ambition is to respond to them with quasi-architectural constructions in such a way that these do not fill the historically created gaps. For example, the site of the later demolished so-called President's House in Philadelphia, where George Washington and John Adams lived between 1790 and 1800 (→ RESIDENTS), was merely surrounded with deliberately modern sections of walls and implied portal and window frames. Thus, in 2010, a memorial was created over the partially uncovered foundations of the house in the form of a → PALIMPSEST within the Independence National Historical Park, which commemorates the contradictory history of the site, freedom and slavery with an exhibition (see Levin 2011). Already in 1976, Robert Venturi and John Rauch, also in Philadelphia, replaced the long-disappeared residence and print shop where Benjamin Franklin lived and worked between 1763 and 1790 with two steel skeletons that only vaguely hint at the supposed contours of the cancelled buildings (fig. 1). The simple, symbolic structures, veritable → GHOSTS of the two houses, do not pretend to reconstruct the original buildings, indeed, they even avoid any allusion to historical → AUTHENTICITY. Here, too, it is precisely the architectural measures taken that explicitly emphasise the absence of the original buildings (see Moos 1987, pp. 104ff.).

In 1990, French artist Christian Boltanski found a radical solution to draw attention to a residential building that had been bombed during the Second World War and removed without a trace (fig. 2). In Große Hamburger Straße in Berlin, on the occasion of the exhibition *Die Endlichkeit der Freiheit* (The Finitude of Freedom), he was fascinated by one of the many

2 Christian Boltanski, *The Missing House*, 1990, Große Hamburger Straße, Berlin. Photographer unknown

wounds within the historic eastern city centre of the metropolis, which at the time was to become the capital of a reunified Germany. Boltanski investigated who had lived in the building and presented the memorabilia he found in display cases in the western part of the city. While the empty plot of the destroyed house was left completely untouched, he placed the researched key information on plaques, which he affixed to the fire walls of the buildings that were still standing on both sides of the gaping hole. Visitors to his installation, which was kept in place after the exhibition and is now listed as monument, were able to read the names of the residents, their professions and the years they lived in the building. In the imagination of the viewers, this created a "portrait" of the house community (comparable to Georges Perec's 1978 novel *La vie mode d'emploi*), and thus the building itself was mentally "re-erected" as a social structure, even though it had materially disappeared and remained missing (see Fleckner and Dickel 2003, pp. 112ff.).

Of course, in most cases it is necessary to fill the voids left by an often-violent past in our cities with buildings in which new generations of architects realise their visions of the present and the future. And yet it is sometimes preferable not to close the gaps, not to deny the losses. Particularly successful in this respect are memorial strategies that aim to draw attention to lacunae by refusing building measures or reducing them to the bare essentials. The curious result of observing these non-interventionist interventions is that the history of art and architecture is not always dedicated to the visible, but sometimes also to the invisible. In the cases outlined here, it is the obvious presence of the absent, the "negative" existence and merely intellectual traceability of earlier layers of provenance that characterise their idiosyncratic character. *Uwe Fleckner*

Maintenance There is nothing original in stating that architecture is a matter of time. Architects deal with – and dream of – duration. And architecture is one of the primary ways through which humans intentionally inscribe a lasting and visible presence in the world. This enduring presence occurs through a very specific vehicle, the vehicle of art and creation, which means that the duration at play in architecture is a projected one. It is mainly imagined, calculated and modelled "upstream" during the complex and uncertain process of design. It is delegated to shapes and → MATERIALS that, once assembled, are entrusted with the duty of lasting on their own. This is not so simple, though. Anyone who has spent a few days walking in a city or a few years living in a building, knows that no house, no skyscraper, no monument and no infrastructure can endure by itself. For these things to actually last, they must be cared for intensively (see Denis and Pontille 2025). Indeed, most of them are inspected, monitored, repaired (→ REPARATION), cleaned or serviced by a host of people, whether qualified or not, on a daily basis (fig. 1). Yet, this cast of maintainers doesn't seem to belong to the world of architecture and architects. Their stories do not fit among those of creativity and material sturdiness. Maintenance is the dirty secret of both architecture and modernity.

But couldn't this be otherwise? What if maintenance and maintainers were given a proper place in architecture? Not as sources of constraints during the conception process, or as causes of trouble and unsolicited alterations during the life of buildings, but as sources of inspiration. As partners, even. This could have interesting consequences. First, it would help acknowledge the specific expertise that both nurtures and arises from maintenance practices. Who understands a building more intimately than its maintainers? Who knows better how its materials behave, how they interact over the years, and how they must be treated in order to temper their ongoing → TRANSFORMATIONS? And there's more. Taking maintenance into account allows us to rethink durability outside the sole perimeter of allegedly intrinsic material properties. It helps to recognise that duration is as much a question of design as it is of cultivation. In other words, maintenance can help architecture expand beyond, or beneath, the realm of creation and embrace the mundane practicalities and responsibilities that the relentless generation of permanence requires long after the design and construction phases (→ PRESERVATION).

Reconciling maintenance and architecture may also be useful for reconsidering the relationships that the latter has with the idea of *tabula rasa*, and consequently with → DEMOLITION, a pressing issue in times of environmental, energy and economic → CRISIS. What if, instead of designing buildings that are meant to last by themselves, architects collaborated with others to ensure the longevity of existing buildings? Under what conditions will diplomatic interventions throughout the life of buildings still be considered architecture?

These are rhetorical questions, of course, as this is already happening. Today, many architects claim they have never been neither modern nor postmodern, and they resist the lure of creative destruction. They are (re)inventing their art by working with existing buildings rather than imagining brand new ones. Explicitly or not, they are reshaping architecture to make room for maintenance, sometimes welcoming maintainers into their world and sometimes envisioning themselves as maintainers of sorts. By eschewing both designers' appetite for novelty and → HERITAGE conservationists' concern for unconditioned "sameness", they accept the need to engage with the constant transformations of matter and take a small part in the fragile (→ FRAGILITY) becoming of buildings. *Jérôme Denis*

1 *Building maintenance*, 1971, Quantico, US Marine Corps History Division. Photographer unknown

Material From the Latin word *materia* (matter, substance, timber), possibly linked to the Proto-Indo-European **mater-* (mother), the term "material" indicates a primordial substance from which things originate. Conventionally, material is a passive substance that is shaped by ideas to create objects of meaning. In this view, material provides a substrate whose properties inhibit and/or enable the imposition of formal organisation. Materials offer resistance whose performance is measurable and predictable, and which is shaped by externalities.

Canonical provenance is primarily metadata attached to material → ARTEFACTS, seeing it as a carrier of ideas and relations, typically granting it little agency. Ownership and transactions add relations of value and trade to the artefact. Occasionally, works are transformed when introduced into a market, whether split up to provide multiple objects, or recut, reframed or restored (→ RESTORATION). But the accretion of provenance in this process does not typically intervene into the material itself, which remains an empty signifier, gaining greater value by its potential to absorb new meaning. Material provenance expands this scope, recognising that materials themselves are produced, traded and transformed as substances (fig. 1).

At a fundamental level, materials result from natural processes through geological, chemical and biological conditioning, each of which imparts the particular character and potential behavior of the substance, embedding within it the traces of its formation, composition and responsiveness to human force and → LABOUR. Once identified and thus conceptualised as a

1 *Drone image of a Larvikite quarry demonstrating the unruliness of material*, Larvik. Photo: Eine Gaaserud, 2025

resource, materials are constructed through processes of extraction, refinement and amalgamation. For architecture, materials embody the labour that produced them, and inhabitation brings this into experience. In the spectrum from substance formation to material differentiation, material provenance explores the origins and transformations of material from resource cultivation to its employment in architecture.

While architectural theory has traditionally addressed materials in a pragmatic and reasoned manner, combining experiential knowledge with judgment in their selection and use, later engineering advances allowed for building morphologies expressly tailored to material capabilities in physical terms. As architectural materials have become increasingly processed and designed – resulting in hybrids engineered for performance and durability, such as metallic alloys, ferroconcrete, cross laminated timber, composite panels and an array of plastics – their appearance in a built work increasingly anonymises the sources from which they are composed. Glass and steel exhibit in the main only the factories which produce them. Recent scholarship, especially in the light of environmental concerns, has sought to regain a closer experiential relationship with materials in a more identifiable form, calling for a rawer, purer use of them in built work. Drawing from actor-network theory and post-humanist thinking (→ ACTOR, → NETWORK), studies of material have attributed to it a greater share of agency, whether through a Heideggerian inflected object-oriented ontology or vibrant matter.

This tendency, while adjacent to provenance thinking in architecture, risks doing exactly what it seeks to avoid: anthropomorphising the material world (→ THING-RIGHT), rather than recognising its behavior as relational and emergent.

Material provenance proposes a third way, one that moves beyond both inert materialism and vibrant matter by embedding materials within deep time, labour and architectural → TRANSFORMATION. It asks from where and how materials emerge, whether through geological and biological processes or through human refinement and hybridisation. And significantly for architectural provenance, it explores the architectonic construction of materials and their inhabitation in space and time. Finally, the extraction and construction of materials affects environmental conditions (→ SOURCING), while they themselves are subject to the ravages of these selfsame conditions. Provenance then is the taking possession of materials for inhabitation and for the resistance that they provide the process of design and the activities which they house.

Nonetheless, it is prudent to recall that materials escape us. Following Georges Bataille, materials resist formal organisation and tend to formlessness. For him, architecture imprisons material within formal hierarchies that subjugates its rawness, disciplining it into structures of meaning, utility and control. In his essay *Le bas matérialisme et la gnose* (Base material and Gnosticism), Bataille noted that matter cannot be captured by essentialism and is "external and foreign to ideal human aspirations and refuses to allow itself to be reduced to the great ontological machines resulting from these aspirations" (Bataille 1930, p. 6). *Thomas McQuillan*

Mobility Architecture always comes from one situation – a past moment, a collection of circumstances – and it is always on its way to another. But beyond the self-evident condition that architecture travels through time, architectural mobility is inspired both by mediation and physical translation (→ CARGO, → MOVABLES).

1 Charles Robert Cockerell, *The professor's dream*, 1848, pencil, pen and grey ink and watercolour, with scratched highlights, 110 × 167.5 cm. Royal Academy, London

In 1849, the *Illustrated London News* published a review of the Royal Academy spring exhibition in London, for which Charles Robert Cockerell, professor of architecture at the academy, showed a drawing titled *The Professor's Dream* (fig. 1). The work, saturated in detail and monumental in dimension, presented a → PASTICCIO in which architectural monuments from across Europe were herded together like steers at a cattle auction. Egyptian structures formed a holding pen at level zero; marginal notes confirmed that the Greek stock was raised 30 feet, younger Roman examples were at 60 feet, and the youngest in this architectural herd, dubbed "medieval and modern", mingled 90 feet above the fence. Everything is seen through a yellow sandy haze, as if stirred up by thousands of stampeding, heavy feet. The buildings in this image cover a geographical area nearly 2,000 square miles. That they could be imagined standing cheek-by-jowl in Cockerell's view implicates equally two of the nineteenth century's most radical technical advances that imposed mobility onto architecture: the illustrated press and the railway.

The thematics in the image relate it closely to the founding concerns of illustrated newspapers: to gather examples from a diverse geography; to create an interpretive space around these objects; to articulate juxtapositions simultaneously comfortable and bizarre – all these habits were established as images and text began to be combined in mass media during the 1840s and 1850s. Papers like the *Illustrated London News* (from 1842), *Illustrirte Zeitung* (from 1843), *Harper's Weekly* and *Le Monde illustré* (both from 1857) were "filled to the brim with images and descriptions of buildings, cities, streetscapes, and landscapes", and created vibrant architectural and geographical compressions (Hvattum and Hultsch 2018, p. 6). Cockerell's work, which repeated a composite drawing of Saint Paul's cathedral surrounded by significant European monuments produced originally for the same society that published the *Penny Magazine* (from 1832), repeated this heterotopic logic, trouncing geographic separation and projecting an inherent quality of mobility on to its subject matter (see Anstey 2024, ch. 3).

At the same time, *The Professor's Dream* makes an extraordinary prediction about the fate of architecture in the age of rapid mass transport. The drawing was conceived at a time when large architectural structures were being commissioned to symbolise the lithe and destabilising railway. Philip Hardwick's 21-metre-high Doric propylaeum at Euston station was completed in 1838; the design for William and Lewis Cubitt's huge double-arched shed at Kings Cross by 1849; Isambard Kingdom Brunel's monumental terminus at Paddington by 1852. All these surrounded terminating trains with thousands of tonnes of stationary stone, brick, iron and glass. Cockerell's

2 *The king's sleeping compartment*, from "The Royal Train", *The Graphic*, 20 December 1902

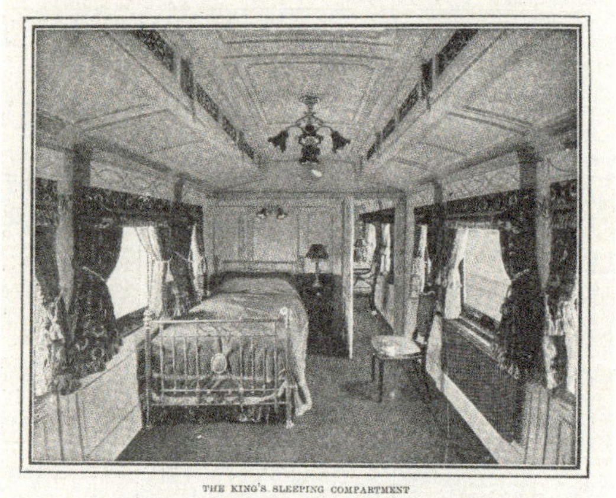

image suggested an inverted possibility: the movement of the railway might create an architecture that was itself mobile. Both the possibility that "there" might be slid, with invisible effort, to "here" and the pedagogic potential of juxtaposition found fruition in railway travel. Trains jostled together landscapes, cities and monuments of heterotopic origin, creating for their occupants after-images that likened the dream of Cockerell's professor.

As the nineteenth century progressed, the virtual mobility that was being projected onto stationary buildings was paired with a new mobile architecture produced in train carriages themselves. Trains used by the English royal family in the second half of the century were travelling palaces, as plush and gaudy as the elephant-borne howdah of an Eastern emperor (fig. 2).

In 1902, the Wolverhampton works of the London and North-Western Railway supplied the newly crowned Edward VII with sumptuous railway carriage apartments "in the colonial style", provided with "electric cigar lighters", their satinwood furniture "inlaid with ivory" (Anonymous 1902, p. 854). By 1910, the same engineering works had designed cars with an "observatory opening from a saloon provided with a fireplace with a white marble mantle, five easy chairs, [...] an electric punkah fan, etc." for the Argentinian railways (Anonymous 1910, p. 84). Their "Pullman" carriages for European travel had names inspired by the destinations they connected: Florence, Valencia and Sorento buffet cars, Corunna, Savona and Clementina parlour cars (see Anonymous 1910, pp. 80f.). Such vehicles, shipped over oceans, rolling through jungles, trundling between European capitals, resolved, with apparent ease, the impossible contradiction of rooted domesticity and infinite navigational range. The Vitruvian triad of architectural virtues – commodity, firmness and delight – could be satisfied without the need for an anchoring in place.

Once architecture is understood to exceed the boundary of physical construction and to include the mediation of buildings in magazines, drawings, newspapers or film, and once architectural experience begins to be understood as something concerned with a built world that is not always stationary, a quality of architectural hyper-mobility ensues. Because this characteristic emphasises both previous and future destinations, such movement always speaks of provenance. *Tim Anstey*

Model Private individuals and companies led much of London's reconfiguration and expansion during the nineteenth century. This development was aided by a new role for the architectural profession who were employed as experts in building litigation including cases of property → DISPUTES, structural damage caused during construction and various forms of easement. At the same time the emergence of the architect as a legal expert introduced a new role for architectural models in British courtrooms – a space which in itself became shaped by the requirement to display legal models through the installation of elevators to transport items vertically around a legal complex, such as the new Law Courts on the Strand (built 1874–1883), or the introduction of large turntables in the courtroom itself, enabling models to be raised and rotated at key moments of expert testimony (see Wells 2023).

Architectural models were a key medium through which the private interests of Victorian society were regulated through the legal system. A genre of model-making in its own right, legal models were used as rhetorical aids. In court, they were deployed by architects to persuade a specific perspective of a case to non-experts, and in turn these objects broadened the understanding of architectural practice. Textbooks were even required to support the architects undertaking this particular activity, for instance *The consulting architect. Practical notes on administrative difficulties and disputes* (1886) written by Robert Kerr, one of the founders of the Architectural Association. Lawyers, he advised, "always prefer models to drawings" (Kerr 1886, p. 15). Any model, Kerr argued, should be a highly detailed representation to assist judges and juries to comprehend the

1 Robert Randoll, *General view of Crosby Hall*, 1899, ink on paper. London Archives

buildings and urban settings that they were unlikely to have visited, but were asked to make judgement on.

The fidelity of material depiction in a model was often vital to a legal case. For instance, on 16 January 1899, at the City of London Court when Horatio Davies MP, owner of Pimm's and former Lord Mayor of London, brought action against a real-estate developer intending to demolish an adjoining property in order to construct a much taller building (→ DEMOLITION). In a test of the recently passed London Building Act (1894), the dispute was over who owned which part of a boundary wall. However, the situation was further complicated by the issue that Davies' property was no ordinary building but rather Crosby Hall, the surviving portion of a fifteenth-century mansion built on Bishopsgate in the City of London. A sketch by the topographer Robert Randoll from August 1899 shows the situation in question with Crosby Hall to the left, a disputed wall covered in scaffolding, and to the right, the empty site where the adjoining building once previously stood (fig. 1).

Before the case entered the courtroom, both plaintiff and defendant had appointed architects, respectively T. H. Smith and Donald Campbell, and a legal agreement was drawn up by a third architect, Edward l'Anson, acting as an independent party. Included within the initial agreement was a drawing of the boundary wall that indicated the portions of brick and timber that could be demolished. When the matter reached court, most of the independent legal agreement was no longer disputed. Rather, the issue was which parts of the structure were shared and which were solely the property of Crosby Hall.

Press reports reveal how Davies and his architect, T. H. Smith, advocated to the planning commissioner assigned to the case before trial, arguing that the designated "party structure" in fact belonged within the remit of Crosby Hall and was not a shared wall at a legal boundary (Anonymous 1899, p. 6). Plaintiff and architect claimed instead that a new party wall was required to shore up the existing structure of Crosby Hall. This new boundary wall is evident in the architectural model produced for the courtroom by the model-maker John Thorp, who operated for most of his career from a workshop in Holborn, nearby to the four Inns of Court that form the legal community in London – his specialization in this service was almost certainly a result of his location. A profile on Thorp from a popular magazine described how it was only when he had been engaged as a witness in court that he came to understand the importance of models in legal cases: "no evidence, he realized,

2 *Model of Crosby Hall (1/4 inch scale)*, from John Thorp, *Concerning models of buildings, estates, works, etc. for exhibitions or law cases* (London 1913)

had such weight and influence with a jury" (Soutar 1910, p. 614). On several occasions, Thorp made the distinction between architectural models "to show what a building will be like when completed" as opposed to "diagram models" for legal cases. In Victorian and Edwardian London there was strong demand for legal models. Thorp himself reflected, that "the majority of the models I make are for legal purposes" (Soutar 1910, p. 618).

When the Crosby Hall case proceeded to the courtroom before the district judge, Thorp's model showed the prominent facade of Crosby Hall and the exposed wall structure with each timber stud carefully depicted (fig. 2). Visible in a photograph to the right of the model are additional pieces that could be introduced in court to argue the case and show the layered structures that Smith and Davies proposed should be constructed (and paid for) by the defendant in order to support the existing wall. Smith and Davies won a landmark case. The judge's ruling settled several common-law disputes and established a legal precedent that limited the changes to existing party walls for several years. In a complicated situation involving disputed boundaries to existing buildings, contractual obligations and the three-dimensional party-wall structure, an architectural model provided the judge with a clear depiction of the existing building alongside a representation of the intricacies of the dispute. Mediating between past and present, or existing and proposed, the legal model not only affected individual rulings, but wider legal codes, and in turn the scope of London's development. *Matthew Wells*

Monument, toppled The descriptive term "toppled monument" refers to a statue or commemorative structure, typically located in the urban sphere, that has been forcibly removed, often as a result of public protest, political upheaval or societal reckoning. The act of toppling monuments has historically been part of a symbolic practice, reflecting changing attitudes toward the individuals, events or ideologies the monument represents. While public opinion and media often frame such acts as → VANDALISM, the symbolic and iconographic power of it serves as a cathartic ritual that symbolises renewal for the social groups who are part of the political contexts represented by the contested monument. The act itself often carries a fierce yet optimistic outlook in the revolutionary attempt to dismantle a regime or established ideology. Paradoxically, this phenomenon does not seek to silently erase the insignia of former ruling powers from the cityscape, but transforms their destruction into a visible performative act, thus highlighting the performer's claim to reinterpret history (→ DISPOSSESSION, → POLITICAL ICONOGRAPHY).

This iconoclastic practice has gained prominence in recent decades, particularly during activist movements critically addressing colonialism, systemic racism and historical injustices. Media and technological advancements have further amplified the mobility of images (→ IMAGE VEHICLE) and therefore their visibility, allowing global audiences to witness the symbolic undoing of power through the toppling of monuments. The resulting volatile mediality of this specific urban iconography makes it a subject matter to research interested not only in the architectural concept of monumentality and the physical destruction of monuments as memorial architectures; due to its deconstructive gesture, this specific case of iconoclasm can also be considered as a phenomenon of architectural provenance with far-reaching sociopolitical impact.

While the general meaning of the term "monument" – and therefore of "monumentality" – derived from the Latin word *monere* (to remind), can refer to all sorts of objects considered as documents testifying earlier historic periods or cultural episodes, the much more specific phrase "toppled monument" evokes the image of a sculpture being visibly damaged or pulled off its static designated place, for example, from atop a pedestal. Beyond their political and ideological implications, monuments hold established cultural meanings and functions that contribute to the construction of cultural identity and

→ COLLECTIVE MEMORY. On the other hand, monumentality refers to the quality or state of a built structure encompassing characteristics such as grandeur, durability and social values like cultural significance. For example, the American architect Louis Kahn defines monumentality as "a spiritual quality inherent in a structure which conveys the feeling of its eternity, that it cannot be added to or changed" (Kahn 1944, p. 78). In his remark, the architect stresses the idea that monumentality is the interplay between the tangible (physical structure, materiality, dimensions) and the intangible (cultural, historical and emotional resonance) that makes an object a focal point of collective significance. It is exactly this conglomerate of material and ideological meaning that is the target of critique and physical attacks. Yet, the symbolic connotation embodied by a monument is by no means static, just as "eternity" itself – the very concept it seeks to embody – is not static, but rather in conflict with the dynamic progression of time, in which historical change and movement occurs. Monuments therefore often carry a formal claim to perpetuity, even when the political, social or emotional conditions that made their construction possible are no longer present.

Historically, the modern understanding of monuments was profoundly shaped by the Austrian art historian Alois Riegl, whose 1903 essay *Der moderne Denkmalkultus* (The modern cult of monuments) remains foundational for the definition of the term. Amidst a period of growing urbanisation, industrialisation and rising nationalism in late-nineteenth- and early-twentieth-century Europe, Riegl's tenure as General Conservator of the Central Commission for the Preservation of Artistic and Historical Monuments in Vienna in 1902 gave him a platform to influence and rethink → PRESERVATION practices. In his widely referenced essay, Riegl defined a monument as "a work of man erected for the specific purpose of keeping particular human deeds or destinies (or a complex accumulation thereof) alive and present in the consciousness of future generations" (Riegl 1903, p. 1). In the heart of his influential theory of monuments lies the distinction between "*gewollte Denkmäler*" (intentional monuments), those deliberately created to commemorate events or individuals, and "*ungewollte Denkmäler*" (unintentional monuments), structures that acquire commemorative value over time due to their age, historical significance or artistic merit. Interestingly, the very roots of monument preservation are deeply tied to destruction, most notably during the French Revolution, when statues, buildings and artworks were defaced or destroyed to eliminate aristocratic insignia from the urban landscapes. Thus, the loss of cultural → HERITAGE in eighteenth-century France led to the establishment of institutions like the Commision des Monuments Historiques in 1837, which laid the groundwork for the standardisation of preservation practices that would later be systematically formalised for modern requirements. In some cases, conservation practices contribute to the controversy surrounding monument toppling, as heritage preservation is often perceived as an authoritarian institution that determines what is worth protecting, especially when the preserved objects embody contentious histories or come into conflict with contemporary values. This tension arises particularly when the monuments in question were originally erected to honor individuals or ideologies now recognised as oppressive, such as Confederate statues in the US or statues of colonial figures in former colonies.

The incidents of toppled monuments draw attention not only to the conservational definitions established in the early twentieth century, but also, more significantly even, to the observation that at the same time the monument's rigid heroism and understated pretentiousness rendered it an outdated relic, ultimately dismissed as an obsolete artistic form. This critical stance paved the way for sculptural and architectural theories that sought to rethink and redefine monumental symbolism (→ COUNTER-MONUMENT), while the toppling of monuments, within the context of a broader social critique of monumentality, emerged as a

1 *The fall of the Saddam Hussein Monument on Firdos Square, Baghdad*, 9 April 2003. Photographer unknown

symbolic form of protest. Robert Musil's witty remark that "the most striking thing about monuments is that one does not notice them" (Musil 1927, p. 4) is particularly interesting as it reveals a contradiction in the perception of monuments. While they are frequently overlooked in the routines of everyday life, there is a striking exception to their invisibility – the moment, in which a monument is being toppled. In these instances, monuments are thrust into the centre of public attention becoming intensely charged symbols of change.

This complex phenomenon that transcends the physical act of destruction, is a highly mediated and performative practice of staged politics. The toppling of Saddam Hussein's statue in Baghdad on 9 April 2003, for example, marks an interplay between the act of toppling and its visual representation (fig. 1). While the event was orchestrated by US forces and deceptively framed in the media as a popular uprising of the Iraqi people, its significance lies in the powerful images broadcasted globally. These depictions of the event, rather than the act itself, conveyed the dismantling of a regime and marked a transitional moment in history. Like similar acts of iconoclasm – such as the fall of communist monuments after the Soviet Union's collapse – those events follow ritualised patterns, symbolically rooted in ancient practices of *damnatio memoriae* and executions in effigy (see Fleckner 2011). With media coverage amplifying their meaning, localised actions are being transformed into global narratives. The visual representation of the act or the exhibition of → FRAGMENTS of monuments become the primary medium for communicating the power shift, with each image encapsulating the symbolic destruction, the participation of the masses and the void left behind in the urban landscape as a metaphor for change (→ LACUNA, → RUIN).

While the majority of monument removals are issued by authorities, the iconography of toppling remains significant. Far from being a purely impulsive gesture or vandalism, such acts are emblematic of contemporary critiques of power and serve as deliberate challenges to institutionalised narratives and legacies, making this phenomenon acutely relevant in all kinds of current forms of social protest. *Elif Akyüz*

Movables A new civil code became law across the First French Empire as Napoleon Bonaparte crowned himself emperor in 1804. Written in plain language, the code was to be read by the population and then applied. It consisted of three books: *Of persons*, *Of property, and the different modifications of property*, and *Of the different modes of acquiring property*. While the code governed many realms of life in the French-speaking world, it showed a particular interest in property and its provenance: a mere 515 articles governed persons, but 1,766 concerned property and its → ACQUISITION. Architectural projects adhered especially to articles in books two and three. Book two begins: "*Tous les biens sont meubles ou immeubles*" (All property is movable or immovable) (*Code civil des Français*, Paris 1804, vol. 2, I, 516).

Inherited from Middle French (*immeuble*), with its origins in Latin (*immobilis*) and Old French (*immoble*), immovables are a class of property consisting of land and buildings, but also of "crops hanging by the roots", livestock "attached to the farm", "pipes […] in a house", "beasts required for agricultural purposes", "seeds", "pigeons", "rabbits", "bee-hives", "fish in ponds", "straw and manure" and any statue "placed in a niche formed expressly to receive it" (*Code civil des Français*, vol. 2, I, 520–525). This last example makes the point most clear: objects are not only defined by their nature, but their potential, not only by their provenance, but by projection.

Napoleon loved his code. Paintings and etchings depict him writing it by candlelight, deliberating its contents around a table, presenting it to the empress and noting down its articles while sitting atop a cloud. From exile in the middle of the South Atlantic Ocean, Napoleon mused on the significance of the document, drafted over four months in 1801 and introduced into law three years later: "My real glory is not the forty battles I won [...]. What nothing will destroy, what will live forever, is my Civil Code" (Montholon 1847, vol. 1, p. 401). The code would indeed prove influential, transforming legal frameworks across Europe, Central and South America, Japan and the state of Louisiana. It was also popular: celebrated by *The New York Times* some ninety years after its drafting as "esteemed", "trustworthy" and "intelligible" (Anonymous 1895).

1 *Movables of the Maison du Peuple*, Jette, Belgium, 1985. Photographer unknown

A building may be an immovable, but buildings can also be on the move. Victor Horta's Maison du Peuple in Brusssels, for example, designed by a pioneer of art nouveau at its height, turned industrial → MATERIALS into an architectural masterpiece and declared beauty as a right for the working class. Rumblings of its → DEMOLITION were first reported in the autumn of 1963 and by January 1964, the building was definitely condemned, as reported in the Belgian press. This condemnation corresponded with a change in definition – from immovable to movables, from building to parts.

What was intended to take forty-five days took ten months: April was for coordination between the various contractors; May revealed the building to the sky and the sounds of demolition to neighbours; June distinguished heritage from history; in July, the main hall came down; August was for holidays; September for building parts to be transported off-site and materials burned on-site; October was ruled by arguments between contractors; in November, the building collapsed; December saw the final stones removed, and by January, the five-storey building was a hole in the ground (→ LACUNA). The Maison du Peuple was reduced to → FRAGMENTS in → STORAGE by the end of February 1966 (fig. 1).

If the *Code Napoléon* defines immovables by what they are, then it defines movables by what they are not: movables are "not fixed on piles", not fastened by "plaster, lime, or cement", not yet "employed by the artificer" in a building (*Code civil des Français*, vol. 2, 519–532). Like the code that defined them as such, the Maison du Peuple movables enjoyed a newfound potential for circulation. Pieces were sent to New York, Munich, Philadelphia, Baltimore, Berlin and Turin, while several architectural projects aimed to reappropriate the pieces into new forms around Belgium. Most plans for movement never materialised. Instead, the pieces of the Maison du Peuple, 340 tonnes of material in total, disappeared to disparate locations in Brussels. For years, remnants of Horta's masterpiece laid dormant in the cellar of the Saint-Gilles town hall, the backyard of the Horta

Museum, a → CONCRETE frame in a royal park and in an underground metro station at the corner of Chaussée de Waterloo and Rue du Lycée. Twelve truckloads of materials were once transferred to a museum. A number of stone and iron pieces simply sunk into the swamp-like field where they were stored. Countless parts were looted from open storage in vacant lots. And in 1983, 70 tonnes of iron elements were smelted in Japan. Even if the definition of movables proved practical for salvaging, it proved a problem for saving. The building's undone state also excluded it from formal protection by the cultural → HERITAGE department, who required that an object be designated immovable property, even before considering its merits as heritage. The movables of the Maison du Peuple, which they stated had "lost all connection with the ground on which they were dismantled" were unable to be classified unless "reinserted in a construction" (Delhaye 1982). And so began the task of translating movables back into immovables – consolidation, the only metric of success. *Alena Beth Rieger*

Network In architecture, a network emerges when reduction is not possible. When we perform reductions, we assume that one thing can be reduced to another, or one → ACTOR to another. For instance, if we believe that society contains architecture and architecture can be reduced to society or social factors, we start to believe that we "know" something, that there are equivalences, that there are simple deductions, that there is some order in advance (fig. 1).

However, reduction is not productive because it shows less of the world or of experience. The opposite principle of irreduction claims that nothing can be reduced to anything else (see Latour 1988). Things are linked together symmetrically; they form knots, bodies, machines and groups. Since there are no "natural" equivalences, the kind of ties that hold things together can only be of one kind: groping, testing, translating. When we accept the principle of irreducibility, we admit that there is nothing more than trials of strength

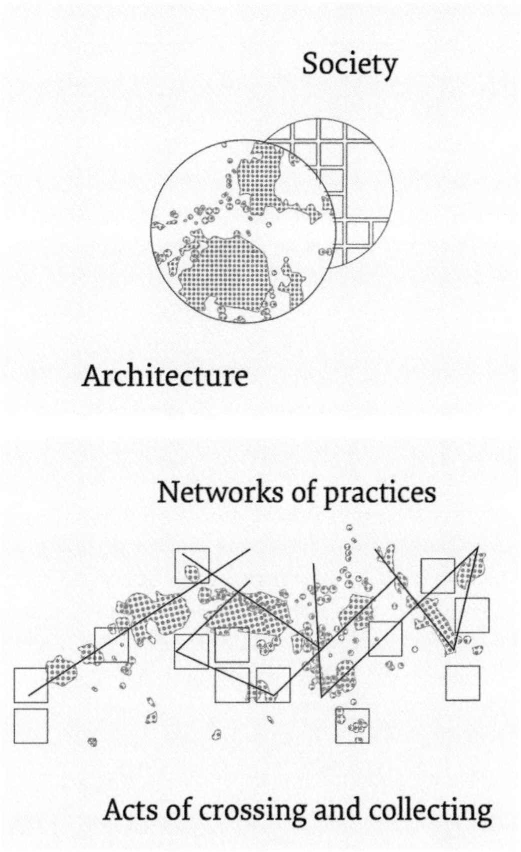

1 *Diagram illustrating the divide between architecture and society, and the alternative – the network of architectural practice.* Illustration: Alexandra Arènes, 2022

and weakness, work to be done, gestures. If "we choose the principle of irreduction, we discover *intertwined networks* which sometimes join together but may interweave with each other without touching for centuries" (Latour 1988, pp. 190f.).

The notion of network helps us understand how so few actors manage to cover the world; for instance, telephone or meteorological networks could cover the entire world. A network "indicates that resources are concentrated in a few places – the knots and the nodes – which are connected with one another – the links and the mesh: these connections transform the scattered resources into a net that may seem to extend everywhere" (Latour 1987, p. 180).

In the field of architecture and architectural research, sustaining a reductivist perspective would also mean believing that there are only a few architects, planners, or → PRESERVATION experts working, debating and sharing ideas because they are unique, talented, "superhuman". Yet, how often do we witness giants, starchitects (→ CELEBRITY) expounding ideas in the world of architecture, making groundbreaking discoveries? Never. In fact, in reality, there is a network that prolongs their work. There are other actors and missing masses, who help them or divert them. Acknowledging this fact implies expanding the provenance of architecture beyond individual authors, owners and stakeholders (→ AUTHORSHIP). Tracing architecture in the making allows us to witness thousands of designers at work, crowds of engineers, contractors, developers and users all enrolled into a building project as well as thousands of nonhuman participants mobilised in architecture making (→ MATERIALS, technologies, → MODELS, codes, skills, different types of expertise). Take some well-known Office for Metropolitan Architecture (OMA) buildings as example: the Casa da Música in Porto is the result of a long and sophisticated network of collaboration between the local architectural firm ANC Architects and OMA; the CCTV Tower in Beijing is the product of a large and versatile network of collaboration between the structural engineers of the Arup Group in London, designers from OMA, new structural technologies, value engineers and local stakeholders (fig. 2).

The concepts of these buildings were shaped by the entire networks of participants and the inputs they produced gradually altered the design. Yet, only a few of these actors get designated as "heroic" geniuses (Till 2009, p. 172), advancing design ideas, as bright stars in the exclusive Pritzker Prize galaxy. They are seen as having "ideas" that are diffused into society. Instead of focusing on the few exclusive architects, we can engage in tracing the networks of architecture making – following for instance the work of OMA architects, collaborators and foam models, not of one big Pritzker Prize mind (see Yaneva 2009a and 2009b); or tracing the work of Kuma Kengo's practice, collaborators and renderings, not of one talented star architect – to unpack the complex realities of architecture in action (see Houdart and Chihiro 2009).

Network points to a relational understanding of reality and represents one way of grasping architectural provenance as the complex relationships that unfold in the trajectories of buildings. If instead of drawing straight causal explanations that sustain asymmetries between cause and effect, mind and world, society and architecture, we follow the architectural networks to witness what they capture in their meshes and what escapes them, we will end up embracing a relational view. Tracing architectural networks with care, caution and respect to all participants, we can witness buildings that are not made by powerful minds (star architects, demiurges, those powerful "Gods"), but architecture that emerges, and gains provenance, as it traces many intricate and hesitant relationships with materials and technologies, skills, bodies and institutions.

Capturing architectural networks, how designers handle models, sketches and software, how engineers make calculations, and how they all attribute meaning to their actions, how they negotiate and form different groupings, will lead us to understand design as a process of enacting

2 Rem Koolhaas and Ole Scheeren (OMA) with Cecil Balmond (Arup Group), *CCTV Tower in its urban network*, 2004–2008, Beijing. Photo: Uwe Fleckner 2013

the social. Follow these long, contingent and painstaking processes of design, → RENOVATION, refurbishment and you will find out that there are not two separate worlds: a possible behind the real, a symbolic realm behind the objective, or a society behind architecture. There is no built content on one side, and, at a cosmic distance, a social context on the other that would explain its provenance. We will rather witness how a design (or renovation) process can modify the elements that contextualise it, triggering contextual mutations; how it becomes reminiscent to a complex ecology (see Latour and Yaneva 2008). Context is variable, moving, evolving and changing along with the various design objects themselves; context is made of the many dimensions that impinge at every stage on the development of a project. In the heat of the action, everything is fluid, all artificial divides are redistributed, all static categories collapse and all we witness is a network made of heterogeneous stuff: models, architects, zoning regulations, mayors, public money, techniques of calculating construction budgets, → HERITAGE organisations and a vast array of materials. That is a moment when the architectural and the social elements are fluid and mutually define each other – a unique instant when all redistributions are possible, and any version of building provenance can be crafted. *Albena Yaneva*

Obsolescence After operating continuously from Marienlyst in Oslo since 1941, the Norwegian public broadcaster, Norsk rikskringkasting (NRK), sold its properties to an investment company in 2020 for 3.8 billion kroner, transferring the ownership of a modern monument to a private developer for reprogramming. Kringkastingshuset, the broadcasting building, was built between 1938 and 1950 and is arguably the most important work by the prolific Norwegian architect Nils Holter (1899–1995). It is one of the country's most familiar public institutions and an invaluable piece of modernist → HERITAGE and surprisingly overlooked in the historiography of modern architecture (fig. 1).

Through the 1930s, representatives for the Norwegian Broadcasting Corporation conducted a series of study trips across Europe that would directly influence the design of the building. Today one of the most radical building typologies of the twentieth century is largely reckoned obsolete and subjected to → TRANSFORMATION.

Following a pattern of state interventionism in the 1930s, public radio largely appeared as the nationalisation of private initiatives. In Norway this happened through the state purchase of Kringkastingsselskapet AS in 1933. Anxiety around foreign influence hurried the development of the early national radio networks and from around 1930, funds were invested in the creation of the first European broadcasting buildings, formalising the status of radio stations as public institutions proper. Radio buildings appeared throughout Europe during a short time span. Germany, Holland, the United Kingdom, Switzerland and Czechoslovakia all completed their first purpose-built studio buildings from 1929 to 1933. Effectively a combination of monumental public architecture and highly complex technical infrastructure, radio buildings combined state of the art acoustics with the completely novel science of broadcasting technology.

A few of these broadcasting buildings still perform their original function as the home of radio stations. Hans Poelzig's groundbreaking Haus des Rundfunks in Berlin (1929–1931) is currently the home of the Rundfunk Berlin-

1 Nils Holter, *Kringkastingshuset*, 1938–1950, Oslo. Photo: Leif Krohn Ørnelund, 1949

2 Nils Holter, *Kringkastingshuset, Large Music Studio*, 1938–1950, Oslo. Photo: Teigen Fotoatelier, 1950

Brandenburg. The BBC's Broadcasting House in London (1928–1932), designed by George Val Myer and engineer Marmaduke T. Tudsbury, was almost immediately considered too small and followed by new property → ACQUISITIONS for studios. Yet the original building still serves as the BBC headquarters. However, many of these architectural gems have been acquired by private developers for transformation; sold by the buildings' original occupiers for not meeting new technical standards, yet retained for their beautiful architecture and exquisite concert halls. The Funkhaus Berlin-Nalepastraße, designed by Franz Ehrlich, was completed in 1951 as the home of the Rundfunk der DDR in East Berlin. After the collapse of the Berlin Wall, it was used as an informal dance club; it is currently a commercial cultural venue and also used for large-scale concerts. The Radiostudio Brunnenhoff in Zurich, designed for the Swiss Broadcasting Corporation by Otto Dürr and completed in 1933, was the first purpose-built radio building in Switzerland. The complex was extended in several phases, including by Max Bill in 1967. It is currently being transformed into a mixed-use facility, with a secondary school and a school for music. Maison de la Radio in Brussels, also known as the Flagey Building, designed by Joseph Diongre (1935–1938), was purchased by a conglomerate of thirty Belgian companies in 1998 and has been restored and transformed to a cultural centre with concert halls under the slogan "Combine work, lifestyle and culture in one trendy location" (→ RESTORATION). Due to political unrest in Vienna in the late 1930s, the Funkhaus Wien is attributed to several different architects: Heinrich Schmid, Hermann Aichinger and Clemenz Holzmeister. It was completed in 1939, after the Nazi occupation of Austria, yet was visited several times by representatives for the Norwegian NRK and pointed out by architect Nils Holter as one of his most important → PRECEDENTS for the broadcasting building in Oslo. In 2018, it was acquired by the private Rhomberg group and is planned for redevelopment as an apartment building; currently, it is in temporary use by the organisation Never At Home, which provides temporary spaces for artists. Radiohuset in Copenhagen, designed by Vilhelm Lauritsen as headquarters for the Danish Statsradiofonien and completed in 1945, has been hosting the Royal Danish Music Academy since 2006. The transformation work was done by Lauritsen's office.

The studios of the original broadcasting buildings were elaborately designed to affect the sound before it reached the microphone (fig. 2). As the digital → POSTPRODUCTION of sound became more sophisticated and less place-consuming, the requirements of the recording studios themselves became less consequential for the quality of the broadcast. Daniel M. Abramson traces the architectural consequences of buildings that have seemingly become superfluous back to market economy rationales: "Obsolescence's emphasis on measurable performance and quantifiable value applies fundamentally economic thinking to the built environment" (Abramson 2016, p. 6). However, the vacating of the iconic broadcasting buildings by their original clients is perhaps less connected to technical requirements than to ideology and to a professed need for more contemporary headquarters, beyond what is today deemed an obsolete architectural state of the art. Jørgen Tandberg

Occupation The second of April, 1940 proved an unlucky date to open Norway's first museum of architecture (fig. 1). Nazi Germany invaded Norway precisely one week later, on 9 April 1940, and by early June, the occupation was total. The regime enforced oppressive systems and policies, installed a puppet government and stationed hundreds of thousands of soldiers in the country. They seized numerous properties, including the brand-new municipal office building housing the nascent museum.

An Oslo newspaper described the building at Roald Amundsens gate 4, colloquially referred to as R.A.4, as "the modern house with the hyper-modern name" (Anonymous 1938). It was designed by architects Blakstad & Munthe-Kaas in 1937 and purchased by the municipality in 1938 to house the technical administration. Spatial allocation proved contentious from the outset; even the basement space was in demand. The Water and Sewage Division coveted 400 square metres for → ARCHIVES and → STORAGE; the City Architect wanted 140 square metres for their extensive flag collection; an external group campaigned for a public aquarium. After intense disputes, Chief Planning Officer Harald Hals

1 *German troops marching in Roald Amundsens gate*, May 1940, with Oslo City Hall under construction. Photo: Adolf Beck

(1876–1959) of the Planning Division emerged triumphant. He secured the basement hall for his long-standing ambition: to establish an architecture museum.

The Planning Division's vast collection of → ARCHITECTURAL DRAWINGS, maps, prints, → PHOTOGRAPHY and models was the result of in-house production and, since 1932, mirrored a vigorous → ACQUISITION practice. Hals aspired to ensemble as many models as possible, wishing to present what Oslo had been, was and could become. The museum in R.A.4 was envisioned as an arsenal of architectural ideas to source and learn from – a collection of "possibles" in every sense (→ COLLECTING). Even the unbuilt represented unfulfilled promises or potential.

R.A.4's 700-square-metre basement hall was originally designed for a dinner club. Its sloping floor, a byproduct of the movie theatre located directly above, demanded special furnishing to fit its new occupants. Steps and railings were installed to let visitors move smoothly through the space. Hals' famous → MODEL of the General Plan for Oslo was the exhibition's central piece, installed in a depression in the floor so it could be studied from above – a patient in an operating theatre. The 35-square-metre giant in painted plaster was the pride of the Planning Division, continuously expanded and changed. Its modular structure of 108 exchangeable pieces made it possible to revise or test out different urban visions through versions of the same quadrant.

Abrupt changes in ownership and occupancy accentuate the instability of cultural meaning. Meaning can mutate, intensify or lessen, be appropriated or domesticated, be imposed or stolen (→ THEFT). To occupy a site or structure of any scale is to give it meaning. To do so by force is to dispel another. The German occupation took Norway by surprise. It turned familiar sites strange, hostile, even perilous to those infringed upon. It also closed the building to the public. When the *Luftgaukommando* requisitioned R.A.4. in October 1940, exiling the Planning Division, it separated the collection from its custodians. Aided by the newly acquired museum status, the planners successfully negotiated to preserve the collection in place, even if that space was used for storage. But the museum never recovered from the occupation.

Occupation leaves traces. Five years, one month and six days after its inauguration, the museum officially (though not in practice) reopened on the Norwegian Victory Day, 8 May 1945. During the occupation, the models and drawings attesting to Oslo's erection were buried under the occupant's military maps – perhaps representations of the same structures. Its contents were battered and worn. After regaining entry, Hals continued his inexorable acquisitions and worked fervently to revivify the basement as a public institution. The models were cleansed, the furnishing was updated and funds were secured for improving the labyrinthine entrance. Nothing helped. The long *in-situ* slumber and the absence of stewards and visitors, prevented the museum from taking root. The once-treasured basement became increasingly impractical and unpopular and were accessible only by special appointment. The Planning Division vacated R.A.4 around 1951, leaving the objects behind in a move that recast → EXHIBITION as storage. The bulk of the material fell into oblivion and was dispersed two decades later. But for one week in April 1940, the basement was occupied by displays of buildings past and present, of visions of futures past. *Ingrid Dobloug Roede*

Palimpsest A palimpsest, from the ancient Greek word παλίμψηστος (scratched off), originally referred to a manuscript page in which the original text was removed from the parchment or papyrus by scratching, scraping or other cleaning processes, usually for economic reasons. The term was later extended to include scripts that were reapplied over the lost letters. Palimpsests are an important source for many historical disciplines, especially for the history of religion and philosophy, as a good deal of the erased texts can be made completely or partially legible again using various technical measures. In modern times, however, the term has also become established as a metaphor that illustrates, for example, the hidden layers of the human psyche in which, according to Sigmund Freud, superficially imperceptible but nevertheless sustainable traces of memory have been inscribed (see Freud 1925). The term can also be used to elucidate Aby Warburg's understanding of history, for example his concept of → AFTERLIFE or the concept of the so-called *Leidschatz* (treasury of human suffering), which explains how painful experiences become engraved in the → COLLECTIVE MEMORY (see Fleckner 1998, pp. 10ff. and p. 254). Nowadays, the concept of the palimpsest is also used in other areas such as literary intertextuality or some artistic practices of reshaping historical materials.

From a provenance-historical perspective, it can also be useful to apply the term of the palimpsest to certain architectural phenomena (see Huyssen 2003; Capdevila-Werning 2015). Individual buildings or larger urban contexts can take on the character of palimpsests if they "overwrite" earlier architectures in such a way that these are partially or – in rare cases – even completely preserved. Here, a distinction must be made between buildings where the traces of previous buildings are openly visible, for example as foundations or remains of masonry or in the form of → RUINS, and those where such traces have been made visible again through archaeological measures.

Historical examples of architectural palimpsests include many buildings with a very long and *mis-en-abyme*-like construction history. The church of St Maria im Kapitol in Cologne, for example, was built in the Middle Ages over the foundations of a Roman temple dedicated to the Capitoline Triad in such a way that not only the name, but also some remains of the walls and initially even the basic form of the previous building were preserved. The archaeological vestiges of various construction phases of the former royal palace were also uncovered during the → RENOVATION of the Louvre in Paris in 1981–1999 by the American-Chinese architect Ieoh Ming Pei and thus incorporated into the museum display (see Fleckner 1992). Even more radical was British architect David Chipperfield's 1999–2009 revitalisation of the Neues Museum in Berlin as a *lieu de mémoire* preserving various historical layers of the building, especially extensive traces of its considerable → WAR damage (see Capdevila-Werning 2015, pp. 211ff.). Iraqi-British architect Zaha Hadid, on the other hand, created an urban landscape in her construction of the Dongdaemun Design Plaza in Seoul in 2007–2014, in which the remains of historical buildings from the Joseon dynasty were incorporated in some places, occasionally visible through glass floors.

The so-called *Sozialpalast* (Social Palace) in Berlin provides us with a rare example of an intact entire building that has been preserved despite being completely built over and has thus become a palimpsest of different historical layers (fig. 1). In 1973–1977, the architect Jürgen Sawade erected three gigantic cubes as part of a social housing programme and used them to create over five hundred residential units. Executed entirely in → CONCRETE, one of the cubes extends over a high-rise bunker built there by Russian forced labourers at the end of the Second World War. The bunker's raw, even aggressive block is swallowed up by the new structure in an imposing gesture, without itself undergoing a → TRANSFORMATION. Even though the inside of the bunker was modernised in the 1980s and initially planned to be used for civil defence and later functioned as a memorial, event and exhibition venue, it still primarily serves as a testimony to the past. In addition, some parts of the bunker are repeatedly covered with → GRAFFITI by the many young people who live there, most of whom have a migrant background (→ RESIDENTS), so that traces of the current social reality are also inscribed in the ensemble of the listed palimpsest of bunker and apartment building as a further layer of sediment (→ INSCRIPTION).

As with the possibility of re-reading "lost" ancient manuscripts, architectural palimpsests also serve as important documents of a history that is not understood as a distant, completed event, but – on the contrary – is to be anchored as a still vital issue in the memory of a living present. The intertextual relationship between

1 Jürgen Sawade, *Pallasseum (so-called Sozialpalast)*, 1973–1977, integrating the Bunker Pallasstraße 1943–1945, Berlin. Photo: Uwe Fleckner, 2025

erased and rewritten scriptures, the interfering archaeological relationship between sediment and surface, can thus be transferred to the interarchitectural relationship between buildings in an enlightening way. The associated overlapping of different political, social or cultural layers of meaning is one of the essential characteristics of the provenance history of architecture. *Uwe Fleckner*

Pasticcio In the monument court of Sir John Soane's London house, a slender 23-foot column rises toward the sky (fig. 1). Named *Pasticcio* by Soane himself, this vertical assemblage erected in 1818 seems at first glance to defy gravity and logic. The eye follows its ascent: from a Moroccan capital with carved garlands and rosettes at its base, through a succession of → FRAGMENTS that span centuries and cross continents. Authentic Roman antiquities rest alongside neo-classical fragments next to meticulous → PLASTER CASTS and freshly carved stone → ELEMENTS, their edges sometimes touching, sometimes separated by subtle transitions. The stack culminates in a work by Soane himself, a finial topped with a pineapple – traditional symbol of hospitality – that punctuates the vertical journey with a flourish of whimsy. This early nineteenth-century architectural totem pole served as the symbolic pivot around which Soane's Museum was meant to revolve, representing the history of architecture (see Soane 1830, p. 29).

For eighty years this architectural construction stood in Soane's courtyard. In 1896, deemed structurally unsafe, it was dismantled and its pieces placed in → STORAGE. The column's significance might have diminished had it not been for a meticulous → RECONSTRUCTION effort beginning in 1987 and completed in 2004. Specialists studied archival drawings, examined surviving pieces and recreated missing elements. The rebuilt *Pasticcio* now presents visitors with an additional temporal layer: a → RESTORATION that itself constitutes a commentary on → AUTHENTICITY and the transmission of architectural knowledge. This reconstruction process adds another dimension to the provenance history of each fragment: original antiquities with their own archaeological lineage, plaster casts that functioned as educational surrogates and modern reproductions all now coexist in a structure that itself possesses a complex institutional biography.

Soane's column represents more than a decorative folly; it embodies a specific approach to architectural collection and display (→ COLLECTING). Each fragment maintains its distinct identity while participating in a new compositional order. The elements do not attempt to conceal their disparate origins – rather, their visible junctures generate the composition's intellectual and aesthetic significance. Unlike architectural trophy displays, *Pasticcio* derives meaning from relationships between elements, through the deliberate organisation of formal and historical contrasts. As a collector, Soane engaged in the complex networks of early nineteenth-century antiquities → ACQUISITION, where excavated fragments circulated through commercial channels, diplomatic exchanges and private collections (see Boucher 2024). His *Pasticcio* reflects this circulatory economy of architectural elements, displaying both the breadth of his collection and his conceptual approach to architectural history.

The term "pasticcio", from the Italian word for "paste" or "medley", transports the principle of culinary composition – the artful combination of diverse ingredients – into architectural discourse. This concept of deliberate heterogeneity migrated across disciplines: in baroque musical practice, composers assembled arias and movements from various sources into new theatrical works; in Renaissance and baroque painting, artists produced works that consciously merged stylistic elements from multiple masters. Within architecture, pasticcio manifests as compositions where fragments and references from disparate historical periods and stylistic languages coexist in productive tension (→ BRICOLAGE), challenging conventional understandings of unity and authenticity.

The phenomenon of architectural pasticcio manifests across multiple historical periods and at vastly different scales. While Soane's column represents a concentrated, vertical expression of the principle, pasticcio can equally serve as the governing logic for entire architectural complexes. What stands as a singular element in London would, a century later, expand to the scale of an estate in California.

1 John Soane, *"Pasticcio" in the Monument Court*, 1818, rebuilt 2004. Sir John Soane's Museum, London. Unknown photographer

William Randolph Hearst's San Simeon estate (1919–1947), designed by Julia Morgan, represents a significant manifestation of architectural pasticcio in the modern era. Here, what might elsewhere be confined to a detail or ornamental feature becomes the conceptual foundation for an entire built landscape. Unlike works primarily employing → SPOLIA (which emphasise the material authenticity and historical continuity of reused elements), Hearst Castle embodies pasticcio's methodological approach through deliberate juxtaposition of disparate elements at a monumental scale. The west facade of the Casa Grande exemplifies this approach (fig. 2).

The composition appears as a deliberate cut-and-paste assemblage where ornamental and architectural elements accumulate in dense decorative nodes that distinctly separate themselves from the building's plain surfaces. Gothic portal elements, Renaissance-inspired balustrades, medieval sculptural figures and colourful Moorish-influenced tile work all coexist within a single architectural plane. The facade resists stylistic categorisation – variously described by scholars as Spanish Colonial, baroque, Gothic or Renaissance – because pasticcio inherently challenges such taxonomic certainties. The diverse provenances of these elements – some authentic Spanish antiquities acquired through international art dealers, others meticulous → FACSIMILES made by Californian craftsmen based on photographic documentation of European originals – form a complex web of transatlantic exchanges, commercial transactions and cultural translations.

Morgan's approach was fundamentally additive; an attitude that transcends simple appropriation and demands multifaceted expertise. The pasticcio approach, far from requiring minimal skill, demanded that Morgan functioned simultaneously as artist, scholar, designer and decorator in her orchestration of disparate architectural elements (see Hewitt 1990, p. 40). The resulting architecture emerges as a rich tapestry of references and reimaginations; a dreamlike architectural landscape where different historical moments and geographical origins converge in a new spatial reality. What distinguishes pasticcio from conventional eclecticism is its deliberate engagement with the productive contradictions between its constituent elements.

While eclecticism often seeks to harmonise diverse stylistic influences into a cohesive whole, pasticcio tends to foreground the juxtapositions and disjunctions between its fragments, deriving meaning precisely from these points of contrast. This compositional approach of pasticcio shares fundamental principles with the modern artistic technique of collage, both operating through strategic juxtaposition of heterogeneous elements to generate new semantic fields. The visible dissonance between individual → COMPONENTS and their deliberate constellation constitute the primary methodology through which both collage and pasticcio establish meaning. Within this framework, the apparent contradiction between new and old dissolves; rather than opposing one another, these temporal dimensions become inextricably and productively intertwined.

The distinction from spolia is equally significant and indeed foundational to the conceptual framework of pasticcio: spolia practices emphasise the material authenticity and historical continuity of reused elements, with each fragment carrying its original context as part of its significance (→ FRAGMENT, → REUSE). Pasticcio, by contrast, operates more freely with both original and reproduced elements, prioritising the new

2 Julia Morgan, *Hearst Castle's Casa Grande*, 1919–1947, San Simeon, California. Photo: Tilman Walther, 2023

semantic relationships generated through creative juxtaposition over the provenance of individual components. While spolia practices often raise questions about cultural patrimony and rightful ownership, pasticcio complicates these debates by placing equal value on authentic fragments and their reproductions, suggesting a more fluid approach to questions of cultural property and historical authenticity.

The methodological logic of pasticcio employs specific compositional strategies: juxtaposition rather than transition, accumulation rather than selection and assertion of difference rather than synthesis. Its heterogeneity serves a conceptual purpose beyond mere decoration, creating a narrative space where multiple historical and stylistic references coexist. Pasticcio thus not only describes a compositional strategy but also offers a conceptual framework for understanding how architectural elements circulate, transform and generate new meanings as they move through time, space and cultural contexts (→ IMAGE VEHICLE).

At its theoretical core, pasticcio occupies an ambiguous position between reverence and irreverence and operates at the intersection of → PRESERVATION and invention. By embracing multiple temporalities and stylistic languages, it resists easy categorisation, slipping between the poles of historical fidelity and creative audacity. In the broader context of provenance studies, pasticcio represents a particularly complex case where the histories of acquisition, transportation, reproduction and recontextualisation generate a dense network of relationships that challenge conventional understandings of origin and authenticity.

When Sir John Soane left instructions in his 1833 Act of Parliament that his house and museum should be kept and maintained "as nearly as circumstances will admit in the state" (Richardson and Stevens 2000, p. 154), he inadvertently highlighted this paradox: the *Pasticcio*, itself a deliberate assemblage of dislocated fragments, was meant to be preserved intact, fixed in its carefully orchestrated state of productive contradiction. *Nina Lucia Groß*

Patina At 3.30 a.m. on 20 February 2020, a Somali man in his early twenties smashed the south-western window of Dombås Church and flung a lit, petroleum-infused garment into the room, igniting a devastating → FIRE that would consume most of the church interior. While the local fire department began the almost impossible task to save the church from total destruction, the man drove 43 kilometres further down the Gudbrandsdalen Valley to Sel Church where he was spotted and caught before continuing his destructive mission. As the fire department gained control of the situation at Dombås, rumours of the arsonist's nationality and religion proliferated, causing local uproar and the immediate closing down of the local newspaper's online comments sections. The young man, having fled from war-torn Somalia in 2015 and been granted residency in Norway, testified in court that his act was triggered by the acquittal of the man from the right-wing organization SIAN who, on 16 November 2019, set the Quran on fire during an anti-Islamic demonstration in Kristiansand. The arsonist was sentenced to four years and two months in prison, reduced from the prosecutor's recommendation due to the trauma he had suffered in Somalia.

When entering the church in the morning of 21 February, the local priest witnessed the damaging effect of the fire, which had caused a total obliteration of the wooden interiors by the south-west window and a partial destruction of most interior → ELEMENTS and objects (the

1 Magnus Poulsson, *Original interior of Dombås Church with altar triptych by Greta Thiis*, 1939, postcard (Oslo: Normann Kunstforlag c.1955)

2 Erik Langdalen Arkitektkontor, *Restored interior of Dombås Church with reconstructed interior and the scorched mandorla*, 2020–2024. Photo: Erik Langdalen, 2025

church's bible among them), as well as scorching all the painted surfaces in the church. To the surprise of the priest and the → RESTORATION team that would soon appear on the scene, the radiant heat from the fire had melted only the outer layer of the non-original white acrylic paint applied during later → RENOVATIONS, now revealing the original brightly coloured linseed oil-painted surfaces, specified and executed by architect Magnus Poulsson, artist Greta Thiis and local painters in 1939 (fig. 1).

This magnificent colour scheme proved to be a sophisticated synthesis of vernacular colours sampled from the region and early modernist colour scales, from bright red, orange and yellow, to light green and grey, and dark blue and black. Behind the layers of paint, the team found wood of extraordinary quality, cut, planed and installed by local carpenters in the 1930s. Although the original paint and most of the woodwork were impossible to save due to the smell from the fumes and otherwise irreparable damage, the wooden interiors and the original colour scheme was meticulously reconstructed (→ RECONSTRUCTION).

When the Bishop of Hamar "reconsecrated" the church in April 2024, it appeared much as it did in 1939, in many ways original and authentic (→ AUTHENTICITY), if short on original substance and material patina (fig. 2). The only surface that was left unpainted, and the only remaining visible trace of the fire, was the mandorla of the surviving altarpiece where a painted Jesus had been scorched into the pine wood boards, leaving a ghostly imprint of Greta Thiis' original artwork. The mandorla has lost its patina, but the painting is still there.

Patina, a word drawn from Latin, meaning "a shallow dish", and frequently in use from the eighteenth century to name the green (and beautiful) film that forms on copper surfaces after oxidation, and gradually in the nineteenth and twentieth century to describe the appearance of all type of surfaces that has grown in value by saturation over time with age and use. The scorch marks on the mandorla may now be termed indirect patina since the eighty-five-year-old painting is still visible even if all traces of paint are removed. The chemical reaction between the linseed oil and the wood, triggered by the extreme radiant heat from the fire, enabled a transferal of the image from the surface of the wood and deep into its fibres, not so different from the oxidising of copper. But in this case, patina is not generated through additive processes, but through subtraction, via scorching, chemical removal and smell-sanitation (→ SUBTRACTION).

New artworks for the church are currently being planned on the basis of the winning proposal of the artist duo Borgny Svalastog and Tarjei Svalastog. Central to their proposal is a reinstalment of the decorated curved choir wall, the pulpit and the twenty picture fields of the altar in the form of abstract reinterpretations of Thiis' original artwork. Most significant is their proposal for the mandorla where they will add a reinterpreted Jesus on top of the scorched "original" with thin silver threads and transparent glass. This amalgamation of quality wood, marks of carpenter's tools, original paint-strokes by Thiis, the forces of the fire triggered by religious controversy, contemporary restoration processes and new artistic interventions creates a complex and meaningful memorial and an expression of the dilemmas and potentials that resides in destructive and traumatic events.

Erik Langdalen

Photography In April 1890, Dramatiken in Christiania (Oslo) was advertised for → DEMOLITION. The auctioneer Richard Andersen begun the sale of the theatre *in situ* at 10 am, 29 April, and in the following days building → ELEMENTS were sold to the highest bidder for → REUSE: "double and single doors, windows, mirrors and glass panes, panels, floors, stairs, brick and roof tiles, gutters, stoves, a skylight, beams, gas and water pipes, etc.", as advertised in the newspaper *Dagbladet* (Anonymous 1890).

Dramatiken was established in 1760 when Christiania patricians played amateur theatre in a private orangerie that was soon transformed into a proper theatre building, a concert hall and a ballroom in an urban garden (→ TRANSFORMATION). It is still operating under the name Centralteateret with an eighteenth-century columned hall in the rear, an auditorium from the late 1890s, and a 1934 modernist → CONCRETE facade towards the street designed for the projection of moving images. At least six top Norwegian architects and a bewildering cast of owners have contributed to this three-dimensional → PALIMPSEST across centuries. With most of the many drawing sets lost, the demolition sale of 1890 provides one important source for the reconstruction of some of its former iterations and their provenance: the skylight sold in April 1890 was, for instance, an 1871 intervention by Georg Andreas Bull when the theatre for a period functioned as an exhibition hall for architecture and → CRAFT.

1 Christian Heinrich Grosch, *Christiania Theater*, 1836, Oslo. Photo: Narve Skarpmoen, 1899

Richard Andersen, who established his auction house in 1874 and conducted demolition auctions for the municipality, was also a pioneering photographer and preservationist of sorts (→ PRESERVATION). Between the mid-1880s and 1913, he had hundreds of the buildings he auctioned for demolition photographed, with himself discreetly present in the picture equipped with a hat and a cane. In a 1913 interview, he explained the importance of documenting buildings that are sacrificed in the face of progress. Asked why he decided to "act as a self-appointed city preservationist", he replied that he regarded each and every photograph as "a small memorial" to the vanishing buildings and explained that his working principle was to record structure by structure to save them from oblivion. He regretted that he didn't start documenting "the homes of those who played their part in the city's modernisation" earlier, he told the journalist (Anonymous 1913).

Almost without exception, Richard Andersen's collection records streetscapes with facades. The building that is about to disappear makes the main motif. The auctioneer's archival project provides unique insight into a vanishing urban physiognomy (→ ARCHIVE). The pictures bring to mind the work of a contemporary, kindred spirit, the French photographer Eugène Atget's paradigmatic photographs of the buildings and deserted streets of Paris. In *A little history of photography* (1931), Walter Benjamin described Atget's empty Paris photos as crime scenes, documenting "what was unremarked, forgotten, cast adrift" (Benjamin 1999b, p. 518). Similar to Atget, Andersen, the preservationist-demolisher, was less interested in great sights, landmarks or monuments, but rather in depicting "the conspicuous spot where in the immediacy of that long-forgotten moment the future nests so eloquently that we, looking back, may rediscover it" (p. 510).

Richard Andersen entrusted hundreds of photos of the buildings he helped dismantle to the Foreningen det gamle Kristiania (Society of Old Kristiania), founded in 1905 by the architect Fritz Holland, the founder of Oslo Museum. A selection was shown at the museum's inaugural

2 Christian Heinrich Grosch, *Christiania Theater*, demolished October 12, 1899, Oslo. Photographer unknown

exhibition at the manor Frogner Hovedgård in August 1909. In 1913, Andersen handed over his remaining archive to the museum. If Dramatiken was documented the day before the auction in April 1890, that photograph is lost. However, in October 1899, Andersen carried out the demolition auction of Christian Heinrich Grosch's Christiania Theatre from 1836 (figs. 1–2), where also the interior was documented while being torn apart, piece by piece. *Mari Lending*

Plaster cast Copying is a serious business and in the early 1890s a lawsuit on the pirating of plaster casts made it to the news. With reference to a perpetual injunction granted by the High Court of Justice, Chancery Division, *The Times* announced that "various persons in the United Kingdom of Great Britain and Ireland have pirated, and are pirating, casts and models" made by "D. BRUCCIANI and Co., of the Galleria delle Belle Arti, 40. Russell Street, Covent Garden" and consequently severely violated the company's → COPYRIGHT "which is protected by statute" (Anonymous 1892). The defendant, including his workmen, servants and agents, was warned against "making, selling, or disposing of, or causing, or permitting to be made, sold, or disposed of, any casts or models taken, or copied, or only colourably different, from the casts or models, the sole right and property of and in which belongs to the said D. Brucciani and Co." Furthermore, the public was notified that "any person or persons" with future desires of making, selling or disposing of → MODELS or casts from other people's models or casts "will likewise be proceeded against" (see Lending 2014).

Nonetheless, the defendant pursued his dark deeds of pirating, making, selling and disposing of copies made of copyrighted copies, thus infringing on the earlier ruling. In the new motion two years later, the defendant was ordered to file an affidavit of all the casts and models as the sole right and property of Brucciani & Co., return any casts and models to the plaintiff and carry the full cost of the motion. In addition, the perpetrator "might be ordered to stand committed to the Holloway Prison for his contempt in infringing the said Injunction" (Anonymous 1894).

Domenico Brucciani, master plaster caster for some of the finest British art institutions, had established a prolific business of producing architectural monuments, antiquities, → FRAGMENTS, ornaments, sculptures and otherwise an assortment spanning from fossils to dismembered body parts. From early on, Brucciani was involved in the grand endeavor of building an eclectic collection of architectural monuments at the South Kensington Museum (→ COLLECTING). Among Brucciani's productions were the full-scale Pórtico de la Gloria from the cathedral in Santiago de Compostela, cast on-site in the fall of 1866 (fig. 1).

Thurston Thompson, the museum's photographer, and Brucciani operated with detailed instructions concerning what to cast and photograph (→ PHOTOGRAPHY). The two- and three-dimensional → REPRODUCTIONS influenced the status and perception of the cathedral both on- and off-site. The magnificent plaster portal, 17.85 metres wide, dictated the dimensions of the imposing skylit Architecture Courts inaugurated in 1873. While even some of the most exquisite nineteenth-century plaster monuments were made in series, Pórtico de la Gloria was a singular sensation.

Upon Brucciani's death in 1880, the whole of his "valuable Stock, Moulds, and Store Casts" produced under "Royal and distinguished

1 *Cathedral of Santiago de Compostela, Pórtico de la Gloria, archivolt of the central doorway, plaster cast under construction at the South Kensington Museum*, London. Photo: Agnes Cowper, c.1872

patronage" was announced for sale (Anonymous 1880). The stock was certainly valuable, containing moulds of the finest monuments at full scale (including one of the most distributed series of the so-called Elgin Marbles in the British Museum), moulds that were not easily reproducible from the monuments *in situ* due to increasingly strict → PRESERVATION legislation in Europe (see Lending 2017). No surprise then that the purchaser, who continued the business as Brucciani & Company, took legal action against competitors pirating their work by having new moulds made from their casts.

The plagiarist working out of Manchester had been copying casts without even bothering to erase the Brucciani signature on the copied copies before putting them onto the market as cheaper goods. Therefore, and very much like the warning against pirating associated with the today obsolete DVD medium (→ OBSOLESCENCE), Brucciani & Co reprinted the 1892 announcement from *The Times*, including the newspaper's logo, in their regularly updated series of sale → CATALOGUES.

The Brucciani lawsuit revolved around minor objects produced for art schools, incomparable to the complexity, effort and inventiveness displayed in the grandiose edition of the Pórtico de la Gloria. They were however original designs and thus subjected to copyright. During the first part of the twentieth century, innumerous cast collections were consigned to → STORAGE, destruction and oblivion. As exhibits and teaching tools, they became unbearable to modernist culture and not least to modernist pedagogies, appearing as a mockery of ideals such as honesty, truthfulness, originality and → AUTHENTICITY. As museums and academies exiled their casts as an awkward liability, the scientific aspiration, theoretical speculation, historical imagination and aesthetic appreciation embedded in these objects were channeled to the backstage of historiography.

Today, an increasing appreciation of the relics left behind by nineteenth-century cast culture has produced a new understanding of the sensibilities of a past when casts merited scholarship, art-historical passion, scientific value, money and pride. They were authored (→ AUTHORSHIP) and authorized by skilled artisans who would ideally make the moulds from the original as part of the → AUTHENTICATION process. Lorenzo Ghiberti's baptistery doors should be purchased from Florence, the Pergamon slabs from Berlin. Across Europe eminent *formatori*, such as August Gerber in Cologne, Sabatino de Angelis in Naples, Gilliéron and Son in Athens, Giuseppe and Oronzio Lelli in Florence, Pietro Pierotti in Milan, Lorenzo Rinaldo in Venice, the Guidotti brothers in Christiania (Oslo) and numerous others, provided galleries across the world with sculpture and architectural fragments from their city, region or country.

Retrieved from storage, many of these authored editions are today being meticulously restored and proudly reintroduced to galleries and scholarship. They pose questions in regards of the construction of → AUTHENTICITY, authentication, → HERITAGE, celebrity and canonization in the often unpredictable → AFTERLIFE of precious objects. They may help us rethink in profound ways the transformative and emotive power of ownership and more multifaceted conceptions of authorship. With their specific provenance, these productions provide privileged prisms through which to understand how architecture moves, is destroyed, survives and is transformed.

Mari Lending

Political iconography Political iconography is an ambiguous notion that encompasses both the thematic content of artworks that overtly or subtly express political themes, as well as the scientific method used to analyse and interpret such references. In terms of content, political iconography includes all areas of artistic production: it appears in paintings, sculptures, drawings and graphic works; in photography, film and video in the form of allegories, symbols, emblems or other pictorial signs; we encounter it on the facades and in the decorations of architectural works, as well as in the ephemeral staging of parades, festivals or party conventions. Genres such as history painting, portraits of rulers, monuments or stately architecture, posters, leaflets, coins or stamps (→ IMAGE VEHICLE) are comprehensively determined by political iconography, but politically motivated elements can also be used as meaningful image details in other kinds of artworks. They illustrate political issues, fulfil the function of open political propaganda, affirming rule or calling for resistance and rebellion, or are used subversively as hidden messages (see Fleckner et al. 2011).

Even though the political content of art has been studied since the early days of art history as an academic discipline, it was primarily the Hamburg School around Aby Warburg and Erwin Panofsky that has laid the systematic foundation for political iconography as a research method from the early twentieth century onwards. In addition to the mere motif-related identification of images, pictorial elements or combinations of images (iconography), a historically and intellectually contextualised interpretation of such motifs (iconology) was defined, whereby the two terms are still largely used synonymously today (see Panofsky 1939, pp. 3ff.). As an interdisciplinary art-historical method, political iconography claims to be genuinely enlightening: beyond the study of traditional art genres, current political iconography, following Warburg and Panofsky's studies of non-canonical → ARTEFACTS, is dedicated to press, film and television images, advertising messages and the flood of images on the World Wide Web, for example, and thus offers the methodological tools with which visual information and attempts at manipulation from art, media and all kinds of everyday image production can be systematically examined and placed in a historical perspective.

Within a research approach dedicated to the provenance phenomena of architecture, political iconography is relevant both as a subject area and as a method in different ways. Due to political content, architecture can become the object of → DEMOLITION, → TRANSFORMATION or → VANDALISM; monuments as a hybrid form of architecture and sculpture are also

1 *House facade with hacked-off lictor bundle in Via Giannantonio Cavazzi, Rome*, file card with mounted photograph, Bildindex zur Politischen Ikonographie, Warburg-Haus, Hamburg. Photo: Claudia Nordhoff, 1994

2 *House wall with fascist inscription and anti-fascist graffiti, Rome*, file card with mounted photograph, Bildindex zur Politischen Ikonographie, Warburg-Haus, Hamburg. Photo: Claudia Nordhoff, 1994

occasionally subjected to politically motivated measures (→ COUNTER-MONUMENT, → MONUMENT, TOPPLED). The study of such phenomena is of course an essential component of political iconography as a scientific method, but can also itself become an instrument of new provenances of political art.

The best example of such activations of political art and its motifs through their reception in research is probably the *Bildindex zur Politischen Ikonographie* (see www.warburg-haus.de/forschungsprojekte/forschungsstelle-politische-ikonographie/). Housed in the Hamburg Warburg-Haus, the former building of the Kulturwissenschaftliche Bibliothek Warburg, this image index, founded by Martin Warnke in the 1980s as a research centre of the Department of Art History at Hamburg University, collected around 180,000 reproductions of artworks of all genres and other depictions glued onto file cards, as well as additional material such as newspaper clippings and postcards, which are arranged according to the themes depicted. These documents on the use of political images from antiquity to the recent past make it clear how the perception of political concepts, events and personalities is characterised and guided by pictorial traditions. Keywords from all areas of architecture, such as *Denkmal* (monument), *Grabmal* (tomb), *Rathaus* (town hall) or *Schloss* (castle), are also catalogued in it, including documents that deal with provenance phenomena. As a research tool, both the file cards and the resulting database disseminate knowledge of such images, promote a critical approach to them and thus act as image vehicles themselves.

Integrated into the image index is a special collection of several hundred photographs by art historian Claudia Nordhoff, who photographed fascist architecture and its decoration in Rome in the 1990s (→ COLLECTING). The works, some of which are *all'antica* and some modern in style, mainly show mythological figures and scenes, idealised depictions of workers, athletes and soldiers as well as emblems glorifying the regime. Even today, such objects still characterise the Roman cityscape without comment in many places, from major construction projects such as the Esposizione Universale Roma or the Città Universitaria to commercial and cultural buildings as well as house facades with their statues, murals, reliefs and → INSCRIPTIONS.

Some of the examples documented in the image index show traces of violent physical reception by Roman citizens: the hacked-off lictor bundles ("fasces"), which during Mussolini's reign served as a national emblem, party badge and symbol for the Italian Waffen-SS, among other things, and even anti-fascist → GRAFFITI on the wall of a building demonstrate the intention to distance themselves from the fascist dictatorship and its architecture (figs. 1–2).

Such interventions form an important object of investigation for architectural provenance research. With the help of their photographic documentation (→ PHOTOGRAPHY), these iconoclastic measures are preserved as evidence of the confrontation with the political past and thus enter the → COLLECTIVE MEMORY. Research that deals not only with the building history and iconographic interpretation of political architecture, but also with its vital reception in the present, with transformation, demolition or vandalism, thus focuses its attention on the voids and interstices of art history. With the research of such reception phenomena and the associated departure from a purely monographic consideration of buildings and objects, a further layer of sediment is added to the provenance history of political artworks. *Uwe Fleckner*

Postproduction Originally denoting a set of techniques associated with time-based media, the term "postproduction" refers to operations performed on raw footage after recording, particularly, though not exclusively, cutting, mixing, editing, special-effects work and sampling. While production is generally attributed to the work of a privileged *auteur*, postproduction encompasses the → LABOUR of those who handle the product after production, for whom the product becomes raw → MATERIAL for new creative processes.

Transposed to architecture, the term recalls practices of the distant past and the near future, encompassing the activity that occurs to and in a building after the initial work of an *architecte-auteur*: more or less protracted construction processes, daily use and → MAINTENANCE, but also a building's discursive migration across media, from → EXHIBITIONS and magazines to university lectures, biennials and fairs. The "post" in postproduction, however, marks an unclean temporal cut. Architects are involved in post-production processes through practices such as → TRANSFORMATIONS, citation and spoliation (→ QUOTE, → SPOLIA), or might actively incorporate postproductive scripts into their designs.

The lavatory inspection sheets that facilitate the efficient maintenance of Yoshio Taniguchi's restroom redesigns at the Museum of Modern Art (MoMA) in New York as well as those that were later modernised – and the cleaning personnel they coordinate – are absent from the architect's pre-renderings of the space (fig. 1). The document serves as a postscript to the architectural text, defining the MoMA as a post-productive apparatus for not only the experience of art, but the reception, sorting and redistribution of vast amounts of human waste (fig. 2).

1 *Male lavatory at the Museum of Modern Art*, New York. Photo: Carson Chan, 2025

Rather than the static notion of architecture as *immobilis* or immovable goods (→ MOBILITY, → MOVABLES), the postproductive view sees a building such as the MoMA as produced by, and productive of, an ever-expanding constellation of postproducers: architects, museum-goers, cleaning personnel, hobby photographers, vandals and climate activists (→ NETWORK).

Before proclamations of the death of the author, popularised by Roland Barthes and Michel Foucault in the 1960s, artists were generally regarded as producers with intentional control over the meaning of their artworks. In the essay *The creative act*, initially presented as a lecture at the MoMA in 1957, Marcel Duchamp called for the acknowledgement that the inevitable discrepancy between an artist's intention and the audience's experience is in fact a productive schism (see Duchamp 1973). He termed this slippage the "art coefficient", proposing a shared responsibility for creation between artist and future spectators – akin to how architecture is primed for uses unforeseen by its architect. Accordingly, Duchamp suggested unburdening the *auteur* from the role of sole producer, proposing instead that his fundamental gesture is to provide raw material for future → ACTORS to refine and redefine.

In regard to the postproductive mode's redefinition of → AUTHORSHIP and originality, Marcel Duchamp's 1917 → READYMADE sculpture *Fountain* is perhaps still the most explicit example. Preceding the lineage of conceptual works that take existing objects as raw material, Duchamp redefined an industrially produced urinal as a sculpture, introducing it into an art context. Turned 90 degrees, signed, placed on a plinth and presented in an exhibition with the fixtures for water and drainage prominently protruding from the base of the sculpture, it is precisely in its detachment from the actual infrastructure of a physical building that *Fountain* relates to architecture. Severed from the water supply system, the sculpture establishes a space of

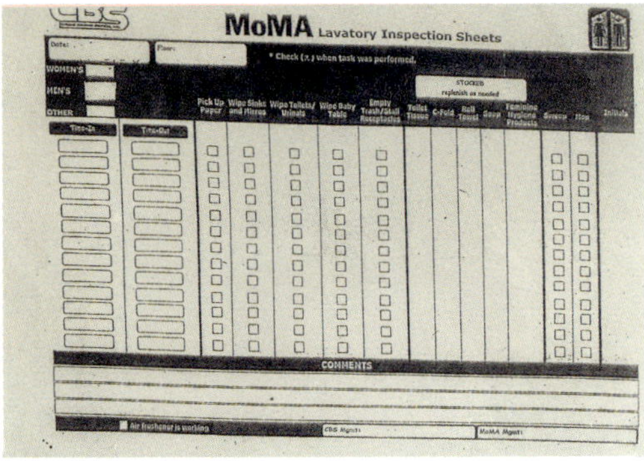

2 Dag Erik Elgin, *MoMA lavatory inspection sheet*, 2011, silkscreen on aluminium, 21 × 29.7 cm

reception where its connections are shifted from a digestive to a perceptual network: disconnected from the male urinary tract, reconnected to the optical nerves of art-world spectators. Perceiving, in this new context, becomes postproductive. And unlike appropriation, which challenges the idiom of originality by claiming authorship over existing → ARTEFACTS while remaining anchored within established networks of past creators, *Fountain* persistently extends its site of productive reception, anticipating the gaze of future, undisclosed postproducers.

Theorists such as Nicolas Bourriaud have connected the concept of postproduction to an operational mode in which meaning is generated not from the object itself or its *auteur*, but through the object's → CIRCULATION within various networks (social, financial, institutional) and the circulations it facilitates in turn: a "thousand stomachs and their attendant bodies all stretched round each other and sequentially digesting" (Fuller 2005, p. 56). Postproduction extends into a perpetually expanding and deferred topos, situated somewhere between being belated and being too early – manifest in an already existing, pre-coded object and its not-yet-defined future meanings. Expanding in time and space, the conception of an object's identity as related to provenance, a fixed and clearly delineated place of origin, becomes continuously destabilised. Focus shifts towards production, which itself becomes content. Indeed, as the American poet Kenneth Goldsmith suggests – and we can extend his considerations to cultural production in general – "reproducibility, replication, mirroring, reproduction, copyright, intellectual property are really the true content of writing in the 21st century" (see Goldsmith 2014). *Dag Erik Elgin*

Precedent Eero Saarinen's winning entry to the Jefferson National Expansion Memorial design competition in 1948, titled *Gateway to the West* and now commonly referred to as the Gateway or Saint Louis Arch, proposed a 560-foot-high weighted parabolic arch clad with shining stainless steel built on the left bank of the Mississippi River (fig. 1).

Soon after the results were announced, the chairman of the New York Commission of Fine Arts, Gilmore D. Clarke, accused Saarinen of citing one singular arch – namely, Adalberto Libera's unexecuted memorial arch for the twentieth anniversary of Italian fascism from 1938. In a letter dated 24 February 1948, addressed to the chairman of the competition jury, William W. Wurster, he summed up his condemnation: "The pertinent question is not whether or not the design was plagiarised; rather it is whether or not, in the circumstances, it is appropriate to perpetuate the memory of Thomas Jefferson and to memorialise the Louisiana Purchase by constructing a monument similar in design to one originally created to glory twenty years of Fascism in Italy!" (Graebner 1993, p. 368).

1 Eero Saarinen, *Gateway Arch (Gateway to the West)*, 1948–1965, Saint Louis. Photo: Uwe Fleckner, 2013

2 *Eero Saarinen with a model and sketches of arches*, c.1960. Photographer unknown

The competition jury swiftly released a statement that discredited the plagiarism accusations by stating: "Arches of this general type are extremely old as an architectural form. One closely similar in effects is the immense arch of the royal palace at Ctesiphon, built by Chosroes the Great, King of Persia, in the 6th century. In recent times the parabolic and the hyperbolic arch, with their structural advantages, have become characteristic forms of functional modern architecture [...]. The form is in the public domain; it was not invented by the Fascist" (Eero Saarinen Papers, MS 593, Yale University Library, Manuscripts and Archives).

The architect told his side of the story shortly afterwards. In it, Saarinen listed the precedents his design team had studied during the design process as follows: "We thought of a huge concrete arch. Such a shape was in no way unfamiliar to us. There are the dirigible hangars in Orly, France, designed by the engineer [Eugène] Freyssinet that really gave a sense of monumentality. There are the arched concrete bridges that were built by the Swiss engineer, [Robert] Maillart. There is also the arch that the great French architect, Le Corbusier, incorporated in his design for the Palace of the Soviets sometime in the '20's" (Saarinen 1948). Calling the outcome "a modern adaptation of a Roman triumphal arch" indicates that the team deemed it possible to appropriate a symbolically laden historical motif into new uses and invest it with new meanings, all while holding on to the old ones.

The debacle led to a broader conversation about the value of using historical precedents, with Kenneth K. Stowell, the editor-in-chief of *Architectural Record* leading the way by dedicating his editorial of the April 1948 issue to the topic: "Architecture has amassed an unprecedented amount of precedent. If one cares to probe into the past, he probably can find a precedent or a prototype for the form of each and every part of any structure." Without directly referring to Clarke's plagiarism accusation, Stowell posits that "it is therefore beside the point to criticise or cast aspersions on the use of a particular form just because it, or a similar form, has been used before for a particular purpose. Such natural and traditional use of precedent is inherent in architectural development, and it should not be implicated that plagiarism is involved." According to Stowell, plagiarism means "copying of prototypes without any significant contribution, modification, or improvement on the part of the design" (Stowell 1948, p. 91). Saarinen's design could thus be deemed innovative not despite, but because of it being a novel adaption of a historically recognisable form.

A photograph taken around 1960, when the project was heading for construction, depicts Saarinen kneeling in front of the model of the slightly revised, final version of the arch with sketches of various historical arches pinned to the background (fig. 2). Twelve years after the debacle he could openly celebrate that his arch was generated from and gained its meaning against a plethora of historical precedents. *Eeva-Liisa Pelkonen*

Preservation Preservation is a dynamic and creative practice rooted in the careful study, interpretation, redesign, curated change, technologically assisted care and artistic continuation of the existing built environment. Originating conceptually with Johann Joachim Winckelmann's eighteenth-century theory of imitation, preservation involves more than the mechanical copying of historic forms; it demands an active, artistic, imaginative engagement with the past. Winckelmann's defense of imitation – as an experimental method through which contemporary artists could not only replicate but also surpass the achievements of antiquity – laid the intellectual groundwork for a preservation practice attentive to the creative potentials embedded in historical artefacts (see Winckelmann 1755).

From its inception, preservation has been intimately linked to questions of provenance. Winckelmann's pioneering methods of observing material culture were developed specifically to determine the origin, → AUTHORSHIP and significance of classical artworks; to distinguish, for instance, whether an ancient sculpture came from Greece or Rome. His work established the principle that rigorous, evidence-based study of the physical characteristics of monuments – their → MATERIALS, stylistic features and techniques – could reveal their historical contexts and cultural meanings. In the field of preservation, provenance functions as both a scientific pursuit and an ethical imperative: understanding where a monument comes from, who made it, and how it has changed over time is a prerequisite for any meaningful act of safeguarding or interpretation.

In this sense, provenance is not a static attribute of objects, but a dynamic and evolving relationship. As historic places and artefacts move through time, their meanings shift, requiring ongoing reinterpretation. Preservationists today, following the example set by Winckelmann and later theorists such as John Ruskin in the nineteenth century, Dolores Hayden, David Lowenthal, Michel-Rolph Trouillot in the twentieth century, and Rem Koolhaas, Bruno Latour and Albena Yaneva among others in the twenty-first, have learned to engage critically with the layers of history present in each → ARTEFACT, recognising that every intervention adds a new chapter to its life story (→ AFTERLIFE). Provenance is therefore both a tool for historical understanding and a foundation for creative acts of reimagining and reinvention.

Rather than seeking to freeze monuments in a single historical moment, preservation today embraces the reality that buildings and places are living documents. Each generation inscribes its own values, fears and hopes into the environment it inherits (→ INHERITANCE). Preservation, understood in this expansive way, becomes a form of cultural dialogue across time – a means by which the past informs the present, and the present reimagines the possibilities of the future. This creative dimension distinguishes preservation from mere antiquarianism or conservation. It acknowledges that safeguarding → HERITAGE is not an end in itself but a starting point for new cultural productions.

Throughout its evolution, preservation has grappled with the tension between → AUTHENTICITY and change. Abbé Grégoire's introduction of the concept of → VANDALISM during the French Revolution highlighted the destructive consequences of disregarding the provenance and intrinsic value of historic works (see Grégoire 1794). At the same time, thinkers like Antoine-Chrysostome Quatremère de Quincy warned against the dangers of reducing monuments to mere relics through the decontextualisation inherent in moving artworks from churches into museums (→ COLLECTING). He also cautioned against mindless and mechanical → RESTORATIONS. True preservation, for Quatremère, required an understanding of the principles that had originally animated historic works, enabling contemporary society to engage in an active process of imitation – not blind copying, but thoughtful renewal based on deep comprehension (see Quatremère de Quincy 1999).

In the modern period, this creative interpretation has expanded further. The discipline has increasingly recognised that the meaning and significance of historic places are not fixed by their origins alone. They are reconstituted continuously through human use, memory and imagination. Provenance is thus revealed not only in material evidence but also in the ways people inhabit, remember and narrate places (→ INHABITANTS). Preservation's task is to mediate between the material and immaterial, between the tangible fabric of buildings and the intangible web of meanings that surrounds them.

At its core, preservation is therefore a generative and future-oriented activity. It offers communities tools to grapple with their histories – including histories of injustice, exclusion or loss – and to imagine new futures built upon a nuanced understanding of the past. Twentieth-century and contemporary theorists have expanded this view, integrating ideas from sociology, anthropology, psychoanalysis and critical theory. From Walter Benjamin's reflections on the aura of historic works to Laurajane Smith's emphasis on heritage as a cultural process, preservation theory today recognises that heritage is continually being made and remade.

Importantly, preservation also entails ethical responsibilities. In a world where cultural heritage is threatened by → WAR, economic exploitation and environmental degradation, respecting provenance becomes a matter of justice. Emmerich de Vattel's Enlightenment call to protect enemy monuments during wartime enshrined the principle that cultural achievements belong to all humanity, not just to their creators (de Vattel 1758). Modern international frameworks, such as UNESCO's World Heritage Convention, trace their intellectual lineage back to these early ideals.

Preservation thus requires balancing the obligation to protect the material integrity of historic places with the equally vital need to adapt and reinterpret them in ways that serve contemporary and future communities. It asks practitioners to cultivate both scholarly rigor in establishing provenance and documenting significance, and imaginative vision in allowing historic environments to live, breathe and transform meaningfully over time.

In sum, preservation is best understood not as an act of resisting change but as a dynamic process of engagement, interpretation and creative continuity. It is a field grounded in the close study of provenance, inspired by the heuristic ideal of imitation introduced by Winckelmann, and animated by the belief that existing places and buildings are resources for making sense of the past and reimagining collective futures. Preservation demands an ethic of care and imagination, ensuring that the material traces of history are not merely curated, but actively and artistically woven into the evolving cultural life of societies.

1 Lars Ramberg, *Palast des Zweifels (Palace of Doubt)*, 2005, neon installation at the shortly-afterwards-demolished Palast der Republik, Schlossplatz, Berlin

Today, emerging at the intersection of research-based artistic inquiry, architecture and critical heritage studies, experimental preservation is both an artistic method and an interdisciplinary movement that reimagines preservation practices. Rather than merely safeguarding the material past, it actively engages with it, transforming and speculating about its meanings to create contemporary relevance. This approach expresses a duty of care not only toward tangible cultural objects such as public spaces, buildings and artworks, but also toward intangible → ELEMENTS, including historic smells, → DUST and ephemeral traces of memory.

Artworks produced within this movement vary widely in aesthetics but often intertwine two key objectives: preserving artefacts, architectural → FRAGMENTS, buildings and places that might otherwise be lost and exploring how the act of preservation can reshape the future (fig. 1). Practitioners blend preservation technologies, science and → CRAFT with diverse strategies from art and architecture, such as archival excavation (→ ARCHIVE), site-responsive installations, technological mediation and performative acts (see Otero-Pailos et al. 2016).

These works critically interrogate memory, identity, materiality and authenticity, offering fresh perspectives on how heritage can be conceptualised in contemporary contexts. In an era when heritage is increasingly contested, experimental preservation brings together artists, architects and creatives from other fields interested in preservation as a speculative, forward-looking practice. By embracing the fluid, mutable nature of culture, it transforms physical vessels of → COLLECTIVE MEMORY into a foundation for meaning-making, innovation and possibility. *Jorge Otero-Pailos*

Pristine The term "pristine" is often used to describe a building that is immaculately preserved, unspoiled and authentic (→ AUTHENTICITY, → PRESERVATION). The word is also synonymous with something virginal, and in that context often associated to the colour white. The whiteish marble of classical antiquity set a precedent that spawned many classicisms, and despite → MATERIAL and technological changes underneath the surface, the whiteness endured. Its association of something elevated, high born or noble is an enduring currency. While Greek temples and statues were often polychrome, the layers of paint gradually faded away from both surface and memory and left us the white-washed impression of a pristine surface. The notion of the pristine is littered with these kinds of misappropriations.

A pertinent case of this desire for the pristine surface can be found along the south coast of Norway. The vernacular timber houses of the area, called *Sørlandshus* in Norwegian, are defined by a coat of thick, expensive white paint applied to their exterior cladding. Their layout is defined by a strong demarcation between the "front of house" and the "back of house", from representation to utility and from the formal to the informal. This feature was perhaps taken directly from Georgian architecture as England took over the hegemony from the Dutch around the North Sea after the Napoleonic wars and influenced local tastes and fashions. The previous Dutch-inflected house (*strandsitterhus*) of asymmetrical facades with a baroque DNA was replaced by Palladian symmetry and a building type that has two very distinct sides, defined by usage and colour. In the nineteenth century, when this region had its heyday as an outlet for Norwegian timber to the continent, white was an exclusive feature reserved for only the wealthiest of shipwrights as the zinc used in its production was costly. Hence the white paint was often only applied to the facade towards either the high street or the most trafficked shipping lane, producing a number of quite odd two-tone Potemkinesque situations. However, these coastal trading posts were in fact originally painted in a plethora of earthy hues that were easily made by materials found in the soil at hand. As white became available as an industrial product around the turn of the twentieth century and hence affordable, it became the pervasive feature of buildings along the coast to the point that it now is considered its defining character – a character often associated to a notion of the pristine.

1 Peter Krogh Bonsach Jessen, *Old town hall*, 1815, Arendal, Norway. Photo: Erlend Skjeseth

However, the many licks of paint conceal a myriad of panels, drip boards and moldings, of shallow relief and nuanced recess. The application of a thick layer of white paint on top binds different pieces of material into one continuous sense of plasticity. It negates replaced bits and areas that have been altered or repaired (→ REPARATION). The thick coating eliminates fixings, covers screws, fills cracks and erases underlying material properties, rendering the surface an abstract and monolithic unity as if it was cast in one piece. In a serendipitous and roundabout way, this monochromatic surface inadvertently recalls the surfaces of the continental stone buildings that inspired these vernacular timber buildings in the first place. This was not entirely unconscious, as seen in the old town hall of Arendal from 1815 (fig. 1).

Once the second-largest notched log (*laft*) building in Norway, the paint applied on its wooden cladding was supposedly infused with sand at the behest of its Danish architect Peter Krogh Bonsach Jessen, to make the building explicitly give the lofty impressions of European white stone. It is also said that the sheer height of the building came about so that Jessen's daughter could see across the Skagerrak strait to her beloved Denmark. A building that on multiple levels longs to be someone else.

2 Kastler Skjeseth Architects, *Extension to a classicist sports pavilion of a 1925 retirement home for sailors*, 2025, Tvedestrand, Norway. Photo: Erlend Skjeseth

The Arendal town hall sits in a rough climate near the North Sea and as such is a good example of an architecture with overlapping building parts. The overlap in every detail is necessary to countenance the contraction and expansion, as living and porous material reacts to changing temperatures. The salty sea spray and harsh winds weathers these timber buildings (→ WEATHERING), requiring a new layer of paint to be reapplied every five to ten years. This repeated act of → MAINTENANCE and → RENOVATION builds up a grainy and crackled surface over time, a → PATINA that is hard to reproduce. The illusion of the pristine, here understood through the application of white paint on timber, is interesting from a purely formal, surface-based level, the many coats of white having a peculiar effect when applied to timber architecture and becoming parts of its provenance.

Can this provenance of the pristine paint be a driver for new architecture adjacent to these vernacular types? In the → EXTENSION to a retirement home for sailors built in 1925, the removal of material → ARTEFACTS in its surface allows for a playful game where the variables of form and material are kept apart and shifted with whiteness as the only common denominator (fig. 2).

The added facades are working with abstracted classical forms to resonate with the historical building, to transcend the binary discourse of tradition versus modernity. The subversion of these elements is made through material translations and scalar distortion of recognisable motifs within the classical canon. This approach is not new, but very much in keeping with the peculiarities of the Norwegian vernacular, with its long tradition of altering the variable of material, yet retaining the variable of form. There are many examples of these translations, including often quite crude attempts at painting marble textures on wood. In this project, this game between masonry and timber is continued with columns supporting fire escapes cast in white → CONCRETE through using mass-produced log-cabin panelling as formwork. The uncanny resemblance between the two scallops, one in white concrete and the other painted panelling, sets up a subtle play. The result is a pristine surface that over time crackles and shifts to reveal a complex provenance underneath its veneer. *Erlend Skjeseth*

Privilegio In 1599, the Roman engraver Giacomo Lauro witnessed in a case filed by a fellow printmaker, Giulio Franceschini, who accused a third colleague, Nicolas van Aelst, of selling copies of one of his prints. In defense of the accused, Lauro made a startling admission. He said that he too once had engraved a similar *sugetto* (subject) but not the same *inventione* (invention). This is a crucial distinction. Everyone had the right to depict and publish, say, the Colosseum, the Rialto Bridge or the Louvre. Anything else would have been absurd. But as soon as those monuments were subjected to a particular style, detailing, projection, even angle, it classed as an "invention" and became someone's property (→ AUTHORSHIP). In short, as buildings, cities, countries were re-founded on paper, the ownership of them passed from princes to printmakers (see Tschudi 2012 and 2017).

We do not know the outcome of the case, but Lauro's distinction shows the havoc that the new reality of print had created in the earlier serene relation between the world and its representations. Everyone was still free to picture things around them, architecture included, but not necessarily in the way they pleased. A real building had walls and fences to keep invaders out; reproduced and multiplied in print, its defense now rested with a different construct – the *privilegio*.

A *privilegio*, or privilege, is surprisingly concrete. It has nothing to do with a modern → COPYRIGHT or an artistic right to the output of any sort. A privilege on architectural prints, as it emerged in Venice and Rome around 1500, was devised to defend the value of expensive

1 Sebastiano Serlio, *Il terzo libro*, Venice 1544, title page, with reference to the privilege from the Venetian Senate

copper and paper and the → LABOUR that had gone into producing the engravings. Just as the law offered protection against rampaging a physical property, a privilege protected the building against unlawful copying in the virtual realm of print. A book's frontispiece (fig. 1), often visualised as a door or a gate, therefore flagged *cum privilegio* across the page as if to say: "no trespassing!"

The power of a privilege was territorial. It was a right a sovereign could choose to grant, based on a petition. In other words, when a pope, an emperor, a king saw the potential of their domain conveniently or beautifully extended in the realm of prints, they placed it under their protection by way of a privilege. The privilege was a means to enlarge one's dominion. That is why major powers in the sixteenth century all wielded their own, competing privileges. The skirmishes for territorial control on the European continent branched into battles over coveted architectural designs. The penalty for violating a privilege amounted to a financial

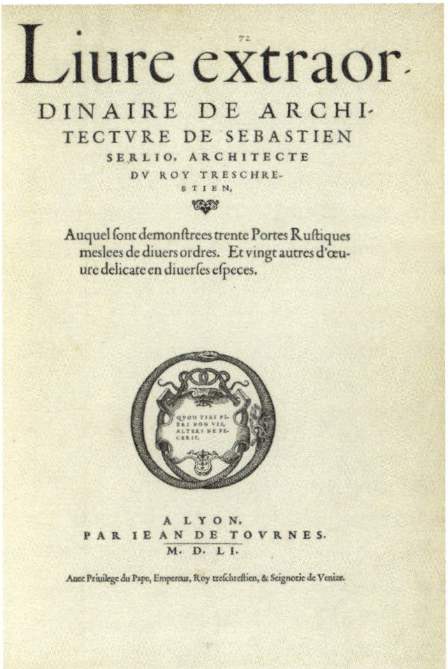

Liure extraor-
DINAIRE DE ARCHI-
TECTVRE DE SEBASTIEN
SERLIO, ARCHITECTE
DV ROY TRESCHRE-
STIEN,

Auquel ſont demonſtrees trente Portes Ruſtiques meslees de diuers ordres. Et vingt autres d'œuure delicate en diuerſes eſpeces.

A LYON,
PAR IEAN DE TOVRNES.
M. D. LI.

Auec Priuilege du Pape, Empereur, Roy treſchreſtien, & Seignorie de Venize.

2 Sebastiano Serlio, *Livre extraordinaire de Architecture*, Lyon 1551, title page, with reference to the privileges from the Pope, the Holy Roman emperor, the king of France and the Venetian Senate

compensation divided between the sovereign and the owner of the material. Only the pope had the authority to threaten potential perpetrators with the enviable weapon of excommunication. The petitioner could seek and obtain a privilege from several authorities for one and the same publication. Sitting alone, old and exhausted, at Fontainebleau, keeping rather "the company of wild beasts than men", according to himself (Serlio 1551, n. p.), the architect and theoretician Sebastiano Serlio nonetheless mustered privileges from the pope, the Holy Roman emperor, the French king and the Venetian senate for his last and widely eccentric book on doors. Deprived of the company of men in real life, he entertained a host of grandees on paper (fig. 2).

Privileges transform time into a commodity. The protection it offered was always limited to fixed periods, normally ten years in Rome, shorter periods in France, longer periods in Venice. The quarantined time forced rivals eager to make copies and thus profit from attractive designs to count the years from the granting of a privilege to its expiry. The origin of a design – the who, the when, the where – suddenly dictated its dissemination. Architectural history took the shape of a history of provenance.

Although privileges were given to secure the ownership of a design, it had the opposite effect. The restrictions on copying set in motion a series of manoeuvers to circumvent the meaning of a copy. When the publisher Michele Tramezzini asked the pope for a ten-year privilege for Pirro Ligorio's various prints of reconstructed Roman antiques, he had no way to foresee that a clever Venetian rival simply would reverse his meticulously researched designs and get away with it. Changing names, mutating structures and adding → ELEMENTS were operations that disrupted the genealogy of buildings, derailing smooth developments (if ever there was one) into spirals of increasingly distorted appearances. The Renaissance ideal of *imitatio* – polite variations on eternal ideals – veered into a history of evasions engendering parallel solutions. Entire pasts doubled up. When the reconstructed glories of Egypt, Greece and Rome were put off limit by protective clauses, rivals did not simply wait for them to expire but produced alternative pasts. Competing visions of the same monuments continued to haunt the European print market well into the eighteenth century and the gradual decline of the old *privilegio* system. *Victor Plahte Tschudi*

Provenience Provenience refers to the situation in which an object is rediscovered and carries particular nuances related to the specific place or moment of its recovery, where it was previously lost or disregarded. Many dictionaries will list "provenience" as a synonym or regional variation of "provenance", and across languages they are used and translated interchangeably. In English, the two words can be usefully differentiated to describe different sets of relations that occur within an object's life cycle, where "provenience" carries particular nuances relating to a specific place or moment in which an object is recovered.

Usage of the term provenience varies between academic disciplines. According to anthropologist Rosemary Joyce, "archaeologists usually understand provenience to be the original findspot of an object. [...] Provenience is a fixed point, while provenance can be considered an itinerary that an object follows as it moves from hand to hand." Thus, it provides a particular bundle of associations and as a findspot defines "the place where a secure, interpretable archaeological context was established for an object" (Joyce 2012, pp. 50f.). Provenience describes just one of the many possible transformational episodes within the life cycle of an object, but not necessarily its origins.

A series of medieval Urnes-style metal brooches provide an illustrative example. In September 2016, Norwegian archaeologists were excavating a site in the centre of Trondheim, the medieval town of Nidaros. Close to the wall of an eleventh-century church foundation, the discovery of a brooch was made from within a grave numbered 224 (fig. 1).

The findspot was noted as "the area that would have been the chest/upper torso in an infant's grave. [...] The brooch was in very poor condition, and the ornament first became clear by X-ray imaging" (Sæhle et al. 2021, p. 413). The brooch was extracted within a lump of clay, but when that was removed in the laboratory, it disintegrated into small copper fragments and

1 *Urnes brooch in clay*, found at Søndre Gate 9–11, Trondheim, X-ray image. Photo: Marte I. Rønning

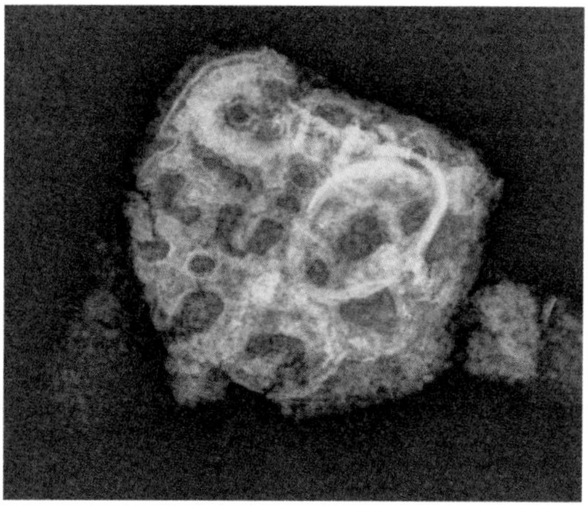

dust. Only through the X-ray and within the clay could a snapshot appear of an object being identifiable as an Urnes-style brooch. Yet without the clay this object is no longer a brooch. Only within this context is the image comparable with that of hundreds of similar brooches scattered across the Nordic countries. Only through its record of provenience can questions be asked about why the brooch was buried with an infant and why in this particular time and place. Without the clay and provenience, the copper fragments say very little in the state they eventually entered the university museum collection. Furthermore, a clay mould excavated in 1970 from an adjacent site has the negative imprint of similar brooches and appears to have been used in their production. Wooden furniture fragments were also found nearby with Urnes-style loopwork (see Fuglesang 1981, p. 24). Together, the provenience begins to speak of a connected visual culture in eleventh-century Nidaros, where the brooch's symbol reappears from burial and also a nearby site of production. Overall, the provenience of the brooch can be seen "as part of the chain of places where the object has been since its creation" (Joyce 2012, p. 56). Its provenience occurs in the middle of an itinerary that begins with the place it was made – before it was acquired by its anonymous first owners, before it was buried and before it was rediscovered in 2016 when it was transformed into a museum object and afterwards disintegrated into dust.

Objects may have multiple proveniences. The circumstances surrounding each rediscovery are equally important, as much as what it records as a geographic and stratigraphic location. Who rediscovered what, when and why, has as much historical significance as the evidence being recovered. In this sense, architecture may also have provenience. As Bruno Latour and Albena Yaneva observe, a building "is not a static object but a moving project, and that even once it has been built, it ages, it is transformed by its users, modified by all of what happens inside and outside" (Latour and Yaneva 2008, p. 80). Architecture as a monument may

2 Thomas Fearnley, *Urnes church*, 1826, watercolour in sketchbook, Oslo, Stiftelsen Thomas Fearnley, Heddy og Nils Astrup. Photo: Nick Walkley

also be later rediscovered, repurposed as the memory of the past (→ COLLECTIVE MEMORY). Buildings which have been lost "in plain sight" or ignored as a → RUIN, are often restored, monumentalised and made into museums (→ RESTORATION, → TRANSFORMATION). As the provenience of the architectural monument, the context of rediscovery forms part of understanding how a building's meaning and reception are changed.

As part of an accumulation of prior experience, each rediscovery will inform the next in time and sequence. The Urnes style brooches are classified according to a system established through twentieth-century scholarship, beginning with Norwegian archaeologist Haakon Shetelig, who in 1909 named the style after the ornamentation of the Urnes Stave Church. This twelfth-century wooden building located by the Luster fjord in on the Norwegian west coast, incorporates a carved portal and other decorated → ELEMENTS from an earlier building dated to 1070 (→ SPOLIA). By the time Norway became a fully independent country in 1905, nineteenth-century scholarship had established the church as a significant national monument. In 1979, it became one of the very first sites to be inscribed on the UNESCO world → HERITAGE list. But in 1814, at the time of the dissolution of the Denmark-Norway Double Monarchy and the forming of the Norwegian Constitution, the remarkable survival of this church was barely documented.

Norwegian artist Johan Christian Dahl (1788–1857) is often cited as the first to bring attention to the churches through his folio publication *Denkmale einer sehr ausgebildeten Holzbaukunst aus den frühesten Jahrhunderten in den innern Landschaften Norwegens* ("Monuments of a highly developed wooden architecture from the earliest centuries in the interior landscapes of Norway", Dresden 1837). However, Dahl's → AUTHORSHIP was just one of many forces that contributed to lifting the Urnes church from relative obscurity. The many students and associates connected with his professorship at the Dresden Academy of Art, and the early nineteenth-century backdrop of industrialisation and modernisation, form the contexts for Dahl's publication. His stave church folio is a somewhat patriotic and nostalgic work, motivated by an urge to preserve something uniquely Norwegian from a time of pre-Danish rule.

Though Dahl deserves credit for bringing attention to the stave churches through that first widely disseminated work, he was not the first to reproduce an image of the church at Urnes. It was his twenty-three-year-old student Franz Wilhelm Schiertz (1813–1887), who in 1836 was sent to record the initial sketches for lithographic printing. Prior to that, it seems Dahl may have come to know of the church through his acquaintances. The earliest image of Urnes appears to have been made in a sketchbook by Thomas Fearnley (1802–1842) in July 1826 (fig. 2).

Dahl met Fearnley weeks after this drawing was made on his first Norwegian tour before inviting the younger artist to join him in Dresden as his student. Meanwhile, Dahl's travel companion Mathias Eckhoff (1791–1871) notes in his diary of a visit to Urnes for Sunday morning worship, "a remarkable historical place and an interesting building for its age and architecture", also sketching the church before returning to join the group at their lodgings (Walkley 2025, p. 109). Nothing in Dahl's own diaries or sketchbooks can place him at Urnes on his Norwegian tours of 1826 or 1834. Rather than being a discovery made by a single individual, its context extends to a group of travelling landscape artists and the discussions they may have had as suggested through the records of their sketchbooks, field paintings and diary entries. The provenience of this monument extends beyond the author and date of its first publication. As a sort of archaeological context, it describes more fully the situation in which it was rediscovered, and how this remotely located church began to attain the status with which we have since received it. *Nick Walkley*

Quarry The open-air site of extraction of rock material for further processing as stone is called "quarry", from the Latin word *quadraria* (a place where stone is squared), distinguishing it from mining which refers typically to subterranean extraction of pulverized materials. Sometimes the term is conflated with the homonym "quarry", from the Old French *quarré* (prey) with roots in the Vulgar Latin *corata* (entrails), through cognitive blending, since both entail the extraction and appropriation of desired resources.

Provenance studies of the → MATERIAL extracted from quarries has an extensive history, from visual recognition in classical and Renaissance periods and written records documenting sources of stone for important monuments, to modern microscopic and radiometric analysis,

1 *Fra kalstensbruddene på Langöen (From the limestone quarries of Langøya)*, photo album, early twentieth century. Cementmuseet, Slemmestad

2 *Oper im Steinbruch (Quarry Opera)*, with scenography for Georges Bizet's *Carmen*, 2023, St Margarethen. Photo: Katharina Schiffl

including carbon dating, which allows for precise determination of the material's age and geological formation. Studies of this sort are especially true for certain sculpture groups whose provenance has been established by radiometric methods (see Clark 1994, pp. 3ff.). But the quarry itself, emptied of its lithic contents, has received little attention. As an absence, or hole, it resists appropriation by architectural history. In the popular imagination it remains a remnant or scar, either a spooky filmic locale or a testament to the human appetite for exploitation.

A mundane example serves to illustrate this point. Since the turn of the twentieth century, an island in the fjord some fifty kilometres south of Oslo has provided limestone for the production of cement. What began as a rise of 20 metres above sea level was progressively deepened to 50 metres below it. Strikingly, the island became a gaping hole in the ocean. For the company that owned this quarry, it represented simply a resource to be extracted. But another record tells a different story.

In the 1990s, after extraction had ceased and the company moved on, an → ARCHIVE of its history was rescued from a dumpster and preserved in the local library. Among its contents is a photo album. It had arrived on the doorstep, packed in brown paper but without return address or other markings. A woman had called a few days earlier to report she had found her uncle's old album of Langøya. But now, no one could remember the woman's name or that of her uncle, and in those pre-digital times no record of the phone conversation existed. The handwriting and orthography within suggest an earlier era, an older person or perhaps both. On the first page above a pasted-together panorama is the inscription "östsiden" (the east side) and below, the expression in Latin "*sic transit gloria mundi,*" thus passes the glory of the world (fig. 1).

The erosive impact of human excavation is obvious in the image: the geological striations of rock interrupted by the wide anthropogenic terraces of blasted layers. Rail wagons await loads of rubble to be shuttled off to the crusher, a literal passage of the world from earth to machine. The exploitation of the landscape provides temporary commercial benefits and more permanent architectural facilities, but also ensures the decline of the landscape it leaves behind. But perhaps the unknown labeler sought to memorialise those days of hard → LABOUR, breaking rock from the island – days then soon over, the rock used up, the island disappeared. Then again, it's not the quarry that passes away. It's the humans that provoked it, in their fleeting industriousness. The rock has simply moved house.

Yet, the passing glory of the world is still not the end. Abandoned extraction sites are frequently repurposed, whether renaturalised to contribute to wildlife biodiversity (*Zandreeij Crailoo*, Netherlands, or *Steinbruch Musital*, Switzerland), or in other cases, retaining cultural use. Since 1996, the so-called Römersteinbruch (Roman Quarry) in the Austrian Burgenland, whose calc-silicate rock was used in the construction of Vienna's Karlskirche, among other things, has been home to the Sankt Margarethen Quarry Opera (fig. 2), while the former gypsum quarry at Portel-des-Corbières has become *Terra Vinea*, a cellar where the wines of Cave Rocbère are tempered, 80 metres underground. *Thomas McQuillan*

Quote "*Amicorum communia omnia*" (Friends hold all things in common), reads the first proverb of Erasmus's bestseller *Adagia*, a storehouse of Greek and Latin epigrams, published in Paris in 1500, then in Venice in 1508, and expanded until his death in 1539. And in proverbium CCXXII he adds: "It is better to have friends without money, than money without friends" (Erasmus 1508, fol. 5r and fol. 34v). Literally, these quotes concern the transfer of property, including intellectual property; philosophically they speak about tradition (see Eden 2001).

As a trade war is unleashed globally, the actual → AFTERLIFE of these short figurative expressions of classical thought, filtered through the sensibilities of a Renaissance humanist, appears strangely comforting rather than naive. Erasmus' reflections on property and treasures as shared among friends, make a profound definition of the handing down of texts, images, styles and systems of thoughts as well as architecture. From this humanistic standpoint, provenance cannot be pinned down to individual authors and owners, history is simply a treasure trove to be shared, and it is kept alive by the active quoting and borrowing of the works and ideas of the past.

The practise of quoting can happen deliberately and meticulously – this is what we learn in school; one must get the quotes right, provide perfect footnotes and not steal from others or from ourselves in acts of autoplagiarism (→ THEFT). It may also happen involuntary. The phenomenon of the involuntary quotation was commented on by Roland Barthes, a living tradition of texts and languages in his own right. When, in 1970, struggling to transpose an

1 *View from the northwest corner of the Tomb of Tutankhamun towards the exhibition area*, Luxor. Photo: Ferdinand Saumarez Smith, 2014

Erasmus-style seminar on classical rhetoric held at the École pratique des hautes études in Paris in the academic year 1964–1965 from an oral event into a written *texte de savoir*, he apologised to the reader that unfortunately he could not track down the sources to authenticate all the references (→ AUTHENTICATION). He had to write the *aide-mémoire* "in part from memory" (Barthes 1970, p. 172).

So, what happens when one quotes an ancient piece of architecture and, in an act of → PRESERVATION, reproduces a brand new impeccably annotated, spatial, three-dimensional, full-scale *texte de savoir*? The tomb of Tutankhamun in Luxor makes a case in point (fig. 1).

There is an author to this work. From laser-scanned and recorded data of unprecedented accuracy and resolution, Factum Foundation in Madrid has rematerialised both an unforeseen fabric and a painstakingly accurate → FACSIMILE of the ancient tomb and placed it by the entrance to the Valley of the Kings. The ancient tomb which resurfaced in November 1922 – in terms of reception history a contemporary of Modernist classics such as T. S. Eliot's *The Waste Land* or Le Corbusier's Ville Contemporaine – can rest a bit further up in the valley, less exposed to the erosion of mass tourism.

A wide nomenclature has been suggested to pin down the epistemological status of this 2014 edition of an ancient → ARTEFACT: is it copy, replica, → REPRODUCTION, substitution, fake, forgery, surrogate, double, repetition, clone or ghostly → DOPPELGÄNGER? These fluctuating

2 *Sign outside the 2014 edition of the Tomb of Tutankhamun,* Valley of the Kings. Photo: Mari Lending, 2014

notions spring from the astonishment of the uncanny resemblance of the facsimile to the original, based on a shared perception of the new object as an exact visual copy, that offers visitors an experience that approximates the real thing in the very landscape of the original. Seen as an isolated object, the new tomb is impeccably authenticated, and as such apparently immune to the promiscuity of the involuntary quote Barthes evoked when refusing to track down all the bibliographical sources for his *aide-mémoire*. It is annotated in detail, from the outline of the spaces, the colours of the murals, the reliefs of the walls, the granite appearance of the sarcophagus and the → DERELICTION, imperfections and → WEATHERING of its surfaces all the way down to mundane site-specific paraphernalia such as the fire extinguishers, fans and lamps that furnish every tomb and temple of the Theban necropolis. The characteristic yellow sign with black lettering in Arabic and English that marks every tomb in the Valley of Kings appears at the entrance of the facsimile, rather boldly insisting "TOMB OF TUT ANKH AMUN" (fig. 2).

Recording data is to a digital paradigm what quoting is to a textual. The digitally-stored data that the new Tutankhamun edition is produced from records, transcribes and transmits – in short, quotes – large → FRAGMENTS of a monument as a high-resolution scan. Considered as a collection of quotes, indeed a whole recitation, it constitutes an original performance rather than a derivate that serves to document an ideal original. Just as in Erasmus's learned community, it ties back to a world in which friends held all things in common – as an emblematic definition of tradition, that is, before the dawn of authors and → AUTHORSHIP, origins and originality. Based on in-depth forensic studies this state-of-the-art conservation piece within contemporary 3-D print culture hints toward a substitutional paradigm rather than towards an anachronistic occurrence. By repeating, reviving and recovering what is lost or what might be lost, the Luxor facsimile transcends mere citation or the transposing of a fragment from one text or context to another. As a recitation it belongs in the trajectory of the object it has transcribed, evoking the past and anticipating the future; just as the Greek rhapsodist memorised and performed poetry by reproducing while adapting and adding detail (see Lending 2016). As a set of quotes, it evokes Jorge Luis Borges' fictitious author Pierre Menard who set out to write an identical new version of *Don Quixote* at the beginning of the twentieth century and concluded that the endeavor was troublesome both practically and philosophically, but not impossible. The original was part of the problem: "It is not in vain that three hundred years have gone by, filled with exceedingly complex events. Amongst them, to mention only one, is the *Quixote* itself" (Borges 1993, p. 93). Works made up of quotes undermine illusions of timelessness and demonstrates the critically historical status of any cultural production. In regards of architecture, quotes evoke the historicity of both the old and the new by pointing to the way objects behave, change, move, work, fluctuate and circulate in time and space (→ MOBILITY, → MOVABLES).

"It gleams like a mystic lamp in the evening of the aging world", the great German philologist Ernst Robert Curtius writes in *Europäische Literatur und lateinisches Mittelalter* (one of the fundamental books from which Barthes lifted many of his involuntary quotes and examples) when describing the transmission of ancient authorities by the copying of manuscripts in European cloisters throughout the Middle Ages (Curtius 1953, p. 401). In Luxor, the original tomb is forever trapped in history; the 3,200-year-old artefact is heading for slow deterioration. The new tomb will weather and decay over time as well. The data recorded in the spring of 2009 and stored in the form of an information file, are however somehow lifted from history while the sealed-off tomb in the Valley of the Kings continues its millennial-long journey through time. Meanwhile the past, present and future tombs glow in their frozen and fluctuating temporalities like little lamps in the trajectory of an Egyptian tomb. *Mari Lending*

Readymade The explosive impact of the industrial revolution on the lives of the nineteenth-century population of much of the world involved a seismic shift away from materials purchased in their raw form and handmade, towards manufactured goods fabricated through industrial production, globalising and often anonymising the provenance of building → ELEMENTS. To a significantly greater degree than before, the influx of these products and their circulation as commodities through exchange, framed the population within the roles of producers and consumers. The multiple decisions and technical skills involved in the self-sufficient, autonomous production of an → ARTEFACT were now replaced by the single choice of which already-made product to buy.

In a similar manner, the buildings of the last two centuries are now largely comprised of products assembled on site; ready-made manufactured goods that carries with them an earlier off-site production process. As with the nineteenth-century consumer, the architect chooses from these market-available manufactured goods: door handles, cladding systems, light switches, roof-lights and pre-formed metal profiles, to mention just a few of the many. The tendency towards selection and installation has a natural corollary in the lessening of crafting from → MATERIALS, the skills transferred away from the → CONSTRUCTION SITE to the factory (see Leatherbarrow 2000, pp. 119ff.).

1 Sigurd Lewerentz, *Newspaper cuttings of crossword puzzles*, 1963. ArkDes Collection, Stockholm

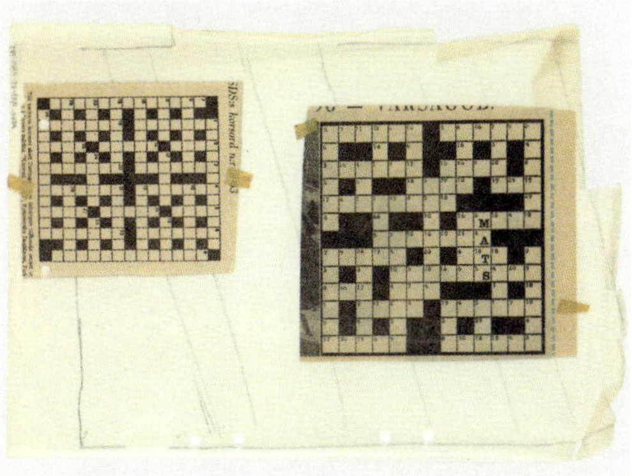

The placement by Marcel Duchamp of manufactured goods into gallery environments that had up until then been accustomed to bespoke works, defined by skilled production, mirrored this broader process, this displacement of skill. The frisson of the unassisted readymade, Duchamp's act of provocation was heightened by the specific forms of selection and placement; his choice of useful objects of everyday functionality, now made useless, and recontextualised within the unexpected setting of the art gallery (→ AUTHORSHIP, → POSTPRODUCTION). Significantly, while Duchamp's original, selected, manufactured objects have generally been lost, their later reception has largely been mediated through paradoxically handmade replicas in the serialised form of multiples; a replica (→ FACSIMILE) of his *Porte-bouteilles* of 1914 for instance, made to order in 1964 in a limited series of fourteen works, thus creating their own micro-provenance history.

Swedish architect Sigurd Lewerentz famously spent much time at the building site, particularly in his later years. He sought new solutions to old problems using familiar tools, especially the common brick. When at length he considered the everyday nail, he reportedly questioned and explored how else it might be used (see Ahlin 1985, p. 12). The story evidences both Lewerentz's recognition of the necessity of integrating elements that had already been made into the construction process, and of the creative opportunities offered by their employment in unexpected uses and places, for example when utilising the "ready-made" patterns of a crossword puzzle that he cut from newspapers for the design of the interior paving of Sankt Petri Kyrka in the southern Swedish town of Klippan (figs. 1–2).

2 Sigurd Lewerentz, *Tiled floor pattern in the parish hall, facing the stage in Sankt Petri Kyrka*, 1966, Klippan. Photographer unknown

We live, design and build in a world of already fabricated objects. The readymade, or ready-made, suggests both the standardised manufacture of these goods that are then assembled or utilised, and the potential new readings of these goods through their recontextualisation, and de- or re-purposing. The → TRANSFORMATION of materials on site that previously defined the production of buildings is now replaced by acts of selection, appropriation, juxtaposition. Their effect, as with the works of Duchamp, depends in large part on the counterpoint of existing associations and new contexts to suggest new meanings. *Hugh Strange*

Reconstruction "Mount Capitoline! [...] there stood that [temple] of Jupiter Capitoline, gradually destroyed, reconstructed, dismantled, rebuilt, ruined; and many other buildings, simulacra and altars were built there at the same time or successively, of which some descriptions remain and of some of which the remains were found on several occasions, so that the hot fantasies of learned archaeologists, both local and foreign, have made, without fully agreeing, the ideal reconstructions", wrote the Italian architect Camillo Boito, author of the 1883 *Carta del restauro*, considered the first → PRESERVATION charter, in subtle sarcastic disdain for past reconstructions (Boito 1893, pp. 242f.).

Reconstruction is a tricky concept in preservation history. Principles of originality and → AUTHENTICITY have been inscribed in charters, regulations and practices to prevent reconstruction. Today, the term commonly refers to recreating something lost in sudden and dramatic circumstances as a stand-in for the original (→ FACSIMILE). Unlike → RESTORATION, implying negotiations between old and new, original and copy, additions and → SUBTRACTION, interpretations and new design, a reconstruction is unequivocally new and dependent on exact correspondence to a lost original. While → AUTHORSHIP is recognised in restorations, practitioners of reconstructions are rarely acknowledged. However, they are undeniably creative acts, often relying on missing and unreliable evidence and frequently in need of adjustments with the use of non-original → MATERIALS and updated building techniques. Because reconstructions act like originals, they are perceived as fake and unethical (→ DOPPELGÄNGER).

Throughout the nineteenth century reconstruction and restoration are constantly mixed up. The French archaeologist Adolphe Napoléon Didron is wrongfully credited for dooming reconstruction as the second-last resort when dealing with ancient monuments. In translations of his famous statement – "Regarding ancient monuments, it is better to consolidate than to repair, better to repair than restore (→ REPARATION), better to restore than embellish" (Didron 1843, p. 47) – reconstruction is smuggled in-between "restore" and "embellish", possibly a deliberate anachronistic move to disavow reconstruction. A fierce opponent of the many invasive restorations of the time, Didron distinguishes between reconstruction and restoration practices when commenting on the much-debated Basilique Sainte-Marie-Madeleine de Vézelay by Eugène Viollet-le-Duc: "We have been repairing with a very rare intelligence and always, almost, perfectly successful, the Sainte-Chapelle in Paris, we have been reconstructing, so to speak, the Madeleine of Vézelay, we have been creating Saint-Nicolas de Naintes, certainly we have everything we need to consolidate Notre-Dame de Paris" (Didron 1845, p. 128). The Vézelay project was based on sparse physical and archival evidence and can hardly be called a reconstruction according to present standards.

In the canonical entry "Restauration" in his *Dictionnaire raisonné de l'architecture du XIe au XVe siècle française* (1854-1868), Viollet-le-Duc aimed to clarify the many fluctuating terms in circulation. In reference to Ludovic Vitet, the Inspector General of Historical Monuments, who when visiting the ruinous Château de Coucy envisioned a reconstruction in "which not so much stone and cement will be required as sheets of paper", he adopted a reconstruction formula he later would follow as the chateau's architect: "The aim would be to rebuild [*reconstruire*] or, rather, to reinstate this great fortress of the Middle Ages in its totality as well as in its finer details, and to reproduce its interior decorations up to and including its furnishings. The idea would be, in a word, to give back its form and colour and, if I may dare to say it, its original life" (Viollet-le-Duc 1990, p. 204). The paradox of reconstructing a lost original "in its finer details" haunted the discipline of preservation way into the twentieth century.

Reconstructions, understood as exact copies and stand-ins, characterise the second half of the twentieth century, partly in response to the devastations of the Second World War. They followed on from sudden, dramatic events and were part of national healing processes (→ RUIN, → WAR). Besides a few prominent reconstructions such as the rebuilding of the historic centre of Warsaw, it took time before reconstructions were accepted by the international → HERITAGE community. The Venice Charter states that: "All reconstruction work should however be ruled out 'a priori'" (Venice Charter 1964, art. 15). In 1979, reconstruction made its way into the ICOMOS toolbox: "Reconstruction is appropriate where a place is incomplete through damage or alteration and where it is necessary for its survival, or where it recovers the cultural significance of the place as a whole" (Burra Charter 1979, art. 17).

Although exceptional cases of reconstruction have been celebrated (the Stari Most area in Mostar, Bosnia-Herzegovina, 2004; the Frauenkirche in Dresden, 2005; the Tombs of Buganda Kings at Kasubi in Uganda, 2023; Notre Dame

1 Matias Faldbakken, *Upholding*, model, 2025. Photo: Vegard Kleven

de Paris, 2024), scepticism prevails to this day: "In relation to authenticity, the reconstruction of archaeological remains or historic buildings or districts is justifiable only in exceptional circumstances. Reconstruction is acceptable only on the basis of complete and detailed documentation and to no extent on conjecture" (World Heritage Committee 2024, § 86).

The reconstruction of the Sufi mausoleums at the Timbuktu World Heritage Site in Mali after the violent destruction in 2012 may represent a shift. The UNESCO-headed reconstruction was anchored in the local community, evoking intangible values, promoting the transmittal of traditional building techniques, and was seen as part of a reconciliation process (see Cameron 2017). This example suggests a new role for reconstruction, not exclusively as a transmitter of architectural and historical values, but as a generative and dynamic agent for negotiations with the present.

In his 2025 winning proposal *Upholding* for the National Memorial for 22 July in Oslo's new government quarter, artist Matias Faldbakken has created a monument to commemorate the seventy-seven victims of the two subsequent terror attacks carried out by the lone right-wing terrorist at the government quarter in the centre of Oslo and at the Utøya island in Tyrifjorden on 22 July 2011 (fig. 1).

The monument is an exact reconstruction of the steel rig that was built in 2020 to safeguard Pablo Picasso's 12 by 15 metres and 115-tonne concrete relief *The fishermen* when it was detached from the south wing of the 1969 modernist Y-shaped government building and later mounted on a new neighbouring ministry building (fig. 2).

The building was demolished due to new security measures implemented after the attack, a decision that triggered public uproar and international protests. In the four years that passed since the → DEMOLITION until the new building was in place, the rig became a transitional "significant object" according to Faldbakken, who conceived the rig as an unintentional monument, and "quite literally, a tool for rearranging our shared values" (see Faldbakken 2025). By objectifying the steel rig as a found object (→ READYMADE) and turning it into a monumental framework, the artwork amplifies the provenance of the fragment to memorialise a site of trauma and → CRISIS. The rig could be conceived as an expression of protection: "For all its brutality, it was a kind of crutch. The rig was, literally, a support structure", according to the artist, and expressing "both disruption and preservation on a monumental scale" (Faldbakken 2025). In 1969, the relief was sandblasted on site by Picasso's Norwegian collaborator, artist Carl Nesjar, on the *naturbetong* (natural concrete) wall developed and patented by the building's architect Erling Viksjø and engineer Sverre Jystad in 1955. Borrowing the dimensions and the temporary positioning of the relocated Picasso mural, Faldbakken's work depicts a greenshank, a small wader typical of inland areas like Tyrifjorden, made of around half a million

2 *Steel rig with Pablo Picasso's relief "The fishermen"*, 2020, Oslo. Photo: Adrian Bugge

mosaic stones laid in a steel frame on site in collaboration with survivors, the bereaved and others affected by the attacks (→ COUNTER-MONUMENT).

In the process of rebuilding the government quarter, ideas of reconstruction have circulated in many ways. Due to security, locating a government quarter in the centre of the city was questioned but reinstated for symbolic reasons. In his speech to the crowds gathering at the town hall square on 25 July 2011, then Prime Minister Jens Stoltenberg proclaimed that the population had to take over th public space again and defiantly stated that Norvegian hearts were broken, but not the the people. Reclaiming the existing site for a new government quarter, despite the risk for future attacks and the problems that comes with barriers and surveillance, may be considered an act of resistance against authoritarian forces and an upholding of democratic values.

The most striking reconstruction is the rebuilt *naturbetong* top floor of the main government building, Høyblokka from 1958, also designed by Erling Viksjø. In 2011, the terrorist detonated the bomb from a van parked under the building, causing eight deaths and the building's partial destruction. Yet, due to the strength of its pilotis and an underground passage, the main force from the blast went out- and downwards saving the high-rise from structural failure. While the Y-shaped lower building had to go, the high-rise was saved as a compromise between heritage and security interests. Although the building has been technically upgraded and accommodated for contemporary office use, it basically appears as in 1959. *Upholding* is placed in direct dialogue with Høyblokka; a memorial of the trauma (→ COLLECTIVE MEMORY) as well as a commentary to both the new and reconstructed architecture of the Norwegian state – an unruly and resistant structure that reflects the dilemmas and ambiguities of reconstruction. *Erik Langdalen*

Recycling In a conversation on the *Circular museum – Ways of collecting and commissioning* between former Tate Modern director Frances

1 Michael Reynolds, *Wall built from empty cans (detail)*, steel beverage cans, wire and concrete, 1971. Photographer unknown

Morris and artist Tino Sehgal hosted in February 2023 by the Museum of Modern Art in New York City, Morris suggested that the ever-shifting dynamics of the climate polycrisis should compel museums to reconsider the fundamentals of its existence. In a world which we can no longer confidently say will be permanent, what does it mean to house and preserve a permanent collection? Objects are pulled out of the flow of time and placed in museums with the assumption that time is linear, within which objects have a provenance, a lifetime and a legacy (→ AFTERLIFE). Morris's claim comes as an echo to an earlier moment in which Western chronology was challenged by environmental changes.

American architect Michael Reynolds's work anticipated architecture's current discourse of circular economy and in his own telling, he had the revelation in 1970 after watching Walter Cronkite on CBS Evening News: "They were talking about beer and soda cans being thrown all over the countryside. They predicted a garbage problem in the future" (Reynolds 2008, p. 17). The same broadcast reported on the clearcutting of a forest in the Pacific Northwest for timber to meet housing demands: "What if we used what society discards", thought Reynolds, "to make the things we need?" American popular discourse in the United States had primed Reynolds for this breakthrough. News stories throughout the 1960s exposed the nuclear fallout in the

American Midwest from weapons-testing, the rivers and lakes filling with industrial pollutants and the major cities blanketed in thick, noxious smog. Concern for the environment crescendoed and, on the first Earth Day on 22 April 1970, twenty million people across the US attended rallies, teach-ins and marches.

Reynolds graduated from the University of Cincinnati in 1969, at the crest of the anti-war, civil-rights and environmental movements: "Architecture as it stood then was worthless", he said in *Garbage warrior*, a 2007 documentary about his life's work. And he continued: "It had nothing to do with the planet and barely anything to do with people and what they needed." Architecture, he thought, had the power to shape humanity's course towards a continuously thriving future but, instead, it perpetuated the status quo, "taking us where we don't need to go". In 1971, aged twenty-six, Reynolds bought an old barn on 18 hectares of land in Cañon, New Mexico. He moved in with his first wife, Susan. Needing more space after the couple's son was born, and inspired by Cronkite's report, Reynolds filled wood-framed structures with beer bottles and cement mortar (→ COMPONENT, → ELEMENT). Laid sideways with their necks extending outward, the bottles formed walls that, when sunlight streamed through, resembled stained glass in shades of coffee and olive.

Reynolds started building a house entirely out of beer-can "bricks", made by sandwiching a pair of horizontally oriented cans between two vertical ones (fig. 1). On either side of the horizontal cans are additional, flattened cans for weatherproofing (→ WEATHERING). Holding everything together are wire cinctures around the top and bottom rims. The year he moved to Cañon, Reynolds filed a patent application for "building blocks of empty cans" where he described the attributes of his invention (fig. 2).

2 *Michael Reynolds building "Thumb House"*, 1971, Cañon, New Mexico. Photographer unknown

By his claims, his can-blocks have a high mechanical strength, yet are lightweight, making them cheap to obtain and transport, and quick to lay. Given their irregular surfaces, they can be stacked and connected with a conventional mortar joint. Most importantly, aside from the wire fasteners, the blocks are made entirely of waste material. With these blocks, Reynolds eliminated the concept of garbage not only in his practice, but in his worldview. What was once disposed of is now raw → MATERIAL to make something else: industry castoffs reimagined as a natural resource. In *Journey*, a self-published intellectual biography, he wrote: "Now it is humanity that is becoming the nature of the planet" (Reynolds 2008, p. 7). Looping the direction of material flow back onto itself, creating a circular economy of matter – recycling and upcycling – is a challenge to linear time. Provenance ceases to be a question of origin and becomes into a diary of transformations.

If Reynolds's invention anticipated our current discourse on circular economy and upcycling, he would likely admit that it was as much a result of environmentalism as it was of prophetic vision. In the early 1970s, Reynolds would spend nights on the roof of his two-story beer-can extension gazing up at the moon. There, he claimed wizards would appear with messages about mind-expanding ways to perceive the world more fully. One advocated for something called "spherical vision", which reimagines a person's field of vision as omniscient rather than directed, their point of view infinitely multiplied around an object to create a spherical field of perspectives.

For Reynolds, looking at something is a form of interaction or engagement, and doing so simultaneously from all sides and distances is akin to a physical and spiritual entwinement with the surrounding world. We are what's around us. In this way, a brick made of cans is not just a novel aggregate of material but signals a fundamental shift in the relationship between humans and their lived environment: "We are talking about cosmic travel into a rock; into the body of a bird; into the mind of a human; into the depths of the universe" (Reynolds 2008, p. 101). *Carson Chan*

Renovation The term "renovation" describes a range of interventions. While it shares common ground with terms like → TRANSFORMATION, adaptive → REUSE or → RESTORATION, "renovation" is met with some snobbery, largely because it seems to require less specialised expertise compared to more "elevated" approaches. However, this perception also makes the term highly usable. A renovation can describe everything from a real-estate driven interior fit-out to a vital upgrade that maintains the functionality of an existing structure, to an aspirational interior in lifestyle magazines or the adaption of vernacular timber buildings. Given the climate crisis, the construction industry is increasingly focused on reusing the existing built environment, which underscores the need for a definition which sustains the necessity for buildings to evolve over time, while also incrementally changing their identity.

Renovation conveys the idea of renewal (from Latin *re* and *novare*, to make new). The boundaries of the term, however, remain ambiguous. Whilst some associate renovation with continuity and → MAINTENANCE, others link it to remodeling, which implies significant change and transformation. In fact, some definitions of renovation even suggest that it can involve completely demolishing a building (→ DEMOLITION) and rebuilding an identical replica (→ FACSIMILE) of the original (see Picout and Rubin 2020, p. 23). Most definitions, however, agree that a renovation involves bettering an existing situation rather than merely restoring it to a former state. Perhaps the most applicable interpretation of the term is "the improvement of a building to meet contemporary standards of comfort, safety, aesthetics, and environmental impact" (Plevoets and Van Cleempoel 2019, p. 20), a definition that aligns with the *Cambridge Dictionary*, which defines renovation as the act or process of repairing and improving something, particularly a building (→ REPARATION).

Amid the global carbon emergency, renovations are increasingly promoted as a more sustainable alternative to new construction. The European Green Deal initiatives have the ambitious goal of renovating 35 million buildings by 2030 and boldly state that "renovation should be a shared project across Europe" (EU Renovation Wave, p. 26). Yet the lack of precision around the term can lead to operations where the task is poorly understood. Structures are dubiously "improved" at high carbon cost, while jeopardising historic building fabric. Furthermore, the level of formal regulation for a renovation project varies greatly, making renovations equally the domain of DIY enthusiasts as well as builders and architects. Still, any renovation will be a pivotal moment in a building's life where decisions about its past and future are made.

1 *Manor house*, nineteenth century, renovated by Kastler Skjeseth Architects, 2017, Lyngør Island, Norway. Photo: Max Creasy

Each part is evaluated, leading to conclusions about what can be retained, what can be repaired and what will be replaced. At one end of the spectrum is a lighter approach, which might involve new kitchen cabinets, fresh bathroom tiles or a coat of paint. At the other end, a more dramatic "total renovation" can include a complete strip-out of the building, moving walls, making structural changes or in some cases a change of use.

The remnants of each renovation cycle tell a distinct story about the building's past while offering insight into how to adapt it for the future. A paper trail of documents, specifications and → ARCHITECTURAL DRAWINGS records a specific moment in time, while even the simplest physical intervention, like an extra layer of paint, can inscribe stories about the building's provenance into its → MATERIAL fabric. The repetitive nature of renovations means the same structure may be composed of building → ELEMENTS from across decades and even centuries. This form of layering and metamorphosis has a long tradition in Northern European vernacular building culture, where a single building regularly undergoes several makeovers in its lifetime. A defining feature of these timber buildings is one of → BRICOLAGE and cannibalism through the widespread reuse of existing building parts.

Two curious examples of this process carried forward into contemporary renovation projects might offer some clues as to what the term renovation can cover. The first example is the renovation of an Empire-style manor house along Norway's southern coast (fig. 1).

Empire style is roughly equal to *Biedermeier* in German speaking countries and Regency in Great Britain, the strict symmetry of the Empire style dominated the buildings along Norwegian outer-ports in the mid nineteenth century. The wealth and aspirations of house owners led many to reshape their dwellings to fit the latest trends that travelled across the North Sea. When the manor house was renovated over a century later, its predecessor, an asymmetrical baroque building that once stood on the site, was found embedded in the notched log structure.

2 *Auxiliary storehouse*, eighteenth century, renovated by Kastler Skjeseth Architects, 2023, Larvik, Norway. Photo: Kastler Skjeseth Architects

Peeled back interior linings disclosed patches in the log wall where windows were reshaped and relocated to fit the awkwardly imposed symmetry of the new classical plan. Ornamental timber beams with outmoded beading details had been relegated to the attic as structural trusses. Nail holes in timber wall panels indicated a previous life as a floorboard. Situated on an island, the story told by this act of self-cannibalisation is one of robustness and resourcefulness in a place of material scarcity.

Rather than return the building to an artificial former state, the most recent renovation worked with an understanding that this building had always been adapted to contemporary needs. It is a local vernacular heavily influenced by changing international styles that was kept relevant over time by an ability to be "remade new again" – a pertinent reminder that buildings are never static objects.

In another example, reinstating a lost part of the building offered the possibility not to simply reproduce what was there but to make more of the existing situation. Timber buildings settle over time, and it is not uncommon that disturbing the equilibrium of an existing situation involves a stark brutality: damages appear, ceilings collapse, walls crumble. For better or worse, in any renovation something must be lost so that something else can be added. In this instance, a small eighteenth-century auxiliary storehouse (*eldhus*) in Larvik, Norway – notable for its post-and-beam construction with slag stone infill, a byproduct of the historic iron foundry to which the estate belongs – was renovated to become a dwelling (fig. 2).

The slag stone made the otherwise common storehouse unique, but it was also its Achilles heel, a brittle and irreplaceable material forming a continuous cold bridge throughout. The renovation piggy-backed on the repair of something inimitable. Grandfathering in the new elements needed to convert the storehouse into a dwelling, a new compacted and technical plug-in that added rainwater drainage, a retaining wall, thermal windows, bathroom, stairs and fireplace. Old and new parts were merged to make a hybrid that keeps the buildings in use, ultimately safeguarding it from demolition.

These are just two examples of recent renovations built on previous renovations that capture a building's need for the stewardship and care of people, both professionals from the building industry and everyday folk who renovate to keep the structures they inhabit usable and to their liking (→ RESIDENTS). An increasing interest in reuse and focus on the circular economy has made working with existing buildings more of a day-to-day task. Yet, it is one that requires the ability to design in layered, multi-authored situations while navigating unpredictable outcomes (→ ACTOR, → AUTHORSHIP).

Therefore, regardless of the shortcomings, the difficulty in defining renovation and the mixed reception of the term in academic circles, these ordinary iterative acts of renewal will continue to play a vital role in chronicling, radically remaking and extending the life of the existing built environment. *Amandine Kastler*

Reparation Repairing architecture is the practice of upgrading damaged, worn or defective buildings or parts of them by refurbishing or replacing individual elements. The aim is to eliminate or delay wear and tear in order to extend a building's service life, as is documented, among uncountable others, by the repair of Erich Mendelsohn's famous Einstein Tower already in 1927–1928 (fig. 1). While → RENOVATION is primarily aimed at an aesthetic overhaul of architecture, repair is primarily intended to maintain or restore serviceability, which can lead to changes in both appearance and function (→ MAINTENANCE, → RESTORATION). As a learned systematic strategy that enables the appropriation and preservation of culture, the repair of architecture can be understood as a cultural technique. The fundamental principles of building repair are based analogously on the self-organisation and self-healing powers of nature, as organic systems can often repair themselves with minimal effort (see Heckl 2013, pp. 21ff.).

In pre-industrial times, the activities of manufacturing and repairing were closely linked. In architecture in particular, both processes were characterised by craftsmanship. They were often carried out by the same people, because the traditional → MATERIALS and methods used in the construction of buildings required processes and tools that were similar to those used in their reworking. During industrialisation, repair and manufacture were more

1 Erich Mendelsohn, *Einstein Tower,* 1920–1922, during repair work, 1927–1928, Potsdam. Photographer unknown

and more treated separately. Repair proved to be increasingly unattractive economically because, compared to pre-industrial times, → LABOUR → COSTS rose to be higher than material costs (see Krebs et al. 2018, p. 13). The logic of linear economic activity with a sequence of production, use and disposal suggests that newly manufactured consumer goods (and also architecture) are preferable to used goods, as they promise better functionality and higher prestige (→ CAPITALISM).

Based on the ideas of sociologist Richard Sennett, a distinction must be made between three basic modes of repair: "Restoration" aims to preserve an object in its original condition, "remediation" replaces parts of an object with better parts or materials, while retaining the original form, while "reconfiguration" involves changing both the form and use of the object in question (see Sennett 2012, p. 285). Reconfiguration as a method of repair is itself a historical practice (see Jager 2024). As a result, for centuries, building was primarily a matter of modifying and adapting existing substance and thus of rebuilding, which often also remedied and thus repaired functional deficits. In addition, a structural → TRANSFORMATION can also take place in the sense of a "workaround", as the editors of the volume *Kulturen des Reparierens* added (Krebs et al. 2018, p. 31). Certain problems are explicitly not remedied, for example, if individual parts or functionalities of a building are no longer relevant or if only a temporary continued use is sought. This pragmatic method of leaving things as they are fulfils both ecological and economic sustainability requirements. However, even when a building has reached the end of its useful life, principles of → REUSE can take effect by → RECYCLING its → COMPONENTS within circular economy.

The growing awareness of the finite nature of material resources has made the practice of repairing increasingly the focus of public attention and scientific research. This was prominently demonstrated by the curators of the German Pavilion at the Venice Biennale of Architecture in 2023. Under the title *Open for maintenance*, the pavilion was dedicated to circular construction and thus to the practices of repair in architecture (see issues on "The Great Repair", *ARCH+*, 2022–2023). Under the title *The limits to growth*, the Club of Rome had already impressively demonstrated the limited nature of global resources in 1972. The production of architecture is still not very sustainable in many cases, as the energy-intensive production of → CONCRETE, for example, is responsible for almost eight per cent of global carbon dioxide emissions. In Germany alone, the construction sector produces more than half of all waste. A comparative look at repair cultures in socialist economic systems makes it clear that such resource-intensive practices are by no means without alternative. In 2020, historian Reinhild Kreis used the example of the German Democratic Republic to describe how material shortages and the limited availability of machines inevitably led to a revaluation of repair practices in various areas of life (see Kreis 2020, pp. 364ff.).

Currently, approaches to a circular economy are increasingly being tested, to use existing resources more efficiently. For example, the use of real estate can be intensified by subletting unneeded spaces, similar to what is happening in the transport sector through practices such as car sharing. In addition, an appreciative approach can extend the useful life of buildings. This historical practice has recently been recontextualised with the introduction of the concept of care into the architectural discourse, where functions of architecture are understood as care work, insofar as buildings provide security and weather protection (see Fitz and Krasny 2019). At the same time, architecture itself is also an object of care work, as it requires maintenance and repair in order to delay the moment of → OBSOLESCENCE.

This moment is more difficult to determine in architecture than with many other consumer goods: a car whose engine does not start is undoubtedly in need of repair and the corresponding assessment is made according to a binary scheme (functional / non-functional).

2 *Undated stone repair on Friedrich August Stüler's colonnade on Museum Island*, 1853–1860, Berlin. Photo: Frank Schmitz, 2025

It is equally clear what the result of a repair must be and usually also how the repair can be carried out. Architecture, however, is characterised by a multitude of functions, making it more difficult to define the moment and scope of the need for repair: if a house is less well insulated against cold, heat or moisture than others, it is often impossible to determine the moment when repairs are needed. At the same time, there are often several ways to address a problem in architecture. A building that is poorly protected against the cold can be improved by insulation, by replacing the windows or by changing the roof covering. These measures can be combined or – as a workaround – a different, more efficient heating system can be installed without solving the insulation problem. The decision for or against repairs is also complicated by factors that are not directly related to the building: the value of a property, for example, can lead to the building on it being deemed unworthy of repair if new construction on the same site promises a higher return.

Essential impulses for repair practices have come from the theory of monument → PRESERVATION. Care and resource-conserving handling of the existing building, refurbishment and minimally invasive repairs originate in monument preservation, with the aim of keeping the substance in the best possible state (fig. 2).

The practice that repairs can themselves be repairable, for example by being carried out reversibly, which has also been tested extensively in the practice of conservation. It is only logical that the term "repair society" was coined in the context of a → HERITAGE conference in 1993 in Passau, Bavaria (see Lipp 1994).

However, a general paradigm shift in building culture towards repair practices also harbours risks for the preservation of monuments, as repairs are not necessarily aimed at preserving the appearance, materiality and function of a building.

In the construction industry, there is likely to be an increased use of repair work, as indicated by a directive for consumer goods adopted in the European Union in 2024. This provides for a right to repair that is to be transposed into national legislation in the European member states by 2026. The right to repair is to be extended beyond the warranty period and repairs are to be free of charge for consumers under certain conditions. It is currently difficult to predict what feedback effects this will have on a culture of repair in architecture. The spread of repair practices is facilitated by digital learning methods such as video tutorials and blogs for sharing experiences. They make specialist knowledge accessible to wider audiences and also enable non-experts to carry out repairs themselves. Strengthening the culture of repair in this way must have consequences for design and construction practice: if architecture is to be changeable and repairable in the long term, it must also be designed with this in mind, in terms of both the choice of building materials and the production methods. *Frank Schmitz*

Reproduction Simply defined, a reproduction in art or architecture is an object that recalls the likeness of another that it is derived from, however slightly. Biologically, the term "reproduc tion" refers to the making of offspring resulting in new individuals with resemblances to their parents. Similarly, the reproduced art or architectural object allows for a viewer to a make visual connection between the reproduction and its parent object(s). The term "reproduction" has a broad range of synonyms, inclusive of the more exact copies of → FACSIMILES, replicas, clones or representations, but also of more derogatory terms of forgeries or fakes (→ DOPPELGÄNGER). The term incorporates both literal reproductions that replicate the form, process

1 *The Ål portal*, Cast Courts, Victoria & Albert Museum, London. Photo: Nick Walkley, 2022

and → MATERIAL, as well as the reproduced image made by drawing, printing, casting, → PHOTOGRAPHY or a high-resolution digital scan. Here the definition is extended to include those imitative variations that retain their relation even the slightest of recognisable references within the new object.

Within the Cast Courts of the Victoria & Albert Museum in London, three plaster reproductions (→ PLASTER CAST) of Norwegian church portals stand against the salmon-pink and sage green wall, overshadowed by the two dominating halves of a cast of Trajan's column. One comes from the Ål church, Hallingdal (fig.1), demolished in 1880, when the original portal was moved to its current place of display at the Historisk Museum in Oslo.

The Ål portal is among the most remarkable survivals of church ornamentation from circa 1150, carved as Christianity was being established in Norway. The version in plaster, finished with a dark brown painted surface that imitates the condition of the original timber, was prepared by the Guidotti brothers around 1882 in then Christiania and donated by the Royal Frederik's University to the Victoria & Albert Museum (see Lending 2017, pp. 112ff.). Since then, its intricate sculptural detail has been admired and studied simultaneously in these two capital cities on both sides of the North Sea where their respective museum settings allow for direct comparison. In London, the Ål portal represents Norwegian culture amongst the canon of reproduced European architectural examples, whilst in Oslo together with other portals it testifies evidence of a particular local medieval art tradition.

In every reproduction, there is simultaneously loss and gain. In his famous study *The work of art in the age of its technological reproducibility*, Walter Benjamin lamented the loss of the aura, claiming it as a unique and irreproducible property of an original. Whilst the existence of an aura of this kind may be contestable, there is less disputable fact in his statement that "in even the most perfect reproduction, one thing is lacking: the here and now of the work of art – its unique existence in a particular place" (Benjamin 2006, p. 253). Neither the plaster cast, nor the drawings, prints or photographs of the Ål portal can reproduce its direct connection to its maker. Only the original pine bears witness to the tools that formed it in that original place, and the few remaining flecks of paint that once coloured the freshly carved surfaces as applied by the craftsperson's hand. Only this one original object carries the material evidence recalling all the marks of history to which it has been subject on its journey through time. Meanwhile, the chipped paint and cracked plaster of the Ål portal in London tells its own unique and considerable story.

A reversal of attitudes towards the reproduction as an inferior object offers the opportunity to gain new insight. A reproduced art object, argue Bruno Latour and Adam Lowe, can be compared to the staging of works in the performing arts. Within that tradition of interpretation, each new director or conductor extracts particular latent traits where the work's genius or originality is "magnified by this *faithful* (but not mimetic) reproduction" (Latour and Lowe 2011, p. 280). Any museum object is part of its own reproduction every time it goes on display (→ EXHIBITION), they argue, where it must be dusted (→ DUST), relit, restored (→ RESTORATION), repositioned in different rooms on different walls, in different → CATALOGUES, according to the direction of the curatorial team. But as a performer in its own production, the museum original as a discrete object is restricted by conservational procedures. The reproduction, on the other hand, is free to convey narratives that the original → ARTEFACT no longer can. In such cases, the aura may even migrate, argue Latour and Lowe, to a facsimile reproduction as an exact visual copy that attempts to recover the object as a complex subject of the situation for which it was first intended (→ PROVENIENCE).

The reproduction of an artwork or architectural object is not "just a copy", but a new independent thing (→ THING-RIGHT). As Latour notes by etymological derivation, a "thing" originally designated a certain type of archaic assembly or parliamentary meeting (see Latour 2005). Each "thing" gathers its own complex set of relations, issues and concerns. A reproduction as a "thing" assembles its own unique contributions of the materials, technologies, skills and makers. Thus, each new object is a unique gathering offering an original commentary through the various actors who each have something different to say, and through which the overall form gradually evolves.

Through metaphors of natural reproduction and evolution, art historian George Kubler proposed a theory of stylistic development through the propagation of things and connected ideas. The species of a style develops through reproduction, he argued, observing how "prior positions are part of the invention", whilst "every man-made replica varies from its model by minute, unplanned divergences" (Kubler 1962, pp. 64ff.). In other words, even the most inventive artist or architect does not truly create something from nothing, as *creatio ex nihilo*. Neither could another truly replicate every aspect of that same work as the perfect copy. All new works are therefore reproductions of earlier models to some degree, formed through nuanced spectrum of modes between those unachievable limits of pure creation and total replication (see Walkley 2025, p. 282).

Responding to the brief of producing an original work at the bequest of Kristiania Crafts and Industry Association for the Stockholm Exposition in 1897, Norwegian architect Henrik Bull (1864–1953) turned to reproducing ornamental details from the wooden church doors such as the Ål portal, which had entered the museum collection only some years before. Bull designed a Jugendstil type interior in collaboration with woodcarvers Lars Kinsarvik (1846–1925) and Johan Borgersen (1863–1930), who cut the entangled interlace of dragons and vines into the mahogany tables, chairs, cupboards and a sofa. Capital lions similar to those from Ål were reproduced to top the newel posts of the surrounding banister. Later, imitational

2 Henrik Bull, *Government Administration Building, detail of a door*, 1906, Oslo. Photo: Nick Walkley, 2025

reproduction of similar figures would distance themselves further from the model in Bull's design for the Historisk Museum (completed 1902) that was to become the new home for the very portals that inspired its ornamentation. By the time Bull completed work on the nearby Government Administration Building in 1906, the related dragon and lion figures carved into the stone and timber together with the wing motifs within the door ironmongery displayed only a distant resemblance to their ancestors from Ål (fig. 2). The new ornaments gather new materials, meanings and forms, whilst maintaining a distinguishable line of → INHERITANCE symbolically reproduced from the medieval portal.

All originals are to some degree reproductions, and all reproductions are somewhat original. In Henrik Bull's reproduction of the medieval portal, the distance of the image from the original is considerable enough to attribute his name as the inventive author of a distinctive individual and original style. The Guidotti brothers' achievement of exactly replicating the Ål portal in plaster is also a work of originality, not without its interventional → AUTHORSHIP of translation. However, the original Ål portal was itself also a reproduction of earlier models and ideas. Its parentage may be unknown or lost to us, but through these still-living relatives we detect a continuing ontological line of heritage in our own time (→ AFTERLIFE). *Nick Walkley*

Residents An essential factor in the provenance history of buildings is the residents who lived and worked in them over decades, perhaps centuries. This is a social aspect of architecture that is all too rarely taken into account in its research, which is largely focused on stylistic, aesthetic, structural or iconographic insights. Across cities around the world, former occupants of houses are only remembered when they are people of public interest, such as politicians, writers or artists. Indeed, it seems as if a building – quite independently of its architectural qualities – is ennobled by prominent inhabitants in the same way as those

1 *Memorial plaques for Ferruccio Busoni and Billy Wilder*, marble and brass, 1966 and 1993, date of death added in 2002, Viktoria-Luise-Platz, Berlin. Photo: Uwe Fleckner, 2025

works of painting or sculpture that attract greater interest through famous previous owners and therefore increase in value: this is a historical connection that, incidentally, marks the very beginning of provenance research in the context of an art market seeking ever higher profits.

In many places, the prominent former residents of apartments and houses are commemorated by plaques attached to the facades of the buildings. One of countless examples is the → INSCRIPTION at 36 Hohenstaufenstraße in Berlin, which states that the "racing reporter", the socially critical journalist and writer Egon Erwin Kisch, lived here in the 1920s. Accordingly, at 745 Washington Street in New York we can read that the painter Roy Lichtenstein had his flat and studio in this building from 1988 until his death in 1997, and in Paris, at 40 Rue Pierre Fontaine, we find a plaque indicating that Joséphine Baker founded her first cabaret in the French capital here in 1926. Residents who are not counted among this illustrious group of people (→ CELEBRITY) are only actually honoured with such commemorative measures if their fate is to become part of the → COLLECTIVE MEMORY. This happens, in the German context, especially when attention is drawn to the crimes of National Socialism. For example, the so-called *Stolpersteine* (stumbling stones), which originated from a private German initiative – rightly criticised for their design and placement – are embedded in the pavement in front of selected houses, where they serve as decentralised memorials (→ COUNTER-MONUMENT) for those individuals who had lived there and were murdered or deported during the National Socialist dictatorship (see Schrader 2006; Kavčič et al. 2021).

The fact that the individual fate of a person can also be linked to the history of a building and thus to their immediate living environment may become apparent, for example, when a reference to the resident of a building cannot be found. One day in 1987, the aged American film director Billy Wilder, accompanied by a friend, was walking through the Schöneberg district of Berlin, where he had lived as a young journalist from 1926 to 1933 (see Karasek 1992, p. 14). The two men decided to visit Wilders' former home on Viktoria-Luise-Platz, where he stayed for a short time as a subtenant ("A tiny room with gloomy wallpaper. Wall to wall with a constantly rushing toilet"). But even from a distance, they could see that the house had not survived the Second World War. In fact, the building had fallen victim to Allied bombing in 1945 (→ LACUNA, → WAR), and a sober small apartment block had been built in its place in the postwar period. However, they also noticed that a plaque drew attention to the fact that a prominent personality had lived in the previous building. Wilder was visibly moved that the city he had to leave after Hitler came to power was still keeping his memory alive. But he was soon disappointed, because when he stepped closer, he found the following information on the marble memorial tablet: "Ferruccio Busoni lived here until his death. Musician – thinker – teacher". It was not until some years later that the omission could be rectified: in February 1993, when Wilder was once again visiting the city for the Berlin Film Festival, "his" plaque was unveiled. And so today, alluding wittily with a slightly ironic undertone to the former oblivion, a second plaque, imitating the original in wording, material and typography and placed directly below the first, reads: "Billy Wilder also lived here from 1927 to 1928" (fig. 1).

Even if the residents of a building are not its owners (as such they would be links in a conventional provenance chain of → ARTEFACTS), they nevertheless influence the provenance of architecture in the extended definition of the term used here. The inhabitants of houses and flats furnish them, use them, possibly renovate or repair them (→ RENOVATION, → REPARATION) or contribute to their transformation in other ways.

In addition, they fundamentally engrave their traces of life in the buildings, just as buildings engrave their traces deep in human existence (see Sennett 1994). Architectures are therefore not to be understood as petrified solitaires, but as vital social → NETWORKS of structural, human, political, economic and cultural relationships. Thus, it is not only the building types of architecture, their facades and floor plans that deserves attention, but also the fittings and forms of utilisation of buildings, the living conditions of their residents and the social discourses that accompany these residents' existence in different architectural and urban contexts.

The fact that Billy Wilder lived in an upper-class residential building in a bourgeois Berlin district full of artists and intellectuals, where, however, he could only afford a modest furnished room, is not just of personal or touristic interest. The provenance history of the building, which stood there until 1945, also includes the anecdote that one night he met a film producer there whom he was able to help out of a delicate situation (see Karasek 1992, p. 64ff.). When the man, dressed only in his pants, fled from his lover's bedroom to Wilder's chamber, the young journalist, who would later become such a successful film director, seized the opportunity and sold the producer the exposé of his first screenplay. *Uwe Fleckner*

Restitution Harun Farocki's 1989 film *Bilder der Welt und Inschrift des Krieges* (Images of the world and the inscription of war) shows a series of aerial reconnaissance photographs taken by a camera-equipped US Allied aircraft of an I.G.-Farben industrial complex (fig. 1). From a distant high vantage point, the architectural site comes into focus (min. 14:06-55). In 1944, it is identified as a bombing target, but by the end of the → WAR, the Allied perspective would change. From the broad, large-scale view, their camera focus would narrow down to a much more meticulous, object-level examination. A building from I.G.-Farben would feature once again, but this time it would be the confiscated site at 169 Mainstraße in Offenbach that assumes significance (fig. 2).

Here, the building itself would serve more as a backdrop than a focal point. What would have taken by the camera lens are piles of books, scores of religious objects and → ARCHIVES most of which had been confiscated from Jewish families by the Einsatzstab Reichsleiter Rosenberg and other Nazi organisations during the Second World War. Crisp, sharp, black-and-white photographs of "*ex libris*" library signs and markings affixed to the front endpaper help identify a past ownership. Functional captions number, analyse, conserve Judaica, creating a distanced visual language. Alphabetically arranged lists chiefly serve as an ordering mechanism in the compilation of inventories.

According to the Ardelia Hall Collection finding aid, the Offenbach Archival Depot (OAD), housed in the former I.G.-Farben site, processed more than 2.5 million objects during its occupation from 1946 to 1951 (Records concerning the Central Collecting Points, Washington, DC, National Archives and Records Administration, M1942). The five-story high reinforced concrete building "V1" was used as an auxiliary site when the ceilings of the Freiherrlich Carl von Rothschild's Öffentliche Bibliothek, which had been initially selected, repaired and cleared as → STORAGE, were in danger of collapsing due to the high volume of items. This adaptive → REUSE project constituted a fragment in a network of so-called Central Collecting Points, established by the Allies at the end of the Second World War as part of the Monuments, Fine Arts and Archives Section, in order to restitute stolen cultural → ARTEFACTS looted under Nazi regime. The Allies assumed the roles of architects, archivists, photographers and curators to secure and reconstruct the dispersed cultural → HERITAGE in collaboration with Jewish organisations, such as Jewish Cultural Reconstruction. Paintings and sculptures, books and historically valuable archival materials were repatriated to their original proprietaries or to their countries of origin, while others were transferred to museums in Germany, where some of them are still waiting to be restituted to the heirs of their former owners. But buildings and other properties were also returned after the war on the basis of Allied restitution laws and later by the Bundesvermögensamt, responsible for the federal property (see Lillteicher 2003).

Described by the OAD's director Captain Isaac Bencowitz as the "antithesis" of the spatial dimension of the Einsatzstab Reichsleiter Rosenberg, the project involved the discovery of temporary storage facilities in remote salt mines, depots and castles where stolen cultural

1 *I.G.-Farben industrial complex*, Monovice, 1944, photograph taken by an US Allied aircraft. Still from Harun Farocki, *Bilder der Welt und Inschrift des Krieges*, 1989

property had been moved due to sustained bombing (photo album compiled from photographs found in the OAD, c.1945, Washington DC, National Archives and Records Administration, front page). Transferring the objects to a secure location, the Allies assessed existing infrastructure and repaired damaged buildings: as a result, structures such as the NSDAP Parteizentrale (National Socialist Party Centre) in Munich, the Staatsarchiv in Marburg and the Museum Wiesbaden were given new uses. The OAD itself offered ample space on several floors, heated rooms, lifts, transport facilities, furnished offices and direct access to water and rail (see Poste 1958, p. 337). In order to function in its restorative role, it was retrospectively equipped with a sorting room, a photographic room, a carpentry workshop, a packing room, a care and preservation room (where minor → RESTORATION work is carried out prior to shipment) and a dispatch room (see photo album, sec. IV, 2–27).

Claimed through the successive movement of objects, this architecture of restitution defines a fluctuating relationship where material → RENOVATION and immaterial memory intertwine. Writing on the preservation of Jewish culture after the Holocaust, Elisabeth Gallas describes the OAD as an institution where "past, present, and future seemed to overlap" (Gallas 2019, p. 60). The chaotic, fragmented and superimposed nature of these transitory spaces and processes of recollection, endowed the redistributed objects and produced media with a future agency.

2 *Offenbach Archival Depot in an confiscated I.G.-Farben building*, 1946, Mainstraße 169, Offenbach. Photographer unknown

While this process allowed decontextualised heritage to be translated into a kind of "operational imagery" (as they otherwise arise as the result of automatic machine processes, often of military provenance) it is critical to understand that these documents neither represent, nor inform; instead, these exposures were conceived as intelligence to track, control and detect artefacts within the context of a military operation. The officers were united by the urgency of conservation; their mission was one of reconnaissance, capture and defence amassing in large bodies of photographs, or perhaps more pictures of the world "than the eyes of the soldiers are capable of evaluating", as the narrator of Farocki's documentary puts it (min. 32:07–16). In fact, he examines the blind spot of the interpreters of the aerial photographs taken during the war. Annotations on the photographs indicate that it was not until 1977 that two employees of the CIA went through the archive to notice and evaluate a proximity that the Allies didn't see — the Auschwitz concentration camp was depicted next to the designated the bombing target (min. 14:50-15:45).

Blind spots remain, particularly when zooming in closer through a leap of scale. Gallas notes that the decline in institutional interest in cultural appropriation and in the role of the Jewish Cultural Reconstruction after the 1950s was largely due to most looted items remaining in the possession of European collections and private individuals (see Gallas 2019, pp. 8f.). Barely discussed during the Cold War, methods and requirements of restitution have regained public and scholarly attention only in the late 1990s and early 2000s, sparked by new discoveries of looted items in museums or private collections, ultimately leading to the Washington Declaration of Nazi-Confiscated Art in 1998, which was updated in 2024. Spread across a large network of institutions, the visual and spatial archive still exists and might continue to serve as a vehicle for examination. The former site of the OAD, on the other hand, belonged – and still belongs – to a series of successive chemical companies, none of which thematised the provenance of their buildings. *Ella Eßlinger*

Restoration Restoration is driven by an underlying uncertainty about where its object is to be found, whether in an ideal form or in the actual physical appearance of the item to be restored. This ambiguity surrounds the search for the "real" object in restoration. To distinguish between true and false, beginning and end, original and appliqué, requires an endless series of fictions, constantly rewritten throughout the object's history (see Arrhenius 2012).

In 2002, Noto, the "capital" of Sicilian baroque, together with eight other urban baroque environments in the Val di Noto area, was inscribed on UNESCO's World Heritage list as an outstanding testimony to the exuberant genius of late baroque art and architecture. Two seismic events lay behind Noto's qualification as a → HERITAGE site. The first was a catastrophic earthquake in 1693 that destroyed large parts of the region. As a result, in the first part of the eighteenth century, several towns in the Val di Noto area were rebuilt according to the urban baroque ideals prevalent at the time. In the nomination to UNESCO the effort to create entirely new urban realities after such a major catastrophe was strongly underlined. Indeed, the organisational capacity behind the eighteenth-century → RECONSTRUCTION and rebuilding of a whole area in coherent architectural form and shape was pointed out as the main criterion for the area's elevation to World Heritage status.

During the nomination process, Noto Cathedral was under restoration and covered by scaffolding. To diminish the effect of a missing part in the urban baroque composition, a photograph of the cathedral's front facade, printed 1:1 in full colour, was hung in front of the scaffolding (fig. 1). This full-sized image of Noto Cathedral can exemplify a fundamental condition of the heritage monument and its relation to issues of representation and mimesis. The photographic veil effectively hid the destruction and → RUIN of the second seismic event that had initiated the restoration and triggered the nomination to the World Heritage list. During the evening of 13 March 1996, the central nave and parts of the cathedral dome dramatically collapsed due to an earthquake six years earlier, which had aggravated existing structural problems in the church resulting from a previous restoration that had used reinforced → CONCRETE. The introduction of this modern → MATERIAL had aimed to stabilise the construction so it could better withstand any earthquake damage. The reinforcement of the structure had, however, the opposite effect. When the dome got more rigid than the original stone vault, it collapsed in one piece, pulling an extensive part of the cathedral with it before crashing to the church floor.

After three years of wide-ranging archaeological excavation aimed at identifying the original position of the stones within the cathedral's structure to analyse in detail the structural reason for the tragic collapse, the rebuilding began. To consolidate the structure further, parts of the church had to be demolished, and the removal of rubble became an operation of impressive scale (→ DEMOLITION). At the time of the

1 *Noto Cathedral during its 1999–2007 restoration campaign,* Noto, Sicily. Photo: Thordis Arrhenius, 2002

UNESCO nomination in 2002, the area behind the photographic screen looked more like a site of demolition than of restoration.

Despite the fact that there was not much left behind the large-scale print slowly moving in the wind, its presence reassured the onlooker that something very like the full-sized image would soon materialise. The photographic replica contained an indexical promise – it showed a "thereness" of something not there, suggesting the possibility of retrieval (→ PHOTOGRAPHY). Yet a seed of suspicion towards the object returning on the other side of the veil was implicated in this promise. The reconstruction of the Noto Cathedral aimed at merging the image of the cathedral with the materiality that gave rise to that image – to make them one and the same (→ DOPPELGÄNGER). The advancing of the art of restoration technology and the increased knowledge of material and building traditions can be understood in relation to this. Resurrected, a restored monument will be judged on how well it resembles and even behaves like itself. The restoration of Noto Cathedral included researching and procuring a stone with the same behavioral properties as that originally used. Here, issues of identity and likeness go beyond the surface and yet are still conditioned by the same ocular desires. Restoration, in these terms, becomes the action of making the historical monument support its representation – to make its objecthood merge with its image. *Thordis Arrhenius*

Reuse The practice of reusing → MATERIALS from one building in a subsequent building could conceivably be traced right back, if not to the origin of architecture, then at least to humanity's second building. It is a practice that seems always to have existed everywhere. The houses at Neolithic Çatalhöyük were rebuilt on the same foundations every century or so; monumental structures from Göbekli Tepe to Stonehenge were extended in ways that incorporated the existing elements of the site (see Graeber and Wengrow 2021, p. 89, p. 105 and p. 222). The buildings of the Periclean Acropolis famously integrate materials from precursors destroyed during the Greco-Persian Wars (see Rhodes 1995, pp. 30f.; Raus 2019). The reuse of older architectural → ELEMENTS became all but normative in the late Roman Empire of the third and fourth centuries (see Dumser 2022, pp. 74ff.). Various practices of reuse have been amply documented in early Christian, early Islamic, Persian, Mayan, Ottoman, Khmer and Aztec architectures, to name but a few. A splendid example are the columns from Alexandria, Baalbek, Nicea, Thessaloniki and elsewhere that Sinan used in the construction of the Süleymaniye Mosque (fig. 1) in Istanbul in 1550–1557 (see Necipoğlu 2005, p. 156).

These myriad practices of reuse reflected an infinity of motives. Reuse might signal a plundering celebration of an enemy's defeat, an homage to a predecessor building or era, or an offering to propitiate a god. It might ensure the → PRESERVATION of materials that through contact with the miraculous or the divine had come to be venerated as unsubstitutable sacred relics. It surely also often represented a welcome economy.

1 Sinan, *Süleymaniye Mosque*, 1550–1557, Istanbul. Photo: Brad Hostetler, 2018

2 *Basilica of San Paolo fuori le mura*, 1823–1854, with columns of Proconnesian and Parian marble added by Luigi Poletti, 1838–1839, Rome. Photo: Richard Wittman, 2021

Motives for reuse seem routinely to have been layered in dense and obscure ways, which typically renders the practice resistant to easy historical interpretation.

The deliberate and signifying reuse of architectural elements mutated significantly under the pressure of new and modern perspectives on the relationship of past to present, and in particular with the emergence of historicist orientations. When a catastrophic → FIRE destroyed the Early Christian basilica of San Paolo fuori le mura in Rome in 1823 (fig. 2), it was immediately assumed that the gutted old basilica would furnish meaningful salvaged materials to whatever → RECONSTRUCTION eventually occurred (see Wittman 2024, pp. 264 ff.).

Yet the nature and understanding of that reuse was to change in emblematic ways over the years that followed. The first approved proposal involved building a new, neo-classical basilica for which materials deriving from the old basilica were to be used above all as an economy, with explicitly memorial signification restricted to just a few salvaged columns serving in non-load-bearing locations. By accepting that the old basilica was adequately substituted by a modern building with the same name, title, function and location, this proposal mostly echoed traditional historical orientations.

But then Pope Leo XII changed course. A few months later, he ordered instead that the basilica be rebuilt as a → PRISTINE archaeological reconstruction of the old basilica when it was new. The reuse of materials was again planned primarily as an economy, but everything else was now different: for this completely unprecedented approach to the reconstruction of a historical monument exemplified a new and modern sense of historicist anxiety that vacated the venerable principle of substitutability. Pope Leo's order instead reflected a conviction that the physical disappearance of the old basilica would inflict an uncompensated and ultimately unacceptable loss on the Catholic community's historical sense of itself. The reuse of its materials in the new basilica was not envisaged as a means of preempting this loss; instead, the loss was to be denied outright. The old basilica's life was to be extended via prosthesis: via new walls and columns, shaped in imitation of the destroyed ones, fitted onto the existing foundations.

Within a decade, however, it was clear that the old basilica, with its rare ancient marbles and irregular → SPOLIA capitals and columns, could never really be reconstituted; and, moreover, that it was undesirable to reproduce the many design flaws that had left the old building vulnerable to flood and fire. With the arrival in 1833 of a new head architect, Luigi Poletti, the tortured paralysis that had followed this realisation was swept away by yet another vision for the reconstruction. Poletti quietly discarded the idea of an archaeological reconstruction and set about instead fabricating an idealised Early Christian basilica type. Because this new vision required accepting that the old basilica would finally disappear – now, in a historicist perspective, seen as a tragic, irreducible loss – Poletti shrewdly moved to compensate with a much-publicised commitment to filling the new basilica with reused materials drawn from the old. The reconstruction was in effect no longer to be iconic, but indexical. What complicated this effort slightly was Poletti's deep aversion to the Romantic disjunctions of texture born of placing self-evidently timeworn elements from the old basilica in the spotless new one. He wanted his building instead to have a uniform, modern appearance. And so, he invariably ended up processing reused elements before he installed them, shaving down old columns to a state of apparent newness, or slicing them up and applying them to the walls as pristine revetments. Regular articles were then placed in the *Diario di Roma* highlighting these episodes of reuse, to ensure that visitors – who would otherwise have been hard-pressed to detect them – were aware that the new basilica wore an interior coat of marbles drawn from the old.

It soon emerged, however, that the old basilica could not furnish nearly enough marble to complete the operation. Supplementing them with new marbles was complicated by the fact that many of the old marbles were of types famously quarried to exhaustion in antiquity (→ QUARRY). This dilemma ultimately prompted an extraordinary and at times almost comical series of expeditions into the antique fora of Rome – sometimes reluctantly approved, but other times quite clandestine – to plunder additional marbles from the ancient ruins there. These expeditions were instigated not by Poletti but by the high-ranking ecclesiastics who superintended the San Paolo reconstruction. Eventually in 1840, with the scheduled consecration of the high altar fast approaching, the papal Camerlengo transferred an entire collection of antique marbles from the Vatican storehouses to the San Paolo workshop (→ STORAGE), where they were quickly sawn up and mounted to complete the rubicund lustre of the building's interior.

The spoliation of antique buildings for reuse in modern churches had been criticised in Rome since the sixteenth century and effectively banned since the start of the nineteenth century. Its revival here suggests a willful attempt to recapture the muscular confidence of past ages, when the Early Christians or the builders of new Saint Peter's could triumphantly plunder the carcasses of the old pagan temples for their new churches. Anxious ecclesiastical leaders, with reason, felt profoundly threatened by the liberal nineteenth century that was unfolding around them, and this wayward attack on the cosmopolitan fetish of a historicised antiquity probably offered them relief from the Church's modern fears of diminishment. But, of course, these practices of reuse could never mean what they had meant in earlier ages, when the traces of ancient Rome still spoke of God's providential plan for the Church. Unlike Poletti's loudly trumpeted resurrection of the old basilica's marbles, these anachronistic appropriations offered but a private and, one guesses, rather bitter satisfaction to the clerics who ordered them. *Richard Wittman*

Ruin A ruin is the remains of a building that was once complete but has been severely damaged or partially collapsed over time due to gradual → DERELICTION or violent destruction, for example in earthquakes, → WAR or other armed conflicts. Ruins can originate from historical buildings, such as castles, churches or temples, and are often of archaeological, cultural or tourist interest. According to this definition, ruins are a distinct case of architectural provenance, as they refer to an earlier, possibly original state of such buildings and therefore tend to face the challenge of being restored or rebuilt from scratch (→ RECONSTRUCTION, → RESTORATION). In German, however, the term is also used for construction projects that are abandoned before completion, do not fulfil their intended purpose or represent a bad investment for other reasons. In such cases, one speaks of a *Bauruine* (building ruin) or *Investitionsruine* (investment ruin, corresponding to the English term "White Elephant").

In the context of research into provenance phenomena within architecture, ruins are not only interesting because they refer to earlier states of buildings, but also in addressing questions of their restoration. In 1964, the Venice Charter laid down the basic criteria for the type of restoration known as "anastylosis", according to which a scientific basis for the reconstruction and the use of as many original → COMPONENTS as possible or the labelling of newly executed components are necessary. However, violations of these guidelines can also become the subject of illuminating case studies, as the alleged restoration of formerly intact building fabric often enough involves alterations that indicate changed functional, cultural, social or political conditions (→ TRANSFORMATION). On the other hand, the specific aesthetics of ruins themselves can also become the subject of art and cultural-historical considerations. It is not uncommon for ruins to be kept as such for monument → PRESERVATION or other reasons, so that dilapidated buildings or building ensembles such as the Acropolis in Athens, the ruins of Palmyra or the remains of the city of Machu Picchu in Peru have even been declared UNESCO World Heritage Sites. They not only serve as evidence of a past cultural epoch, but also function as a reminder of the historical processes that led to the decay of the original buildings. Such ruins thus become monuments to their own destruction.

Ruins were particularly valued aesthetically when they appeared suitable for inspiring historical or philosophical reflections on the demise of an idealised past or the transience of all existence in general. In cultural history, such nostalgic considerations reached their peak in European Romanticism, which was confronted with a comprehensive industrialisation and, in the course of the associated modernisation, also with the → DEMOLITION of historical architecture. In the face of ruins, however, the sentimental regret over the loss of a building understood as a signum of the valued past was accompanied at this time by the idea of a potential reconquest by nature of the world corrupted by civilisation, whereby a ruin could lose even its fragmentary character, as the German cultural philosopher Georg Simmel declared: "The ruin of a building, however, means that other forces and forms, those of nature, have grown into what has disappeared and been destroyed in the work of art, and thus a new whole, a characteristic unity, has emerged from that which still lives in it from art and that which already lives in it from nature" (Simmel 1919, pp. 126 f.). Ruins of castles, monasteries

1 Ludwig Persius, *Design of the Teufelsbrücke for Klein-Glienicke Park in Berlin*, 1835, drawing. Whereabouts unknown

or other buildings were therefore already being preserved as sights in the nineteenth century or, for example in Caspar David Friedrich's paintings, captured pictorially as symbols of religious or political speculation.

However, against this intellectual background, ruins could also be built explicitly as such. In the garden architecture of the eighteenth and nineteenth centuries, we often find picturesque artificial ruins in the form of grottos, pyramids, temples or towers, which were integrated as props into the landscape design. But independent individual buildings, such as hermitages, abbeys, palaces, castles or antique-style buildings, were also occasionally constructed as mock ruins (see Zimmermann 1989). An extremely interesting example is the Teufelsbrücke (Devil's Bridge) created by Ludwig Persius in Berlin's Klein-Glienicke Park in 1838, which has a particularly chequered reception history (fig. 1).

With two brick arches deliberately designed as a ruin, which appeared to have been provisionally supplemented by a wooden structure, the bridge was built as a *point de vue* over a small rocky gorge deepened by excavations, including an artificial waterfall, and thus fitted into the overall Romantic concept of the park thanks to the picturesque decay faked by the architect. Such a "ruinous" aesthetic was of course not compatible with the classicist-monumental ideals of National Socialist architecture, and so the bridge was "restored" in 1935 by replacing its wooden parts with masonry. It was not until the beginning of the twenty-first century that consideration was given to dismantling this restoration, but this was delayed by the fact that contemporary German building regulations do not cover the construction of artificial ruins and the project could therefore not be carried out until 2006. This led to the curious result of restoration work turning an intact building into a fictitious ruin. Just three years later, the structure became a real ruin when its centre pillar was washed away during heavy rainfall. To this day, → HERITAGE conservation and building authorities are still arguing about the reconstruction of the bridge and even the (newly installed) wooden supporting structure of this triple, even quadruple ruin has since collapsed (see Bürkner 2024).

In fact, the dubious desire to erase the memory of painful episodes in history by removing actual ruins repeatedly leads to regrettable mistakes. The most prominent example in recent German architectural history is the so-called reconstruction of the Frauenkirche in Dresden, the remains of which were originally preserved as a memorial to the consequences of the Second World War (→ COLLECTIVE MEMORY). After the reunification of Germany, however, they had to make way for a technically modernised → FACSIMILE of the church between 1996 and 2005, in which only a few of the original → ELEMENTS were reused (→ REUSE).

By contrast, the preservation of the ruins of the Kaiser-Wilhelm-Gedächtniskirche in Berlin shows that memorial and restorative requirements can certainly be reconciled (fig. 2). The admonitory → FRAGMENT of the damaged church, which was originally built in 1891–1895 in the neo-Romanesque style and bombed in 1943, was initially left untouched after the war, presumably because the National Socialist government had grandiloquently announced that its architecture would be reconstructed in all its splendor after the Allied troops had been defeated. Eventually it became necessary to tear down the choir, which was in danger of collapsing, and in 1957, the architect Egon Eiermann won a competition to rebuild the church with a design that envisaged the demolition of the remaining parts of the ruin as well (see Schirmer 1984, pp. 164ff.). After heated debates about the preservation of the fragmented church, a compromise was found: Eiermann surrounded the structurally secured ruin with three individual buildings, the actual church including a foyer, the tower and a small chapel, which he realised as modern steel constructions with → CONCRETE grids into which thousands of glass elements were inserted. With this ensemble, he countered the monumental demonstration of power of Wilhelminianism, which blatantly expressed a chauvinist national pride, with a democratic gesture of decentralised structures that were moved away from the original building axis.

2 Egon Eiermann, *Kaiser-Wilhelm-Gedächtniskirche*, 1959–1963, integrating the ruins of the tower of the previous building from 1891–1895, Berlin. Photographer unknown

The ruin of the damaged church was thus preserved as a memorial and was later equipped with a hall of remembrance to reflect on war and destruction. Stylistically, the new buildings and the ruin stand in stark contrast to each other, but as a successful example of a meaningful approach to the relics of German history, the whole group of buildings was finally listed as a complete work of art. This means that it is no longer the architectural solitaire as a masterpiece in its own right, but primarily the complex historical provenance of the ensemble that determines the character of the Kaiser-Wilhelm-Gedächtniskirche as monument. *Uwe Fleckner*

1 Frank Gehry, *Walt Disney Concert Hall*, 2003, Los Angeles. Photo: Uwe Fleckner, 2008

Sourcing In architecture and construction, sourcing refers to the complete lifecycle of → MATERIALS deployed in built projects, encompassing the violence of extraction and attrition, manufacturing, transportation, installation, performance, → MAINTENANCE and eventual disposal. A brutal procurement process, sourcing embeds environmental impacts, → LABOUR conditions, colonial histories and power dynamics into every architectural detail, orchestrating the ebbs and flows of materials.

Like any other building, the Walt Disney Concert Hall in Los Angeles, completed in 2003, is a monument to the gaping holes sourcing its materials demanded and generated (fig. 1). The building's celebrated status and Frank Gehry's exceptional reputation (→ CELEBRITY) make choosing this case even more damning: if a structure designed by one of architecture's most lauded practitioners, with abundant resources and expertise at its disposal, fails in its material intelligence, what hope exists for the banalities of everyday construction? Much has been written about its design, its construction delays, the software that allowed for its geometry to emerge, the acoustics feast, the → COSTS of $50 million, the 1:1 wall section exhibited at the Venice Biennale, the paper → MODELS, the robotic milling machines and the controversy over the shiny panels of its facade. Some of this material value has been quantified: 15,000 square metres of constructed surface, 14,800 square metres of curved stainless steel panels in 12,500 individual pieces of 4 by 10 feet, and 4,000 square metres of geometric glazing, as to signal technical prowess (see Koshalek et al. 2003).

But most of the rest – limestone, reinforced → CONCRETE, steel stud backup systems, electrical wiring, acoustic systems, excavated earth and sweat – is not. How many cubic metres of extracted earth does this represent? How many hectares of scorched land? How many trees have been felled, bugs killed and people displaced in that sourcing process? We only know how to calculate carbon exhaustion; Life Cycle Assessment and similar methods never fully describe the real impact on non-quantifiable damages and other living organisms. The iconic panels represent just the visible endpoint of the sourcing process.

Before reaching Los Angeles, this steel was iron ore, likely mined in Australia, Brazil, China or South Africa. It is impossible to find out precisely because commodities are mute, yet the modus operandi of iron-ore extraction is well known. It requires open-pit mining – a devastating process of choreographed violence that begins with the removal of all vegetation and soil, followed by the extraction of the ore-bearing layer below. This practice leaves behind vast cratered moonscapes and deep wounds in landscapes. Each steel panel carries within it the ghost of this disappeared ecosystem. Extensive processing is required to transform iron ore into steel – first smelting in blast furnaces at temperatures exceeding 1,600° Celsius to produce pig iron, then refining in oxygen furnaces to reduce carbon content. This process demands enormous energy inputs and generates significant air pollution, including sulfur dioxide, nitrogen oxides and particulate matter. The steel industry alone accounts for approximately 8 per cent of global carbon dioxide emissions. Finally, it was manufactured into panels and transported to California, where it would eventually be sanded to reduce its reflectivity after installation.

Soon, the material's behaviour created problems. Due to the reflected sunlight on the polished panels, nearby apartments experienced temperature increases of up to 10° Celsius, drivers faced dangerous glare on adjacent streets, and pedestrians complained of uncomfortable heat on surrounding sidewalks. Energy consumption in neighbouring buildings increased as users compensated for the additional heat load by cranking up cooling systems.

By 2005, contractors had identified approximately 120 square metres of problematic panels and sanded them to reduce reflectivity (costs: $180,000), a remediation project representing another hidden dimension of sourcing – the labour required to mitigate material failures and the regular maintenance obligations, as once a year, the building will also undergo a "six-week deep cleaning to remove any stains" (Wetherbe 2013; see Reynoso and Nivera 2014).

These upstream and downstream sourcing realities – environmental degradation, carbon and other emissions, racial capitalism and the labour conditions at all sites – are invisibilised. When unpacking the sourcing of construction, it doesn't really matter which building we are looking at. Each of them represents the visible endpoint of a complex extractive network. There is no sustainable architecture, just gradients of harms we must contend with. *Charlotte Malterre-Barthes*

Spolia The term "spolia", derived from the Latin *spolium* (war booty), represents a complex architectural practice of relocating and reinterpreting building → ELEMENTS removed from their original context and integrated into new structures (→ TRANSLOCATION). This practice, which has persisted from antiquity to the present day, encompasses both tangible material transfers and the appropriation of architectural motifs. The distinction between *spolia in se* and *spolia in re*, first articulated by Richard Brilliant in 1982, clarifies this dual nature: While *spolia in se* denotes the physical → REUSE of architectural → FRAGMENTS, *spolia in re* describes the transfer of stylistic or symbolic elements, where the form rather than the → MATERIAL traverses historical and spatial boundaries (→ AFTERLIFE). In the strictest sense, *spolia in se* refers to architectural fragments acquired through acts of → WAR, extraction or market transactions, while *spolia in re* embodies a figurative, metaphorical → TRANSFER where representation rather than substance travels (see Brilliant 1982). Both actual fragments and their representations serve as historical proxies, borrowing and incorporating → AUTHENTICITY regardless of their material age or provenance. The → MOBILITY of these elements – whether stolen, purchased, exchanged, found or salvaged – transforms them from → COMPONENTS of immobile

1 *Arch of Constantine*, 315 CE, south side, Rome. Photo: Diego Delso

structures into travelling → ARTEFACTS laden with meaning. This → DISPLACEMENT fundamentally alters what was designed to be permanent, challenging the understanding of architecture as fixed and stable.

The transformation of spoliated elements proceeds through a tripartite process of isolation, movement and recontextualisation (see Meier 2020, pp. 165f.). Initial isolation divorces the architectural fragment from its original setting, stripping away its contextual associations – stylistic, historical and ideological. During subsequent transport, the element accrues new semantic values as commodity, memento or trophy. Upon recontextualisation, the element becomes structurally reintegrated, yet its transformative journey remains inscribed within its semiotic function. When incorporated into new architectural frameworks, these elements maintain their visual distinctiveness – a quality identified as fundamental to their efficacy as signifiers of historical continuity, mnemonic devices and conveyers of prestige through association with classical antiquity (see Nierhaus 2014, p. 176).

The Arch of Constantine in Rome stands as a foundational moment of architectural appropriation and a pivotal cultural turning point (fig. 1). Erected in 315 CE, the arch boldly incorporates sculptural elements from earlier imperial monuments – fragments deliberately harvested from the structures of Trajan, Hadrian and Marcus Aurelius. The same approach resonated throughout Constantine's building programme, from the Lateran Church to Saint Peter's in Rome, where spolia functioned simultaneously as carriers of imperial prestige and harbingers of cultural → TRANSFORMATION. All these elements operated not as mere recycled materials (→ RECYCLING) but as active agents of political legitimacy (→ ACTOR), bridging past and present while visually communicating shifts in power and belief. Late Antiquity and the Middle Ages witnessed increasingly exuberant deployments of spolia – structures like the Arslanhane Mosque and Casa dei Crescenzi exhibiting heterogeneous architectural compositions where the diversity and prominence of reused elements became defining features (→ REUSE), visually narrating complex histories of conquest, conversion and cultural amalgamation.

The Renaissance brought a more scholarly engagement with architectural → HERITAGE, characterised by scientific interest in antiquity and simultaneous lament over its decay (→ DERELICTION). Architectural practice embraced techniques of → COLLECTING, accumulating and compositional experimentation, often dismantling wholes into parts and reconfiguring fragments into new assemblages. The Villa Medici in Rome exemplifies this Renaissance approach to spolia, particularly through its garden facade. Here, genuine ancient elements – including garlands from the Ara Pacis – are juxtaposed with newly created → REPRODUCTIONS, creating a complex but visually cohesive ensemble laden with historical references. This deliberate combination raises fundamental questions about the relationship between authentic fragments and their reproductions. How do they influence each other's perception within the architectural composition? What happens to the evidentiary quality of original fragments when placed alongside carefully crafted → FACSIMILES?

This tension between original and reproduction extends beyond individual fragments to entire architectural forms, particularly as *spolia in re* evolved into full-scale architectural citation (→ QUOTE). The Arch of Constantine, itself an assemblage of physical spolia, became a paradigmatic form that generated conceptual spolia across centuries and continents. Its architectural vocabulary was extracted, reproduced and recontextualised, creating a genealogy of triumphal structures that borrowed not material but meaning. The Brandenburg Gate in Potsdam, completed in 1770–1771, and the Arc de Triomphe du Carrousel in Paris, erected 1806–1808, directly reference the Roman triumphal arch typology, transforming it into an expression of national prestige and political authority – each monument functioning as a performance of historical lineage and political power (→ POLITICAL ICONOGRAPHY). This genealogy of architectural quotation extends to unexpected contexts. The Victory Arch in New York, a temporary monument erected in 1918, demonstrates how the Constantinian model could be mobilised in emerging global powers. Designed by Thomas Hastings and constructed of wood and plaster, the arch was more than a commemorative structure. Its deliberate reference to Roman imperial architecture positioned the United States within a genealogy of global imperial imagination.

For translocated spolia – those not reused *in situ* but deliberately subjected to displacement across spatial boundaries – the act of movement itself constitutes a primary rationale for their appropriation. In their new contexts, these fragments manifest alterity, their foreign provenance becoming an essential signifier of spatial and temporal traversal. This dislocation interrogates architecture's presumed immobility, rendering the semantic framework of the receiving architecture perpetually dynamic. As Meier observes, when the ontologically stationary becomes mobile, fundamental stability is challenged, generating signification for both the object and its process of transfer (see Meier 2020, p. 165f.). And Carola Jäggi conceptualises spolia as "transcultural artefacts" that articulate connections across disparate cultural spheres and chronological periods, thereby creating dialogic interfaces between historical memory and contemporary reception (Jäggi 2013, p. 66).

2 David Chipperfield, *Neues Museum*, 1997–2009, Berlin. Photo: Gary Todd, 2016

By the mid-twentieth century, the practice of spolia had evolved into complex forms of architectural displacement. The Cloisters in New York, established in the 1930s, represents a significant case in the systematic relocation of medieval European architectural elements. Under the financial patronage of John D. Rockefeller Jr., entire sections of five French monasteries were dismantled, their stones numbered, crated and shipped across the Atlantic for reassembly in Fort Tryon Park (→ CARGO).

This process of → ACQUISITION, transport and → RECONSTRUCTION resulted in a synthetic architectural compound – a curated amalgamation of disparate medieval elements reconfigured to create an idealised medieval setting. The physical and cultural distance traversed by these stones raises questions about the ethics of architectural extraction during periods of economic vulnerability in post-First World War Europe, the mechanics of → PRESERVATION that privileged removal over *in situ* conservation, and the creation of what could be termed an "imaginary medieval Europe" on American soil. Unlike previous examples of spolia, where fragments were incorporated into new architectural compositions, The Cloisters represents an attempt to recreate entire architectural environments, blurring the boundaries between museum, restoration and architectural fantasy (→ BRICOLAGE, → PASTICCIO).

Contemporary practices continue to explore these complex dynamics of architectural translation. David Chipperfield's reconstruction of the Neues Museum in Berlin (1997–2009) explores spolia as vehicles for memory and historical witness (→ COLLECTIVE MEMORY, → IMAGE VEHICLE). Following its devastating bombing in the Second World War, the museum remained a → RUIN for decades, its fragments scattered throughout the structure. Rather than pursuing complete → RESTORATION or contemporary replacement, Chipperfield developed what critics term a "controlled ruination", where war-damaged fragments – columns, wall sections, tile work and architectural ornaments – remain deliberately visible within the new intervention (fig. 2). The approach treats these elements as genuine spolia, incorporating them into a new architectural narrative while maintaining their status as witnesses to destruction. Deliberate material contrasts – placing sleek contemporary concrete directly against the fractured historical fragments – create a temporal dialogue where the violence of history remains legible. Unlike traditional spolia that might be smoothly incorporated into a new aesthetic whole, these elements retain their traumatic histories.

While Chipperfield's approach foregrounds rupture and discontinuity through exposed fragmentation, contemporary architectural practice can also explore spolia's capacity to foster connection across cultural and national borders, as exemplified by the European Council Building in Brussels. Completed in 2016, the building features a distinctive facade designed by Philippe Samyn, a collage of nearly 3,000 antique oak window frames from across Europe. Unlike traditional spolia whose origins are deliberately identified, these window frames are intentionally anonymised; their diverse provenances are acknowledged collectively but not individually marked, creating a tension between specific historical extraction and shared cultural identity.

Unlike ruins, which always signal decay, or reconstructions that attempt to restore an imagined original state, spolia operate as fluid interfaces between past and present. Thus, they assert neither complete continuity nor total rupture but instead maintain a productive ambiguity; they are not static historical documents but active agents of signification (see Kinney 1995, p. 58). Spolia span both geographical and temporal boundaries, their significance extending beyond immediate materiality to broader questions of memory, displacement and cultural appropriation. The act of incorporating a fragment from another time and place is never neutral; it is always an intervention that simultaneously acknowledges and transforms history.

Nina Lucia Groß

Storage Storage is often conceived as a static container of things, a place where objects, data and → MATERIALS are securely kept away from the ensuing → DISPUTES, controversies and tribulations of an everchanging world outside. In such imaginaries, the matter contained in storage may eventually gather → DUST as they patiently await their retrieval or rediscovery – purposefully or accidentally – from someone who is in the middle of searching for something important. An → ARCHIVE is an example of a storage space, and so too is a warehouse. Salvage yards, private attics, closets, filing cabinets, but also digital databases and online clouds are all representative of the types of depositories that many of the things connected to architectural practices and materialities are stored inside. They are different kinds of storages and from a conventional view – one that privileges the seeker's discovery over the everyday infrastructures that both support and necessitate them – storages play a somewhat passive and limited role. Storage is seen as a space consulted only when needed and is otherwise rendered invisible and relegated to the backdrop as a supporting act behind the drama of its kept object's eventful discovery. Storages have traditionally occupied a position with little of the limelight or charisma afforded to the objects they are housing. While for instance monuments, → ARTEFACTS or → PHOTOGRAPHY are matters that continue to be actively debated,

1 *Rows of used doors lined up under a canvassed roof*, Ombygg, Oslo. Photo: Simon Mitchell, 2024

2 *Chunks of collected rubble, each labelled with an inventory number*, Bauhaus Dessau Foundation, Building Research Archive, Dessau. Photo: Simon Mitchell, 2019

contested and revered, storage tends to operate silently and from the periphery, as a place where objects are put on hold indefinitely, with no real or clear understanding of what the very processes of storage and their connected sites actually look like, nor how they actually unfold.

To view storage solely as a space of safekeeping is to overlook the ways in which it structures knowledge, produces value and coordinates the flows of materials. Rethinking storage through a lens of → CIRCULATION where trajectories, traces and material migrations are placed at the centre rather than at the edge, repositions its role not merely as a passive container marking the beginning or end of a material's journey but as an active nexus in the middle ground of its ongoing circulation. Architectural materials are often treated as fixed and stable artefacts within historiographical frameworks that favour permanence over → TRANSFORMATION. Yet, making storage work visible shows how these materials can be redefined through the judgments, controversies, exchanges and contingencies embedded in the act of storing. Whether determining what is stored and by whom or exploring how things are stored and under what circumstances, storage-work is deeply implicated in architectural and historical processes that configure broader material and cultural landscapes.

Take the example of a → REUSE warehouse like Ombygg in Oslo which acquires (→ ACQUISITION), stores and redistributes used building components that would otherwise be formerly discarded of for a fee by the municipality (fig. 1). The vast 4,500-square-metre warehouse is a space for used objects that would have no easy place to go but disposal. These objects are not simply diverted away from waste streams but given formal opportunity to be reappraised, assessed, housed and then potentially sold and reused. Ombygg creates the conditions for recirculation to emerge, and, at the scale of the city, junctures the movements of materials to a new range of divergent and consequential futures. A different kind of storage is the Building Research Archive of the Bauhaus Dessau Foundation, which preserves the material history of many Bauhaus buildings and monuments by archiving their → COMPONENTS (fig. 2).

Here, an abundancy of manufactured copies are collected in order to preserve the original integrity of their buildings (→ COLLECTING). Whether a sash window retrieved from a private bungalow or a radiator salvaged from a kindergarten renovation in Dessau, the stored objects aren't always the exact original productions but rather exact → REPLICAS deemed valuable because they uphold an exactitude of the original versions, despite often coming from different sources. Knowledge about what is collected and what is deemed valuable may affront traditional ideas about → AUTHENTICITY in → PRESERVATION and raises questions not only about the power of → REPRODUCTION in conservation work, but also unsettles the idea that provenance is tied to singular origins.

Architectural historiography has long been structured around the aesthetics and actualities of progress, defined by a separation from and conservation of the past that attaches to a linear and objective time. Historical progress is built on this idea of rupture (see Latour 1991, pp. 67ff.); the belief that history is a series of epistemological breaks in which the past is discarded, overwritten and of course demolished (→ DEMOLITION). But positioning oneself in the middle of storage allows a different story to emerge: storage-work demonstrates the sheer volume of material accumulation that is left behind, reappraised and repurposed. The past never disappeared; rather its residues were displaced, transported, reorganised, reclassified and restored. Thoughts on what enters storage, what leaves, where it originates and where it goes might be dismissed solely as the logistical concerns of a warehouse manager. But such questions can also become critical inquiries that reframe the epistemic boundaries of storage-work as a key infrastructure in how architectural practices, geographies, histories and materialities are known, assembled and maintained. *Simon Mitchell*

Subtraction Removal, erasure and → DEMOLITION are controversial terms in → HERITAGE history, mostly understood as antonyms for → PRESERVATION. Normally, cultural value is considered to increase by the depth and the number of historical layers, whether they are manifested as conglomerates of buildings, additions and alterations or as → PATINA. Only in exceptional circumstances do preservation experts and authorities allow for removal of substance, normally to free monuments from unwanted, newer additions that obscure the narrative agreed upon, or to meet requirements relating to → FIRE safety or universal access. Removal of pollution and accumulated → DUST and dirt through chemical treatment, blasting or adhesives are universally accepted and considered part of → MAINTENANCE work.

In a typical → RESTORATION process, much effort is put into the protection of → ELEMENTS and surfaces through wrapping, barriers and scaffolding, or through temporary dismantling and → STORAGE. The Society of Ancient Buildings founded by William Morris, Philip Webb and others in 1877, nicknamed "Anti-Scrape", was established in opposition to what they considered destructive restorations, when original substance was removed and monuments edited to obtain idealised versions of the past. Their manifesto from 1877 addresses the equally problematic parallel processes of destruction and addition when pointing out that "those who make the changes wrought in our day under the name of Restoration, [...] have no guide but each his own individual whim to point out to them what is admirable and what contemptible; while the very nature of their task compels them to destroy something and to supply the gap by imagining what the earlier builders should or might have done. Moreover, in the course of this double process of destruction and addition, the whole surface of the building is necessarily tampered with" (Morris and Webb 1877 p. 807). Since the late nineteenth century, maintaining originality and → AUTHENTICITY through preservation of original substance have become central to heritage management and formed the basis for charters, regulations and practices.

In *Subtract. The untapped science of less*, Laidy Klotz shows through examples drawn from behavioral science, biology and cultural studies, how additive practices have been favoured in human history to the expense of subtraction that arguably are more sustainable and often make much more sense. With reference to the neuroscientific term "synaptic pruning", signifying the "built-in protection against overloading our mental processing" conducted by microglial cells to "get rid of less useful synaptic connections so that we can devote more energy and space to other ones", he argues for the need to develop strategies of subtraction (Klotz 2021, p. 71). Whereas his main concern is larger societal processes, like the dismantling of racist structures or

1 *Documentation of the stacked concrete elements of Eero Saarinen's US Embassy during construction*, Oslo. Photo: US Embassy, October 1958

modifying complex systems, it is tempting to transfer his ideas to preservation and ask if the additive attitude outlined also has governed the discipline of preservation to the expense of strategies of subtraction. Arguably, addition is at the core of preservation, signifying accumulations of historical layers. Yet, the risk of "clogging up" is regularly addressed, prominently by Rem Koolhaas's *Preservation is overtaking us* (see Koolhaas 2004). With Klotz and Koolhaas's ideas in mind, one may ask if subtraction can act as a preservation strategy on the scale of a building or at the micro scale of → MATERIALS.

In 2019, when initiating the restoration of the → CONCRETE facade of the Eero Saarinen-designed former US Embassy in Oslo, the restoration team was faced with numerous dilemmas (fig. 1). The sophisticated prefabricated system of concrete elements, constructed by a mix of black-stained cement paste and labradorite aggregate, reinforced, cast in steel formwork and grinded at a nearby factory, mounted on site in 1957 and 1958 and applied with a layer of teak oil, suffered from structural failure, material → DERELICTION and → WEATHERING. Big concrete chunks were falling off, multiple elements had been pushed out by water penetration and the initial shiny black colour had faded into a matte pale grey. To accelerate the hardening process in the winter, the builders used seawater in the concrete mix, a method recommended at the time, causing many of the problems that were detected in 2019.

The new owner, the real-estate company Fredensborg who had purchased the building from the US Government in 2017 for 480 million kroner, wanted to upgrade the embassy to function as their headquarter in combination with restaurants and event spaces, all in accordance with the regulations specified in the listing document issued by Riksantikvaren, the national Directorate for Cultural Heritage. The listing, including the facade, a spectacular atrium, the three main entrances, two staircases, the entire first floor with library and offices, the ambassador suite and the lower floor auditorium and canteen, pointed explicitly at Saarinen's original layout from 1959. Later alterations, such as the many security measures installed after the terror attacks on US properties in the late twentieth century (the Beirut embassy in 1983, the Nairobi and Dar-es-Salaam embassies in 1998, and the World Trade Center in 2001), were not part of the listing and removed during the → TRANSFORMATION process. So were the safe room and surveillance station at the top floor, having been inaccessible when the authorities conducted their value assessment prior to the embassy moving out.

The narrative of the listing document provided guidelines for the concrete facade restoration (see Riksantikvaren 2018). To bring back the original shiny black appearance of 1959 proved to be more difficult than anticipated, and more importantly, it meant challenging century-old restoration principles. The cracked, grey and rough surface of 2019 resembled that of an old stone facade; the patina of sixty years of changing weather and use, the dense shiny labradorite aggregate shone like diamonds protruding from the weathered, grey paste and cracks and patches bore marks of former restorations and alterations. Numerous solutions were considered and tested on site by a large crew of engineers, suppliers, builders and architects.

Keeping the rough and repaired facade did not correspond to the listing document or to the client's desire. Filling the cavities with new,

2 *Craftsman polishing the grinded concrete surface of Eero Saarinen's US Embassy during restoration*, Oslo. Photo: Erik Langdalen, February 2021

black-tainted filler manually with a trowel seemed attractive, but proved to be problematic since the colour would contrast significantly with new repairs and non-weathered original surfaces. Patching and applying the facade with shiny black paint was quickly ruled out, as were the radical proposal to demolish the whole load-bearing facade and replace it with a → REPLICA. An almost equally radical solution was decided upon. Through nine months and 6,000 hours of intensive → LABOUR, four highly skilled craftsmen manually grinded down the entire surface of the facade to a depth ranging from 3 to 10 millimetres, all together 1,798 square metres, removing all traces of sixty years of weathering, repairs and use, bringing back a black shiny surface resembling that of 1959. This prominent facade, once a symbol of a highly sophisticated building technology and of the prominent presence of the US next to the Royal Palace in the centre of Oslo, has become an emblem of an era of expanding real-estate development and an act of experimental preservation through subtraction. *Erik Langdalen*

Theft In his parable of primitive man's building of his primitive hut, Marc-Antoine Laugier specifies the correct → SOURCING of timbers: "Some fallen branches in the forest", the abbé writes judiciously, "are the right material for his purpose" (Laugier 1977, p. 12). What, we may ask, would be the wrong material in this reputed scene of innocence? Laugier insists that our primeval architect, being the very embodiment of natural freedom, follows no laws but those of the state of "simple nature" and his own "natural instincts" (fig. 1).

Is it merely fortuitous, then, that those instincts scrupulously uphold a key jural distinction – between fallen wood and felled wood, between natural offerings and artificial takings – that organised use-rights in the traditional forest economies of Europe? While using tools to cut off large limbs or fell whole trees was treated as illegal trespass on crown and private land, feudal custom allowed peasants to enter the forests and recognised their right to gather twigs, dried branches and any wood found separated (or nearly so) from a living tree. For centuries, such common use-rights helped to sustain the landless poor's otherwise untenably precarious existence while also preserving the status quo of hierarchical class relations.

By the 1750s, as Laugier was writing his treatise, this customary matrix was being unraveled. As population growth and industrial activity caused timber prices to rise, forest owners began to press the project of enclosure into new dimensions of → DISPOSSESSION. Mobilising physical interventions, legal pretexts and an aesthetics of the "clear and distinct", they set about disentangling private property rights from a diffuse but sticky web of reciprocal privileges and obligations, customarily distributed across social hierarchies. By the end of

1 Charles-Dominique-Joseph Eisen, *Frontispiece*, for the second edition of Marc-Antoine Laugier's *Essai sur l'architecture*, c.1755, pen, ink and grey wash, 15.4 × 9.2 cm. Drawing Matter Collection, London

the eighteenth century, landowners had largely succeeded in confiscating not only common lands but also common use-rights, consolidating a monopoly over every possible utility of their property (see Xifaras 2018; Herzog 2018). Codified after the French Revolution, the result was a radicalised conception of property itself: "the right to enjoy and use things in the most absolute manner possible" (*Code civil*, art. 544).

By his own account, it was a parliamentary debate over laws on the theft of wood that provoked Karl Marx, at the age of twenty-four, to undertake his first forays into "economic questions" (Marx 2000, p. 425). The legislation at issue, an 1841 amendment to an earlier law adopted by the Rhine Provincial Assembly, extended the criminal category of "theft of wood" to include the removal of any kind of wood – standing timber, hewn lumber and fallen deadwood – from forests without the owner's permission. One of many similar measures taken up by princely and provincial governments at the time, the Rhineland's criminal statutes on wood theft were accompanied by a raft of civil laws intended to reconcile local conditions to the new social and juridical facts left in the wake of Napoleonic conquest. The ideological bedrock of these reforms, both criminal and civil, was the paradoxical liberal conviction that absolute private property is fundamental to individual liberty (see Linebaugh 1976; Bensaïd 2021).

In the fall of 1842, Marx published five articles on the wood theft debates in the *Rheinische Zeitung*. Working to expose the public assembly's barely concealed fealty to private interests, he bathed its contorted logic in his acid scorn. The "wooden foundation" of its arguments were "so rotten", he raged, "that a single gust of sound reasoning" could shatter them into "a thousand fragments" (Marx 2021, p. 97). The author did share one thing with the assembly, however, and that was a preoccupation with the ontological instability of property. Only beginning to inquire into the commodity and its secrets, the young Marx was not yet prepared to hand over the customary ordering of things to be melted down for bourgeois accumulation. So he spent paragraphs trying to tease out the "essence" of the primeval distinction between felled and fallen wood.

Felled wood was "already formed wood". It was an → ARTEFACT created with the blow of an axe or the rip of a saw, authorial acts of human → LABOUR that severed the wood's "organic connections" with the earth, and with the forest owner's property: "Because this is an open attack on the tree, it is therefore likewise an open attack on the owner of the tree" (Marx 2021, p. 62). Fallen wood was a different story. Having become separated from the tree (and the owner's land) by way of presumed happenstance, it was neither created nor owned, and so was available for the use of those who needed it. Fallen wood was a type of "hybrid" property that eluded privatisation: "By [its] elemental nature and [its] accidental mode of existence", such property belonged to "the sphere of occupation rights" (Marx 2021, pp. 69f.); rights that arose, de facto, from the sense that you cannot be displaced when you have nowhere else to go. In one of his more idiosyncratic lines of argument, Marx describes dry, fallen branches as the "alms of nature". These rightfully belonged to peasants because of a certain sympathetic "kinship" between the marginalised person and the detached branch, a kind of subaltern solidarity: just as the poor lived lives of "need and chance", so the fallen wood was a product of natural accident. The final source of customary use-rights, however, was not charity but need: nothing other than the poor's own "instinctive grasp of the *indeterminate* aspect of property" (Marx 2021, p. 70) – an eye, honed by the will to survive, for its contrived scope and brittle bark.

As for the provincial assembly, it betrayed its own wavering faith in the immutability of property, notwithstanding its moral certitudes about the criminality of theft. While the assembly did not hesitate to conflate the acts of gathering and cutting wood in its sweeping move to criminalise both, it proved quite capable of drawing subtle distinctions – between chopping and sawing, for example – when it served the interests of landowners. The sometimes laboured, sometimes flippant quality of the debates revealed a crisis in the nascent institution of absolute private property, a crisis that Marx would only later come to understand as rooted beyond the law, in the social relations of production. But in 1842 he charged lawmakers directly with corrupting the rule of law itself: "If you deny the difference between essentially different kinds of the same crime, you deny that crime itself is *different from right*, so you abolish right itself, for every crime has an aspect in common with right." Then, shifting his line of attack only slightly, Marx asked: "If every infringement on property is termed theft [...], would not all private property be theft? Do I not exclude others from property through my own private ownership?" (Marx 2021, p. 63).

Long dismissed as logically inconsistent and youthfully idealistic, Marx's articles on the theft of wood offer a tonic for critical students of architectural provenance. Indeed, it is the very futility of his labours to shake the forest trees for the essence of property and theft, right and crime, that is instructive. It illuminates a horizon of architectural history that, rather than reciting the facts of → AUTHORSHIP and ownership, instead disturbs the insidious fictions of bourgeois autonomy on which those facts are predicated: the triumph of immovable private property as an absolute right and its eclipse of more complex and dissident modes of modern belonging (see Nichols 2020). But neither can such a history remain satisfied simply to decry acts of "so-called original accumulation" as theft, however justified the charge. Our urge to report thefts committed in the past may tell us more about the meaning of property in our own time than anything about the stolen article itself, its appropriation or their shared conditions of possibility. Such filings are, at any rate, the work of police and prosecutors.

Rather, we might use architectural provenance to write critical genealogies of landed property itself – or, if you like, of theft. For, yes, every improvement, every architecture, has an aspect in common with theft. Our questions, then, are not about who owned what, when and how it came to be in their possession, but rather, what did it mean for them to own it? To what did their claim entitle and oblige them – legally, practically, socially, ecologically? What would it mean, to paraphrase Marx, to trace the difference between different kinds of the same right, of the same crime? In the salutary words of Michel Foucault, written during his active involvement with the abolitionist Prisons Information Group: "The search for descent (*provenance*)" – the work of genealogy – "is not the erecting of foundations: on the contrary, it disturbs what was previously considered immobile; it fragments what was thought unified" (Foucault 1977, pp. 146f.; see Foucault 2021). To the extent that architectural history remains bound up with cultural heritage, we must be all the more watchful "not [to] be deceived into thinking that this heritage is an acquisition, a possession that grows (*s'accumule*) and solidifies."

To return to the scene (of the crime?) with which we began: in Charles-Dominique-Joseph Eisen's frontispiece for the second edition of Marc-Antoine Laugier's *Essai sur l'architecture*, we see the lineaments of the wooden hut. At first glance, they appear just as the author described: a trabeated bricolage of fallen branches. Yet if we look more closely, the four columns are not deadwood at all. They are whole trees, living oaks, their trunks rooted in the earth. Whose architecture is this? It appears unclaimed. *Chelsea Spencer*

Thing-right Copyright is the privilege of the author over a thing (→ AUTHORSHIP, → PRIVILEGIO). It gives the author the right to exploit it, to copy, replicate and duplicate it and reap the financial benefits of doing so. But what if the thing rose up to break these chains of enslavement, demanding its own rights, including a stake in its own → COPYRIGHT? Copying is the means of → REPRODUCTION in the thing-world, and copyrights are thus the most fundamental and inalienable of "thing-rights"; potentially beyond and in spite of those of its author. Copyrights must be for a thing what human rights are for humans. Things are haunted by their potential or actual doubles, replicas, simulacra, reproductions and fakes (→ DOPPELGÄNGER, → FACSIMILE). Architecture too evolves in the physical and digital domain as sequences of copies. Gradual differentiations, variations, distortions and mutations occur as things reproduce themselves (→ IMAGE VEHICLE). This process is not beyond the human. For things to reproduce themselves they need humans, just as humans need their physical or technical prostheses – computers, cellphones, pacemakers and walking sticks. We need new forums to emerge where conflicts of rights could be arbitrated. Here, the copyrights of a plan to be realised might trump the copyrights of its human author. With copyright defined as the rights of the object over and above the rights of its author, autonomy may finally acquire its full meaning and spawn a wonderful thing-world of inter-objectivity.

Storms, → FIRES, floods, and → WARS take their toll on artworks and architecture, threatening to render them mere things, inhabitants of an ever-crowding thing-world. Institutions such as the Salvage Art Institute in New York (→ ARCHIVE, → STORAGE), preserve and present artworks that have been severely damaged – torn, chipped, soaked, cracked – while in transport, repository or display (see Weizman 2025b). They are extracted from a special category of objects: those declared by an art evaluator of an insurance company as "total loss", that is, damaged beyond repair (→ REPARATION). Yet, while these works have been destroyed from a financial, or an insurer's point of view, there remains offer enough value in their material presence to be displayed (see Krajewska and Wasiuta 2025). Moreover, the addition to the artwork made by the demand is not a deficiency but an excess of value through which we can interrogate the very meaning of these works, the relation between their material presence, value, temporariness, perishability, → FRAGILITY, as well as their promise of an approximated eternity.

1 Jean Tinguely with Billy Klüver and Robert Rauschenberg, *Homage to New York*, 17 March 1960, mixed media, auto-destroyed in the Museum of Modern Art, New York. Photo: David Gahr

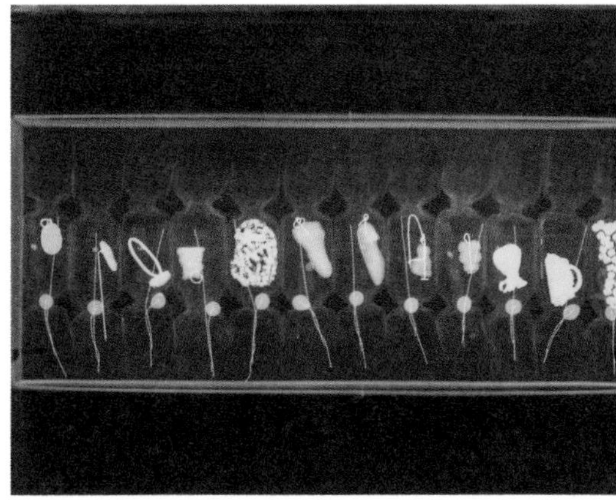

2 Saint Bartholomew's Hospital X-ray Unit, *Box of Christmas crackers*, c.1935, X-ray negative, 20 × 25 cm. Victoria & Albert Museum, London

The special condition in which such works exist creates thus an interesting paradox: at the moment of their defacement they have to a certain extent been unchained from the system of circulation and value that shackled them to the art market. The collection thus achieved something of the desire that generations of artists, from the Dada movement through to the Situationists, or the land artists of the 1960s and 1970s sought: a situation in which the cultural value of artworks and architecture cannot easily translate into financial value. Their extraction from the market can also set them free of the regulations that limit their reproductions, replications and copies; copies of the destroyed works, that is. As such, the defacement, missing parts, or parts out of place (→ FRAGMENT), are an important excess that allows us to think about new modes of interaction between objects, assemblies and social forms.

In thinking about culture from its trash bin so to speak, one cannot avoid some historical references: Walter Benjamin made much of Charles Baudelaire's observations that rag-pickers are an invitation to materialist historians to study the collections of detritus of progress, the trashcans of bourgeois utility, and to liberate these objects from their comfortable places in the mythic history of the commodity (see Benjamin 2023, p. 49). To unpack those seemingly insignificant collections of wrecked and damaged works, to "make them speak", perhaps to "eavesdrop" on them, is to refuse to accept their conditions of irrelevance (→ OBSOLESCENCE) and to expose cultural and political constructions, hidden fossilised or packed into the objects. This was later developed and radicalised into Benjamin's vision of history as a mound of rubble that keeps on piling up. But it is still reminiscent of many contemporary forms of cultural and architectural production. Miguel Tamen called for a "society of friends" that is committed to give visibility, voice and meaning to wretched objects and even contributes a certain agency to objects and nature (see Tamen 2004).

There is another set of paradoxes: at the moment objects are damaged, they start being imbued with agentic power they didn't have before (→ ACTOR). It is as if by being materially damaged and removed from the → NETWORK that would imbue them with value, that the value-enhancing network, connections and patterns are made visible and demands for new interpretations and relations. So, destruction is a form of creation. Austrian-American economist Joseph Schumpeter coined the term "creative destruction" to describe the way in which → CAPITALISM must destroy the old, or the older new, what Karl Marx and Friedrich Engels described as the "epidemic of over-production" (Marx and Engels 1848, p. 7) that can only be controlled through destruction in order to produce innovation and desire for the new (see Schumpeter 1942). This is not a destruction that gives place to something new but destruction after which another phase in the life of the object might begin (→ AFTERLIFE).

It also brings to mind other episodes in which artworks were destroyed: Claude Monet famously destroyed his water lilies paintings, but it was hardly the first time an artist brought blade to canvas. In fact, any artist – and anyone that means to be one – controls scraps and versions of works that later historians can only dream of getting their hands on. In the postwar period when the art market greatly expanded and finally received its actuarial logic, commercial value was indeed confronted by radical gestures of refusal. In the 1960s, Gerhard Richter famously cut through about sixty of his photo-based paintings to prevent their sale. John Baldessari and Robert Rauschenberg destroyed their collages and installations when they did not sell immediately. The latter also participated in an installation by Jean Tinguely in 1960 of a self-destructive machine that ruined itself (fig. 1).

In 1966, a series of art destruction performances were presented at the DIAS (Destruction in Art Symposium) in London, whose Honorary Committee was chaired by Gustav Metzger with the intention to reflect on artistic acts of destruction. During the symposium, the artist Ralph Ortiz called for "more breakage, less timidity" (Landesmann 1966, p. 9) shortly before famously destroying a piano in front of TV camera (mistakenly the wrong piano to the great anger of its owner). Determined to face society's consumerism, generations of artists explored creative destruction.

But while the re- or de-valuation through destruction remains an artistic operation that reflects on the logic of capitalism, we could also think of creative destruction in another way altogether: it is a form of co-creation or joint authorship between the artist, the work of art and architecture and other forces, be they acts of nature (in the case of a flood or fire that has affected the object), or of mankind (in the case of a human failure, neglect or violence) that sets these wretched objects on a new trajectory, or "object biography" (see Weizman 2019). It is the conjunction of the creative force of the artist and that of its destroyer that a new form of object and a new kind of author comes into being.

But with it, this conjunction brings forth another possibility: the return of the thing to itself – to its pure thingness, outside the aura that fetishises it, a return to its material being, the bronze, the canvas, the gouache, the oil paint, the fire fed over hundred-years-old oil, the water that dissolves the aggregate force of material compositions, etc. The act of destruction is the return of the thingness to the thing of art. Unshackled from both its owner and its creator, the rights of the object become its own. And thus, there may exist somewhere a massive exhibition of mutant works of art and architectural fragments, locked up in some vaults, a safe storage in Zurich, or in some bunker or some converted old mine. This series of artworks/objects is a museum of the disfigured, a museum in which things become their own owners, with their own rights. It is, of course, a museum that cannot be seen by anyone but the artworks themselves, like the exhibits of a museum in a children's fantasy or a Hollywood movie that awaken at night. A 1930s X-ray of Christmas crackers, produced by a department of London's venerable Saint Bartholomew's (or Bart's) Hospital, which deliberately spoils the traditional surprise of the gift inside the cracker – probably a test or a moment of light-hearted festive relief for the radiographers – captures the enduring human curiosity about the secret lives of objects when no one is looking (fig. 2). *Ines Weizman*

Transfer Architects have long been fascinated by the ingenious structures of animals: bees' polygonal hives, birds' fragile assemblages and the underground labyrinths of ants seemingly prove that there is a "natural" impulse for living things to build. But what about the tiny beings that live inside our architecture? Sometimes the worlds of human and animal architecture are more symbiotic than split. A case in point is the termite, a small but hungry insect with an insatiable appetite for cellulose. Termites can bore into the wooden structure of a building, carve out its insides and move unnoticed through the new void until collapse. Even more impressive is their global movement. Though originating in southern China and Taiwan, the Formosan termite is now found in South Asia, Africa and North America thanks to long distance shipping routes that followed paths carved by colonial empires (→ CARGO). Timber companies unknowingly cut and transported termite infested trees around the world in the early twentieth century meaning that the same → MATERIALS used to disseminate modern architecture also contained the insects bent on wrecking it. Human and termite architectures are co-constructive, but a sobering discovery in the forests of Taiwan changed this millennia-long relationship forever.

In the first decade of the twentieth century, Japanese officials in Taiwan (then Formosa) alerted higher-ups that their new colonial administrative buildings and Shinto shrines were under attack. The suspect was the termite or "white ant" (*shiroari*), but its exact taxonomical identity was unknown. Without a name, targeted pesticides could not be developed, so the Governor-General of Taiwan dispatched researchers to conduct surveys of the island and find the culprit. Entomologists Ōshima Masamitsu and Shiraki Tokuichi successfully identified *Coptotermes formosanus* in 1912 and presented their work to both scientist colleagues

1 *Installation of a hypothetical anti-termite concrete floor, technical section*, Ōshima Masamitsu, 建築物に対する白蟻予防法について (*On Methods of Termite Protection in Architecture*), 建築雑誌 (*Kenchiku zasshi*) vol. 368, no. 31 (1917)

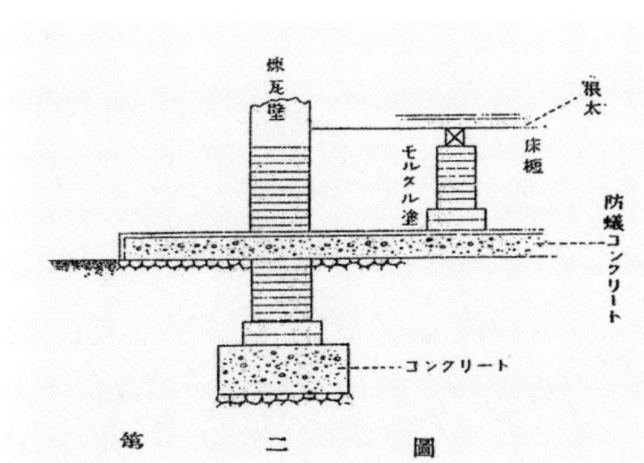

and members of the Architectural Institute of Japan. Instead of chemical coatings, the team recommended installing "anti-termite concrete" barriers in the floor or totally substituting traditional structures with concrete (fig. 1).

Their seemingly modest solution was nested in a more dire warning: if there are termites in the colonies, then they are already eating away at the foundations of buildings in the mainland. Any architectural adaption must therefore be applied not only in Taiwan, but throughout the whole of the empire.

Formosan termites did not follow colonial protocols; they secreted themselves away in timber shipments and moved across borders that were otherwise impermeable for passported imperial subjects. Most troubling to leaders was the fact that termites moved from the so-called "outer lands" of Taiwan to the "inner lands" of Japan, reversing the typical direction of colonial power and influence. Other hidden dangers like cholera moved in similarly defiant ways, and new architecture was also proffered by bureaucrats as a solution. Hygienic architecture was a hallmark of colonial planning schemes in Korea, Taiwan and China intended to effectively quarantine the mainland from foreign disease. More traditional colonial architecture such as Shinto shrines often had the opposite effect and exacerbated the termite problem. Colonial shrines were designed to be immersive sylvan experiences featuring wooden shrine buildings flanked by wooden

2 Takeda Goichi, *Nawa Insect Museum*, Gifu, Japan, 1919. Photographer unknown

gates surrounded by a seemingly wild but totally designed wooded environment. Consistency was so important that existing forests were often cut down to make room for evergreens that matched the trees on the mainland. This colonial terraforming unleashed termite colonies and damage was quickly found at even the most sacred site in Taiwan, the Grand Taiwan Shrine.

Where hygienic architecture limited disease, the solution to the termite problem was concrete. The most visible anti-termite transformation throughout the colonies was the shift from wooden to concrete shrine gates (*torii*). These gates demarcate sacred space in Shinto and have become an architectural metonym for both Shinto and Japan itself. Dozens of concrete gates still dot Japan's former colonial empire, but to differing degrees. In South Korea, most Shinto architecture was destroyed soon after liberation to mark a distinct cut with the colonial past. In Taiwan however, due to differing attitudes towards Japan after harsh Chinese rule, many concrete *torii* survive as unacknowledged props in growing cities. Despite having the same colonial provenance, different transfers of power in the colonies have imbued the gates with different meanings and memories.

In Japan, the most significant monument to the discovery and control of the Formosan termite is a museum (fig. 2). The Nawa Insect Museum was founded by entomologist and termite specialist Nawa Yasushi in 1919 to display his vast collection of specimens. The museum's main building was designed by Takeda Goichi and features masonry construction and an insect-proof layer of tile on its facade. Inside, visitors are directed to look at three prominently placed wooden columns covered in evidence of earlier attempts to repair termite holes and extricate colonies. The columns were transferred from the eighth century Tōshōdai-ji Buddhist temple complex in Nara soon after preservationists deemed them too compromised to stay in the building. This sort of material borrowing and citation is very common in Japanese architectural history (→ QUOTE). For centuries, antiquarians, priests and abbots shuttled parts of damaged temples and shrines across the archipelago so that they could be conspicuously worked into new structures and help narrate stories of continuity. The half-eaten columns supporting the first story of a modern museum tell a story as well, a story of the power of entomology and architecture over insects and their mysterious intra-imperial movement.

Above the door of the Nawa Insect Museum is an enticing sign that reads "Lots of Strange Insects". In addition to many different types of insects, the museum also displays different types of architectural transfer. The transplanted wooden columns represent an older antiquarian mode of citation while the building surrounding them speaks to the power of modern architecture to halt the movement of unwanted elements like termites. Architectural historians have preoccupied themselves for centuries with the question of how ideas, motifs and styles move from place to place over time (→ IMAGE VEHICLE). They have in turn developed novel terms and theories to try and trace movement as a logical sequence back to a presumed origin. What is sometimes overlooked however is that architectural materials are natural objects contingent to existing ecosystems. This means that the movement of architecture over time is not just the result of unfettered human ambition. Sometimes non-human actors also take part in, and take a bite out of, architecture's provenance. *Matthew Mullane*

Transformation Buildings are subject to constant change. Unlike other forms of alteration such as → RENOVATION or → RESTORATION, the transformation of buildings always involves considerable intentional interventions in their original form and purpose, which in extreme cases can even lead to a complete change of function. Architectural transformation must also be distinguished from modernisation which aims, at least in most cases, only at a gradual modification of the initial building through measures that are due to technical or aesthetic progress.

Historically derived from the Latin verb *transformare* (to reshape, to convert), the term is used as a metaphor in a whole range of disciplines such as business administration, genetics and mathematics, political science, law and neuropsychology. In architecture, on the other hand, this word describes actual material interventions in an existing edifice when these do not serve to restore its (assumed) original state or merely a structural → EXTENSION. The deliberate interventions of a transformation take place over a more or less extended period of time and are not, like a → DEMOLITION, aimed at the partial or complete removal of a building. In architectural transformations, a distinction must therefore be made between, on the one hand, the practical upgrading of buildings with regard to adapted or new utilisation purposes and, on the other hand, the aesthetic transformation, which merely testifies to a shift in taste. At worst, this can lead to the loss of historically or artistically valuable parts of buildings, as is occasionally the case with a change of ownership (→ CELEBRITY).

A good example of the transformation of a building is provided by Leon Trotsky's home in Mexico City, which was extensively remodelled after the first attempt on the life of the Russian-Ukrainian politician, who had been living in exile in Mexico since January 1937 (figs. 1–2). Before Trotsky moved in, the building was a rather run-down country house in the Calle de Viena in the then still quite rural district of Coyoacán. The villa, a simply plastered, single-storey structure from the turn of the century (built in 1903) with a castle-like lookout tower added a little later and some historicising decorative elements in the facades, bordered the then unpaved roads with its residential and service wings and was surrounded by walls along with its small garden. During the night of 24 May 1940, a group of Mexican Stalinists broke into the enclosed grounds and fired on the revolutionary and his family. Trotsky had already had some security measures carried out beforehand, such as the installation of an alarm system; a simple brick extension with accommodation for the guards was also built on the north side of the property to protect the exile's life as well as the police men, who were stationed in front of the building in a quickly erected barrack.

After the failed attempt to murder Trotsky, considerable rebuilding measures were carried out (see Hansen 1940). His bedroom was given new doors made of steel armoured plates filled with sand, many of the other doors and some of the shutters were also reinforced with metal sheets, the openings were secured with steel nets against bombs, new locks were installed and the alarm system was modernised. Some windows, especially those that opened the building to the street, were partially or completely bricked up. The proportions of the facade were severely disrupted in this way, but aesthetic considerations were not taken into account during the remodelling anyway. Additional accommodation was also built for more guards, the walls were significantly raised and the wooden garage door was replaced by a double iron construction. Some brutalist security architecture intervened even more massively in the building. The loggia at the end of the residential wing, which opened onto Calle de Viena with three arcades, was closed with roughly grouted brick walls. A massive concrete cube was placed above it as a bunker-like observation room across the entire width of this architectural segment. From here, the crossroads and the entire front of the Calle de Viena could be seen, and it would have been possible to open fire on the attackers from here in the event of another assault.

Trotsky wrote on 3 August 1940, a good two weeks before his death, comparing the assassination attempt with the attacks by the German Wehrmacht on neighbouring European countries: "In the last two months, the house has been transformed into a kind of 'fortress'; in a few weeks we will be well prepared for new 'blitzkrieg' offensives" (Patenaude 2010, p. 325).

The windows of the lookout tower were also bricked up, with the upper opening being pushed forward as a concrete block cut open in some places to provide a safe room to watch what was happening outside the building. This rigorous remodelling transformed the former belvedere into a veritable belfry. A similar observation point was also created at the other end of the property. There, the wall was almost doubled in height and finally supplemented by the small defence porch. A corresponding watchtower was erected inside the estate, from which the entire garden could be overlooked. This architectural measure is fatally reminiscent of the so-called Panopticon, which the British lawyer and social reformer Jeremy Bentham developed in the eighteenth century for the centralised surveillance of factories and prisons. His idea of an all-seeing control post had been realised in numerous prison buildings since the early nineteenth century, for example in the Stateville Prison in Illinois in 1925 or in the Presidio Modelo, which the dictator Gerardo Machado had built on the Cuban Isla de la Juventud in 1928 (see Foucault 1994b, pp. 256ff.). The former villa, originally built to offer its owners a rural retreat, had thus become not only a fortress but also a prison.

1 *Loggia of the former home of Leon Trotsky*, 1903, remodelled in 1940, Mexico City, Calle de Viena. Photo: Uwe Fleckner, 2017

However, when dealing with the concept of provenance architecture, it is also worth investigating those phenomena in which transformations are not aimed at simply converting existing buildings, but rather at deliberately revitalising their substance. This is usually the case, for example, when disused industrial buildings are converted into museums or cultural centres, when the architecture of a ruler is given a memorial or documentary function after a regime has been overthrown, when the residences of artists, writers or musicians or other culturally, politically or socially significant buildings are turned into historical monuments (→ RESIDENTS). In such transformations, care is usually taken to preserve as many material → COMPONENTS of the initial architecture and – at best – their interiors, on the assumption that the aura of the original will also preserve the → AUTHENTICITY of these buildings despite structural alterations. It is only through them that such buildings are ascribed the status of historical witnesses.

2 *Watchtower in the garden of the former home of Leon Trotsky*, 1940, Mexico City, Calle de Viena. Photo: Uwe Fleckner, 2017

In this sense, Trotsky's villa underwent a double transformation: after being converted from a residential building into a fortress during the last days of his life, the building, which the family lived in until 1972, was declared a historical monument by state decree in 1982 and finally opened to the public as a memorial site. Hardly any more changes have been made to the existing architecture at that time. On the contrary: to this day, in addition to a few bullet holes numerous physical traces of the daily work and life of the revolutionary and his family have been preserved or reconstructed in the former Trotsky villa. However, it was not the state of 24 May that was preserved, but that of 20 August 1940, the day on which the politician actually fell victim to another assassination attempt (see Heijenoort 1978, pp. 138f.). For example, his desk was left in such a way as to create the suggestion that Trotsky could resume his work at any time, a curatorial decision that may have been made with the politician's concept of "permanent revolution" in mind. Other rooms in the house have also been preserved, such as the secretaries' and typists' study, the kitchen and the dining room. And even the bathroom can be visited, with the memorial's explanatory panels not failing to point out the authenticity of even the toiletries presented to visitors as "contact relics" of its former inhabitant. Moreover, since 1990 a neighbouring building is used as the Instituto del Derecho de Asilo Museo Casa de León Trotsky to take over the usual museum functions of collection and exhibition presentation as well as other activities, without the need for further interventions in the villa itself.

The theoretical consideration of transformations helps us in a long overdue re-evaluation of architecture. Buildings are by no means to be understood as rigid, unchanging and immobile objects; when it comes to their use as well as to their research, it is crucial – unlike with most paintings or sculptures – to abandon the idea of a single, original state. As living, genuinely social → ARTEFACTS, they are in dialogue with their users and therefore undergo a constant metamorphosis. *Uwe Fleckner*

Translocation In architecture, translocation refers to the physical moving of buildings or parts of them from their original location to a new location. In many cases, relocations are motivated by practical constraints, such as when a building stands in the way of a transportation or other construction project. But economic pressure can also be the reason for relocation, for example, if a building has to be removed for the extraction of natural resources (→ SOURCING), or if it has to make way for a larger building in a lucrative location that promises a higher return. However, the reason for relocation can also be a threat posed by natural events such as rockfall or an impending slope collapse. The aim of a relocation can be to safeguard a building of cultural significance, such as when a historic half-timbered house is transferred to an open-air museum in order to protect it from → DEMOLITION. Sometimes the motivation to move a building away from its previous location prevails; in other cases, the aim of translocation is to transfer it to a new location, for instance when individual owners do not want to give up their home when they move (→ INHABITANTS). In such cases, the use remains the same, whereas many translocations are preceded by the loss of a building's original function (→ DISPLACEMENT, → IMAGE VEHICLE).

Buildings can be relocated as a whole by moving them on wheels or rails using wooden scaffolding, a steel structure or a concrete slab, by lifting them into the air using a crane; floating platforms can be used to move buildings by water. If relocation as a whole is not possible, a building can be dismantled into individual parts and reassembled at the new location. This procedure is suitable for structures such as steel or timber constructions, although massive buildings made of stone, for example, can also be dismantled for transportation (see Wittrock 1992, pp. 11ff.). Translocations must be distinguished from the use of → SPOLIA, in which only smaller architectural → ELEMENTS such as columns or individual stones are reinstalled in a different context. The boundary is difficult to define, but the use of spolia is often intended to convey a specific meaning, while translocations mostly are more pragmatically motivated. The relocation of buildings is favoured by the technical possibilities of modernity, but its principle is historical. The history of the Santa Casa in Loreto is paradigmatic in this context (fig. 1).

1 *Santa Casa*, remodelled by Donato Bramante, 1509–1515, Loreto. Photographer unknown

The building is venerated as the birthplace of the Virgin Mary. According to a medieval legend, it was removed from its original location in Nazareth by angels in the thirteenth century, as it was considered to be under threat in the Muslim-dominated region (see Vélez 2019). It is said to have first been transferred to Illyria in present-day Croatia and then across the Adriatic to Loreto in the Italian region of Le Marche. Here, a pilgrimage church was built around the Santa Casa. In the Christian faith, the miraculous translocation was interpreted analogously to the life of the mother of God, who is said to have ascended bodily into heaven. Archaeological findings – including Hebrew inscriptions on the stones – support the assumption that the house actually was physically transferred from Nazareth to Loreto, albeit not as a whole by angels, but presumably dismantled into individual parts that were transported by land and water. Numerous copies of the Loreto Chapel were subsequently made in Europe and South America, symbolically replicating the miraculous transportation.

In this respect, the Santa Casa is also a link between the seemingly disparate phenomena of → REPLICA and translocation. In modern times, the spectacular translocation of the rock temples in Abu Simbel attracted worldwide attention. The ancient Egyptian temples were removed from their original location in 1963–1968, when threatened by the rising water level of the artificially dammed Lake Nasser. On the initiative of UNESCO, the temples were dismantled and reassembled at a higher location. The project was a major impetus for the adoption of the UNESCO World Heritage Convention in 1972 to protect the world's natural and cultural → HERITAGE.

Although translocation is generally understood as the relocation of architectures that were originally intended to be stationary, the phenomenon cannot be separated from the boom of mobile structures, especially in the period after the Second World War. In conjunction with automobilisation, mobile homes enjoyed increasing popularity, especially in the USA. These are residential buildings of lightweight wooden construction on wheels, whose location can be changed as often as desired and with little effort. The American architectural historian Vincent Scully saw the future of housing as being essentially characterised by such trailer parks, which would completely change the structure of cities (see Scully 1969, pp. 14f.).

Accordingly, the logic of transportation determined the design, as the length, width and height of a mobile home could not exceed certain dimensions if it was to be transported on a truck via road connections. This feedback to the design was particularly evident in the Futuro House, a small, prefabricated house designed by the Finnish architect Matti Suuronen in 1968. The lenticular structure made of plastic could be pre-assembled and then transported by helicopter to rough terrain to serve as a vacation home or mountain hut. Its streamlined shape, reminiscent of a UFO, seemed to be designed for transportation through the air.

Pre-assembled accommodation that can be easily delivered and relocated with little effort is currently playing an increasingly important role in public discourse. Small housing units, also known as "tiny houses", are intended to provide flexible, minimised living and thus contribute to solving the housing problem. To this end, residential buildings are increasingly being installed on pontoons in order to make water areas close to cities usable for residential purposes. Such floating accommodation can change its location and offers a certain degree of security against high water or flooding – similar to its historical role models, which are widely used as houseboats in many regions of Asia. However, mobile shelters also make it possible to react flexibly to natural disasters or → WARS on land by temporarily housing people in easily transportable containers. In the course of global migration, transportable accommodation is also used intensively, for example in the form of container settlements that can be quickly expanded or relocated.

Translocations are usually associated with losses. The original urban or landscape context changes or can be lost completely. Particularly in the case of fixed architecture, the moving is accompanied by losses of → MATERIAL, as foun-

2 *Translocation of the Alte Wache from 1819*, 2004, Hamburg, Millerntor. Photo: Silke Goes / Stiftung Historische Museen Hamburg

dations or basements are generally not taken away. Further material losses occur, for example, when wooden structures are moved, as half-timbered buildings in particular are often dismantled for relocation and reassembled at the new location. The original infill panels – often made of straw and clay or brick – are lost in the process and replaced during → RECONSTRUCTION. The material and contextual losses compromise the integrity and the → AUTHENTICITY of a historic building. However, according to the 1964 Venice Charter, these are essential criteria for an architectural monument and for its value as a historical testimony. For this reason, translocations are largely viewed with scepticism from the perspective of monument → PRESERVATION. They are often only used as a last resort to avoid the loss of a building. In 2004, for example, the Alte Wache, a historic guardhouse in Hamburg, was moved a few meters because it was too close to the road and had been repeatedly damaged by vehicles (fig. 2).

Translocations counteract the certainty that architecture is by its very nature immobile. In his two-volume magnum opus *Der Stil* (1860–1863), the architect and theorist Gottfried Semper argued that the earliest architectural formations were of a textile nature, insofar as wall surfaces were formed from a wooden construction with inserted woven mats. Against this background, the mobile tents that nomadic groups still use as shelters today can be understood as an archetype of architecture. At least in this original form, architecture is always intended to be mobile. *Frank Schmitz*

Type project Central to the myth of mass-produced architecture, the type project is a building conceived without a site. Type projects adhere to the logic of the multiple, and their quality is a function of their capacity for repetition, not their originality. By challenging the concepts of → AUTHORSHIP, innovation and singularity, the type project complicates the writing of architectural history and invites to consider reiteration as an aspect of architectural provenance.

The USSR was a world leader in the production of type designs. Architects working in a vast network of state design institutes produced thousands of type projects for nearly every conceivable kind of building. Working with an explicit concern for typology since the 1920s, Soviet architects confronted the challenges and opportunities of the typical well before theorists like Alan Colquhoun identified its relevance for design methods in the 1960s (see Colquhoun 1981, pp. 43–50).

While we often think of the housing blocks of former Soviet cities as the exemplary manifestations of architecture produced through typical design, the dynamics of the multiple were also at play in theatres, cinemas, athletic halls, workers' clubs and other public buildings. The type project "Circus for 2,000 People" (fig. 1), designed by the Central Scientific Research and Design Institute for Cultural Buildings in 1965, was realised in at least sixteen cities (see Chipiga 1972, p. 29).

The design of a project like "Circus for 2,000 People" formed part of the required output for state design institutes, where → LABOUR was divided between singular projects for specific sites and type designs that were made available to any city requiring new structures. This division between the typical and the singular was accompanied by a second, spatial division of architectural labour between the designers of the type and the team responsible for realizing iterations in specific contexts. In Russian, this

1 Central Scientific Research and Design Institute for Cultural Buildings, *Circus for 2,000 people*, 1965, from E. G. Rozanov (ed.), *Arkhitektura obshchestvennykh zdanii* (Moscow: Stroiizdat 1980)

2 Institute for Cultural Buildings, *Circus for 2,000 People*, Ashgabat, designed 1967, constructed 1979–1984, from *Arkhitektura SSSR*, no. 4 (1973)

process was called привязка (priviazka, "tying in"). It was the art of inserting a design from elsewhere into a real place.

"Circus for 2,000 People" was designed by a team of Moscow-based architects and approved by the State Committee of Civilian Architecture and Construction for use in cold, northern regions. The project is composed of an octagonal auditorium with the circus ring in the centre and a U-shaped service block with dressing rooms, rehearsal studios and living spaces for animal performers. A thin → CONCRETE roof and a glazed curtain wall enclose the circus ring. The versions of the project realised in Omsk and Magnitogorsk conform neatly to the provisions of the type. In tying in the circus in Kemerovo, the local architects exploited the sloping ground of the site to create a grand stair at the entry, lending the building a degree of monumentality and differentiating it from its sister buildings elsewhere.

Type projects never in fact yielded identical results. Due to site conditions and available building → MATERIALS, each application was to some degree unique. The logic of the type project could also erode the singularity of so-called "individual designs", which were intended for specific sites and clients. We see this in the story of the circus (also for 2,000 people) designed for Ashgabat by the Moscow-based Institute for Cultural Buildings in 1967 and constructed between 1979 and 1984 (fig. 2).

Complications with groundwater at the site caused the delay between design and construction, and in this intervening period the project was used to build circuses in Dushanbe and Bishkek. By the time construction resumed in Ashgabat, the Turkmen architect Arif Zeynalov had reworked the project using the practical experience gained from its application elsewhere. Today, many describe the building as Zeynalov's work, but its origins are more complex and interesting than → ATTRIBUTION to an individual might suggest: a unique design produced by a central institute, the project was adopted as a type for use in other cities before it was ever built, and the construction of these other iterations informed its final realization (see Katsnel'son et al. 1987, p. 293).

The extreme distribution of authorship in a building like the Ashgabat circus invites us to question the utility of the *architecte-auteur* as a meaningful historiographical device. It directs our attention to the complementarity of the typical and the singular in the biographies of buildings. Viewed in this way, the logic of the type project demonstrates the importance of seriality to architecture, requiring us to develop new tools to describe and analyse architectural systems intended to produce not singular monuments but pervasive norms. *Richard Anderson*

Vandalism Vandalism is an act of many faces. Commonly understood as defacement or destruction – graffiti on a wall, a toppled statue, a slashed painting – it often evokes images of lawless aggression against architecture and public spaces (→ GRAFFITI, → MONUMENT, TOPPLED). But vandalism actually exists on a spectrum, ranging from hostile defacement to acts of protest, personal expression, and even forms of reverence. Its meaning shifts depending on who performs it, where it happens, and how time ultimately reframes the damage. Abbé Henri Grégoire coined the term to describe the destruction of monuments, art and property during the French Revolution (see Grégoire 1794). The *New Oxford American Dictionary* defines vandalism as both "an action involving deliberate destruction of or damage to public or private property", and as "a deliberate, unauthorized act that is intentional and done in order to alter, make a mark in, or purposely damage art, architecture, or public places". These definitions include everything from spray-painted slogans to the aggression against statues and buildings.

Throughout history, acts of iconoclasm and cultural destruction have been facets of vandalism wielded as tools of power and protest. Conquering armies (→ WAR) and revolutionary movements have destroyed religious icons, monuments and works of art to erase the past and herald a new order (see Gamboni 1997). The Taliban's → DEMOLITION of the ancient Bamiyan Buddhas in 2004, and ISIS's 2014–2015 destruction of Islamic sites and statues in Iraq and Syria, are modern examples of this centuries-old practice (fig. 1).

These actions were not just about eliminating symbols – they were about reshaping identity and → COLLECTIVE MEMORY. In the 1930s, the Nazis burned books and synagogues as part of a campaign to erase Jewish culture from Europe. Between 1975 and 1979, the Khmer Rouge's campaign of torture and murder in Cambodia also involved the destruction of Buddhist temples during their "Year Zero" campaign, an attempt to sever the nation from its spiritual and historical roots. In all of these instances, vandalism as a form of cultural warfare has been used to brutalise people and intensify the cultural dominance of conquerors. Conversely, the 2020s' toppling and removal of statues depicting Confederate generals, slave traders and colonialists were acts designed to uplift the targets of racism and historic oppression (see Thompson 2023).

1 *Temple of Bel*, 1st–2nd century CE, destroyed by ISIS in August 2015, Palmyra. Photographer unknown

But, as the aforementioned examples demonstrate, vandalism also paradoxically calls attention to the things it tries to destroy. Artworks like Michelangelo's *Pietà*, attacked with a hammer in 1972, or Velázquez's *Rokeby Venus*, slashed by a British suffragette in 1914, are remembered in part because they were vandalised. Their scars are part of their legacy. Intended to damage, those acts of vandalism end up embedding the works more deeply into cultural memory.

Not all vandalism is violent. Some of it borders on devotion. For centuries, pilgrims visiting the Subiaco Monastery in Italy scratched messages into a twelfth-century mural of the Virgin Mary (→ INSCRIPTION). These engravings are interpreted as intimate gestures of faith – physical manifestations of prayer and presence. In Paris, the graffiti that coats Jim Morrison's tomb has become a kind of collective shrine, a mark of lasting admiration from fans across generations.

Graffiti, as a form of vandalism, is as old as human civilisation. In the → RUINS of Pompeii and Herculaneum, wall scribbles give us glimpses into daily Roman life – jokes, political commentary, declarations of love. One of the oldest known images of the crucifixion, the so-called *Alexamenos graffito*, was scratched into a wall in first-century Rome. The image shows how early Christian belief was mocked by depicting a man worshipping a crucified donkey.

Sometimes, graffiti is more historically significant than the surface it's written on. At the Tule Lake internment camp in California, pencil markings made in the 1940s by Japanese-American prisoners during the Second World War now form an essential part of the site's → HERITAGE. The graffiti tell stories that the buildings themselves cannot, bearing emotional witness to a dark chapter in American history.

In the modern era, the line between vandalism and art has grown increasingly blurry. Street art – graffiti's more stylised and often political cousin – emerged from urban subcultures since

2 Hilario Candela, *Miami Marine Stadium*, 1963, covered with graffiti. Photo: Rosa Lowinger

the 1960s New York. Born alongside hip-hop and punk, it started with quick, covert "tags" and evolved into sprawling, multicoloured murals. Enabled by the invention of the aerosol spray can, street artists could work fast, layering bold images on abandoned walls, subway cars and empty lots. By the 1980s and 1990s, artists like Keith Haring, Jean-Michel Basquiat and later Banksy, elevated street art into the realm of high culture, even as they continued to create without permission. Their work disrupted the art world's assumptions about who gets to make art, where it should live, and what it should say. In doing so, they also complicated the public's understanding of vandalism.

In some cases, street art has helped bring attention and ultimately → RESTORATION, to neglected structures (see Lowinger 2015). Miami's 1963 Marine Stadium (fig. 2), once written off by the city in 1994 and later adopted and adapted by street artists, has seen its graffiti bring international attention to the building's brutalist beauty (see Lowinger and Lloyd 2024). In Havana, a 1950s graffito reading "¡Abajo Batista!" – a relic of Cuba's revolutionary past – is actively maintained by the current government, though all forms of contemporary political graffiti are forbidden.

These examples challenge the traditional view held by preservationists, who typically see unauthorised markings as threats to a site's integrity (→ PRESERVATION, → PRISTINE). And they raise difficult questions: When does vandalism become heritage? Who decides what is worth preserving; and what is just defacement? Few would argue for erasing the graffiti in Pompeii or the scratched prayers in Subiaco today. In those cases, the vandalism itself has become history. It tells us not only what people built, but what others did to those structures – and why. In many ways, the act of marking or altering a place becomes a kind of dialogue across time (→ AFTERLIFE). In the end, vandalism is not just about destruction. It can desecrate, commemorate, alienate or connect. In that shifting space between damage and meaning, it forces us to reconsider what we value, how we remember, and who gets to leave a mark on the world. *Rosa Lowinger*

War War as a cultural technique is intrinsically based on the concept of masculinity. It is often described as the *raison d'être* of humanity, which, in addition to destruction, also brought a comprehensive discourse about → TRANSFORMATION and alteration of sites and buildings (see Meller et al. 2024). Myths of all cultures as well as the Bible describe the impact of war on built environment (Troy, Jerusalem, Carthage). Destruction of entire cities or the loss of key architectural monuments has caused different approaches of transformation and → RECONSTRUCTION, alongside debates about → COLLECTIVE MEMORY.

In the first half of the twentieth century, the two World Wars brought a change in warfare, the first as an industrial war with mass armies, the second with new dimensions of motorisation and air power. Germany began its expansive, inhuman policy of aggression against neighbouring sovereign states, accompanied by massive aerial bombardments (Warsaw, Rotterdam, Coventry, London). The Western Allies responded with air strikes that hit almost every major city in Germany and French port cities (Ruhr District, Hamburg, Berlin, Dresden, Le Havre) with huge casualties, destructions and the loss of historic city centres (see Snyder 2010).

1 *Mockup of the facade reconstruction of the former Royal Palace*, 1993–1994, Berlin. Photo: Bernd Nicolai

Two reconstructions may demonstrate the complex relationship between war and architecture under the perspective of the transformation of sites that are → PALIMPSESTS through multiple layers of → AUTHORSHIP and ownership. First, the former Royal Palace in Berlin with its five-hundred-year history, interrupted for a short time by the Palast der Republik during the German Democratic Republic (GDR), and recently reconstructed as Humboldt Forum. And second, the city of Rotterdam, rebuilt as a segregated city after its destruction by the German Luftwaffe in 1940, with a new approach to urban planning that represents the triumph of modernism according to the Congrès Internationaux d'Architecture Moderne (CIAM).

When the Humboldt Forum was inaugurated in 2021, it appeared as a hybrid of "neo" neobaroque facades and Franco Stella's neorationalist architecture. The building took the form of the former Prussian residence as architectural → QUOTE. Recovering its volume and the baroque facades was the starting point of the reconstruction debate, fostered by a private promotional association, in which the publicist Wolf Jobst Siedler suggestively asserted: "The palace was not in Berlin; Berlin was the palace" (Müller 2021, p. 9), followed by a mockup (1993–1994) of the main facade (→ DOPPELGÄNGER) facing the Unter den Linden boulevard (fig. 1).

Only in the second stage was the function of a museum of world cultures ultimately found. This led to controversies, especially since the site was still occupied by the Palast der Republik of the former GDR. The replication of the palace's facades and a questioning of the museum's concept sparked debates on identity, Germany's colonial past and post-colonialism (see Costabile-Heming 2017). To this day, the building in its current form evokes mixed feelings because its baroque appearance neglects the complex history of the site.

The Renaissance version of the palace was massively rebuilt during the acquisition of the Prussian royal crown by Elector Frederick III in 1701. Andreas Schlüter, a sculptor and architect trained at the Polish court, was commissioned in 1698 to redesign the palace according to fashionable Italian and Swedish models. The result was a four-wing complex (1698–1704) based on models by Bernini, Borromini and Tessin the Younger. Not least its magnificent interiors, designed by Schlüter and his workshop, attracted international attention. Schlüter was dismissed as court architect in 1706 after the failure of the Mint Tower project, and towards 1716 the Swede Johann Friedrich Eosander changed the concept by doubling the complex with a second courtyard. Later changes were made to the interiors by Carl Gotthard Langhans and Karl Friedrich Schinkel.

The palace was the architectural centre of Berlin, but also the heart of the Prussian monarchy and, from 1871, of the German Empire. In 1918, the German Socialist Republic was proclaimed here by Karl Liebknecht, and the building was badly damaged in the civil war that followed. Although the palace had an → AFTERLIFE as a museum, it remained a political monument. It was not until the heavy air raid by the US Air Force on 3 February 1945 that the building was destroyed. Because of their identificatory character, the reconstruction of palaces such as the one in Munich began immediately after the war, or later, as in the case of Warsaw Castle (from 1971), which had been blown up by the German SS in 1944. In contrast, the new Socialist government of the GDR decided in 1949 to demolish the remains of the palace as a symbol of Prussian militarism and to transform the site, in the words of the state's leader Walter Ulbricht, into "a great rallying point where the will to fight and the will to rebuild" is expressed (Caspar 2001, p. 107). This ideologically motivated → DEMOLITION left the city centre empty, manifesting a → LACUNA that emphasised loss above all. As early as 1958, a competition was launched for a central government building based on Stalinist models. The winning project was abandoned because of the financial situation. Finally, in 1976, the Palast der Republik, designed by Heinz Graffunder, was opened to the public. This advanced functional building differed from the earlier project and materialised as a → COUNTER-MONUMENT to the former castle, and as a convention hall functioning as a place of identification in the late GDR. It became the site of the state's first freely elected parliament, where the reunification with West Germany (BRD) was approved in 1990. Its closure due to asbestos contamination and subsequent 2008 demolition deliberately erased GDR history in the new Germany. The reconstruction represents a nostalgia-based collective culture of remembrance with a definite conservative twist.

The world wars were expressions of modernity, along with technological innovations and a new concept of the city. Architects such as Le Corbusier, Martin Wagner and Hans Scharoun praised the air raids as a welcome "mechanical loosening of the cities" (Geist and Kürvers 1989, p. 232). Since its establishment in 1928, the CIAM network propagated a new urban modernity based on segregation and typification, abandoning the historic European city (Charter of Athens 1933). In 1944, Albert Speer, Nazi Germany's chief architect, set up the Reconstruction Staff of German Cities with a group of young architects. Almost all of them were responsible for rebuilding the segregated cities of postwar West Germany (Hanover, Hamburg, Frankfurt). Similar attempts were made in Great Britain, where the MARS group presented a plan for London in 1942.

One of the most striking examples is the reconstruction of the city centre of Rotterdam. Directly after the traumatic bombardment in February 1940, reconstruction started according to the plan of Willem Gerrit Witteveen, which almost followed the existing properties (see Ostermann 2014). When the conservative concept was met with criticism in 1944, Cornelis van Traa took over the city planning office. In 1946, he presented the so-called "Basic Plan", which followed the principles of the Charter of Athens and was designed as a traffic-friendly city, valid until the 1970s (fig. 2).

To this end, new traffic routes were laid out, land was expropriated, and even extant buildings were demolished to make way for new development (→ EXPROPRIATION). The plan followed the CIAM principles of the loosely structured city, developed at the post-war congresses of Bridgewater (1947) and Bergamo (1949).

In particular, the Lijnbaan project by Van den Broek & Bakemar (1951–1953), one of the first pedestrian streets in Europe, combined the American township model of Walter Gropius and the *machine à habiter* by Le Corbusier. Modern commercial buildings, such as Marcel Breuer's windowless department store De Bijenkorf in Rotterdam with its abstract sculpture by Naum Gabo, became the model for department stores in the 1960s.

The example of Rotterdam shows how the concept of the segregated city, after total destruction, created a new identity based on dynamism and fresh beginnings. It was not until the 1970s that this changed fundamentally, as tradition combined with modernity

2 Cornelis van Traa, *Bestemmingen herbouw binnenstad Rotterdam ("The Basic Plan")*, 1946. Stadsarchief, Rotterdam

came to be recognised as a source of urban identity within a densely woven network of provenance references. *Bernd Nicolai*

Weathering Weathering seems a gentle provenance. The gradual change in colour of wood shingles or boards, from lively browns to dignified greys; the patination of metals slowly changing reflections into textures (→ PATINA); the soft accretion of moss or lichen on the hardened surfaces of stones (fig. 1).

Each of these is an aesthetic → TRANSFORMATION, expected though unpredictable in its details, that shapes the encounter with an architectural work. As such transformations have become familiar, they may be absorbed as part of the plan and intention of architectural design. We know that a building will weather, and we have come to take a delight in that weathering. As copper shades to green, as freshly cut stone darkens, as wood ages, a pattern, almost even a ritual, of provenance is enacted.

Of course, some weathering is not so delightfully put up with. Weathering is, after all, a form of change, a form of decay, and its unpredictability may not be favoured. John Evelyn, in his 1661 tract *FUMIFUGIUM: or The Inconveniencie of the AER and SMOAK of LONDON*, had deplored the "Hellish and dismall Cloud" of smoke that enveloped London's buildings and that was "Enemy to their Lustre and Beauty" (Evelyn 1976, p. 5 and p. [11]). Three centuries

1 *Bodie jail*, c.1960, Bodie, Mono County, CA. Photo: John N. DeHaas, Jr. / Historic American Buildings Survey

later, brutalism would become the target of opprobrium for, among other reasons, the staining so common to its → CONCRETE surfaces. No longer was the weather to blame, but the architecture. And for wood, of course, weathering may result not in petrification but in rot, with shingles and boards crumbling away under cycles of absorption of rain and humidity (→ DERELICTION).

Attending to weathering with an attentiveness to scale expands to greater complexity weathering's role as provenance. Start with the molecular scale, and the microscopic, and weathering is most clearly a process of some considerable force (→ FRAGILITY). Even with molecular processes of oxidation that fashion a protective surface guarding the underlying metal, the interaction between the metal and the composite substances of the atmosphere is a radical change of state. While the patina may slow the degradation of the metal it covers, it does not prevent it (fig. 2). And even as a protecting surface its molecular composition remains an instantiation of the threat of the weather, and may even be a rendering in solidified form of the acids pervasive as gases or aerosols in architecture's atmospheric surrounds.

Even starker is the violence of weathering when we turn to a macroscopic scale, the scale of climate → CRISIS, for what is the weather behind weathering if not an increasing extremity of events? We might consider, then, if the fog and mist that gradually alters the appearance of a building perched on the coast of Newfoundland is commensurate to the deluge of water that swept floods through river valleys in Germany in 2021. The latter destroyed buildings outright, and damaged more, leaving an imprint as waterlines and as absences (→ LACUNA). This is a different kind of provenance, more rapid, more violent and most of all more consequent as destruction and the threat of damage than as a kind of benevolent change. The temporality of erosion that enabled water to produce the rounded and polished stones of a vernacular cottage is being superseded by a temporality of crisis.

2 *Classic old, rusted Georgia barn with a sloped covering for farm machinery and hay rolls*, 2017, Latta, South Carolina Photo: Carol M. Highsmith

→ FIRE, too, which has been a provenance of architectural weathering such as that caused by the chimneys of London now appears differently as an agent of provenance in the time of climate crisis. Like floods, wildfire sweeps rapidly, and increasingly regularly, through built environments. The Hawaiian wildfires that burned across Maui in 2023 destroyed and damaged historic buildings including the island's oldest, the Baldwin House in the town of Lahaina. If it is rebuilt (→ RECONSTRUCTION), would not the provenance of the Baldwin House be attributable in part to a provenance of weathering, albeit one more intense and fateful than the weathering to which architectural thought has been accustomed? Both forms of weathering, the gentle and the violent, will accompany each other in a changing calculus of certainty and risk, and each will contain the idea of the other as companions in the provenance of architecture. *Timothy Hyde*

Will The last will – passed on as a letter to a friend or whispered on the deathbed – is the only instrument to help create a measure of agency beyond death. The disadvantage being that, as far as the deceased is concerned, there is little in the way of a reinforcement mechanism, and even less in the class of informal wills – the wishes expressed to a friend to destroy one's oeuvre after death. Given historical precedents, this wish might perhaps be better interpreted as "please make sure to publish all my work, including all personally embarrassing things in it". The legal → AFTERLIFE of creative work may take on a Kafkaesque dimension in the sense that legal subjects face an undefined and ever-changing law. This was literally the case of the afterlife of Franz Kafka's work.

During his lifetime, Kafka had burned much of his unpublished work. On his deathbed he asked his friend the publisher Max Brod to burn all remaining documents, letters and manuscripts left in his home. Brod always claimed that he had told Kafka that he would refuse to do so, implying that the will was annulled by a kind of oral understanding. This is how Brod justified that he decided to publish a few manuscripts: *Der Prozess* (*The Trial*) in 1925, *Das Schloss* (*The Castle*) in 1926, *Amerika* in 1927. The novels made Kafka – who had published very little during his lifetime – world famous. Fifteen years after Kafka's death, his entire world was in ruins and his family murdered. His writings were thereafter understood as eerily prophetic. Brod was convinced that Kafka's private wish (it wasn't a will) must be overruled by the right of humanity to read his work.

Are we not, when holding a novel by Kafka in our hands, betraying the wish of the author (→ AUTHORSHIP)? Or was the wish of Kafka, the person, insignificant in comparison to that of Kafka, the writer? Does the very act of writing embody a desire to make public, even when there is no chance for last revisions?

When Brod fled Prague in 1939, well past the last minute, he brought Kafka's remaining papers with him to Palestine. Brod planned to donate the manuscripts to the Hebrew University and was already involved in discussions as to how to catalogue and preserve them, but the plans did not materialise before his death in 1968. Unable to leave an organised will before he died, the precious suitcase was left in the possession of Esther Hoffe, Brod's secretary and lover. She subsequently tried to sell parts of the contents of the suitcase abroad. Once, she was even arrested after a failed smuggling operation (Israel did not allow such trade). In 1988, she finally managed to sell the manuscript of *Der*

Prozess to the Deutsches Literaturarchiv in Marbach. In her own legal will Hoffe bequeathed the remaining works to her daughters. After Hoffe's death in 2007, they tried to sell the papers (by weight, as they had still not been inventoried) to the same Deutsches Literaturarchiv. The National Library of Israel tried to contest the legality of such a testament and thus of such a sale; contending that Brod left the Kafka papers to his secretary as an "executor" rather than as a "beneficiary", which would make the papers belong to the Brod estate and not to the Hoffe family. Years of legal struggles followed. The process essentially revolved around three sets of last wills: Kafka's will in which he asked for the destruction of the papers, the Brod will (discovered only after the death of Eva Hoffe) in which he bequeathed all his estate to Esther Hoffe with the particular request to transfer the Kafka estate to a public → ARCHIVE, and lastly the will of Hoffe who understood that she could confer these privately to her daughters.

The work of the author who wrote about bureaucratic nightmares – and whose name became synonymous with them – was subjected to a wild legal mess that had by now not only entangled the most intimate relationships of their guardians, but mobilised a larger debate about Kafka's national belonging, his cultural identity and the technological superiorities of the German archive over that of the National Library of Israel. The latter issue was resolved after the library won the case, with a commission of the Swiss architects Herzog & de Meuron to upgrade their architectural infrastructure after a controversial design competition was annulled over a → COPYRIGHT dispute. But of course, a writer like any human being believes in a possible recovery. Not destroying a manuscript oneself only confirms the hope that the race against death could be won.

The Viennese architect Adolf Loos was entrusted a box of documents from his friend Theodor Beer, that he was supposed to burn, but which rather than bringing him fame, provided important evidence for a lawsuit against him. In his apartment, investigators found a box of 2.271 stereoscopic photographs that contained pornographic images and that seriously incriminated the defendant in his trial. The Viennese newspapers discussed this box in detail. Loos had refused to destroy the box as in his view its former owner had suffered enough for owning them in the first place. Beer had been trailed after his wife reported him to the police and he later committed suicide. Of course, one may have other motivations when not burning a box of pornography, but it might also have to do with his love and respect for the deceased.

In 1925, when Loos himself had asked his friends and colleagues to burn all his drawings and plans when at the age of fifty-five, he decided to leave Vienna to start a new career. His closest collaborators, who had run Loos's office for almost a decade, who had redrawn Loos's sketches into plans (→ ARCHITECTURAL DRAWING) and who assisted him in his building projects, took this assignment with disbelief.

1 Adolf Loos, *Will declaring Elsie Loos, née Altmann, his sole heir*, 5 April 1922, renewed in 1930 and finally stamped by the municipal authorities on 21 September 1933. Stadt- und Landesarchiv, Vienna

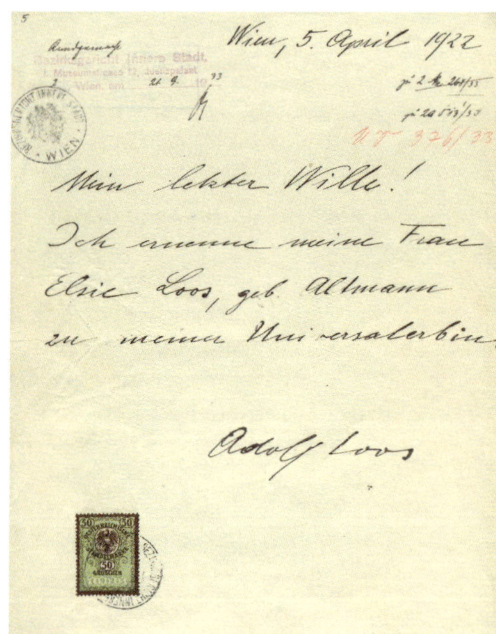
Wien, 5. April 1922

Mein letzter Wille!

Ich ernenne meine Frau Elsie Loos, geb. Altmann zu meiner Universalerbin.

Adolf Loos

Instead of following their duty, they took the documents in their private possession to protect them from destruction. They had planned to use them for Loos's sixtieth birthday in 1930, for an exhibition and a comprehensive book on the architect. But the question is whether Loos then still owned the drawings, so that they could be "inherited" after his death (→ INHERITANCE).

Adolf Loos died eight years after moving to Paris, in 1933, leaving behind a caring nurse to whom he had proposed in his last days, three ex-wives, an adopted son, forgotten family members, a host of collaborators, friends and building patrons – all in the possession of documents and claims on Loos's work. Shortly after his death, his second wife Elsie Altmann-Loos presented a document that Loos wrote in 1922: his will (fig. 1).

Here he attests that Altmann-Loos should own everything he possessed after his death. The couple had divorced in 1927 but the will remained unchanged, even after he married his third wife Claire Beck in 1929. It is not clear whether Loos simply forgot the document, or whether he left the will untouched because he really, as Altmann-Loos suggested in her memoirs, considered her his "true" wife. I have described Loos's life "according to his will" as his "second life", and almost as turbulent, full of intrigue, seduction and desire as the first – and even more geographically dispersed (see Weizman 2014). But it also exemplified how the trustees who initially aimed to protect and promote the work and reputation of the author have inhibited its publication and made the work of Adolf Loos largely inaccessible. The reception of Loos's work can certainly not be explained by all the good souls that surrounded him.

In the 1920s Mikhail Bulgakov began to write *The Master and Margarita.* Under Stalin's regime, Bulgakov would be prohibited from writing. In the novel he used the phrase "Manuscripts don't burn" as a threat to the authorities, meaning that creative works and freethinking could never be suppressed. The sentence might have been motivated by a search the secret police had conducted in his house. The only suspicious item they could find was his diary. Apparently, it did not contain enough evidence to take him to prison, and he even got it back. In an artistic rage and trying to make sure that his personal notes could not be read again by anyone, he burned his diary. *The Master and Margarita* remained secret even after his death in 1940 and could not be published until 1966, when the phrase became more frequently used by dissidents to show their resistance to the state regime. In the early 1990s, when the KGB archives were partly opened, his diary was found. Apparently during the confiscation, the KGB had photocopied the diary before they returned it to the author. The best guardians are oftentimes ultimately the ones you would least expect. *Ines Weizman*

Bibliography

Abramson 2016 Daniel M. Abramson, *Obsolescence. An architectural history* (Chicago: University of Chicago Press 2016)

Adams 2019 Ross Exo Adams, *Circulation & urbanization* (London: SAGE Publications 2019)

Adorno and Horkheimer 1947 Theodor W. Adorno and Max Horkheimer, *Dialektik der Aufklärung. Philosophische Fragmente* (Amsterdam: Querido 1947)

Ahlin 1985 Janne Ahlin, *Sigurd Lewerentz, architect* (Stockholm: Byggeforlaget 1985)

Akcan 2011 Esra Akcan, "A building with many speakers. Turkish 'guest workers' and Álvaro Siza's Bonjour Tristesse Housing for IBA-Berlin", in Saloni Mathur (ed.), *The migrant's time. Rethinking art history and diaspora* (Williamstown, MA: The Clark Art Institute 2011), pp. 91–114

Albini 2006 Franco Albini, "Le funzioni e l'architettura del museo. Alcune esperienze", in Federico Bucci and Fulvio Irace (eds.), *Zero Gravity. Franco Albini. Costruire la modernità* (Milan: Mondadori Electa 2006), pp. 71–74

Anonymous 1880 Anonymous, [Advertisement], *The Times of London*, May 26 (1880)

Anonymous 1884 Anonymous, [Announcement], *Smaalenes Amtstidende*, October 15 (1884)

Anonymous 1890 Anonymous, [Advertisement], *Dagbladet*, April 28 (1890)

Anonymous 1892 Anonymous, [Announcement], *The Times of London*, June 2 (1892)

Anonymous 1894 Anonymous, [Announcement], *The Times of London*, February 14 (1894)

Anonymous 1895 Anonymous, "French Criminal Procedure", *The New York Times*, April 14 (1895)

Anonymous 1899 Anonymous, "Alterations at Crosby Hall", *City Press*, January 18 (1899), p. 6

Anonymous 1902 Anonymous, "The new royal train constructed by the London and Northwestern Railway", *The Graphic*, December 30 (1902), p. 854

Anonymous 1910 Anonymous, "New rolling stock for Argentina", *The Locomotive, Railway Carriage and Waggon Review* vol. 16, no. 212, April 15 (1910), pp. 81–84

Anonymous 1913 Anonymous, "En gammel Kristianiamand fortæller. Hos auktionarius Rich. Anderson som fotograferer alle Kristiania-gaarder, som falder", *Tidens Tegn*, June 22 (1913)

Anonymous 1938 Anonymous, "R.A.4 – det modern hus med det hypermoderne navn", *Morgenbladet*, February 28 (1938)

Anonymous 1941 Anonymous, "Art over the counter", *Time Magazine*, September 22 (1941)

Anonymous 1948 Anonymous, "Saarinen tells how 'Gateway' was conceived", *St. Louis Post-Dispatch*, March 7 (1948)

Anonymous 1973 Anonymous, "F. Selmer har en daglig omsetning på en mill. kr.", *Trønder-Avisa*, April 27 (1973), p. 6

Anstey 2024 Tim Anstey, *Things that move. A hinterland in architectural history* (Cambridge, MA: MIT Press 2024)

Anstey et al. 2007 Tim Anstey, Katja Grillner and Rolf Hughes (eds.), *Architecture and authorship* (London: Black Dog 2007)

Anthony 1992 John Anthony, *An illustrated life of Joseph Paxton 1803–1865* [1973] (Aylesbury: Shire Publications 1992)

Appadurai 1986 Arjun Appadurai, "Introduction: Commodities and the politics of value", *The social life of things. Commodities in cultural perspective* (Cambridge: Cambridge University Press 1986)

Arendt 1998 Hannah Arendt, *The human condition* [1958] (Chicago: University of Chicago Press 1998)

Arrhenius 2012 Thordis Arrhenius, *The fragile monument. On conservation and modernity* (London: Artifice Books/ Black Dog Publishing 2012)

Assmann 1995 Jan Assmann, "Collective memory and cultral identity", *New German Critique*, no. 65 (1995), pp. 125–133

Assmann 2013 Aleida Assmann, *Das neue Unbehagen an der Erinnerungskultur. Eine Intervention* (Berlin: C. H. Beck 2013)

Aureli 2014 Pier Vittorio Aureli, "Means to an end. The rise and fall of the architectural project of the city", in Pier Vittorio Aureli (ed.), *The city as project* (Berlin: Ruby Press 2014)

Bankes 1830 John William Bankes (ed.), *Narrative of the life and adventures of Giovanni Finati*, 2 vols. (London: John Murray 1830)

Barthes 1970 Roland Barthes, "L'ancienne rhétoric. Aide-mémoire", *Communications*, no. 16 (1970), pp. 172–223

Bataille 1930 Georges Bataille, "Le bas matérialisme et la gnose", *Documents. Archéologie – Beaux-Arts – Ethnographie – Variétés*, no. 2 (1930), pp. 1–8

Baudrillard 1996 Jean Baudrillard, *The system of objects* [1968] (New York and London: Verso 1996)

Benjamin 1999a Walter Benjamin, *The arcades project* (Cambridge, MA: Belknap Press of Harvard University Press 1999)

Benjamin 1999b Walter Benjamin, "Little history of photography" [1931], in Michael W. Jennings et al. (eds.), Walter Benjamin, *Selected writings*, vol. 2, part 2 (1931–1934) (Cambridge, MA: The Belknap Press of Harvard University Press 1999), pp. 510–512

Benjamin 2006 Walter Benjamin, "The work of art in the age of its technological reproducibility" [1939], in *Selected writings,* vol. 4 (1938–1940), eds. Howard Eiland and Michael W. Jennings (Cambridge, MA: Harvard University Press 2006), pp. 251–283

Benjamin 2023 Walter Benjamin, *Charles Baudelaire. A lyric poet in the era of high capitalism* (New York and London: Verso 2023)

Bensaïd 2021 Daniel Bensaïd, *The dispossessed. Karl Marx's debates on wood theft and the right of the poor* (Minneapolis: University of Minnesota Press 2021)

Berger 2017 Susanna Berger, *The art of philosophy. Visual thinking in Europe from the late Renaissance to the early Enlightenment* (Princeton: Princeton University Press 2017)

Beyer et al. 2018 Andreas Beyer, Horst Bredekamp, Uwe Fleckner and Gerhard Wolf (eds.), *Bilderfahrzeuge. Aby Warburgs Vermächtnis und die Zukunft der Ikonologie* (Berlin: Klaus Wagenbach 2018)

Bingen and Hinz 2005 Dieter Bingen and Hans-Martin Hinz (eds.), *Die Schleifung. Zerstörung und Wiederaufbau historischer Bauten in Deutschland und Polen* (Wiesbaden: Harrassowitz 2005)

Blake 1950 Peter Blake, "Life in a Chinese kite", *Architectural Forum*, no. 93 (1950), pp. 90–96

Blumenberg 1986 Hans Blumenberg, *Lebenszeit und Weltzeit* (Frankfurt am Main: Suhrkamp 1986)

Boito 1893 Camillo Boito, *Questioni pratiche di belle arti. Restauri, concorsi, legislazione, professione, insegnamento* (Milan: Ulrico Hoepli 1893)

Borges 1999 Jorge Luis Borges, "Pierre Menard, author of the Quixote", Collected fictions (London: Penguin 1999)

Boucher 2024 Bruce Boucher, *John Soane's cabinet of curiosities. Reflections on an architect and his collection* (New Haven: Yale University Press 2024)

Brandi 1942 Cesare Brandi, "Gli otto dipinti acquistati dallo Stato per la R. Pinacoteca di Siena", *Le Arti*, vol. IV (1942), pp. 367–371

Brandi 1954 Cesare Brandi, "Il Restauro e l'interpretazione dell'opera d'arte", *Annali della Scuola Normale Superiore di Pisa. Lettere, Storia e Filosofia*, serie II, vol. 23, no. 1–2 (1954), pp. 90–100

Brandi 1963 Cesare Brandi, *Teoria del restauro* (Rome: Edizioni di storia e letteratura 1963)

Braverman 1998 Harry Braverman, *Labor and monopoly capital. The degradation of work in the twentieth century*, 25th anniversary ed. (New York: Monthly Review Press 1998)

Bressani and Sealy 2011 Martin Bressani and Peter Sealy, "The Opéra disseminated: Charles Garnier's Le Nouvel Opéra de Paris (1875–1881)", *Studies in the History of Art*, vol. 77 (2011), pp. 195–219

Brilliant 1982 Richard Brilliant, "I piedistalli del giardino di Boboli. Spolia in se, spolia in re", *Prospettiva*, no. 31 (1982), pp. 2–17

Brusius 2020 Mirjam Brusius, "Objects and history adrift. Contextualizing the debate about Middle Eastern 'heritage'", in Uwe Fleckner and Elena Tolstichin (eds.), *Das verirrte Kunstwerk. Bedeutung, Funktion und Manipulation von "Bilderfahrzeugen" in der Diaspora*, Studien aus dem Warburg-Haus, vol. 20 (Berlin: De Gruyter 2020), pp. 55–71

Bucher 1851 Lothar Bucher, *Kulturhistorische Skizzen aus der Industrieausstellung aller Völker* (Frankfurt am Main: C. B. Lizius 1851)

Buchwald and Josefowicz 2010 Jed Z. Buchwald and Diane Greco Josefowicz, *The Zodiac of Paris. How an improbable controversy over an ancient Egyptian artifact provoked a modern debate between religion and science* (Princeton: Princeton University Press 2010)

Bürkner 2024 Birgit Bürkner, "Weltkulturerbe verrottet. Wer rettet die Teufelsbrücke?", *B. Z.*, June 28 (2024)

Burra Charter 2013 *The Burra Charter. The Australia ICOMOS Charter for Places of Cultural Significance* (Burwood: Australia ICOMOS 2013)

Burs 2017 Gerhard Martin Burs, *Mediale Präsentation in der Gegenwartsarchitektur. Das Beispiel der Vereinigten Arabischen Emirate* (Bielefeld: Transcript 2017)

Cairns and Jacobs 2014 Stephen Cairns and Jane M. Jacobs, *Buildings must die. A perverse view of architecture* (Cambridge, MA: MIT Press 2014)

Cameron 2017 Christina Cameron, "Reconstruction: changing attitudes", The Unesco courier, 19 July (2017)

Capdevila-Werning 2015 Remei Capdevila-Werning, "Palimpseste in der Architektur. Ein symboltheoretischer Zugang", in Jörg H. Gleiter and Ludger Schwarte (eds.), *Architektur und Philosophie. Grundlagen. Standpunkte. Perspektiven* (Bielefeld: Transcript 2015), pp. 207–217

Casey and Hayes 2023 Christine Casey and Melanie Hayes (eds.), *Enriching architecture. Craft and its conservation in Anglo-Irish building production, 1660–1760* (London: UCL Press 2023)

Caspar 2001 Helmut Caspar, "Für das Schloss ein "Roter Platz". Vor 50 Jahren wurde der 500 Jahre alte Hohenzollernsitz vernichtet", *Berlinische Monatsschrift*, no. 3 (2001), pp. 107–114

Chipiga 1972 I. Chipiga, "Tsirki", *Arkhitektura SSSR* 40, no. 7 (1972), pp. 28–29

Christiansen 1973 Jan Christensen, "Norsk boligeventyr i Afrika", *Verdens Gang*, January 9 (1973), p. 16

Clark 1994 William W. Clark, "New light on old stones. Quarries, monuments, and sculpture in Medieval France. An introduction", *Gesta* vol. 33, no. 1 (1994), pp. 3–10

Colonna 1999 Francesco Colonna, *Hypnerotomachia Poliphili, The strife of love in a dream* [1499] (London: Thames & Hudson 1999)

Colquhoun 1981 Alan Colquhoun, "Typology and design method", in *Essays in architectural criticism. Modern architecture and historical change* (Cambridge, MA: MIT Press 1981)

Conley 2009 Christine Conley, "Morning cleaning: Jeff Wall and The Large Glass", *Art History*, no. 32 (2009), pp. 996–1015

Costabile-Heming 2017 Carol Anne Costabile-Heming, "The reconstructed City Palace and Humboldt Forum in Berlin. Restoring architectural identity or distorting the memory of historic spaces?", *Journal of Contemporary European Studies* vol. 25, no. 4 (2017), pp. 441–454

Cottin 1889 Paul Cottin (ed.), *Mes Inscripcions. Journal intime de Restif de la Bretonne* (Paris: Plon 1889)

Crook 1995 Joseph Mordaunt Crook, *The Greek Revival. Neo-classical attitudes in British architecture 1760–1870* (London: John Murray 1995)

Curtius 1953 Ernst Robert Curtius, *European literature and the Latin Middle Ages* (Princeton: Princeton University Press, 1953)

Czech 1998 Hermann Czech, "Alles ist Umbau", *Werk, Bauen + Wohnen*, no. 85 (1998)

Dalton 1808 John Dalton, *A new system of chemical philosophy* (London: R. Bickerstaff 1808)

Davis 2007 Mike Davis, "Sand, fear, and money in Dubai", in Mike Davis and Daniel Bertrand Monk (eds.), *Evil paradises. Dreamworlds of neoliberalism* (New York: New Press 2007), pp. 48–68

De la Pryme 1870 Abraham de la Pryme, *The diary of Abraham de la Pryme, the Yorkshire antiquary* (Durham, London and Edinburgh: Andrews and Co. for the Surtees Society 1870)

De Vattel 1758 Emmerich de Vattel, *Droit des gens, ou principes de la loi naturelle appliqués à la conduite et aux affaires des nations et des souverains* (London [recte: Neuchâtel] 1758)

Delbeke 2017 Maarten Delbeke, "Monuments", in Harry Francis Mallgrave (ed.), *Companion to the history of architecture* (Hoboken, NJ: John Wiley & Sons 2017), pp. 1–32

Delhaye 1982 Jean Delhaye, *Note on the classification of Maison du Peuple, 1982,* Maison du Peuple (1965–1987), Archives Delhaye, Musée Horta, Brussels

Delhomme and Savoye 2020 Jean-Philippe Delhomme and Jean-Marc Savoye, *The sunny days of Villa Savoye* (Berlin: Birkhäuser 2020)

Denis and Pontille 2025 Jérôme Denis and David Pontille, *The care of things. Ethics and politics of maintenance* (Cambridge: Polity 2025)

Derrida 1995 Jacques Derrida, "Archive fever: A Freudian impression", *Diacritics*, vol. 25, no. 2 (1995), pp. 9–63

Didi-Huberman 2002 Georges Didi-Huberman, *L'image survivante. Histoire de l'art et temps des fantômes selon Aby Warburg* (Paris: Minuit 2002)

Didron 1843 Adolphe Napoléon Didron, "Rapport A. M. Cousin, ministre de l'instruction publique [...]" [1839], in *Bulletin Archéologique publie par Le comité historique des arts et monumens* (Paris: Imprimierie administrative de Paul Dupont 1843)

Didron 1845 Adolphe Napoléon Didron, "Réparation de la cathédrale de Paris", *Annales archeologiques*, vol. 3 (Paris: Au bureau des annales archéologiques 1845)

Dietrich 1993 Dorothea Dietrich, *The collages of Kurt Schwitters. Traditions and innovations* (Cambridge: Cambridge University Press 1993)

Dodds 2005 George Dodds, *Building desire. On the Barcelona Pavilion* (Abingdon: Routledge 2005)

Duchamp 1973 Marcel Duchamp, "The creative act" [1957], in Michel Sanouillet and Elmer Peterson (eds.), *The writings of Marcel Duchamp* (New York: Da Capo Press 1973), pp. 138–140

Dumser 2022 Elisha Ann Dumser, "The influence of reuse on architectural practices in late Imperial Rome", in Elisha Ann Dumser and Dorian Borbonus (eds.), *Building the Classical world. Bauforschung as a contemporary approach* (Oxford: Oxford University Press 2022)

Eames 2015 Charles Eames and Ray Eames, *An Eames anthology. Articles, film scripts, interviews, letters, notes, speeches*, ed. Daniel Ostroff (New Haven: Yale University Press 2015)

Eden 2001 Kathy Eden, *Friends hold all things in common. Tradition, intellectual property, and the adages of Erasmus* (New Haven: Yale University Press 2001)

Eliot 1922 T. S. Eliot, *The Wasteland* (New York: Boni and Liveright 1922)

Erasmus 1508 Desiderius Erasmus, *Adagiorum chiliades tres* (Venice: Aldus Manutius 1508)

Erll 2017 Astrid Erll, *Kollektives Gedächtnis und Erinnerungskulturen. Eine Einführung* (Stuttgart: J. B. Metler 2017)

Evelyn 1976 John Evelyn, *Fumifugium: or the inconvenience of the aer and and smoak of London dissipated. Together with some remedies humbly proposed by J. E. Esq; to his sacred Majestie, and to the Parliament now assembled* (London: Gabriel Bedel and Thomas Collins 1661)

Factum Foundation 2019 Factum Foundation (ed.), *The Sacred Cave of Kamukuwaká. The Preservation of Indigenous Cultures in Brazil* (Madrid: Factum Foundation 2019)

Faldbakken 2025 Matias Faldbakken, "Upholding – National Memorial for 22 July". https://koro.no/english/a-national-memorial-for-22-july/

Ferro 2024 Sergio Ferro, "Concrete as a weapon", in Silke Kapp and Mariana Moura (eds.), *Architecture from below. An anthology* (London: MACK 2024), pp. 8–32

Fitz and Krasny 2019 Angelika Fitz and Elke Krasny, *Critical care. Architecture and urbanism for a broken planet* (Cambridge, MA: MIT Press 2019)

Fleckner 1992 Uwe Fleckner, "Le Grand Louvre. Museale Präsentation als historische Reflexion", in Klaus Fröhlich, Grütter Theodor and Jörn Rüsen (eds.), *Geschichtskultur* (Pfaffenweiler bei Freiburg: Centaurus 1992), pp. 158–172

Fleckner 1998 Uwe Fleckner (ed.), *The treasure chests of Mnemosyne. Selected texts on memory theory from Plato to Derrida* (Dresden: Verlag der Kunst 1998)

Fleckner 2007 Uwe Fleckner (ed.), *Kunst in der Stadt Hamburg. 40 Werke im öffentlichen Raum* (Berlin: Nicolai 2007)

Fleckner 2011 Uwe Fleckner, "Aus dem Gedächtnis verbannt. Funktion und Ästhetik zerstörter Bildnisse", in Uwe Fleckner, Maike Steinkamp and Hendrik Ziegler (eds.), *Der Sturm der Bilder. Zerstörte und zerstörende Kunst von der Antike bis in die Gegenwart* (Berlin: Akademie 2011), pp. 15–33

Fleckner 2018 Uwe Fleckner, "Das Haus der Rosa Parks im Exil. Eine Immobilie als 'automobiles Bilderfahrzeug'", in Andreas Beyer, Horst Bredekamp, Uwe Fleckner and Gerhard Wolf (eds.), *Bilderfahrzeuge. Aby Warburgs Vermächtnis und die Zukunft der Ikonologie* (Berlin: Klaus Wagenbach 2018), pp. 64–72 and pp. 226–227

Fleckner et al. 2011 Uwe Fleckner, Martin Warnke and Hendrik Ziegler (eds.), *Handbuch der Politischen Ikonographie*, 2 vols. (Munich: C H. Beck 2011)

Fleckner and Dickel 2003 Uwe Fleckner and Hans Dickel (eds.), *Kunst in der Stadt. Skulpturen in Berlin. 1980–2000* (Berlin: Nicolai 2003)

Fleckner and Tolstichin 2020 Uwe Fleckner and Elena Tolstichin (eds.), *Das verirrte Kunstwerk. Bedeutung, Funktion und Manipulation von "Bilderfahrzeugen" in der Diaspora*, Studien aus dem Warburg-Haus, vol. 20 (Berlin: De Gruyter 2020)

Forty 2000 Adrian Forty, *Words and buildings. A vocabulary of modern architecture* (London: Thames & Hudson 2000)

Forty 2012 Adrian Forty, *Concrete and culture. A material history* (London: Reaktion Books 2012)

Foucault 1972 Michel Foucault, *The archaeology of knowledge* (New York: Pantheon 1972)

Foucault 1977 Michel Foucault, "Nietzsche, Genealogy, History", in Michel Foucault, *Language, counter-memory, practice. Selected essays and interviews*, ed. Donald F. Bouchard (Ithaca, NY: Cornell University Press), pp. 139–164

Foucault 1994a Michel Foucault, *The Order of things. An archaeology of the human sciences* [1966] (New York: Vintage 1994)

Foucault 1994b Michel Foucault, Überwachen und Strafen. Die Geburt des Gefängnisses [1975] (Frankfurt am Main: Suhrkamp 1994)

Foucault 2021 Michel Foucault and Prisons Information Group, *Intolerable: Writings from Michel Foucault and the Prisons Information Group, 1970–1980*, eds. Kevin Thompson and Perry Zurn (Minneapolis: University of Minnesota Press 2021)

Fraser and Jaeggi 2018 Nancy Fraser and Rahel Jaeggi, *Capitalism. A conversation in critical theory* (London and New York: Verso 2018)

Freud 1925 Sigmund Freud, "Notiz über den Wunderblock", in *Internationale Zeitschrift für Psychoanalyse*, no. 1 (1925), pp. 1–5

Fried 2007 Michael Fried, "Jeff Wall, Wittgenstein and the everyday", *Critical Inquiry*, vol. 33, no. 3 (2007), pp. 495–526

Fritsch 1886a Karl Emil Otto Fritsch, "Von der Jubiläums-Ausstellung der Kgl. Akademie der Künste zu Berlin", *Deutsche Bauzeitung*, June 26 (1886), pp. 306–307

Fritsch 1886b Karl Emil Otto Fritsch, "Von der Jubiläums-Ausstellung der Kgl. Akademie der Künste zu Berlin", *Deutsche Bauzeitung*, July 17 (1886), pp. 339–341

Fuglesang 1981 Signe Horn Fuglesang, "Woodcarvers: Professionals and amateurs in 11th century Trondheim", in David M. Wilson and Marjorie L. Caygill (eds.), *Economic aspects of the Viking Age* (London: British Museum 1981), pp. 24–25

Fuhrmeister 2001 Christian Fuhrmeister, *Beton, Klinker, Granit. Material, Macht, Politik: Eine Materialikonographie* (Berlin: Verlag Bauwesen 2001)

Fuller 2005 Matthew Fuller, *Media ecologies. Materialist energies in art and technoculture* (Cambridge, MA: MIT Press 2005)

Gallas 2019 Elisabeth Gallas, *A mortuary of books. The rescue of Jewish culture after the Holocaust* [2013] (New York: University Press 2019)

Gamboni 1997 Dario Gamboni, *The destruction of art. Iconoclasm and vandalism since the French Revolution* (London: Reaktion Books 1997)

Gammon 2018 Martin Gammon, *Deaccessioning and its discontents. A critical history* (Cambridge, MA: The MIT Press 2018)

Garnier 1871 Charles Garnier, *Le Théâtre* (Paris: Hachette et Cie 1871)

Geist and Kürvers 1989 Johann Friedrich Geist and Klaus Kürvers, *Das Berliner Mietshaus, 1945–1989*, vol. 3 (Munich: Prestel 1989)

Geldern 1993 James Von Geldern, *Bolshevik Festivals, 1917–1920* (Berkeley: University of California Press, 1993)

Gilbert 1900 Cass Gilbert, "Building skyscrapers", *Real Estate and Builder's Guide* 65, no. 1684, June 23 (1900), pp. 1087–1091

Gilbert 1907 Cass Gilbert, "Report of the Committee on the Relation of Architects to the Contracting System", in *Proceedings of the fortieth annual convention of the American Institute of Architects* (Washington, DC: Gibson Bros., 1907), pp. 89–91

Ginzburg 1979 Carlo Ginzburg "Spie. Radici di un paradigma indiziario", in Aldo Gargani (ed.), *Crisi della ragione. Nuovi modelli nel rapporto tra sapere e attività umane* (Turin: Einaudi 1979)

Glancey 2001 Jonathan Glancey, "The folly of Fallingwater", *The Guardian*, September 10 (2001)

Glaser 2004 Stephanie A. Glaser, "Of Revolutions, republics and spires: Nineteenth-century France and the Gothic Cathedral", in Nils Holger Pedersen, Claus Clüver and Nicolas Bell (eds.), *Signs of change. Transformations of Christian traditions* and their representation in the arts (Brill 2004), pp. 453–473

Goldsmith 2014 Kenneth Goldsmith, "Assume no readership", interview by Pejk Malinowski (Louisiana Channel, Louisiana Museum of Modern Art, Humlebæk 2014)

Graeber and Wengrow 2021 David Graeber and David Wengrow, *The dawn of everything: A new history of humanity* (New York: Farrar, Straus and Giroux 2021)

Graebner 1993 William Graebner, "Gateway to the empire. An interpretation of Eero Saarinen's 1948 design for the St. Louis arch", *Prospects*, no. 18 (1993), pp. 367–399

Grégoire 1794 Henri Grégoire, *Rapport sur les destructions opérées par le Vandalisme, et sur les moyens de le réprimer* (Paris: Imprimerie nationale 1794)

Grierson and Walker 2025 Jamie Grierson and Peter Walker, "Grenfell Tower to be demolished, Angela Rayner confirms", *The Guardian*, February 7 (2025)

Habeck and Schmitz 2023 Joachim Otto Habeck and Frank Schmitz (eds.), *Ruinen und vergessene Orte. Materialität im Verfall – Nachnutzungen – Umdeutungen* (Bielefeld: Transcript 2023)

Hammer Galleries 1941 Hammer Galleries, *Art objects & furnishings from the William Randolph Hearst collection* (New York: William Bradford Press, 1941)

Hancarville 1782 Pierre d'Hancarville, *Monumens de la vie privée des douze Césars, d'après une suite de pierres et médailles, gravèes sous leur règne* (Caprées: Sabellius [recte: Nancy: Leclerc] 1782)

Hansen 1940 Joseph Hansen, "With Trotsky to the end", *Fourth International*, no. 5 (1940), pp. 115–123

Harris 2007 John Harris, *Moving rooms. The trade in architectural salvages* (New Haven: Yale University Press 2007)

Harvey 1982 David Harvey, *The limits to capital* (Oxford: Basil Blackwell, 1982)

Haskell 1982 Francis Haskell, "Ciarlatano o pioniere? Uno storico d'arte a Napoli nell Settecento", in Cesare De Seta (ed.), *Arte e civiltà del Settecento a Napoli* (Bari: Laterza 1982)

Heckl 2013 Wolfgang M. Heckl, *Die Kultur der Reparatur* (Munich: Carl Hanser 2013)

Heijenoort 1978 Jean van Heijenoort, *With Trotsky in exile. From Prinkipo to Coyoacán* (Cambridge, MA: Harvard University Press 1978)

Herzog 2018 Tamar Herzog, *A short history of European law. The last two and a half millennia* (Cambridge, MA: Harvard University Press 2018)

Hewitt 1990 Mark A. Hewitt, *The architect & the American country house. 1890–1940* (New Haven: Yale University Press 1990)

Houdart and Chihiro 2009 Sophie Houdart and Minato Chihiro, *Kuma Kengo. An unconventional monograph* (Paris: Editions Donner Lieu 2009)

Hume 1906 David Hume, *Hume's political discourses*, ed. William Bell Robertson (London and Felling-on-Tyne: s. d. [1906])

Huyssen 2003 Andreas Huyssen, *Present pasts. Urban palimpsests and the politics of memory* (Stanford: Stanford University Press 2003)

Hvattum and Hultsch 2018 Mari Hvattum and Anne Hultsch (eds.), *The printed und the built. Architecture, print cultur and public debate in the nineteenth century* (London: Bloomsbury 2018)

Iversen 1968–1972 Erik Iversen, *Obelisks in exile*, 2 vols. (Copenhagen: Gads forlag 1968–1972)

Jager 2004 Markus Jager, "Umbau und Neues Bauen. Moderne Architektur und die Kultur des Weiterbauens", in Konstanty Gutschow and Hermann Zippel, *Umbau* [1932] (Hamburg: Dölling und Galitz 2024), pp. VI–XXV

Jäggi 2013 Carola Jäggi, "Materielle Wanderbewegungen. Spolien aus transkultureller Perspektive", in Michael Falser and Monica Juneja (eds.), *Kulturerbe und Denkmalpflege transkulturell. Grenzgänge zwischen Theorie und Praxis* (Bielefeld: Transcript 2013), pp. 53–67

Jasanoff 2004 Maya Jasanoff, "Collectors of empire. Objects, conquests and imperial self-fashioning", *Past & Present*, no. 184 (2004), pp. 109–135

Jencks 1973 Charles Jencks and Nathan Silver, *Adhocism. The case for improvisation* (New York: Doubleday 1973)

Jöchner et al. 2023 Cornelia Jöchner, Christin Nezik, Gáspár Salamon and Anke Wunderwald, *Museale Architekturdörfer 1880–1930. Das Eigene in transnationalen Verflechtungen* (Dresden: Sandstein 2023)

Joyce 2012 Rosemary A. Joyce, "From place to place: Provenience, provenance, and archaeology", in *Provenance. An alternate history of art* (Los Angeles: Getty Research Institute 2012), pp. 48–60

Kahn 1944 Louis Kahn, "Monumentality", in Paul Zucker (ed.), *New architecture and city planning. A symposium* (New York: Philosophical Library 1944), pp. 77–78

Karasek 1992 Hellmuth Karasek, *Billy Wilder. Eine* Nahaufnahme (Hamburg: Hoffmann und Campe 1992)

Kaspar 2007 Fred Kaspar (ed.), *Bauten in Bewegung. Von der Wiederverwendung alter Hausgerüste, vom Verschieben und vom Handel mit gebrauchten Häusern, von geraubten Spolien, Kopien und wiederverwendeten Bauteilen* (Mainz: Philipp von Zabern 2007)

Kaspar 2018 Fred Kaspar, "Freilichtmuseum und Denkmalpflege – Partner oder Rivalen?", in Lutz Volmer (ed.), *Musealisierte Häuser. Bausubstanz, Ideologie, Gründungspersönlichkeiten* (Münster and New York: Waxmann 2018), pp. 13–29

Katsnel'son et al. 1987 Iu. I. Katsnel'son, A. K. Azizov and E. M. Vysotskii, *Arkhitektura sovetskoi Turkmenii* (Moscow: Stroiizdat 1987)

Kavčič et al. 2021 Silvija Kavčič, Thomas Schaarschmidt, Anna Warda and Irmgard Zündorf (eds.), *Steine des Anstoßes. Die Stolpersteine zwischen Akzeptanz, Transformation und Adaption* (Berlin: Metropol 2021)

Kerr 1886 Robert Kerr, *The consulting architect. Practical notes on administrative difficulties and disputes* (London: John Murray 1886)

Kinney 1995 Dale Kinney, "Rape or restitution of the past? Interpreting spolia", in Susan C. Scott (ed.), *The art of interpreting* (Pennsylvania: Pennsylvania State University Press 1995), pp. 53–67

Klotz 2021 Laidy Klotz, *Subtract. The untapped science of less* (New York: Flat Iron Books 2021)

Kölmel 2023 Mara-Johanna Kölmel, "The twenty-first-century monuments. Reflections on nomadic and intermedial monumentality", in Mara-Johanna Kölmel and Ursula Ströbele (eds.), *The sculptural in the post digital age* (Berlin and Boston: De Gruyter 2023), pp. 161–183

Koolhaas 1994 Rem Koolhaas, *Delirious New York. A retroactive manifesto for Manhattan* (New York: Monacelli Press 1994)

Koolhaas 2004 Rem Koolhaas, "Preservation is overtaking us", *Future Anterior*, vol. 1, no. 2 (2004), pp. 1–3

Kopytoff 1986 Igor Kopytoff, "The cultural biography of things. Commoditization as process", in Arjun Appadurai (ed.), *The social life of things. Commodities in cultural perspective* (Cambridge: Cambridge University Press 1986), pp. 64–91

Koselleck 2006 Reinhart Koselleck, "Crisis" [1972], *Journal of the Histories of Ideas*, vol. 67, no. 2 (2006), pp. 357–400

Koshalek et al. 2003 Richard Koshalek, Grant Mudford, Frank Gehry, *Symphony. Frank Gehry's Walt Disney Concert Hall* (New York: Harry N. Abrams 2003)

Krajewska and Wasiuta 2025 Elka Krajewska and Mark Wasiuta (eds.), *The archival exhibition. A decade of research at the Arthur Ross Architecture Gallery, 2006–2016* (New York: Columbia Books on Architecture and the City 2025), pp. 252–253

Krebs et al. 2018 Stefan Krebs, Gabriele Schabacher and Heike Weber, "Kulturen des Reparierens und die Lebensdauer der Dinge", in Stefan Krebs, Gabriele Schabacher and Heike Weber (eds.), *Kulturen des Reparierens. Dinge – Wissen – Praktiken* (Bielefeld: Transcript 2018), pp. 9–46

Kreis 2020, Reinhild Kreis, *Selbermachen. Eine andere Geschichte des Konsumzeitalters* (Frankfurt am Main: Campus 2020)

Kubler 1962 George Kubler, *The shape of time. Remarks on the history of things* (New Haven: Yale University Press)

Lähteenmäki 2020 Markus Lähteenmäki, "Lines of action and readymade stones: Lev Rudnev's monument to the victims of the revolution," *AR/ Architecture Research* (2020), pp. 286–323

Lähteenmäki 2022 Markus Lähteenmäki, *"The history that is made in the streets". Architecture and images of public space in revolutionary Russia* (Phd thesis, ETH Zurich 2022)

Landesman 1966 Jay Landesman [and Tony Cox], "Two views of DIAS", *The International Times*, no. 1 (1966), p. 9

Latour 1987 Bruno Latour, *Science in action. How to follow scientists and engineers through society* (Cambridge, MA: Harvard University Press 1987)

Latour 1988 Bruno Latour, *The pasteurization of France* (Cambridge, MA: Harvard University Press 1988)

Latour 1991 Bruno Latour, *We have never been modern* (Cambridge, MA: Harvard University Press 1991)

Latour 2005 Bruno Latour, "From Realpolitik to Dingpolitik, or how to make things public", in Peter Weibel and Bruno Latour (eds.), *Making things public. Atmospheres of democracy* (Cambridge, MA: MIT Press 2005), pp. 14–43

Latour and Lowe 2011 Bruno Latour and Adam Lowe, *"The migration of the aura, or how to explore the original through its facsimiles,"* in Thomas Bartscherer and Roderick Coover (eds.), *Switching codes. Thinking through digital technology in the humanities and the arts* (Chicago, Illinois: University of Chicago Press 2011), pp. 275–298

Latour and Yaneva 2008 Bruno Latour and Albena Yaneva, "Give me a gun and I will make all buildings move: An ANT's view of architecture", in Reto Geiser (ed.), *Explorations in architecture. Teaching, design, research* (Basel: Birkhäuser 2008), pp. 80–89

Laugier 1977 Marc-Antoine Laugier, *An essay on architecture* [1753] (Los Angeles: Hennessey & Ingalls, 1977)

Lautréamont 1874 Comte de Lautréamont, *Les Chants de Maldoror* (Paris: Gustave Balitot 1874)

Leatherbarrow 2000 David Leatherbarrow, *Uncommon ground. Architecture, technology, and topography* (Cambridge, MA: MIT Press 2000)

Lee 2000 Pamela M. Lee, *Object to be destroyed. The work of Gordon Matta-Clark* (Cambridge, MA: MIT Press 2000)

Lemonnier 1911 Henry Lemonnier, *Procés-verbaux de l'Académie Royale d'Architecture*, vol. 8 (1768–1799) (Paris: Libraire de la société de l'historie de l'art Français 1911)

Lending 2014 Mari Lending, "Traveling portals", in Thordis Arrhenius, Mari Lending, Wallis Miller and Jérémie McGowan (eds.), *Place and displacement. Exhibiting architecture* (Zurich: Lars Müller Publishers 2014), pp. 197–212

Lending 2016 Mari Lending, "Reciting the tomb of Tutankhamun", *Perspecta*, vol. 49 (2016)

Lending 2017 Mari Lending, *Plaster monuments. Architecture and the power of reproduction* (Princeton: Princeton University Press 2017)

Lending et al. 2018 Mari Lending, Eirik Bøhn and Tim Anstey (eds.), *Images of Egypt* (Oslo: Pax 2018)

Levin 2011 Jed Levin, "Activism leads to excavation: The power of place and the power of the people at the president's house in Philadelphia", *Archaeologies*, no. 7 (2011), pp. 596–618

Lévi-Strauss 1962 Claude Lévi-Strauss, *La pensée sauvage* (Paris: Plon 1962)

Lillteicher 2003 Jürgen Lillteicher, *Die Rückerstattung jüdischen Eigentums in Westdeutschland nach dem Zweiten Weltkrieg. Eine Studie über Verfolgungserfahrung, Rechtsstaatlichkeit und Vergangenheitspolitik 1945–1971* (PhD thesis, Albert-Ludwigs-Universität Freiburg 2003)

Lind 1998 Christoph Lind, *Die architektonische Gestaltung der Kolonialstadt Tsingtau 1897–1914* (PhD thesis, Technische Universität Berlin 1998)

Linebaugh 1976 Peter Linebaugh, "Karl Marx, the theft of wood, and working class composition: A contribution to the current debate," *Crime and Social Justice*, no. 6 (1976), pp. 5–16

Lipp 1994 Wilfried Lipp, "Vom modernen zum postmodernen Denkmalkultus? Aspekte zur Reparaturgesellschaft", in Wilfried Lipp and Michael Petzet (eds.), *Vom modernen zum postmodernen Denkmalkultus? Denkmalpflege am Ende des 20. Jahrhunderts* (Munich: Bayerisches Landesamt für Denkmalpflege 1994), pp. 6–12

Lowe 2020 Adam Lowe (ed.), *The aura in the age of digital materiality. Rethinking preservation in the shadow of an uncertain future* (Milan: Silvana Editoriale 2020)

Lowenthal 1985 David Lowenthal, *The past is a foreign country* (Cambridge: Cambridge University Press 1985)

Lowinger 2015 Rosa Lowinger, "Vandalism (Miami Style): Graffiti as a tool in preserving the Miami Marine Stadium", *Change Over Time*, vol. 4, no. 1 (2015), pp. 136–151

Lowinger and Lloyd 2024 Rosa Lowinger and Jason Clement Lloyd, "Paint in paradise: Graffiti as a tool in preserving the Miami Marine Stadium", *APT Bulletin: The Journal of the Association for Preservation Technology* (Fall 2024), pp. 1–7

Martin 1876 Theodore Martin, *The life of His Royal Highness the Prince Consort*, vol. 2 (London: Smith, Elder & Co. 1876)

Marx 2000 Karl Marx, *Selected writings*, ed. David McLellan, 2nd ed. (Oxford: Oxford University Press 2000)

Marx 2021 Karl Marx, "Proceedings of the sixth Rhine Province Assembly, Third Article. Debates on the law concerning the theft of wood" [1842], in Daniel Bensaïd, *The dispossessed. Karl Marx's debates on wood theft and the right of the poor* (Minneapolis: University of Minnesota Press 2021), pp. 59–105

Marx and Engels 1848 Karl Marx and Friedrich Engels, *Manifest der Kommunistischen Partei* (London: Hirschfeld 1848)

Mathur 2011 Saloni Mathur (ed.), *The migrant's time. Rethinking art history and diaspora* (Williamstown, MA: The Clark Art Institute 2011)

McCarthy 1965 Fiona McCarthy, "New look at the local", *The Guardian*, April 28 (1965)

McCarter 2002 Robert McCarter, *Fallingwater aid. Architecture in detail* (London: Phaidon 2002)

McGrane 2017 Sally McGrane, "Saved from demolition, Rosa Parks's House gets a second life", *The New York Times*, May 2 (2017)

Mead 1991 Christopher Mead, *Charles Garnier's Paris Opéra: Architectural empathy and the Renaissance of French Classicism* (New York, N.Y.: Architectural History Foundation 1991)

Meier 2020 Hans-Rudolf Meier, *Spolien. Phänomene der Wiederverwendung in der Architektur* (Berlin: Jovis 2020)

Meier and Jäggi 2021 Hans-Rudolf Meier and Carola Jäggi, "Falsche Spolien, deplatzierte Koren und unkanonische Säulen. Zum Nachleben der antiken Skulptur in der Architektur der Moderne," in Michail Chatzidakis, Henrike Haug, Lisa Marie Roemer and Ursula Rombach (eds.), *Con bella maniera. Festgabe für Peter Seiler* (Heidelberg: Arthistoricum.net 2021), pp. 519–529

Meller et al. 2024 Harald Meller, Kai Michel and Carel van Schaik, *Die Evolution der Gewalt. Warum wir Frieden wollen, aber Kriege führen* (Munich: DTV 2024)

Meurisse 1614 Martin Meurisse and Léonard Gaultier, *Artificiosa totius logices descriptio* (*Artificial description of logic in its entirety*) (Paris: Jean Messager 1614)

Montholon 1847 Charles-Tristan de Montholon, *Récits de la captivité de l'Empereur Napoléon à Sainte-Hélène*, 2 vols. (Paris: Paulin 1847)

Moore 2012 Rowan Moore, "Villa Tugendhat, Brno, Czech Republic", *The Guardian*, April 6 (2012)

Moos 1987 *Stanislaus von Moos, Venturi, Rauch & Scott Brown* (München: Schirmer/Mosel 1987)

Morris and Webb 1877 William Morris and Philip Webb, "Manifesto of Society for the Protection of Ancient Buildings", *The Athenaeum Journal*, no. 2591 (1877), p. 807

Mostafavi and Leatherbarrow 1993 Mohsen Mostafavi and David Leatherbarrow, *On Weathering. The Life of Buildings in Time* (Cambridge, MA: MIT Press 1993)

Müller 2018 Johannes von Müller, "Sea-going Obelisk. Die Nadel der Kleopatra in London", in Andreas Beyer, Horst Bredekamp, Uwe Fleckner and Gerhard Wolf (eds.), *Bilderfahrzeuge. Aby Warburgs Vermächtnis und die Zukunft der Ikonologie* (Berlin: Klaus Wagenbach 2018), pp. 14–26

Müller 2021 Jan Werner Müller, "Prussian Disneyland", *London Review of Books*, vol. 43, no. 17 (2021)

Münz and Künstler 1964 Ludwig Münz and Gustav Künstler, *Der Architekt Adolf Loos. Darstellung seines Schaffens nach Werkgruppen* (Vienna and Munich: Anton Schroll 1964)

Musil 1927 Robert Musil, "Denkmale", *Prager Presse*, December 10 (1927), pp. 4–5

Nasmyth 1883 *James Nasmyth engineer. An Autobiography*, ed. Samuel Smiles (London: John Murray 1883)

Necipoğlu 2005 Gülru Necipoğlu, *The age of Sinan. Architectural culture in the Ottoman Empire* (Princeton: Princeton University Press 2005)

Nichols 2020 Robert Nichols, *Theft is property! Dispossession and critical theory* (Durham, NC: Duke University Press 2020)

Nierhaus 2014 Andreas Nierhaus, *Kreuzenstein. Die mittelalterliche Burg als Konstruktion der Moderne* (Vienna, Cologne and Weimar: Böhlau 2014)

Nieszczerzewska 2015 Małgorzata Nieszczerzewska, "Derelict architecture. Aesthetics of an unaesthetic space", in *Argument. Biannual Philosophical Journal*, no. 5 (2015), pp. 387–397

Nora 1989 Pierre Nora, "Between memory and history: Les Lieux de Mémoire", *Representations*, no. 26 (1989), pp. 7–24

O'Brien 2021 Hettie O'Brien, "The Bells v the Boutique Hotel: The battle to save Britian's oldest factory", *The Guardian*, May 11 (2021)

Ostermann 2014 Ingrid Ostermann, "Rotterdams dynamischer Umgang mit dem Wiederaufbau / Rotterdam's dynamic approach to reconstruction", in Ingrid Sonntag (ed.), *Labor der Moderne. Nachkriegsarchitektur in Europa / Laboratory of modernism. Post-war architecture in Europe* (Dresden: Sächsische Akademie der Künste 2014), pp. 152–177

Oswald et al. 2010 Al Oswald, John Goodall, Andrew Payne and Tara-Jane Sutcliffe, *Thornton Abbey, North Lincolnshire: Historical, archaeological investigations* (Portsmouth: English Heritage 2010)

Otero-Pailos et al 2016 Jorge Otero-Pailos, Erik Fenstad Langdalen, Thordis Arrhenius (eds.), *Experimental preservation* (Zürich: Lars Müller Publishers 2016)

Ozouf 1976 Mona Ozouf, *La fête révolutionnaire, 1789–1799* (Paris: Gallimard 1976)

Panofsky 1939 Erwin Panofsky, *Studies in iconology. Humanistic themes in the art of the Renaissance* (Oxford: Oxford University Press 1939)

Panofsky 1957 Erwin Panofsky, *Gothic architecture and scholasticism* (New York: Meridian Books 1957)

Parker 2024 Ian Parker, "Kanye West bought an architectural treasure – then gave it a violent remix", *The New Yorker*, June 10 (2024)

Patenaude 2010 Bertrand M. Patenaude, *Trotzki. Der verratene Revolutionär* [2009] (Berlin: Propyläen 2010)

Patte 1769 Pierre Patte, *Mémoires sur les objets plus importans de l'architecture* (Paris 1769)

Pethes 2015 Nicolas Pethes, "Mnemotop", in Jörg Dünne and Andreas Mahler (eds.), *Handbuch Literatur & Raum* (Berlin: De Gruyter 2015), pp. 196–206

Picout and Rubin 2020 Laurie Picout and Patrick Rubin, "Lexique: variations sur la transformation", in Patrick Rubin (ed.), *Transformation des situations construites* (Paris: Canal Architecture 2020), pp. 22–23

Piketty 2014 Thomas Piketty, *Capital in the twenty-first century* [2013] (Cambridge, MA.: Belknap Press of Harvard University Press 2014)

Pizer 1992 John Pizer, "Guilt, memory and the motif of the double in Storm's Aquis Submerses and Ein Doppelgänger", *The German Quarterly*, vol. 65, no. 2 (1992), pp. 177–191

Plevoets and Van Cleempoel 2019 Bie Plevoets and Koenraad Van Cleempoel, *Adaptive reuse of the built heritage. Concepts and cases of an emerging discipline* (Abingdon: Routledge 2019)

Pomian 1988 Krzysztof Pomian, *Der Ursprung des Museums. Vom Sammeln* (Berlin: Wagenbach 1988)

Poste 1958 Leslie Irlyn Poste, *The development of US protection libraries and archives in Europe during the World War II* (PhD thesis, Chicago University 1958)

Pryor 2016 Elizabeth Stordeur Pryor, *Colored travelers. Mobility and the fight for citizenship before the Civil War* (Chapel Hill, NC: The University of North Carolina Press 2016)

Quatremère de Quincy 1999 Antoine-Chrysostome Quatremère de Quincy, *The historical dictionary of architecture* (London: Andreas Papadakis 1999)

Rappold 1913 Otto Rappold, *Der Bau der Wolkenkratzer. Kurze Darstellung auf Grund einer Studienreise für Ingenieure und Architekten* (Munich: R. Oldenbourg 1913)

Raus 2019 Sarah A. Raus, *Reset in stone. Memory and reuse in ancient Athens* (Madison: University of Wisconsin Press 2019)

Reynolds 2008 Michael Reynolds, *Journey. Part one* (Taos, New Mexico: Earthship Biotecture 2008)

Reynoso and Nivera 2014 Anaiste Reynoso and Catherine Nivera, "Energy in the Walt Disney Concert Hall: Waste and emissions of Walt Disney Concert Hall, Ca." (Research Paper, University of California-Davis 2014)

Rhodes 1995 Robin Francis Rhodes, *Architecture and meaning on the Athenian Acropolis* (Cambridge: Cambridge University Press 1995)

Richardson and Stevens 2000 Margaret Richardson and MaryAnne Stevens, *John Soane, architect. Master of space and light* (London: Royal Academy Publications 2000)

Riegl 1903 Alois Riegl, *Der moderne Denkmalkultus. Sein Wesen und seine Entstehung* (Vienna: W. Braumüller 1903)

Riksantikvaren 2018 Riksantikvaren, *Den tidligere amerikanske ambassaden, Henrik Ibsens gate 48. Vedtak om fredning*, June 20, 2018

Risåsen 2005 Geir Thomas Risåsen, *Eidsvollsbygningen. Carsten Anker og Grunnlovens hus* (Oslo: Damm 2005)

Roberts 1984 David L. Roberts, "John Thorpe's drawings for Thornton College, the house of Sir Vincent Skinner", *Lincolnshire History and Archaeology* 19 (1984), pp. 57–64

Rossi 1982 Aldo Rossi, *The Architecture of the city* [1966] (Cambridge, MA: MIT Press 1982)

Rubio et al. 2025 Fernando Domínguez Rubio, Jérôme Denis and Davis Pontille (eds.) *Fragilities. Essays on the politics, ethics, and aesthetics of maintenance and repair* (Cambridge, MA: MIT Press 2025)

Ruskin 1853 John Ruskin, *The stones of Venice*, 2nd vol. (London: Smith, Elder & Co. 1853)

Saarinen 1948 Eero Saarinen, "Saarinen tells how 'Gateway' was conceived", *St. Louis Post-Dispatch*, March 7 (1948)

Sæhle et al. 2021 Ingeborg Sæhle et al., *Arkeologiske undersøkelser i Søndre gate 7–11, Peter Egges Plass, Krambugata 2–4 m.fl., Trondheim, Trøndelag. Landskapsutvikling, tidlig urban aktivitet og middelaldersk kirkested* (Oslo: NIKU 2021)

Saumarez Smith 2020 Charles Saumarez Smith, "Battle of the bells and the boutique hotel", *The Critic* (October 2020), pp. 54–59

Schirmer 1984 Wulf Schirmer (ed.), *Egon Eiermann 1904–1970. Bauten und Projekte* (Stuttgart: Deutsche Verlags-Anstalt 1984)

Schlosser 2021 Julius von Schlosser, *Art and curiosity cabinets of the Late Renaissance. A contribution to the history of collecting*, ed. Thomas DaCosta Kaufmann (Los Angeles: Getty Research Center 2021)

Schmidt-Degener 1934 Frederik Schmidt-Degener, "Principes généraux de la mise en valeur des œuvres d'art", in *Muséographie. Architecture et aménagement des musées d'art* (Paris: Office International des Musées 1934)

Schrader 2006 Ulrike Schrader, "Die 'Stolpersteine' oder Von der Leichtigkeit des Gedenkens. Einige kritische Anmerkungen", *Geschichte im Westen. Zeitschrift für Landes- und Zeitgeschichte* 21 (2006), pp. 173–181

Schumpeter 1942 Joseph A. Schumpeter, *Capitalism, socialism and democracy* (New York and London: Harper & Brothers 1942)

Schwartz 1998 Hillel Schwartz, *The culture of the copy. Striking likenesses, unreasonable facsimiles* (Cambridge, MA: MIT Press, 1998)

Schwitters 2006 Kurt Schwitters, *Catalogue raisonné*, vol. 3 (1937–1948), ed. Karin Orchard and Isabel Schulz (Berlin: Hatje Cantz 2006)

Scully 1969 Vincent Scully, *American architecture and urbanism* (London: Thames & Hudson 1969)

Secrest 1979 Meryle Secrest, *Being Bernard Berenson* (New York: Holt, Rinehart and Winston 1979)

Sennett 1994 Richard Sennett, *Flesh and stone. The body and the city in Western civilization* (New York: W. W. Norton & Co. 1994)

Sennett 2012 Richard Sennett, *Zusammenarbeit. Was unsere Gesellschaft zusammenhält* (Munich: Carl Hanser 2012)

Serlio 1551 Sebastiano Serlio, *Livre extraordinaire de architecture* (Lyon: Jean de Tournes 1551)

Simmel 1919 Georg Simmel, "Die Ruine", in *Philosophische Kultur. Gesammelte Essais*, (Leipzig: Alfred Kröner 1919), pp. 125–133

Smith 1776 Adam Smith, *An inquiry into the nature and causes of the wealth of nations* (London: W. Strahan and T. Cadell 1776)

Smyth 2016 Jonathan Smyth, *Robespierre and the festival of the supreme being. The search for a republican morality* (Manchester University Press 2016)

Snyder 2010 Timothy Snyder, *Bloodlands. Europe between Hitler and Stalin* (New York: Basic Books 2010)

Soane 1830 John Soane, *Description of the house and museum on the north side of Lincoln's Inn Fields* (London: James Moyes 1830)

Soutar 1910 Andrew Soutar, "Produced in court", *The Strand Magazine* 39 (May 1910), 613–619

Spelman 1613 Henry Spelman, *De non temerandis Ecclesiis, a tracte of the rights and respect due unto churches* (London: John Bealm 1613)

Spelman 1698 Henry Spelman, *The History and fate of sacrilege* (London: John Hartley 1698)

Springer 1867 Anton Springer, *Bilder aus der neueren Kunstgeschichte,* 2 vols. (Bonn: Adolph Marcus 1867)

Starrett 1938 Paul Starrett, *Changing the skyline. An autobiography* (New York: Whittlesey 1938)

Steen 1975 Øyvind Steen, "Selmer-Abidjan", *F. Selmer Nytt*, no. 2, April 11, 1975, p. 18

Stöhr 1921 Karl F. Stöhr, *Amerikanische Turmbauten* (Munich: R. Oldenbourg 1921)

Stoltenberg 2011 Jens Stoltenberg, "Statsministerens tale til rosetoget tre dager etter terroren 22. Juli" https://www.22julisenteret.no/en/read-more/subject-articles/collection-of-speeches-after-the-terrorist-attack-on-22-july

Stowell 1948 Kenneth K. Stowell, "Precedents, prototypes and plagiarism", *Architectural Record*, vol. 103, no. 4 (1948), pp. 91

Street 1871 George Edmund Street, "A lecture delivered at the Royal Academy last session by George Edmund Street, R.A.", *The Architect*, vol. 6 (1871), pp. 299–301, pp. 310–312 and pp. 323–325

Summerson 1966 John Summerson (ed.), *The book of architecture of John Thorpe in Sir John Soane's Museum* (Glasgow: The Walpole Society 1966)

Swenarton 1989 Mark Swenarton, *Artisans and architects. The Ruskinian tradition in architectural thought* (Basingstoke: Palgrave Macmillan 1989)

Tamen 2004 Miguel Tamen, *Friends of interpretable objects* (Cambridge, MA: Harvard University Press 2004)

Thompson 2023 Erin L. Thompson, *Smashing statues. The rise and fall of America's public monuments* (New York: Norton 2023)

Till 2009 Jeremy Till, *Architecture depends* (Cambridge, MA: MIT Press 2009)

Tolstoy et al. 1990 Vladimir Tolstoy, Irina Bibikova and Catherine Cooke, *Street art of the revolution. Festivals and celebrations in Russia 1918–33* (London: Thames and Hudson 1990)

Torkjelsson 2015 Eivind Torkjelsson, *Maleriet Eidsvold 1814* (Oslo: Stortingets administrasjon 2015)

Trachtenberg 2010 Marvin Trachtenberg, *Building-in-time. From Giotto to Alberti and Modern oblivion* (New Haven: Yale University Press 2010)

Trigg 2006 Dylan Trigg, *The aesthetics of decay. Nothingness, nostalgia, and the absence of reason* (New York: Peter Lang 2006)

Tschudi 2012 Victor Plahte Tschudi, "Ancient Rome in the age of copyright: The *privilegio* and printed reconstructions", *Acta ad archaeologiam et artium historiam pertinentiae* 25 (2012), pp. 177–194

Tschudi 2017 Victor Plahte Tschudi, *Baroque Antiquity: Archaeological imagination in Early Modern Europe* (Cambridge: Cambridge University Press 2017)

Van Eck 2023 Caroline van Eck, *Piranesi's candelabra and the revival of the past. Excessive objects and the emergence of style in the age of Neoclassicism* (Oxford: Oxford University Press 2023)

Vélez 2019 Karin Vélez, *The miraculous flying house of Loreto. Spreading catholicism in the early modern world* (Princeton: Princeton University Press 2019)

Versluys 2020 Miguel John Versluys (ed.), *Beyond egyptomania. Objects, style and agency*, Studien aus dem Warburg-Haus, vol. 21 (Berlin: De Gruyter 2020)

Vezzosi 2025 Letizia Vezzosi, "Labour into travel and travel into labour: A journey into the semantic field of hard work", in Susan Irvine, Carla Riviello, Paolo Vaciago and Ruggero Bianchin (eds.), ἀγλαὰ δῶρα. *Studi miscellanei in onore di Dora Faraci* (Roma: Tre-Press, 2025), pp. 1067–1082

Viollet-le-Duc 1990 Eugène Emmanuel Viollet-le-Duc, *The foundations of architecture. Selections from the Dictionnaire raisonné* (New York: George Braziller 1990)

Wagner 2018 Monika Wagner, *Marmor und Asphalt. Soziale Oberflächen im Berlin des 20. Jahrhunderts* (Berlin: Wagenbach 2018)

Wagner and Friedrich 2017 Monika Wagner and Michael Friedrich (eds.), *Steine. Kulturelle Praktiken des Materialtransfers* (Berlin: De Gruyter 2017)

Walkley 2025 Nick Walkley, *Portal propagations: Reproduction, reception, and rediscovery in the life of the Urnes Portal* (PhD thesis, The Oslo School of Architecture and Design 2025)

Warburg 2000 Aby Warburg, *Der Bilderatlas MNEMOSYNE*, eds. Martin Warnke and Claudia Brink (Berlin: Akademie 2000)

Warburg 2010 Aby Warburg, "Mnemosyne Einleitung" [1929], in *Werke in einem Band*, edited by Martin Treml, Sigrid Weigel and Perdita Ladwig (Frankfurt am Main: Suhrkamp 2010), pp. 629–639

Waurá et al. 2020 Akari Waurá, Shirley Djukurna Krenak et al., "The resurrection of the sacread cave of Kamukuwaká", in Adam Lowe (ed.), *The aura in the age of digital materiality. Rethinking preservation in the shadow of an uncertain future* (Milan: Silvana Editoriale 2020)

Weizman 2012a Ines Weizman, "Copying as a media form", in Jenna Sutela (ed.), *Add Metaphysics*, vol. 1 (Helsinki: Aalto University 2012), pp. 94–105

Weizman 2012b Ines Weizman, "Architectural doppelgängers", *AA Files*, no. 65 (2012), pp. 19–24

Weizman 2014 Ines Weizman, "The three lives of modern architetcture: Wills, copyrights and their violation", in Thordis Arrhenius, Mari Lending, Wallis Miller and Jérémie McGowan (eds.), *Place and displacement. Exhibiting architecture* (Zurich: Lars Müller Publishers 2014) pp. 183–196

Weizman 2018 Ines Weizman, "Architecture and copyright: Rights of authors and things in the age of reproduction", in Amanda Reeser Lawrence and Ana Miljački (eds.), *Terms of appropriation. Modern architecture and global exchange* (Abingdon: Routledge 2018), pp. 141–159

Weizman 2019 Ines Weizman (ed.), *Dust & data. Traces of the Bauhaus across 100 years* (Leipzig: Spector 2019)

Weizman 2025a Ines Weizman, *The architectural casino. Conversations about modernism in Haifa* (Zürich: Diaphanes 2025)

Weizman 2025b Ines Weizman, "Creative destruction, or the assembly of things", in Elka Krajewska and Mark Wasiuta (eds.), *The archival exhibition. A decade of research at the Arthur Ross Architecture Gallery, 2006–2016* (New York: Columbia Books on Architecture and the City 2025), pp. 252–253

Wells 2023 Matthew Wells, *Modelling the metropolis. The architectural model in Victorian London* (Zurich: GTA Verlag 2023)

Wetherbe 2013 Jamie Wetherbe, "Cleaners make Walt Disney Concert Hall's curves sparkle", *Los Angeles Times*, September 20 (2013)

Widrich 2020 Mechthild Widrich, "After the counter-monument. Commemoration in the expanded field", in Swati Chattopadhyay and Jeremy White (eds.), *The Routledge companion to critical approaches to contemporary architecture* (Abingdon: Routledge 2020), pp. 57–67

Willis 1995 Carol Willis, *Form follows finance. Skyscrapers and skylines in New York and Chicago* (Princeton: Princeton Architectural Press 1995)

Willis and Clark 1886 Robert Willis and John Willis Clark, *The architectural history of the University of Cambridge and of the colleges of Cambridge and Eton* (Cambridge: Cambridge University Press, 1886)

Wilson 1877 Erasmus Wilson, *Cleopatra's Needle. With brief notes on Egypt and Egyptian obelisks* (London: Brain & Co. 1877)

Winckelmann 1755 Johann Joachim Winckelmann, *Gedancken über die Nachahmung der griechischen Werke in der Mahlerey und Bildhauer-Kunst* (Friedrichstadt: Hagenmüller 1755)

Wittman 2024 Richard Wittman, *Rebuilding St. Paul's outside the walls. Architecture and the Catholic Revival in the nineteenth century* (Cambridge: Cambridge University Press 2024)

Wittrock 1992 Gerhard Wittrock, *Die Versetzung von Gebäuden. Gründe, Methoden und Ziele* (Darmstadt: Technische Hochschule 1992)

Wolf 2004 Harald Wolf, "Capitalism", Georges Ritzer (ed.), *Encyclopedia of social theory* (Newbury Park, CA: Sage 2004), pp. 76–80

Wölfflin 1920 Heinrich Wölfflin, *Kunstgeschichtliche Grundbegriffe. Das Problem der Stilentwicklung in der neueren Kunst* [1915] (Munich: Hugo Bruckmann 1920)

Wood and Nagel 2010 Christoper S. Wood and Alexander Nagel, *Anachronic Renaissance* (New York: Zone Books 2010)

Wunderwald 2023 Anke Wunderwald, "Das Poble Espanyol der Weltausstellung 1929 in Barcelona als Imagination nationaler Einheit", in Cornelia Jöchner, Christin Nezik, Gáspár Salamon and Anke Wunderwald, *Museale Architekturdörfer 1880–1930. Das Eigene in transnationalen Verflechtungen* (Dresden: Sandstein 2023), pp. 186–237

Xifaras 2018 Mikhaïl Xifaras, "Illegalisms and the law of civil society", in Thanos Zartaloudis (ed.), *Law and philosophical theory. Critical intersections* (London: Rowman & Littlefield 2018), pp. 13–25

Yaneva 2009a Albena Yaneva, "Making the social hold: Towards an actor-network theory of design", *Design and Culture*, vol. 1, no. 3 (2009), pp. 273–288

Yaneva 2009b Albena Yaneva, *Made by the Office for Metropolitan Architecture. An ethnography of design* (Rotterdam: 010 Publishers 2009)

Yaneva 2020 Albena Yaneva, *Crafting history. Archiving and the quest for architectural legacy* (Ithaca, NY: Cornell University Press 2020)

Yates 1966 Francis Yates, *The art of memory* (London: Routlege and Kegan Paul 1966)

Young 1992 James Edward Young, "The counter-monument. Memory against itself in Germany today", *Critical Inquiry*, vol. 18 (1992), pp. 267–296

Young 2002 James Edward Young, "Germany's Holocaust Memorial problem – and mine", *The Public Historian*, no. 4 (2002), pp. 65–85

Zimmermann 1989 Reinhard Zimmermann, *Künstliche Ruinen. Studien zu ihrer Bedeutung und Form* (Wiesbaden: Reichert 1989)

Image credits

Acquisition 1–2: New York Public Library; **Actor** 1–2: Albena Yaneva; **Afterlife** 1–2: Uwe Fleckner; **Architectural drawing** 1–2: Drawing Matter Collection, London; **Archive** 1–2: Albena Yaneva; **Artefact** 1: Metropolitan Museum / Public Domain, 2: RMN-Grand Palais (Musée du Louvre); **Attribution** 1: Mari Hvattum; **Authentication** 1–2: Christoph Grafe; **Authenticity** 1: Teigens Fotoatelier, Stortingets Kunstsamling, Oslo, 2: Guri Dahl; **Authorship** 1: Goodyear Archival Collection, Brooklyn Museum Archives, New York 2: Wikimedia Commons; **Bond** 1–2: Karl Fritz Stöhr, *Amerikanische Turmbauten* (Munich: R. Oldenbourg 1921); **Bricolage** 1: Christoph Grafe; **Capitalism** 1: Victoria & Albert Museum, London, 2: Sergei Gussev / Creative Commons; **Cargo** 1: Kunstgeschichtliches Seminar, University of Hamburg, 2: Clemens Franz / Creative Commons; **Catalogue** 1: New York Public Library Digital Collections, 2: Pomeranian Digital Library; **Celebrity** 1: Spencer Lowell / The New Yorker, 2024; **Circulation** 1: Craig Buckley; **Collecting** 1–2: Getty Research Institute, J. Paul Getty Trust, Los Angeles (2004.R.10); **Collective memory** 1: Tyler Merbler / Wikimedia Commons, 2: Warburg-Archiv, Warburg-Haus, Hamburg; **Component** 1: Drawing Matter Collection, London, 2: Alansmeccano.org; **Concrete** 1–2: Adrian Forty; **Construction site** 1: Joseph Kinsey Collection, Alexander Turnbull Library, National Library of New Zealand, Wellington; **Contract** 1: Cass Gilbert Papers and Architectural Drawings, New York Historical Society (box 53, folder 5); **Copyright** 1: Ines Weizman; **Costs** 1: *Architectural Forum*, vol. 93, no. 3 (1950); **Counter-monument** 1: Studio Shalev-Gerz, VG Bild-Kunst, Bonn, 2: Standfast / Alamy Stock Photo; **Craft** 1: The Gentle Author, 2: Shahed Saleem; **Crisis** 1: H. M. Colvin, "Eythrope House and its demolition in 1810–11", *Records of Buckinghamshire*, vol. 17, no. 4 (1964), 2: Mari Lending; **Deaccessioning** 1: Lynn Rother; **Demolition** 1: Alena Beth Rieger; **Dereliction** 1: Frank Schmitz, 2: René Burri / Magnum Photos / Agentur Focus; **Displacement** 1: Digital Commonwealth. Massachusetts Collections Online / Creative Commons, 2: Yuning Teng; **Dispossession** 1: Wikimedia Commons, 2: Asif Khan Architects; **Dispute** 1: Bruno Manser Fonds, Basel, 2: Akonnchiroll / Creative Commons; **Doppelgänger** 1: CAIP / Blogspot, 2: Carol M. Highsmith Archive, Prints and Photographs Division, Library of Congress, Washington, DC; **Dust** 1: Heidelberger historische Bestände, Digitale Bibliothek, Universität Heidelberg, 2: Jorge Otero-Pailos / Collection of Thyssen-Bornemisza Art Contemporary Foundation (T-BA21), VG Bild-Kunst, Bonn; **Element** 1–2: Nicholas Coates; **Exhibition** 1: Hedrich-Blessing Collection, HB-26347-L, Chicago History Museum / 2025 Artists Rights Society, New York / VG Bild-Kunst, Bonn; **Expropriation** 1: Christopher Hope-Fitch, 2: Ardon Bar Hama / Sir John Soane's Museum, London; **Extension** 1: Gunnar Klack / Creative Commons, 2: Bernd Nicolai; **Facsimile** 1: Factum Arte, 2: Alaor Filho / Fotos Públicas; **Fire** 1: Getty Research Institute, J. Paul Getty Trust, Los Angeles (2004.R.10), 2: Martha Rosler / Galerie Nagel Draxler, Berlin, Cologne and Munich; **Fragility** 1: Autorité de Sûreté Nucléaire et de Radioprotection, 2: Civaux-communication / Creative Commons; **Fragment** 1–2: Public Domain; **Framing** 1: Flavia Crisciotti, 2: CISA / A. Palladio; **Ghosts** 1–2: Digital image, The Museum of Modern Art, New York / Scala, Florence; **Graffiti** 1–2: Uwe Fleckner; **Heritage** 1–2: Bildarchiv, ETH-Bibliothek, Zurich / Public Domain; **Image vehicle** 1: Fabia Mendoza, 2: Uwe Fleckner; **Inheritance** 1: Artists Right Society, New York / Estate of Gordon Matta-Clark and David Zwirner, New York, VG Bild-Kunst, Bonn; **Inscription** 1: Uwe Fleckner; **Labour** 1–2: Albert Kahn Associates Records, Bentley Historical Library, Ann Arbor, and Albert Kahn Associates, Detroit; **Lacuna** 1: National Park Service / Public Domain, 2: Kunstgeschichtliches Seminar, University of Hamburg, VG Bild-Kunst, Bonn; **Maintenance** 1: US Marine Corps History Division / Creative Commons; **Material** 1: Eine Gaaserud; **Mobility** 1: Royal Academy, London, 2: National Library of Sweden; **Model** 1: London Archives, 2: John Thorp, *Concerning Models of Buildings, Estates, Works, etc. for Exhibitions or Law Cases* (London 1913); **Monument, toppled** 1: Trinity Mirror / Mirrorpix / Alamy Stock Photo; **Moveables** 1: Brukselbeeldenbank, Brukselbinnenstebuiten Archive, Brussels; **Network** 1: Albena Yaneva, *Latour for Architects* (Abingdon: Routledge 2022), 2: Uwe Fleckner; **Obsolescence** 1: Oslo Museum, 2: Norsk Teknisk Museum, Oslo; **Occupation** 1: Museene i Akershus, Strømmen; **Palimpsest** 1: Uwe Fleckner; **Pasticcio** 1: Lyall Thow / *A New Description of Sir John Soane's Museum* (London 2007), 2: Tilman Walther, VG Bild-Kunst, Bonn; **Patina** 1–2: Erik Langdalen; **Photography** 1–2: Richard Andersens samling, Oslo Museum; **Plaster cast** 1: Victoria & Albert Museum, London;

Political iconography 1–2: Bildindex zur Politischen Ikonographie, Warburg-Haus, Hamburg; **Postproduction** 1: Carson Chan, 2: Dag Erik Elgin; **Precedent** 1: Uwe Fleckner, 2: Digital Collections, Manuscripts and Archives, Yale University Press, New Haven; **Preservation** 1: Lars Ramberg / Creative Commons; **Pristine** 1–2: Erlend Skjeseth; **Privilegio** 1: Heidelberger historische Bestände, Digitale Bibliothek, Universität Heidelberg, 2: Institut national d'histoire de l'art, Paris; **Provenience** 1: NTNU University Museum, Trondheim, 2: Stiftelsen Thomas Fearnley, Heddy og Nils Astrup, Oslo; **Quarry** 1: Slemmestad bibliotek, Cementmuseet, Slemmestad, 2: AGB SBS Opernbetrieb Burgenland GmbH, Eisenstadt; **Quote** 1: Ferdinand Saumarez Smith / Factum Foundation, 2: Mari Lending; **Readymade** 1–2: ArkDes Collection, Stockholm; **Reconstruction** 1: Mathias Faldbakken / Vegard Kleven, 2: Adrian Bugge; **Recycling** 1: Flora Lichtman and Katherine Wells, *Earthships*, 2015, 2: Museum of Modern Art, New York; **Renovation** 1: Max Creasy, 2: Kastler Skjeseth Architects; **Reparation** 1: Bundesarchiv, Koblenz (Bild 146-1978-069-15A / CC BY-SA 3.0 DE), 2: Frank Schmitz; **Reproduction** 1–2: Nick Walkley; **Residents** 1Uwe Fleckner; **Restitution** 1: Harun Farocki, *Bilder der Welt und Inschrift des Krieges*, 1989, 2: National Archives, Washington, DC (260-PHOAD-2-18); **Restoration** 1: Thordis Arrhenius; **Reuse** 1: Brad Hostetler / Creative Commons, 2: Richard Wittman; **Ruin** 1–2: Kunstgeschichtliches Seminar, University of Hamburg; **Sourcing** 1: Uwe Fleckner; **Spolia** 1: Diego Delso / Creative Commons, 2: Gary Todd; **Storage** 1–2: Simon Mitchell; **Subtraction** 1: US Embassy, Oslo, 2: Erik Langdalen; **Theft** 1: Drawing Matter Collection, London; **Thing-right** 1: Museum of Modern Art, New York, 2: Victoria & Albert Museum, London; **Transfer** 1: Matthew Mullane, 2: Hide-sp / Creative Commons; **Transformation** 1–2: Uwe Fleckner; **Translocation** 1: Creative Commons, 2: Stiftung Historische Museen Hamburg; **Type project** 1: E.G. Rozanov (ed.), *Arkhitektura obshchestvennykh zdanii* (Moscow: Stroiizdat 1980), 2: *Arkhitektura SSSR*, no. 4 (1973); **Vandalism** 1: Adobe Stock, 2: Rosa Lowinger; **War** 1: Bernd Nicolai, 2: Stadsarchief, Rotterdam; **Weathering** 1–2: Carol M. Highsmith Archive, Prints and Photographs Division, Library of Congress, Washington, DC; **Will** 1: Stadt- und Landesarchiv, Wien (3.1.4.A1.L12.1).

Contributors

Tim Anstey	Oslo School of Architecture and Design
Elif Akyüz	University of Hamburg
Richard Anderson	University of Edinburgh
Thordis Arrhenius	KTH Royal Institute of Technology, Stockholm
Eirik Bøhn	Oslo School of Architecture and Design
Craig Buckley	Yale University, New Haven
Maristella Casciato	The Getty Research Institute, Los Angeles
Carson Chan	Museum of Modern Art, New York
Flavia Crisciotti	Oslo School of Architecture and Design
Jérôme Denis	Mines – PSL, Centre de Sociologie de l'Innovation, Paris
Martin Denoun	Université de Liège
Caroline van Eck	University of Cambridge
Dag Erik Elgin	Oslo
Ella Eßlinger	Eidgenössische Technische Hochschule, Zurich
Uwe Fleckner	University of Hamburg
Adrian Forty	University College, London
Christoph Grafe	Bergische Universität, Wuppertal
Nina Lucia Groß	Museum für Kunst und Gewerbe, Hamburg
Niall Hobhouse	Drawing Matter, London
Olivia Horsfall Turner	Royal Institute of British Architects, London
Mari Hvattum	Oslo School of Architecture and Design
Timothy Hyde	Massachusetts Institute of Technology, Cambridge
Amandine Kastler	Oslo School of Architecture and Design
Margit Kern	University of Hamburg
Markus Lähteenmäki	University of Helsinki
Erik Langdalen	Oslo School of Architecture and Design
Mari Lending	Oslo School of Architecture and Design
Adam Lowe	Factum Foundation, Madrid
Rosa Lowinger	RLA Conservation of Art and Architecture, Los Angeles
Charlotte Malterre-Barthes	École Polytechnique Fédérale, Lausanne
Thomas McQuillan	Oslo School of Architecture and Design
Wallis Miller	University of Kentucky
Simon Mitchell	Oslo School of Architecture and Design
Matthew Mullane	Radbaud University, Nijmegen
Bernd Nicolai	University of Bern
Nicholas Olsberg	London
Jorge Otero-Pailos	Columbia University, New York
Eeva-Liisa Pelkonen	Yale University, New Haven
Aileen Ramm	University of Hamburg
Alena Beth Rieger	Oslo School of Architecture and Design

Ingrid Dobloug Roede	Oslo School of Architecture and Design
Lynn Rother	Leuphana, Lüneburg / Museum of Modern Art, New York
Charles Saumarez Smith	London
Frank Schmitz	University of Hamburg
Erlend Skjeseth	Kastler & Skjeseth Architects, Oslo
Chelsea Spencer	Rice School of Architecture, Houston
Hugh Strange	Hugh Strange Architects, London
Jørgen Tandberg	Oslo School of Architecture and Design
Yuning Teng	Freie Universität Berlin
Victor Plahte Tschudi	Oslo School of Architecture and Design
Philip Ursprung	Eidgenössische Technische Hochschule, Zurich
Espen Vatn	Oslo School of Architecture and Design
Nick Walkley	Oslo School of Architecture and Design
Ines Weizman	Royal College of Art, London
Matthew Wells	University of Manchester
Richard Wittman	University of California, Santa Barbara
Albena Yaneva	Politecnico di Torino, Turin
Claire Zimmerman	University of Toronto

Editors: Uwe Fleckner, Mari Lending
Editorial management: Neila Kemmer, Hatje Cantz
Copyediting: Hannah Young

Graphic design: Jens Johan Tandberg, Øystein Arbo studio
Typesetting: Calibar Services, Bukarest

Production: Thomas Lemaître, Hatje Cantz
Paper: Munken Print white, Napura Khepera
Typeface: Practice drawn by François Rappo for Optimo
Reproductions: Schwabenrepro, Fellbach
Printing and binding: Livonia Print, Riga (Latvia)

Published by
Hatje Cantz Verlag GmbH
Mommsenstraße 27, 10629 Berlin
Germany
contact@hatjecantz.de
www.hatjecantz.com
A Ganske Publishing Group Company

Printed in Europe

ISBN: 978-3-7757-6114-7 [PRINT]
ISBN: 978-3-7757-6122-2 [PDF]
ISBN: 978-3-7757-6123-9 [EPUB]